MW01194471

The Story of God Bible Commentary Series Endorsements

"Getting a story is about more than merely enjoying it. It means hearing it, understanding it, and above all, being impacted by it. This commentary series hopes that its readers not only hear and understand the story, but are impacted by it to live in as Christian a way as possible. The editors and contributors set that table very well and open up the biblical story in ways that move us to act with sensitivity and understanding. That makes hearing the story as these authors tell it well worth the time. Well done."

Darrell L. Bock
Executive Director of Cultural Engagement, Howard G. Hendricks
Center for Christian Leadership and Cultural Engagement,
Senior Research Professor of New Testament Studies
Dallas Theological Seminary

"The Story of God Bible Commentary series invites readers to probe how the message of the text relates to our situations today. Engagingly readable, it not only explores the biblical text but offers a range of applications and interesting illustrations."

Craig S. Keener
Professor of New Testament
Asbury Theological Seminary

"I love the Story of God Bible Commentary series. It makes the text sing, and helps us hear the story afresh."

John Ortberg
Senior pastor of Menlo Park Presbyterian Church,
and author of *Who Is This Man?*

"Bible study leaders, Christians searching for a devotional guide, and pastors who know the importance of expositional preaching will all benefit from this clearly written, theologically perceptive guide through Paul's letter to the Christians in Philippi. Lynn Cohick brings not only her valuable expertise in the language and culture of the New Testament to Philippians, but also her Christian experience and mature theological reflection. The result is a clear, helpful guide through this small but rich part of God's Word."

Frank Thielman
Professor of Divinity
Beeson Divinity School

"The Story of God Bible Commentary series is unique in its approach to exploring the Bible. Its easy-to-use format and practical guidance brings God's grand story to modern-day life so anyone can understand how it applies today."

Andy Stanley
Senior Pastor
North Point Ministries

"I'm a storyteller. Through writing and speaking I talk and teach about understanding the Story of God throughout Scripture and about letting God reveal more of His story as I live it out. Thus I am thrilled to have a commentary series based on the Story of God—a commentary that helps me to Listen to the Story, that Explains the Story, and then encourages me to probe how to Live the Story. A perfect tool for helping every follower of Jesus to walk in the story that God is writing for them."

Judy Douglass
Author, Speaker, Encourager
Office of the President, Cru
Director of Women's Resources, Cru

"The Bible is the story of God and his dealings with humanity from creation to new creation. The Bible is made up more of stories than of any other literary genre. Even the psalms, proverbs, prophecies, letters, and the Apocalypse make complete sense only when set in the context of the grand narrative of the entire Bible. This commentary series breaks new ground by taking all these observations seriously. It asks commentators to listen to the text, to explain the text, and to live the text. Some of the material in these sections overlaps with introduction, detailed textual analysis and application, respectively, but only some. The most riveting and valuable part of the commentaries are the stories that can appear in any of these sections, from any part of the globe and any part of church history, illustrating the text in any of these areas. Ideal for preaching and teaching."

Craig L. Blomberg
Distinguished Professor of New Testament
Denver Seminary

PHILIPPIANS

The
Story of God
Bible Commentary

PHILIPPIANS

Lynn H. Cohick

Tremper Longman III & Scot McKnight
General Editors

ZONDERVAN

Philippians
Copyright © 2013 by Lynn H. Cohick

This title is also available as a Zondervan ebook. Visit www.zondervan.com/ebooks.

Requests for information should be addressed to:
Zondervan, *Grand Rapids, Michigan* 49530

Library of Congress Cataloging-in-Publication Data

Cohick, Lynn H.
      Philippians / Lynn H. Cohick.
         p. cm. — (Story of God Bible commentary; 11)
      ISBN 978-0-310-32724-0 (hardcover)
      1. Bible. Philippians — Commentaries. I. Title.
   BS2705.53.C64   2013
   227'.6077 — dc23   2013008290

Cover design: Ron Huizinga
Cover imagery: iStockphoto®

Printed in the United States of America

---

13 14 15 16 17 18 19 /DCI/ 24 23 22 21 20 19 18 17 16 15 14 13 12 11 10 9 8 7 6 5 4 3 2 1

To Dave and Denise (January 5, 1955 – March 23, 2013) Fisher

Models of Christ's love, faithfully striving
toward the goal to win the prize (Phil 3:14)

Old Testament series

1 ■ Genesis — *Tremper Longman III*
2 ■ Exodus — *Christopher J. H. Wright*
3 ■ Leviticus — *Jerry E. Shepherd*
4 ■ Numbers — *Jay A. Sklar*
5 ■ Deuteronomy — *Myrto Theocharous*
6 ■ Joshua — *Lissa M. Wray Beal*
7 ■ Judges — *Athena E. Gorospe*
8 ■ Ruth/Esther — *Marion Taylor*
9 ■ 1 – 2 Samuel — *Paul S. Evans*
10 ■ 1 – 2 Kings — *David T. Lamb*
11 ■ 1 – 2 Chronicles — *Carol M. Kaminski*
12 ■ Ezra/Nehemiah — *Douglas J. Green*
13 ■ Job — *W. Eric Smith*
14 ■ Psalms — *Elizabeth R. Hayes*
15 ■ Proverbs — *Ryan P. O'Dowd*
16 ■ Ecclesiastes/Song of Songs — *George Athas*
17 ■ Isaiah — *Mark J. Boda*
18 ■ Jeremiah/Lamentations — *Andrew G. Shead*
19 ■ Ezekiel — *D. Nathan Phinney*
20 ■ Daniel — *Wendy L. Widder*
21 ■ Minor Prophets I — *Beth M. Stovell*
22 ■ Minor Prophets II — *Beth M. Stovell*

New Testament series

1 ■ Matthew — *Rodney Reeves*
2 ■ Mark — *Timothy G. Gombis*
3 ■ Luke — *Kindalee Pfremmer DeLong*
4 ■ John — *Nicholas Perrin*
5 ■ Acts — *Dean Pinter & Cherith Fee Nordling*
6 ■ Romans — *Michael F. Bird*
7 ■ 1 Corinthians — *Justin K. Hardin*
8 ■ 2 Corinthians — *Love L. Sechrest*
9 ■ Galatians — *Joel Willitts*
10 ■ Ephesians — *Mark D. Roberts*
11 ■ Philippians — *Lynn H. Cohick*
12 ■ Colossians/Philemon — *Todd Wilson*
13 ■ 1 – 2 Thessalonians — *John Byron*
14 ■ 1 – 2 Timothy, Titus — *Marius Nel*
15 ■ Hebrews — *Radu Gheorghita*
16 ■ James — *Mariam J. Kamell*
17 ■ 1 Peter — *Dennis Edwards*
18 ■ 2 Peter, Jude — *C. Rosalee Velloso Ewell*
19 ■ 1 – 3 John — *Constantine R. Campbell*
20 ■ Revelation — *Jonathan A. Moo*
21 ■ Sermon on the Mount — *Scot McKnight*

Contents

Acknowledgments

Obligatory acknowledgments run the risk of sounding disingenuous, which is why Zondervan decided to make this page optional to its contributors. I am grateful for that decision so that I can express, without any hint of compulsion, my deep gratitude to the several people who were influential in the writing of this work. My involvement with this series began over a delightful lunch with Katya Covrett, senior acquisitions editor at Zondervan, who asked me if I would be interested in working on a new commentary series. I am grateful for her excellent service leadership in guiding the commentary's New Testament editorial board. My deep appreciation extends to Scot McKnight, series senior editor and good friend, for his unfailing support and encouragement of me, and more broadly, of Christian women in the academy. To Mike Bird and Joel Willitts, members of the editorial board, thank you for your voices of wisdom that helped me think more deeply about God's Word.

The final copy of the commentary owes much to the artful hand of senior editor-at-large, Verlyn Verbrugge, in reining in my word count to manageable page limits, and in the process making my thoughts on the page read more clearly. I am grateful for the insightful suggestions of Greg Thellman, my TA at Wheaton College, that sharpened my thinking, and for his careful reading of the manuscript that prevented numerous errors. To Sam Knutson, thank you for tirelessly double-checking and rereading the manuscript.

I'm grateful for the living examples of Christ's love shown to me by my parents, Scott and Sally Harrison, who model Paul's injunction to strain toward what lies ahead, the hope of resurrected life in Christ. My children, Charles James and Sarah, graduated from college during the writing of the commentary, and they continue to prove true Paul's word that "he who began a good work in you will carry it on to completion until the day of Christ Jesus" (Phil 1:6). I share this journey of faith with my husband, Jim, whose example of Christian joy and peace made my reflections on Philippians all the richer.

The Story of God Bible Commentary Series

The Word of God may not change, but culture does. Think of what we have seen in the last twenty years: we now communicate predominantly through the internet and email; we read our news on iPads and computers; we can talk on the phone to our friends while we are driving, while we are playing golf, while we are taking long walks; and we can get in touch with others from the middle of nowhere. We carry in our hands small devices that connect us to the world and to a myriad of sources of information. Churches have changed; the "Nones" are rising in numbers and volume, and atheists are bold to assert their views in public forums. The days of home Bible studies are waning, there is a marked rise in activist missional groups in churches, and pastors are more and more preaching topical sermons, some of which are not directly connected to the Bible. Divorce rates are not going down, marriages are more stressed, rearing children is more demanding, and civil unions and same-sex marriages are knocking at the door of the church.

Progress can be found in many directions. While church attendance numbers are waning in Europe and North America, churches are growing in the South and the East. More and more women are finding a voice in churches; the plea of the former generation of leaders that Christians be concerned not just with evangelism but with justice is being answered today in new and vigorous ways. Resources for studying the Bible are more available today than ever before, and preachers and pastors are meeting the challenge of speaking a sure Word of God into shifting cultures.

Readers of the Bible change, too. These cultural shifts, our own personal developments, the progress in intellectual questions, as well as growth in biblical studies and theology and discoveries of new texts and new paradigms for understanding the contexts of the Bible — each of these elements works on an interpreter so that the person who reads the Bible today asks different questions from different angles.

Culture shifts, but the Word of God remains. That is why we as editors of The Story of God Bible Commentary series, a commentary based on the New International Version 2011 (NIV 2011), are excited to participate in this new series of commentaries on the Bible. This series is designed to address this generation with the same Word of God. We are asking the authors to explain what the Bible says to the sorts of readers who pick up commentaries so they can understand not only what Scripture says but what it means for today. The Bible does not change, but relating it to our culture changes constantly and in differing ways in different contexts.

When we, the New Testament editors, sat down in prayer and discussion to choose authors for this series, we realized we had found fertile ground. Our list of potential authors staggered in length and quality. We wanted the authors to be exceptional scholars, faithful Christians, committed evangelicals, and theologically diverse, and we wanted this series to represent the changing face of both American and world evangelicalism: ethnic and gender diversity. I believe this series has a wider diversity of authors than any commentary series in evangelical history.

The title of this series, emphasizing as it does the "Story" of the Bible, reveals the intent of the series. We want to explain each passage of the Bible in light of the Bible's grand Story. The Bible's grand Story, of course, connects this series to the classic expression *regula fidei*, the "rule of faith," which was the Bible's story coming to fulfillment in Jesus as the Messiah, Lord, and Savior of all. In brief, we see the narrative built around the following biblical themes: creation and fall, covenant and redemption, law and prophets, and especially God's charge to humans as his image-bearers to rule under God. The theme of God as King and God's kingdom guides us to see the importance of Israel's kings as they come to fulfillment in Jesus, Lord and King over all, and the direction of history toward the new heavens and new earth, where God will be all in all. With these guiding themes, each passage is examined from three angles.

Listen to the Story. We believe that if the Bible is God speaking, then the most important posture of the Christian before the Bible is to listen. So our first section cites the text of Scripture and lists a selection of important biblical and sometimes noncanonical parallels; then each author introduces that passage. The introductions to the passages sometimes open up discussion to the theme of the passage while other times they tie this passage to its context in the specific book. But since the focus of this series is the Story of God in the Bible, the introduction leads the reader into reading this text in light of the Bible's Story.

Explain the Story. The authors follow up listening to the text by explaining each passage in light of the Bible's grand Story. This is not an academic series, so the footnotes are limited to the kinds of texts typical Bible readers and preachers readily will have on hand. Authors are given the freedom to explain the text as they read it, though you should not be surprised to find occasional listings of other options for reading the text. Authors explore biblical backgrounds, historical context, cultural codes, and theological interpretations. Authors engage in word studies and interpret unique phrases and clauses as they attempt to build a sound and living reading of the text in light of the Story of God in the Bible.

Authors will not shy away from problems in the texts. Whether one is examining the meaning of "perfect" in Matthew 5:48, the complexities with Christology in the hymn of Philippians 2:6–11, the challenge of understanding Paul in light of the swirling debates about the old, new, and post-new perspectives, the endless debates about eschatology, or the vagaries of atonement theories, the authors will dive in, discuss evidence, and do their best to sort out a reasonable and living reading of those issues for the church today.

Live the Story. Reading the Bible is not just about discovering what it meant back then; the intent of The Story of God Bible Commentary series is to probe how this text might be lived out today as that story continues to march on in the life of the church. At times our authors will tell stories about what this looks like; at other times they may offer some suggestions for living it out; but always you will discover the struggle involved as we seek to live out the Bible's grand Story in our world.

We are not offering suggestions for "application" so much as digging deeper; we are concerned in this section with seeking out how this text, in light of the Story of God in the Bible, compels us to live in our world so that our own story lines up with the Bible's Story

SCOT MCKNIGHT, general editor New Testament
LYNN COHICK, JOEL WILLITTS, and MICHAEL BIRD, editors

Abbreviations

AB	Anchor Bible
ANTC	Abingdon New Testament Commentary
AYB	Anchor Yale Bible
b.	*Babylonian Talmud*
BECNT	Baker Exegetical Commentary on the New Testament
BNTC	Black's New Testament Commentary
BTB	*Biblical Theology Bulletin*
BTCB	Brazos Theological Commentary on the Bible
CIL	*Corpus inscriptionum latinarum*
DPL	*Dictionary of Paul and His Letters*
ESV	English Standard Version
HTR	*Harvard Theological Review*
ICC	International Critical Commentary
IVPNTC	InterVarsity Press New Testament Commentary
JETS	*Journal of the Evangelical Theological Society*
JSPHL	*Journal for the Study of Paul and His Letters*
KJV	King James Version
LCL	Loeb Classical Library
NETS	New English Translation of the Septuagint
LXX	Septuagint
m.	*Mishnah*
NIB	*New Interpreter's Bible*
NICNT	New International Commentary on the New Testament
NIGTC	New International Greek Testament Commentary
NIV	New International Version
NIVAC	NIV Application Commentary
NRSV	New Revised Standard Version
NPNF[1]	*Nicene and Post-Nicene Father*, series 1
PNTC	Pillar New Testament Commentary
RB	*Revue biblique*
SBG	Studies in Biblical Greek
SBLAB	Society for Biblical Literature Academia Biblica
SGBC	Story of God Bible Commentary
SNTSMS	Society for New Testament Studies Monograph Series
SP	*Sacra pagina*
THC	Two Horizons Commentary
TynBul	*Tyndale Bulletin*
WBC	Word Biblical Commentary

Introduction to Philippians

Life is full of "what if" scenarios. Some are exciting—what if I had not visited that church? I never would have met my husband. Some are tragic—what if she had missed that bus that later crashed on the icy roads? She would still be with us today. Some represent the vagaries of history—what if the Bedouin had not found the first fragments of the Dead Sea Scrolls? And some are of immense theological import—what if Paul had not written his letter to the Philippians? What if Philippians was absent from our New Testament? Several aspects of God's character, his redemptive plan for the world, and the believer's response to such audacious and marvelous news would be shifted to the realm of speculation and surmise. Paul speaks to the character of God, the character of the believer in Christ, and the character of believers together in Christ, and he invites theological reflection on the good news of the gospel of Jesus Christ.

The character of God. In four short chapters, Paul describes the wonder and beauty that is God. His character shines forth in the Christ hymn (2:6–11), which displays the self-emptying, non-grasping, humble servant who is Christ Jesus. This portrait reveals God's character, not simply Jesus' full humanity and full divinity. It advocates that "humiliation belongs to the identity of God as truly as his exaltation does."[1] As Gorman explains concerning the hymn, "Christ's divinity, and thus divinity itself, is being narratively defined as kenotic and cruciform in character."[2] That is, God's very nature is self-emptying and self-humbling. As Jesus himself indicated, "Anyone who has seen me has seen the Father" (John 14:9).

The nature of our salvation. Paul reflects on the wonder of the incarnation; very God takes on real humanity, the purpose of which is humanity's salvation. Accomplishing such salvation required humiliation and obedience, suffering death on a cross. Yet death does not have the final word. Christ stands exalted now, having defeated death, and all creation will recognize his exaltation (2:11). The "day of Christ Jesus" (1:6) is eagerly anticipated by his followers (3:20). Paul describes the intricate and lovely salvation plan designed

---

1. Richard Bauckham, *God Crucified: Monotheism and Christology in the New Testament* (Grand Rapids: Eerdmans, 1998), 61.

2. Michael J. Gorman, *Inhabiting the Cruciform God: Kenosis, Justification, and Theosis in Paul's Narrative Soteriology* (Grand Rapids: Eerdmans, 2009), 25. Gorman speaks of kenosis as Christ's exercising his divinity, his equality with God (p. 27), rather than as an emptying of divinity.

by God in and through Christ: from Christ's incarnation to his exaltation, then to the second coming and to believers' own transformed, resurrected bodies fit to enjoy life forever with their Savior (3:21).

The character of the believer in Christ. Such salvation, Paul declares, sets the image and goal of each believer's life. If God's character is self-giving and self-humbling, believers should expect their own journeys to reflect selflessness and generosity. Yet the journey is not simply about the here and now, for Paul pushes the Philippians to take an eternal view of their life. He does not write a self-help booklet about gaining prosperity or success, for that would betray gospel truth. Instead, he speaks of partnership in the struggles and sufferings that characterized the Savior's life and thus are a hallmark of his church's testimony to the world.

Paul's deep reflection on his own story helps the Philippians make sense of their own situation. His life as a Pharisee provided the necessary groundwork and perspective from which to recognize the magnificence of God's Messiah, Jesus, and to "serve God by his Spirit" (3:3). His Roman imprisonment galvanized the local church to stand fast and to preach Christ (1:15–16). And Paul's conviction that Christ's resurrection promises his own new and transformed life permeates and shapes his daily life (3:13–14).

The letter to the Philippians reveals a fundamental reality of the gospel: Jesus' story reshapes our story. A believer's past, present, and future take on redeemed significance as Jesus' story infuses our story. Or better said: our story takes on eternal significance because Jesus' story gathers up our individual stories, our individual past and present, into his story of redemptive love. Jesus' story of incarnation, cross, resurrection, and glorification establishes that a believer's past need not define his or her future — sins forgiven, fellowship with God restored. Jesus' story of obedience and suffering reinterprets believers' present struggle, pain, and heartache. Jesus' story reminds us that his final destruction of sin and death lies in the future. Thus the present is marred by evil and suffering, yet Jesus' story ends not with the cross, but with glorification, and his resurrection points to this glorious event when all will confess Jesus as Lord (2:11).

The character of believers together in Christ. While Paul encourages each believer to reconsider their own stories through the lens of Jesus' story, he stresses just as strongly that an individual believer's story is inextricably tied with other believers who make up the local church. Indeed, Jesus' story includes creating a people of God united by their belief and God's Spirit, a people whose identity is tied to the new heavens and new earth. In each chapter, Paul uses the word group *koinōnia* (fellowship/partnership/participation, 1:5; 2:1; 3:10; 4:15), praising the church's commitment to Paul's ministry, and encouraging them to unify more deeply within their local community.

This unity means more than laboring together on community service projects, as important as such outreach is. A Christlike attitude includes humbly serving other believers, sharing godly love and pursuing the good of others. Even as a sports team cannot long withstand grumbling and grousing in their midst, so too the local church cannot thrive amidst gossip and griping (2:14).

This is especially true in settings where the church is small and is a minority in its setting. A friend of mine worked for several years overseas in a city divided between Christians and Muslims, serving in a church of about twenty believers. It was the only church in a Muslim area—no alternative if a disagreement arose, or the music was not to your taste, or the children's ministry was unsatisfying. The choices were three: stop going to church, tear the church apart over the disagreement, or strive with urgency toward unity.[3] The Philippians' circumstances mirrored my friend's experience. Paul asks that believers have the same mind in Christ, avoiding schisms but rather laying down one's own vain pursuits and ambitions (2:3). It means a harmony built on self-giving love.

An invitation to theological reflection. Participating in Christ's story as individual believers and together as a local church includes embracing theological reflection. For those of us in the West who created an eleventh commandment, "thou shalt be efficient," this call for reflection is often shifted to one side as unproductive. But like the Philippians, we too must appreciate the link between our actions and attitudes. Broadly speaking, Paul invites us (1) to consider God's activities and purposes in creation and salvation, (2) reflect on God's calling in our own lives, and (3) embrace a mind-set that privileges others above ourselves.

Paul's theological reflection on God's salvation story reaches back before time and forward beyond the end of time. He speaks of Christ Jesus as "being in very nature God" (2:6), a member of the Trinity, who exists outside of time and is unconstrained by space. He reflects on God's giving of the law to Israel (3:5–6) and on Jesus Christ's incarnation and life of obedience even to death on a cross (2:6–8). Paul regarded the law's subsequent status at the coming of Christ Jesus and the Spirit (3:3–7). He considered God's present working in the Philippians, energizing them to great sacrifices as they gave from their poverty and embraced even more poverty as part of their public confession of Christ (4:14–19). Paul thought about the common values shared by Christians and others in Philippi (4:4–8).

Paul's theology cannot be separated from his views on a believer's spiritual growth. To speak of Christology is to speak of the believer's life in Christ. To

---

3. From a conversation with my TA, Greg Thellman, 1/16/2013.

speak of the Holy Spirit is to speak of its empowering presence in the believer's life. To speak of the Father is to speak of the glorious, gracious plan of salvation that overcomes all evil and makes all things new. God works, God wills, God has a purpose — one that is good and includes our participation (2:13). Paul's theology, then, is not separate from God's story of redemption, and thus our individual story of redemption in Christ becomes another note in the grand symphony God composes down through time. This goes beyond imitation of discrete actions to embracing Christ's story, such that a believer's life becomes a "*living exegesis*" of Christ's story.[4] Morna Hooker sums up this point well in her analysis of the hymn/poem of Christ in 2:6 – 11:

> The pattern of Christ's self-humiliation is the basis of the Christian's life and of his dealings with his fellow men. This is not simply a question of following a good example: he *must* think and behave like this, because the behaviour of Christ is the ground of his redemption; if he denies the relevance of Christ's actions to his own, then he is denying his very existence in Christ.[5]

These important theological themes must always be in our peripheral vision. They are tethered to the specific situation addressed by Paul as one "in chains." Thus we now turn to examine historical questions concerning the writing of the letter to the Philippians.

Why Paul Wrote Philippians

No serious questions challenge Pauline authorship of Philippians,[6] and all commentators place the letter toward the end of Paul's ministry, at least in his third journey if not during his imprisonment in Rome (cf. Acts 28). This latter theory is defended below, placing the date of Philippians to about AD 60 – 62.

Paul wrote this letter to the Philippians because he could not travel to speak with these believers personally. He was imprisoned, something similar to house arrest, which restricted his movement but not his writing. Paul also wrote to address the Philippians' concern for his well-being. Their anxiety

---

4. Michael J. Gorman, *Cruciformity: Paul's Narrative Spirituality of the Cross* (Grand Rapids: Eerdmans, 2001), 92, italics original.

5. Morna D. Hooker, *From Adam to Christ: Essays on Paul* (Cambridge: Cambridge University Press: 1990), 25.

6. For a general introduction to letter writing at the time of Paul, see E. Randolph Richards, *Paul and First-Century Letter Writing: Secretaries, Composition and Collection* (Downers Grove, IL: InterVarsity Press, 2004). See also P. T. O'Brien, "Letters, Letter Forms," in *DPL*, 550 – 53.

had several layers, based on their limited knowledge of his situation, their continued financial support, and apparent hearsay about the local church's responses to his imprisonment (1:12–18, 23; 4:10, 14). Paul wants to reassure them of his good health, his confidence in their support, and his own likely release from prison.

Paul's Imprisonment on Behalf of the Gospel

Paul states that he is "in chains" (1:13, 17) in the proximity of the Praetorian Guard (NIV "palace guard," 1:13; cf. also 4:22). This was the elite guard of Caesar, stationed in Rome. But the term could also describe a provincial governor's headquarters and troops (see Mark 15:16; John 18:28, 33; 19:9; Acts 23:35, which speak of Roman troops in the *imperial* province of Roman Palestine).[7] When considering Paul's location in writing Philippians, most note he likely wrote Philemon during the same imprisonment, and some argue that he also wrote Colossians, and perhaps Ephesians.[8] Moreover, Timothy co-wrote the letter with Paul; regardless of how one explains Timothy's contribution, clearly he is with Paul as the letter is written (1:1; 2:19). Such details limit possible locations to either Ephesus or Rome (Caesarea Maritima is unlikely).[9]

The city of Ephesus is much closer to Philippi than Rome. Some argue that this is the likely spot for Paul's imprisonment, for such proximity would better accommodate the journeys between Philippi and Paul's place of imprisonment made by Epaphroditus and Timothy. Additionally, Acts indicates that Paul visited Philippi three times, including his initial visit (Acts 16:12; 20:1, 3, 6). Second Corinthians also suggests that Paul visited several times (2 Cor 1:16; 2:13; 7:5; 13:1), but Philippians itself seems silent about any subsequent visits. If the letter was written before 2 Corinthians (dated to ca. AD 55), during a time of imprisonment in Ephesus, such silence is understandable.

---

7. Imperial provinces such as Judea carried the emperor's mediated rule through governors, whose headquarters were designated as a *praetorium*.

8. The latter two epistles are often considered deutero-Pauline. I have elsewhere defended the Pauline authorship of Ephesians (see *Ephesians* [New Covenant Commentary; Eugene, OR: Cascade, 2010]) and consider Colossians as Pauline. But decisions on Philippians do not depend on conclusions reached on the authorship of Ephesians and Colossians. General discussions on Pauline authorship include Terry L. Wilder, *Pseudonymity, the New Testament, and Deception: An Inquiry into Intention and Reception* (Lanham, MD: University Press of America, 2004); Hans-Josef Klauck, *Ancient Letters and the New Testament: A Guide to Context and Exegesis* (trans. Daniel P. Bailey; Waco, TX: Baylor University Press, 2006).

9. Caesarea Maritima is an unlikely candidate: (1) Paul's mention of the Praetorian Guard and "Caesar's household" (1:13; 4:22) would have sounded pretentious since Caesarea was considered a frontier or backwater town, especially to Philippian ears; (2) Acts 24:26; 25:27 indicate that Paul did not face serious threats of execution at Caesarea; (3) the travel between Philippi and Caesarea is the most difficult of the three possible cities. See Marcus Bockmuehl, *The Epistle to the Philippians* (BNTC; Peabody, MA: Hendrickson, 1998), 29–30.

Moreover, Ephesus is close to Colossae, about a hundred miles away, which makes it a likely place for Paul to meet Onesimus, the slave of Philemon.[10]

Yet critical points speak against Ephesus, especially since we have no evidence that the Praetorian Guard was stationed in Ephesus, a city located in a *senatorial* province.[11] Second, we have no evidence that Paul was imprisoned in Ephesus, although it is entirely possible that he spent some time in jail there.[12] But the imprisonment described in Philippians extended over many months and was based on a capital charge. As a Roman citizen, it would be unlikely for Paul to be imprisoned for any length in Ephesus on a capital charge; rather, he would have been transported to Rome.

Rome is thus the more likely city from which Paul wrote Philippians, connecting the writing of this letter with the imprisonment noted in Acts 28:14–31. Not only does Rome fit most naturally with the mention of the Praetorian Guard, but it also explains the numerous believers near Paul, some of whom have no apparent loyalty to the apostle (1:15–17). Additionally, those of "Caesar's household" (4:22) most likely hail from Rome.[13]

Moreover, travel between Philippi and Rome was quick by ancient standards, given that the well-traveled *Via Egnatia* ran right through the city and on to points east to Byzantium and west to the port city of Dyrrhachium on the Adriatic Sea.[14] A typical courier using a chariot could make eighty kilometers a day, and a person walking could average thirty kilometers. Sea travel was much faster; travel by boat from the port at Neapolis (twelve miles from Philippi) to Rome via Corinth was a matter of a week or so. Perhaps Epaphroditus traveled by road to western Greece, and from there by ship to Brundisium, a port city on the eastern coast of Italy, a day trip if the winds were good. From there it was about a three-week journey west to Rome (approximately 350 miles). Then, as now, it is not merely the miles that one travels, but the accessibility to good roads and ships that determines travel times.[15] Philippi

---

10. Often Onesimus is labeled a runaway slave, and thus fleeing to Ephesus would be more likely than making it all the way to Rome. I suggest Onesimus is not a runaway, but was sent by Philemon to help Paul in Rome, in his imprisonment; see Cohick, *Ephesians*, 28–30.

11. Bockmuehl, *Philippians*, 28, notes that the three inscriptions from Ephesus mentioning a *praetorianus* were speaking about the man's previous position, not his current role in Ephesus.

12. Paul indicates he had many opportunities to preach the gospel in Ephesus and remained there longer to take advantage of these open doors (see Acts 19:8–22).

13. Bockmuehl, *Philippians*, 31, highlights that approximately 70 percent of all first-century inscriptions indicating someone from Caesar's household are located in Rome, and fully 96 percent come from Rome, Italy, and North Africa.

14. The distance from Philippi to Dyrrhachium was about 350 miles, see J. B. Lightfoot, *St. Paul's Epistle to the Philippians* (London: Macmillan, 1868), 37, n 1.

15. L. J. Kreitzer, "Travel in the Roman Empire," *DPL*, 945–46, offers a useful summary of travel by sea and road in the ancient world. See also Lionel Casson, *Travel in the Ancient World* (Baltimore, MD: The Johns Hopkins University Press, 1994).

to Rome would have presented many options for travel and courier service, making communication relatively simple between the two cities during Paul's two years of imprisonment in Rome.

Paul's Encouragement to the Philippians

As Paul continues to preach and teach under house arrest in Rome, stories of his situation float back to Philippi, creating concern and nervousness among his partners in the gospel. Paul's letter addresses these accounts by supporting their basic outline but putting them into gospel perspective. Yes, he has faced opposition, but it has had the pleasant consequence of emboldening some believers (1:15–18). Yes, he could be executed, but this knowledge has served to clarify more completely his own activities as Christ's apostle (1:19–26). Yes, Epaphroditus was quite ill, but God healed him (2:25–30). Yes, he received the gift from them, and he rejoices in their sustained and deep friendship (1:3–4; 4:10).

Paul also encourages the Philippians to consider their own circumstances from a gospel vantage point. Seventeen times in this short letter he repeats the call for a mind-set or disposition that rightly reflects the character of those who claim to be followers of Christ.[16] For Paul, loving actions spring from a heart and mind centered in the reality of Christ's salvation. The call for theological reflection is strongest in 2:1–5.[17] Paul asks that the church reflect on the ramifications of their unity with Christ and on how they function together. Moreover, a sharing of the Spirit, a unity with Christ, an experience of God's love should result in a humble mind-set evidenced by seeking the good of others. This sort of thinking is not switched on for a half hour during one's private devotions or for the hour spent at church worship Sunday morning. Rather, it permeates a believer much as a high school crush consumes its victim's thoughts and behavior, or as an infant absorbs its mother's every waking thought.

Paul's Composition of Philippians

In our day of texting, tweeting, and photo sharing, the art of letter writing has become a quaint pastime, a carryover from the worlds of Jane Austen or later Victorians. The modern reader is unprepared for the level of scholarly discussion and disagreement surrounding Paul's letters as relates to their form and argumentation. Two particular concerns receive focused attention in relation

---

16. Ten times in this letter Paul uses the verb *phroneō* ("think [rightly], be wise, comprehend, purpose such and such things), see 1:7; 2:2 (2x), 5; 3:15 (2x), 19; 4:2, 10 (2x). Paul uses *hēgeomai* in 2:3, 6, 25; 3:7, 8 ("consider, regard") and *logizomai* in 3:13; 4:8 ("count, think").

17. Here *phroneō* and *hēgeomai* occur five times in as many verses.

to Philippians: (1) the genre of the letter, specifically whether it should be identified as a friendship letter, and (2) the integrity of the canonical letter to the Philippians, whether it is a compilation of several letters sent to the Philippians. Both of these questions have profound influence on how the letter is understood.

We will only briefly touch on the second question, as detailed explanations can be found elsewhere.[18] We will treat the letter as a unity for several reasons. First, every ancient manuscript has it as a single letter. Second, we have no historical parallel of an editor taking a collection of letters and stitching them together. Third, postulating an editor to explain the abrupt transitions (e.g., 3:1 to 3:2) or Paul's failure to thank the Philippians at the beginning of the letter only kicks the interpretive task can further down the exegetical road. Stronger and more solid arguments support the letter's unity;[19] specific issues on abrupt transitions and Paul's placement of his thanksgiving will be dealt with in the commentary.

The first question about labeling Philippians as a friendship letter must be carefully examined. These issues include whether this letter exhibits specific literary characteristics defining the subgenre "friendship letter" known from the ancient world. Second, does Philippians show informal use of friendship categories without framing them in a friendship letter genre? Third, how does Paul envision the paradigm of friendship based on the reality of the gospel?

(1) Several commentators argue that Philippians is best read as a friendship letter. Walter Hansen notes ten expressions of friendship found in Philippians that parallel Hellenistic conventions, including the affection and partnership shared by Paul and the Philippians, the struggles against common enemies, and a desire to be united in spirit and share the same virtues.[20] But a close examination of the letter reveals that Paul does not use the form or structure of a friendship letter. "Philippians ill fits the examples of such a letter type in the theorists handbooks, and one wonders if such letters ever were written and were not simply for schoolboy exercises and a classification scheme seldom found in 'pure' form."[21] For example, we do not find in Paul's letters the terms

---

18. John Reumann offers a defense of Philippians as a composite letter (*Philippians* [AYB; New Haven, CT: Yale University Press, 2008], 8–18. Bockmuehl, *Philippians*, 20–25, summarizes the arguments and defends the letter's unity.

19. Gordon Fee, *Paul's Letter to the Philippians* (NICNT; Grand Rapids: Eerdmans, 1995), 22–23, argues for the letter's unity, noting the common vocabulary throughout all four chapters.

20. Walter Hansen, *The Letter to the Philippians* (PNTC; Grand Rapids: Eerdmans, 2009), 6–11.

21. John Reumann, "Philippians, Especially Chapter 4, as a 'Letter of Friendship': Observations on a Checkered History of Scholarship," in *Friendship, Flattery, and Frankness of Speech: Studies on Friendship in the New Testament World* (ed. John T. Fitzgerald; Leiden: Brill, 1996), 105. See also

philia or *philos* — the two terms translated as friendship/love. James 4:4 is the only place in the New Testament to use the noun *philia*: "*Love/friendship with the world means enmity against God.*" Although arguments from silence are often weak, the term's non-appearance may be due to a deliberate choice by early Christians to distance themselves from direct connection with the Greco-Roman friendship construct.[22]

Moreover, the ancient convention configures friendship as between two socially equal adult males. Yet in Philippians, Paul remains the senior partner in their fellowship, even though he and Timothy do not use the title "apostle" in this letter. Bockmuehl argues that Paul does not use the social paradigm of mutual reciprocity that governed ancient friendships.[23] Moreover, the ancient friendship included an element of competition between the friends for honor and wealth; such agonistic elements are absent from Philippians.

(2) If not a formal letter of friendship, might the general social conventions of friendship have guided Paul? These cultural conventions were drawn from Aristotle's description of three types of friendships: (a) based on utility, (b) based on pleasure, and (c) based on virtue.[24] Clearly Paul sought a friendship based on Aristotle's third option, a virtuous partnership together in the gospel (see 4:10 – 20, where Paul speaks to the Philippians' financial gift giving toward his ministry, a repeated activity that cemented their friendship). The tone of the letter is warm and friendly. Finally, Paul's call to stand with each other in unity (2:1 – 5) draws on the fact that friendship is tested over the long haul; good friendships take time to build.

(3) We are well reminded that, while Paul is not bound by existing categories, he is also connecting with real people who have particular social dispositions and assumptions that must be accounted for, whether accepted or rejected. That is, Paul's readers would have specific assumptions about how a relationship works. As we understand those assumptions, we are better able to see how Paul overturns or reconfigures ancient friendship.[25] Indeed, even Fee, who argues strongly for Philippians as a friendship letter, in the end carefully

---

Stanley Stowers, *Letter Writing in Greco-Roman Antiquity* (Philadelphia: Westminster, 1986), 60: "Although there are no letters of friendship in the New Testament, some letters employ commonplaces and language from the friendly letter tradition." L. Michael White, "Morality between Two Worlds: A Paradigm of Friendship in Philippians," in *Greeks, Romans, and Christians: Essays in Honor of Abraham J. Malherbe* (ed. D. Balch et al.; Minneapolis: Fortress, 1990), 206, writes that Philippians exhibits "an emphasis on terms associated with the virtue of friendship."

22. Bockmuehl, *Philippians*, 34.

23. Ibid., p. 35.

24. Aristotle, *Nichomachean Ethics* 1155a3, 1156a16 – 1156b23 (LCL). Aristotle pronounced that "to a noble man there applies the true saying that he does all for the sake of his friends . . . if need be even to the point of death" (9.1169a).

25. See further discussion on friendship and patronage in Phil 4.

nuances this label with the additional notes that this is Christian friendship, and it is hortatory.[26] We must be alert to the emphases for Christian formation stressed in Philippians.

Content of Philippians

One Sunday morning as I was writing this introduction, my husband, Jim, decided to read Philippians all in one sitting. Later I asked him what struck him as central to the letter. He quickly answered that it was Paul's single-minded direction toward Christ, his belief that he could do all things through Christ's strength. Yet those "things" were not typical of the world's definition of success; rather, they were in spite of the trials within and outside the church. He recognized Paul's counterintuitive viewpoint, the disregard for notoriety or even appreciation, and the joyful freedom that surrender to Christ brings. Jim grasped the essence of Philippians' power, namely, its ability to draw readers into Paul's story, which is part of the larger story written by God for the church.

As I reflected on Jim's response, two additional ideas came to mind. First, Paul's appeal comes in part from his candid description of his ministry—the ups and downs, the apparent failures and struggles; here is a man writing that he can do all things, and yet he has been under house arrest for months. Second, Paul is vulnerable and open to an entire community, not just to his best friend or in a private prayer to God. What follows are brief observations summarizing Paul's call for Christian formation, based on his theological convictions.

Paul's Injunctions to the Philippians

The category of friendship captures Paul's warm tone, the evident strong relationship between Paul and the Philippians, and the language of fellowship and giving and receiving (including financial gifts). These add up to a letter that should shape our understanding of relationships between believers in Christ. Fowl suggests the church today would benefit from a long, deep drink from this well.[27] Christian formation such as Paul describes it here is bound up with friendship—a believer's spiritual growth is irreducibly linked to Christian care of one another. The West's reflexive individualism often blinds us to the reality that true piety is gained in community. Paul insists that to grow spiritually, to live into God's story for the church, believers *must* foster and cultivate

---

26. Fee, *Philippians*, 14.
27. Stephen E. Fowl, *Philippians* (THC; Grand Rapids: Eerdmans, 2005), 208–9.

friendship. Philippians offers a concise summary of what godly friendship looks like—and this vision challenges the church today.

Christian formation includes at least four elements: steadfastness (1:27–30), blamelessness (2:15), submission to one another (2:2–4),[28] and joy (3:1; 4:4). Each of these is inextricably bound up in community, in friendship, and in the call for unity (2:2–5). The Philippians are called to stand firm as one unit against the onslaughts from the wider world (1:27–30). Their blameless and pure lives are shaped in the crucible of real-life interaction with each other and in the wider society in Philippi. Paul relates their blamelessness to their refusal to grumble or argue. Instead of arguing, Paul invites the Philippians to value others above their own ego or public honor (2:2–4). All this leads to deep-seated joy, such that grows more satisfying as it develops and bears fruit in the steadfast hope of the coming of the Savior (3:20–21).

Challenges to Community Building

The challenges to our way of thinking about friendship and community come in several forms. First, the friendship Paul talks about is not a matter of like-minded people gathering together for a specific purpose, such as worship. The community Paul envisions is comprised of those who proclaim Jesus as Lord, the one who makes of each individual someone new. Thus believers are organically connected with others who are new creatures in Christ. Friendship as Paul imagines it is not part of a "to do" list that believers prioritize based on their circumstances and personal proclivities. Entering God's story with the declaration that Jesus is Lord radically changes who we are and makes us part of a new family, a new social entity, a new eschatological reality. "Entering into friendships in Christ such as Paul, the Philippians and we do is not simply an added benefit of the Christian life; it is constitutive of the Christian life."[29]

Second, we tend to think of Christian friendship through the prism of the old saying, "You can choose your friends, but you are stuck with your family." Thus we think of friendship in church as something we decide to enter into, and do so for our own pleasure or enrichment. The friendship displayed on the pages of Philippians, however, stresses that Christ *chose* us. This reshapes what friendship is all about—service, not self.

What might this look like? Fowl mentions two examples. A reshaped view

---

28. Submission to others in our fallen world can lead to being abused. Certain safeguards include constructing friendships not as sets of pairs but as several individuals in community. Second, continue to study Scripture and stand on the foundational Christian teachings such as the Trinity, the atonement in Christ alone, and the second coming of Christ. Third, set godly boundaries, recognizing that submission does not mean that abuse is acceptable. Christian counselors can be of great help in discerning whether particular relationships are toxic.

29. Fowl, *Philippians*, 215.

of friendship should reframe our conversations from a primary focus on our own stories to a decidedly God-focused content. We see ourselves and fellow believers as part of God's story, and we encourage, challenge, and exhibit behavior that matches such reality.[30] A second example centers on the makeup of the Philippian church—a complex, heterogeneous mixture of Jews and Gentiles, slaves and free. Friendship is hard in that context, and today, in pursuing the laudable goal of growing church attendance, we might choose to build homogeneous communities rather than wrestle with the rich complexity that is Christ's church.[31]

A missionary working in central Europe among a Muslim population found himself facing such a challenge. The gospel message attracted many Muslim gypsies, a group generally looked down upon by the wider Muslim society. If this small church welcomed the Gypsies, would they alienate the majority Muslim population? After much deliberation about the church's call to love and unity, the believers embraced the Muslim gypsies, even with the added struggles that decision brought in reaching the majority of Muslims in the area.[32]

Paul suggests that friendship is one of God's ways to mature us as believers. He sees community and unity as opportunities to change from the old (selfish) way of thinking about the world and one's place in it, to a new, joy-filled, selfless way of engaging others in Christ. Friendship allows us to be stretched, to confess our anger, to repent of our sense of being unappreciated. It grooms us to not insist on our own way, but to march to someone else's drum for a bit. It invites real service, the kind that only the heavenly Father knows about.

This sounds like Jesus' command to his disciples that they love each other (John 15:9–17). Jesus defines ultimate love as laying down one's life for one's friends. This is precisely what he did with his death on the cross. Three terms connect this passage with Philippians: *love*, *friend*, and *joy*. First, Paul prays that the Philippians' *love* will abound in knowledge and insight (Phil 1:6) that comes from Christ for God's glory (1:11). He calls for the steadfast to stand firm alongside a fellow believer when opponents batter their business or slander their good name (1:27–29). He asks Euodia and Syntyche to lay down all "rights to be right" and instead seek a singular purpose in Christ (4:2–3). Second, Jesus identifies the disciples as no longer servants but *friends*. So too, Paul will repeatedly encourage the Philippians to think differently, to consider their world in light of the gospel. Third, Jesus promises complete *joy* to those disciples who remain in his love. Paul takes hold of this promise, stressing

---

30. Ibid., 223.
31. Ibid., 216.
32. Conversation with Greg Thellman, 1/16/2013.

that such joy should be characteristic of a believer's posture (joy is a theme of this letter).

Paul's Theological Claims

Not only are Paul's injunctions about Christian formation rooted in Christ's commands that believers love each other with the self-sacrificial love demonstrated by Christ on the cross, but they are also to remain in him as the branches remain in the vine (John 15:1–11). This image of salvation can be identified as participatory, for the emphasis is on the mutual indwelling of Christ and believers.[33] This picture is especially helpful in reading Philippians, where the theological reality of "union with Christ" best describes Paul's theological emphasis. It is also useful in explaining the lack of typical salvation verbs and terms such as "faith" (3:9 [2x]) and "grace" (1:7) in this epistle, because "union with Christ" language in its complexity and nuance encompasses the breadth of salvation theology even as it also presupposes and builds on the historical reality of Christ's death and resurrection.

Believers "in Christ"

There are several ways in which the phrase "in Christ" and related phrases ("in the Lord," "in him")[34] function as Paul's theological "shorthand" for the actions of God the Father and Christ the Son in our redemption and new life. First, being "in Christ" involves union, participation, identification, and incorporation into Christ's life.[35] These terms capture the multifaceted redemption brought by Christ. Moreover, they suggest that relationship is possible; notice that Paul wants to *know* Christ and to *gain* Christ (3:8). The relationship is made possible by the incarnation and made salvific by Christ's death on the cross (2:6–8), resurrection (3:10), exaltation (2:9), and future return when all things will be brought under his control (3:21).

Second, the prepositions in these phrases (such as "in," "by," "with," "into," "through") present different angles from which to view our relationship with Christ. These include (but are not limited to) a locative sense, which emphasizes the sphere of influence or realm of Christ (4:1), as well as causal, which focuses on something being true *because* of Christ (3:1).[36] Union with Christ involves both the static or objective place held by a believer based on Christ's resurrection (3:10), and the dynamic, participatory nature of being found in

---

33. Brenda B. Colijn, *Images of Salvation in the New Testament* (Downers Grove, IL: InterVarsity Press, 2010), 248–50.

34. Paul uses such phrases about twenty-one times in Philippians. See Fee, *Philippians*, 49.

35. Constantine R. Campbell, *Paul and Union with Christ: An Exegetical and Theological Study* (Grand Rapids: Zondervan, 2012), 29.

36. Ibid., 161–62.

Christ (3:9). As Campbell observes, "To know Christ is not the same as being found in him, since the former concept holds Christ as object, while the latter notion partakes in him."[37]

As we explore Philippians, then, we must be alert to the language of union with Christ. Talk of union, however, should not blind us to Paul's assumptions underlying his thought about the uniqueness of Christ's person and work. Christ has life in himself, for Christ is God, and God is life. Humans share in that life through Christ, but we do not have this life apart from God's grace. This means that our union with Christ is not identical to the union shared by the Father and the Son, which is marked by *perichoresis* or the mutual indwelling of the Father, Son, and Spirit. At best, our union with God in Christ is merely analogous in a limited way to the perichoretic union that exists within the Godhead because we do not share in the life of the Godhead by nature as God does. Our life, or the life of the church, unites with the Godhead strictly through the power and grace of the latter.

Perichoresis is related to the Greek term "to dance around," so if we build on this image, perhaps we can imagine the church's indwelling or abiding with the Trinity, much as a couple dances together holding their baby in their arms. The baby has no power to dance in herself; she is completely dependent on her parents. Yet, through the actions of her parents, she is also participating in her parents' dance (probably with a big smile!)

Paul stresses Christ's vicarious atonement even as he expounds on union with Christ. He does this by emphasizing that Christ achieves salvation on behalf of humanity, and no individual believer contributes to his or her forgiveness of sins before God. Thus our participation in Christ is of a particular sort; it is "the gracious inclusion in the achievements of another,"[38] with Christ as our representative, acting on our behalf, but with us and in us. The church father Athanasius argued, "The achievements of the Savior, effected by his incarnation, are of such a kind and number that if anyone should wish to expound them he would be like those who gaze at the expanse of the sea and wish to count its waves."[39] Using another metaphor, we might think of a believer in Christ as an echo of Christ's work; the echo imitates the original sound but is always secondary to it.

The goal of union with Christ is not a happier, more prosperous life here and now; indeed, Paul speaks of participation in Christ's sufferings (3:10). The aim is transformation — the sort that is accomplished only at Christ's

---

37. Ibid., 234.
38. Ibid., 351.
39. Athanasius, *On the Incarnation* 54 (trans. and ed. by John Behr; Yonkers, NY: St. Vladimir's Seminary Press, 2011), 167.

return (3:21). Thus Paul emphasizes in his theological reflection the day of Christ (1:6) and the return of the Savior (3:20–21) as he thinks theologically about God's salvation plan. Said another way, in Philippians, eschatology (the study of the end things) sounds a consistent note through each chapter. To make sense of God's character and to understand who Jesus Christ is, Paul points us to the final phase of the redemption story. Once we know where we are going, we understand more fully Paul's specific comments about God, Christ, and the gospel. Union with Christ highlights God's character as it relates to all aspects of redemption and our inclusion in the gospel story. As Colijn remarks, "For Paul, 'being in Christ' is not a transaction but a real spiritual union between Christ and the believer that determines the believer's identity and shapes all of the believer's life."[40]

Whom Paul Addresses in the Letter

The Philippian church has the honor of being the first church established by Paul in Macedonia. The story of its beginnings occupies most of Acts 16 and includes several unusual features that mark the church's special character. The letter does not connect immediately with the Acts account, nor does it contradict it. Rather, these two chapters in the church's life stand side by side as windows into its life experiences and theological expressions.

This brief overview of the Philippian church serves more than to satisfy historical curiosity. First, it represents the theological conviction that the letter spoke to real believers in a real time in history. Its language conveyed gospel truth in culturally accessible ways to believers eager to grow in Christ. The insistence on the historical importance of the first-century Philippian context reinforces the historical reality of Christ's own life, death, and resurrection. Christianity is a faith rooted in historical events and insists those events shape human history. Second, the interest in the historical Philippian church imposes an interpretive lens that seeks to understand the text as it would have been understood to the initial reader/listener. That is, it insists on authorial intention; it holds that Paul the apostle wrote this letter with particular ideas in mind that he was able to communicate to his first-century audience.

The Philippian Church from Acts 16 and Philippians

The coming of the gospel to Philippi in Acts 16:9–40 began with a vision. Paul saw a man from Macedonia (the Roman province in which Philippi was located) beckon him to come and help. Without delay, Paul and his

---

40. Colijn, *Images of Salvation*, 250.

companions set off for Philippi. To understand the impact of Paul's message, we must appreciate the social and political makeup of Philippi in the first century AD, specifically its Roman colony status, its mixture of Roman, Greek, and foreign communities, and its Jewish inhabitants.[41]

Acts 16:13, 16 identifies the gathering of the Jews on the Sabbath as a *proseuchē* ("house of prayer") and notes that Paul spoke only to women gathered at the river. From these details some postulate that this group had fewer than ten Jewish men and thus lacked the minimum number established in the rabbinic texts to form a *minyan* or quorum.[42] However, this position fails to appreciate that *proseuchē* was a common term used to identify Diaspora meetings, and *synagōgē* ("house of assembly") was the preferred choice for those gatherings in Judea.[43] Additionally, Luke states that Paul spoke with the women there; he does not state that few men were present. Luke's emphasis on women here counterbalances his later emphasis on the Philippian jailer. Luke often pairs stories about men and about women; thus, his focus on Lydia as one among this group of women matches his wider practices.[44] We need not read into his argument from silence that Jewish men were not present or were few in number.

Jews in Paul's day were not only part of a religion; they were also an ethnic group that had a political presence in Roman cities and often had limited self-governing privileges. Jews were one of many Eastern ethnic groups that puzzled and intrigued Romans. Today some Christians, especially those without many Jewish neighbors, tend to see Jews only through the lens of religion, but the ancient world held a broader definition of what constituted a Jew and the Jewish community.

Philippi as a Roman Colony

Philippi had the unusual distinction of being a Roman colony; that is, it carried the status of a city on Italian soil. It is the only city with this status that Paul visited (outside of Rome, of course). A close examination of the archaeological finds, inscriptions, and social studies of first-century Roman towns suggests that about 1 percent of the population (about 100) were retired

---

41. About 5,000–10,000 people lived in the city and surrounding suburbs of Philippi. See Peter Oakes, *Philippians: From People to Letter* (Cambridge: Cambridge University Press, 2001), 45.

42. See *m. Megillot* 4.3; *m. 'Abot* 3.7.

43. Lee I. Levine, "Common Judaism: The Contribution of the Ancient Synagogue," in *Common Judaism: Explorations in Second-Temple Judaism* (ed. Wayne O. McCready and Adele Reinhartz; Minneapolis: Fortress, 2008), 43.

44. Ben Witherington III, *The Acts of the Apostles: A Socio-Rhetorical Commentary* (Grand Rapids: Eerdmans, 1998), 328. Ann Graham Brock, "Luke the Politician: Promoting the Gospel by Polishing Christianity's Rough Edges," in *Early Christian Voices: In Texts, Traditions, and Symbols* (ed. David H. Warren, Ann Graham Brock, and David W. Pao; Leiden: Brill, 2003), 94.

Roman military men,[45] and about 23 percent of the population were colonists.[46] This small percentage, however, retained its strong Roman identity, as indicated by *Latin* inscriptions during the next two centuries.[47] Perhaps these men were descendants of those who fought in the battles outside Philippi between Octavian and Marc Antony against Brutus and Cassius (42 BC), or ten years later in the battle of Actium, in which Octavian bested Antony and Cleopatra. It was after this second battle that Octavian, now Caesar Augustus, renamed Philippi after himself, *Colonia Iulia Augusta Philippensis*. Retired Roman soldiers were given land there.

The Philippian Church

Although much is made of the Roman identity of Philippi, it is unlikely that Roman veterans were part of the early church or even part of the audience targeted with the gospel.[48] From the various groups that made up first-century Philippi, Paul would likely have had more access to those who worked in the city rather than those who commuted to the farming lands around the city. He would have interacted most with craftsmen, shopkeepers, and slaves, as well as any Jews and Gentile God-fearers such as Lydia (Acts 16:14). Perhaps the church had one or two elite members among the fifty to one hundred congregants. A third of the church may have been Roman citizens, taken from the service groups and the freed slaves who gained citizenship upon manumission; they would likely be quite poor.[49]

This general picture fits well with the few details we have of individual believers in Philippi. Lydia from Thyatira in Asia Minor (Acts 16:14) was at least fairly well off, if not elite, and likely her household included three or four relatives and perhaps half a dozen slaves. Euodia and Syntyche (Phil 4:2–3), as well as Epaphroditus, the deliverer of the gift to Paul (2:25–30), were also Greek, but their social status is unknown. We do not know if the slave girl healed by Paul joined the church (Acts 16:16–18), but it would fit the picture of the church including slaves. Another possible slave is the Philippian jailer (16:23, 27–34).[50]

---

45. Oakes, *Philippians*, 2. Unfortunately we do not have much evidence from the first century AD; see 38–39.

46. According to Oakes (ibid., 51–52), elite families, military families, and average farming families made up this percentage.

47. By the second century, Romans in cities such as Corinth often used Greek in their inscriptions (ibid., 36–37).

48. See Oakes, *Philippians*, 53.

49. Ibid., 62.

50. Ibid., 65. Davorin Peterlin, *Paul's Letter to the Philippians in the Light of Disunity in the Church* (Leiden: Brill, 1995), 144–50, suggests that the jailer was a public slave, for if he was freed, he would not have remained as jailer.

The Roman dominance over the Greek population was felt keenly, as Philippi's Roman colonial status included a strong emphasis on Latin and the reality that Romans owned most of the land, controlled the city's politics, and had a monopoly on the city's wealth.[51] Most in the church probably felt ambivalent toward Rome and the empire, especially the 60 to 65 percent who were non-Romans. Even some of the Roman believers, drawn from the service class and freed slaves, might also have had mixed emotions toward the Roman elite.

The Imperial Cult in Philippi

The imperial cult deserves special mention because it factors so extensively in current conversation about Paul and his context.[52] Scholars argue that Paul directly targets Caesar and the imperial cult in his message to the Philippians (and in his other letters). In shorthand, when Paul writes, "Jesus is Lord" he also intends "and Caesar is not." Does the evidence bear this out?

The archaeological evidence for the mid-first century in Philippi is meager, but a tentative consensus has emerged that two of the temples in the forum were dedicated to the imperial cult. Because the architecture is similar to other pagan temples, identification as an imperial cult temple usually relies on inscriptions.[53] An inscription, likely from the mid-first century, was discovered in Philippi's port, Neapolis, which identified Cornelia Asprilla as a priestess of Livia Augusta.[54] This information highlights an often forgotten fact about the imperial cult — it venerated members of the imperial family. By Paul's day, when Nero was emperor, not only Augustus, but his wife Livia and grandson Claudius had been deified, following Julius Caesar, Augustus's adopted father.

Since the people of Philippi lived amidst Roman imperial propaganda of all sorts, including the imperial cult, it seems incontrovertible that the Philippian believers made connections and drew distinctions between Paul's declaration of Jesus Christ as Savior and Rome's claims to bring peace and prosperity. That Paul would contrast the pagan rulers' claims for honor with God's rightful reception of honor fits well with his Jewish heritage, as Jews have a long history of rejecting paganism and promoting God as the true King over all creation.

---

51. Oakes, *Philippians*, 74.

52. For a careful discussion of this topic, see Scot McKnight and Joseph B. Modica, ed., *Jesus Is Lord, Caesar Is Not: Evaluating Empire in New Testament Studies* (Downers Grove, IL: InterVarsity Press, 2013).

53. Erik M. Heen, "Phil 2:6–11 and Resistance to Local Timocratic Rule: *Isa theō* and the Cult of the Emperor in the East," in *Paul and the Roman Imperial Order* (ed. Richard A. Horsley; Harrisburg, PA: Trinity Press International, 2004), 135.

54. Peter Pilhofer, *Philippi* (Tübingen, Mohr Siebeck, 2009), 2:2–3.

Additionally, much of the imperial cult's power was exercised through the patronage system, which reinforced the social hierarchy and stratification of individuals based on the world's assessment of social value. Paul has no patience for believers continuing the social hierarchy of the day (1 Cor 11:17–22). Yet I do not find compelling the argument that Paul has Caesar as his target as he establishes the identity of Jesus Christ.[55] Rather, Paul speaks more generally against the paganism of his time, distinguishing Jesus Christ as God's true revelation.

Summary of the Social and Political Realities in Philippi

Understanding the social and political realities within Philippi helps us appreciate Paul's call to unity and his encouragement to endure suffering. In Philippi, we have a wide array of social and economic classes, as well as a built-in tension between Romans and Greeks (and perhaps Jews and God-fearers), that makes unity hard to imagine outside of Christ. Again, service providers and shopkeepers lived a precarious economic existence, inasmuch as they were beholden to their trade guilds and to patrons. Confessing Christ was one way to scare away patrons and often resulted in the believer leaving the pagan trade guild or being ostracized from others doing similar work. In other words, economic hardships were a real dilemma for these earliest Gentile believers. The cost of following Jesus was not only in broken familial and professional relationships, but had a steep price tag attached in jobs lost.[56]

My own privileged position creates a blind spot to the reality of economic suffering in the pages of the New Testament, and I have a tendency to spiritualize the suffering motif. My shortsightedness was brought home to me during an exchange with an African sister in Christ, who responded to my question about how her village was coping with the two-year long drought. She said, "God is so good; no one has died of starvation." I think the Philippians would have understood her statement well.

The Opponents of the Philippian Church

The identity of those who oppose the Philippians has generated much discussion, and I confess none of the arguments fully convinces me. The verses that mention opponents include 1:27–30; 3:2; and 3:18–19.[57] The difficulties

55. Lynn H. Cohick, "Philippians and Empire: Paul's Engagement with Imperialism and the Imperial Cult," in *Jesus Is Lord, Caesar Is Not: Evaluating Empire in New Testament Studies* ed. Scot McKnight and Joseph B. Modica; Downers Grove, IL: InterVarsity Press, 2013), 166–82.

56. Oakes offers a detailed description of the possible economic suffering faced by Philippian believers. See *Philippians*, 89–93.

57. Paul also notes personal enemies who preach to gain some advantage over him (1:15–17). Yet they preach Christ and thus are part of the church, however "un-Christian" they are behaving towards the apostle. See commentary.

arise primarily because the data seem to point in different directions, or connect groups thought not to share similarities.

In general, two options are available. One theory argues that the opponents are Gentiles promoting Roman imperial propaganda, who persecute the believers. This theory draws on the verb *politeuomai* (meaning "live as citizens") in 1:27.[58] The verb carries the sense of being part of a commonwealth or civic group; a similar noun, *politeuma* ("citizenship") is used in 3:20.[59] This theory suggests that Paul draws on Philippi's special status as a Roman colony with Italian citizen privileges in distinguishing Gentile opponents from the church's primary allegiance to Christ. This reading makes good sense of these two rare terms in Paul by connecting them with the political and social reality in Philippi. It also stresses the real struggle the early church faced against paganism, including the growing imperial cult. Modern Western interpretation has tended to read back into the first century our own separation of religion and politics. In so doing we miss the religious support of political power and the belief among many that rulers were in some way divine.[60] Yet, as I noted above, this evidence can be pushed too far.

A second theory suggests that Jewish agitators promoting circumcision for Gentile believers are stirring up trouble within Paul's congregation. The specific evidence includes Paul's statements about the "dogs" that are a threat (3:2). In this theory, they are "enemies of the cross," who have twisted the gospel message to their own destruction (3:18–19). They have their minds on earthly things, while Paul stresses one's citizenship is in heaven. Thus the language of *politeuma* ("citizenship") is related to Diaspora Jewish experience, not to Roman citizenship. This theory accounts for Paul's lengthy discussion of Judaism in chapter 3 and connects these agitators with a similar group that invaded the Galatian churches. But it does not explain the opponents in 1:28 who appear to be frightening the Philippians with hardships and sufferings.[61]

In the end, I suggest that Paul has in mind two different groups, but gives a similar response to both. Specifically, Paul encourages the Philippians to stand firm in their faith against the onslaught of Gentile pagan opponents who promote Roman imperial propaganda and back it up with threats of

---

58. The verb is found only here and in Acts 23:1, "My brothers, I *have fulfilled my duty* to God in all good conscience to this day." English readers can see the roots of our term "politics" here.

59. The noun *politeia* ("citizenship") is found in Acts 22:28; Eph 2:12.

60. Jews were an obvious exception to this tendency; instead, they sacrificed *to God* each day an offering on behalf of the emperor.

61. Frank Thielman, *Philippians* (NIVAC; Grand Rapids: Zondervan, 1995), 19–21. Thielman connects the discussion of opponents noted in chapter 3 with his claim of an Ephesian origin to this letter, concluding that Paul warns the Philippians not to fall victim to the errors of the Galatian and Corinthian congregations.

violence and social and economic pressures. The same response—standing firm—is enjoined when faced with teaching that promotes circumcision as the path to full fellowship with God and God's people (3:2–3, 18–19). This group, made up of either Gentile believers who promote Jewish practices or Jewish believers doing the same,[62] is either a threatening danger on the horizon, or a danger that already has a foothold inside the city walls. " 'Persecution for the cross of Christ' (Gal 6:12) could therefore arise for Gentile Christians from the Roman state for Roman reasons; and for Jewish Christians like Paul, who advocated fellowship with Gentiles and thus the dismantling of Judaism's ethnic boundaries, from the synagogues for Jewish reasons."[63] In any case, Paul is clear on what believers should know and do: believers are the true "circumcision" (3:3), who embrace the cross (3:11, 18, by implication) and look beyond this moment to the day of Christ, our Lord and Savior (1:6; 3:21).

Format of This Commentary

Philippians offers a treasure trove of "good news" to the church today, even as it spoke welcome words of comfort, encouragement, and exhortation to the first-century believers in Philippi. This commentary examines Paul's teachings and biographical notes always with an eye to the church today—the men and women who desire a deeper relationship with God, a stronger foundation for their walk, and a clearer vision for God's working in the world beyond their immediate circle—according to the commentary pattern described in the introduction to The Story of God Bible Commentary series.

---

62. Bockmuehl, *Philippians*, 186, notes that the opponents who promote circumcision could be Gentile believers who had undergone circumcision to join the synagogue. These men now resent Paul's gospel message that Gentiles need not be circumcised to join God's family.

63. Ibid., 190.

CHAPTER 1

Philippians 1:1-2

 LISTEN to the Story

¹Paul and Timothy, servants of Christ Jesus,
To all God's holy people in Christ Jesus at Philippi, together with the overseers and deacons:
²Grace and peace to you from God our Father and the Lord Jesus Christ.

Listening to the text in the Story: Slaves: Numbers 12:7; Jeremiah 25.4; Romans 6:19; Philippians 2:7; Saints: Exodus 19:5–6; Deuteronomy 7:5–6; Acts 15:14; Timothy: 2 Timothy 1:5; Acts 16:1–3.

In his opening address to the Philippian church, Paul offers important personal, ecclesial, and theological hints about which he will expound in greater depth. Paul foreshadows here his forthcoming magnificent proclamation of Jesus as both God and human (2:6–11) by introducing the term "servant" ("slave"). With "grace" and "peace" Paul encapsulates his gospel message (3:8–11), and with his declaration that Philippian believers are "holy people" ("saints"), he prepares them for his discussion on godly living. Finally, declaring Jesus as "Lord" implies a distinction between the claims of Christ and the claims of Nero, the Roman emperor, and the pagan, imperial establishment.

EXPLAIN the Story

Servants (1:1)

Turning to the issue of slavery and the term "slave" (*doulos*), we should point out that though some English texts translate this as "servant" (see NIV), this weakens the force of the term in the minds of modern readers. A slave in Paul's day was owned legally by another and had no freedom apart from what the owner allowed.[1] In Paul's churches, some members were slaves, perhaps

---

1. As much as one-third of the population in Rome and perhaps 20 percent in Philippi were

owned by other church members; the most prominent example is Philemon and his slave Onesimus. Paul and Timothy use the historical force of such reality when they speak symbolically of being slaves of Christ. Paul elsewhere develops that every believer is a slave of righteousness (see Rom 6:19). Moreover, we should not forget that the common word for a slave owner is *kyrios* ("lord"; see Eph 6:9). Thus the terms "slave" and "Lord/lord" had an extensive tradition in the Greco-Roman culture, which Paul mines to highlight aspects of the gospel.

Ancient Israel practiced slavery, and the Old Testament includes numerous stories about it. One of the most famous slaves is Hagar, the mother of Ishmael, Abraham's first son (Gen 16:1–15). Recall too Israel's enslavement in Egypt, the defining moment in their history when God delivered them out of Egypt, "the land of slavery," and brought them to the land he had promised (Exod 12:40–13:3). Thus at key points in Israel's history, slavery played a role. But later Israelites owned other Israelites or Gentiles, who were enslaved through wars or to pay debts. Laws established appropriate treatment of slaves and restricted abuse (21:1–27). God's people were to release fellow slaves in the seventh year of their enslavement (Lev 25:39–43).[2]

In addition, in the Old Testament the terms "slavery" and "slave" are used metaphorically, often translated as "the servant of the LORD" (*'ebed yhwh*). Such a person had divine authority from God to speak and act on his behalf. For example, Numbers 12:7 speaks of his servant/slave Moses, who was faithful in God's house and to whom God spoke face to face (see also Jer 25:4; Ezek 38:17). Drawing on the Exodus narrative, Israel understood itself as God's slave, based on the exclusive covenant that Israel's God had established at Mount Sinai. Like a slave, Israel was to obey their God in all things, especially by rejecting idolatry.[3]

Paul probably had both the literal and the metaphorical uses of the term in mind when he described himself and Timothy as slaves of Christ.[4] This phrase is used several times in the New Testament, primarily referring to apostles and

---

slaves (Oakes, *Philippians*, 49). Freed slaves owed their masters certain obligations, which kept them tied to the owner's family even after their manumission.

2. Gentile slaves were not similarly released (Lev 25:44–6). If the slave did not wish to be freed, the owner was obligated to keep them for life (see Exod 21:3–4; Deut 15:12–18).

3. Interestingly, rarely do we find pagans referred to as slaves of a deity; see Dale B. Martin, *Slavery as Salvation: The Metaphor of Slavery in Pauline Christianity* (New Haven, CT: Yale University Press, 1990), xv–xvi.

4. For a discussion of the hermeneutical issues surrounding slavery in the New Testament, see William Webb, *Slaves, Women & Homosexuals: Exploring the Hermeneutics of Cultural Analysis* (Downers Grove, IL: InterVarsity Press, 2001). For different approaches to the use of this term, see John Byron, *Slavery Metaphors in Early Judaism and Pauline Christianity* (Tübingen: Mohr Siebeck, 2003), and Martin, *Slavery as Salvation*.

Christian leaders.[5] He will soon emphasize the socially demeaning aspect of slavery when he reinforces the point that Jesus Christ took on flesh and made himself nothing, a mere slave (Phil 2:7).

Holy People (1:1)

If the slave image draws from the lowest rung of the social ladder, Paul's description of the Philippian believers as "holy people" ("saints," *hagioi*) conveys a portrait of those at the top. Our modern understanding of the term carries a sense of human perfection preserved in stained glass windows — a far cry from our average existence. But not Paul's audience; in Exodus 19:5 – 6, God declares that if Israel will keep his commandments, they will be his treasured possession, a priestly kingdom, and a holy nation. Moses reiterates this in Deuteronomy 7:5 – 6, explaining that idolatry has no place among them for they are a people holy to the Lord. Paul indicates that the Philippians are "holy in Christ Jesus." Chrysostom, a fourth-century presbyter of Antioch and later bishop of Constantinople, notes that Paul had to distinguish the holy ones he spoke of as those in Christ, for Jews were likely to have used the label for themselves.[6]

Paul's intention in using the term *hagioi* and what it came to mean within church tradition do not line up. With the veneration of martyrs in the second century, the church began to develop what is now an elaborate system of canonization to sainthood in both Roman Catholicism and Eastern Orthodoxy. They define a saint as one who has demonstrated extraordinary piety, such as Mother Teresa, or attribute to him or her miracles based on their intercession before God. The modern structure of sainthood, however, should not be imposed back into Paul's day.

Overseers and Deacons (1:1)

To this community of believers in Philippi Paul bestows "grace and peace." He replaces the typical Greek "greetings" (*chairein*) with the word "grace" (*charis*) and thereby transforms the mundane for the gospel. Each letter, each message, is shaped by the grace of God shown in Christ Jesus (2 Cor 5:16 – 17).

Having so carefully stated his own status as a slave of Christ, it seems a bit ironic, if not contradictory, for Paul to mention the two leadership titles

---

5. Murray J. Harris, *Slave of Christ: A New Testament Metaphor for Total Devotion to Christ* (Downers Grove, IL: InterVarsity Press, 1999), 133. He notes that "slave of Christ" occurs ten times and "slaves of Christ" three times.

6. Chrysostom, "Homily I on Philippians," in *NPNF¹*, 13:184. See www.ccel.org/ccel/schaff/npnf113.pdf.

in the Philippian church: "overseers [bishops] and deacons." These terms are used infrequently in the New Testament, which makes it difficult to be precise about their meaning. Peter describes Jesus as the "Shepherd and Overseer" of believers' souls (1 Pet 2:25). In Acts 20:28, Paul addresses the Ephesian elders as "overseers" who shepherd both themselves and the church *among* (not *over*) whom the Holy Spirit has placed them. The image of the caring shepherd who lovingly attends to the sheep permeates these texts (see also Rom 16:1; 1 Tim 3:1–13; Titus 1:7).

Neither "overseer" nor "deacon" is found in the list of spiritual gifts; some have suggested that the terms are parallel to helpers and guides in 1 Corinthians 12:28.[7] Chrysostom suggests that the bishops (overseers) and deacons were responsible for collecting funds and sending Epaphroditus to support Paul while he was imprisoned. Although Paul does not mention these groups again when he thanks the community in 4:10–20, the Greek text of 1:3 can be understood as Paul thanking the Philippians for remembering him, in which case Paul would be connecting "the overseers and deacons" with the gift sent by the church to aid him in his chains. Because both words are plural, Paul is not speaking of a single bishop or overseer. Moreover, he does not speak of the "office" of bishop.[8] Therefore it is best to see these words as functions of administration and leadership within the Philippian community.

A final question relates to Timothy's role in this letter. At first glance it appears as if Paul and Timothy coauthored the letter.[9] This would match the practice in 1 and 2 Thessalonians. But in Philippians 1:3, we find the singular pronoun "I," not "we," where Paul is perhaps alluding to the gift that the Philippians extended to him while in prison. Perhaps, then, Timothy functions as Paul's secretary, so his own expressions intertwine with Paul's thoughts in this letter.

 LIVE the Story

One can hardly enter a bookstore or public library without noticing the numerous titles dealing with leadership. Moreover, the internet is filled with websites promising leadership training, and colleges and churches are estab-

---

7. Gerald F. Hawthorne, *Philippians* (rev. Ralph Martin; WBC; Nashville: Nelson, 2004), 7, notes this possibility, but does not endorse it.

8. First Timothy 3:1 in the NIV reads "office of bishop," but the term "office" is not in the Greek text.

9. Coauthoring a letter was uncommon in the ancient world. We have no extant examples of such, and only a single reference by Cicero to the practice, when he notes that Atticus wrote some letters in conjunction with others, *Att.* 11.15.1 (LCL 2.363).

lishing leadership programs. The task before us is to describe Paul's vision of godly leadership. In general, leadership carries with it responsibilities and the authority to get done what is required in the organization. We understand intuitively the need for moral character in our leaders,[10] but again, not everyone who lives uprightly is what people would call a leader. In fact, leadership is a rather slippery term; it is difficult to isolate specific leadership characteristics. Said another way, those characteristics we want in a Christian leader — trustworthiness, kindness, goodness — we hope to find in all believers.

Robert Greenleaf (1904 – 1990)[11] was a world-renowned teacher and writer who coined the phrase "servant leadership." In the 1960s he observed that corporations were not run with an eye to the public's needs. He advocated a leadership style that focused on making sure that both their constituents' needs and those of their employees were met. Many Christians gravitated to this message and found support for his principles in the Bible. Soon "servant leader" became the buzzword for describing Christ's own leadership style, but as with any term used too frequently, much of its content has become diluted. It has been used to reinforce an individualistic model of leadership that plagues some Western or American church structures. Moreover, often the description of "servant leader" is so general as to apply to all believers.

"Servant" functions as an adjective in the phrase "servant leader," so perhaps we would do better to speak of "service leaders," which suggests action and behavior rather than flat description. Additionally, because "servant" should be characteristic of every believer, the definition of "leader" becomes crucial, and we are back to the question we began with, namely, what is leadership, and more specifically, what is good or godly leadership.

Paul is described as a great leader because of his singleness of purpose. But is that characteristic of all good leaders? Or at times does leadership need to be flexible and innovative, not only in terms of method but also of goals? Others declare Paul's driven spirit makes him an effective and efficient leader. But this might say more about our Western admiration for efficiency and productivity. Paul seems to speak more about forming and maintaining relationships with his churches (see 1 Cor 3:1 – 4:16). And there is perhaps nothing less efficient than maintaining relationships, then and now.

Paul's understanding of his own leadership is complex. He does not hesitate to make known his calling as an apostle, but he sees that position not as

---

10. Nancy Beach, *Gifted to Lead: The Art of Leading as a Woman in the Church* (Grand Rapids: Zondervan, 2008). See also Joel Manby, *Love Works: Seven Timeless Principles for Effective Leaders* (Grand Rapids: Zondervan, 2012), e-pub edition.

11. Robert K. Greenleaf, *On Becoming a Servant Leader* (ed. Don M. Frick and Larry C. Spears; San Francisco: Jossey-Bass, 1996).

one that provides perks or even personal respect. An apostle is only as good as the one who called him (2 Cor 11:13–15). Paul describes himself as a clay jar (4:7), a weak vessel filled with a precious message. His mighty strength comes from the gospel, and if he preaches out of human resources or from human wisdom, the powerful message of the cross is eviscerated (1 Cor 1:17, 2:2–5).[12]

To the Philippians, Paul identifies himself and Timothy as slaves of Christ Jesus. The departure from his usual pattern of describing himself as an apostle is noteworthy. Indeed, nowhere in this letter does Paul use the label "apostle" for himself. The predominant reason given for the absence of "apostle" is that Paul is on such good terms with the Philippians that he did not need to bring up his superior status. While it is true that Paul seems at one mind and purpose with the Philippians, the supposition that he mentions his apostleship in his other letters as a push for his authority fails to appreciate his understanding of his apostleship and the role of apostle.

First, Paul maintains that his apostolic authority is from God, and he has no special rights to it (1 Cor 15:8–9). Second, in a poignant snapshot he likens apostles to those prisoners of war paraded through the streets and mocked by the conquerors (4:9). Third, while he insists that apostles establish the correct foundation for the church (3:10; Eph 2:20), his point is not that apostles are better or have more authority, but that apostles must get it right, or the entire building will be off kilter because of a weak or faulty foundation.

Associating Paul's claims about his apostleship to notions of authority skews the vision of service leadership that infuses Paul's understanding of apostleship. The force of his authority is Christ, and the power of the gospel is in its shame and weakness (1 Cor 1:17–18; 2:1–5). Then, as now, we tend to associate authority with dominance and thus conclude that the absence of a power struggle means the absence of the need to stress apostleship. Paul instead emphasizes the weakness of his apostleship, so that the power of God's kingdom might be evident (4:20).

Paul's use of the slave/servant metaphor is critical to his authority among the Philippians. As suggested by Romans 1:1 and Titus 1:1, "apostle" and "servant/slave" inform each other. The mixture of service and authority is nowhere better seen than in Christ Jesus, who "came not to be served, but to

---

12. John Ortberg ("The Strong-Willed Leader" (www.christianitytoday.com/le/currenttrends columns/leadershipweekly/thestrongwilledleader.html) argues that leaders should exhibit a surrendered will, not a weak will. He cites Jesus as demonstrating an indomitable will, a deep courage in following his Father's will over against opposition to authorities and public opinion. While this does accurately reflect Jesus' obedience, I wonder if that courage is leadership or perhaps better discipleship.

serve, and give his life as a ransom for many" (Mark 10:45). The picture of Christ assuming a slave's posture in washing the disciples' feet speaks volumes (John 13:4 – 17). In the beautiful hymn celebrating the incarnation in Philippians 2:6 – 11, Paul highlights Christ's perfect demonstration of authority: to embrace the form of a slave and, in obedience to God, endure death on a cross.

What does this type of leader look like today? One characteristic is a *lack of fear*. The leader Paul envisions is one who is unafraid of a congregation's negative appraisal (1 Cor 4:3). Indeed, the fearless leader does not navel-gaze at his or her work or person. Paul declares that he does not judge the worth of his assignments, or even if he has accomplished them; he leaves that to the Lord (4:4 – 5). In plain English, the godly leader focuses on obedience, not success as typically defined by material goods or social prestige. Their obedience is driven by love — first God's perfect and effective love for them, and then their imperfect response of love. As John notes, "perfect love casts out fear" (1 John 4:18). A godly leader, then, freely gives and freely submits to God in obedience.

A second characteristic is *perseverance*. The godly leader stays the course and stays in step both with God and with the Christian community. The temptation to run ahead of God's timing or to prod the community to keep up signals a failure to appreciate the service nature of leadership. Paul is clear that the overseers and deacons serve from among the congregation, not above them. To explain this aspect of leadership, the analogy of a shepherd with his sheep rose easily in the first-century Jewish mind. The shepherd theme comes from a rich tradition within the Old Testament. In Ezekiel 34, after chastising the shepherds of the people for growing fat and failing to feed the sheep, God declares that he will be the shepherd of his sheep (34:15). The Lord God continues, "I will place over them one shepherd, my servant David, and he will tend them ... and be their shepherd" (34:23). Jesus describes himself as the good shepherd who lays down his life for his sheep (John 10:11, 14).

The good shepherd demonstrates godly character. Too often leaders, including biblical leaders such as King David, assume that as long as they basically serve the people, they are above God's moral law. Today some Christian leaders rationalize adultery or theft as insignificant compared to their great service to the larger community. Paul's strong words in 1 Corinthians 11:1, "Follow my example, as I follow the example of Christ," stand in judgment.

A third characteristic of leadership is embracing an *attitude of humility*. Probably this was the hardest posture to accept in Paul's day, because his was an honor/shame culture. In this setting, people were taught to honor or respect their community and to avoid any behaviors that deviated from the group's values. Honor was gained and retained in competition with others. While today in the West we still want to do what is honorable and avoid the shameful, we tend to focus more on what is right or wrong, and our focus on individual rights lessens the importance of a community's assessment.[13] However, the display of humility is perhaps as difficult an idea to swallow today as it was then. For example, it can be humbling to accept the lower wages paid by Christian nonprofits. The temptation is to announce that one could certainly "do better" but is "choosing" to earn less. Instead, the gospel calls believers to embrace the "shame" of a lower salary as a signal that priorities are rightly placed.

I also suggest that humble leadership is marked at *the passing of the baton*, when new leaders take hold of running a ministry. John Stott, a remarkable Christian pastor, preacher, and teacher, showed humble leadership in his willingness to let go of the reins and honor the person taking them up.[14] Chris Wright, the current International Director of Langham Partnership International, recalls two situations where Dr. Stott (Uncle John) humbly stepped aside for new leadership. In the first case, a new vicar, Michael Baughen, was chosen to lead All Souls Church in London. As Wright puts it, "from the start he [Stott] insisted that while he remained as a senior presence at the church ... he would never undermine or overrule Michael's role as the final authority in the church's affairs.... He did not try to play 'queen mother,' or the 'power behind the throne.'" Wright credits Stott's actions as a key reason for continued unity within All Souls.

A second situation is more personal, as Dr. Stott handed the leadership of Langham Partnership over to Wright. As Wright recalls, at board meetings Stott would say with a smile, "'Chris is the leader' or words to that effect. He would introduce me as such in public meetings ... insisting that he had handed over leadership to me." Dr. Stott would participate in the meetings, and when the two met for breakfast (as they did regularly), Stott would have questions, and Wright would give an update on his travels and the issues facing Langham. "But although I [Wright] was like a Timothy to his Paul, he never pulled rank or corrected or queried any of my decisions or directions, but supported and prayed and enquired." Wright has carried on for over a decade in leading Langham Partnership, and during that time until Dr. Stott's

---

13. See David A. DeSilva, *Honor, Patronage, Kinship & Purity: Unlocking New Testament Culture* (Downers Grove, IL: InterVarsity Press, 2000), 23–42.

14. Two biographies of note have been written about John Stott, a two-volume work by Timothy Dudley-Smith, *John Stott: The Making of a Leader* (Downers Grove, IL: InterVarsity Press, 1999), and *John Stott: A Global Ministry: The Later Years* (Downers Grove, IL: InterVarsity Press, 2001); Alister Chapman, *Godly Ambition: John Stott and the Evangelical Movement* (Oxford: Oxford University Press, 2011). See also www.christianitytoday.com/ct/2011/julyweb-only/john-stott-obit.html.

death in July 2011, he never reasserted himself into the captain's chair. Such humility in leadership is a rare commodity, but one the church needs desperately as it strives for unity within its ranks and as it testifies to the humble love of its Savior.[15]

Martin Luther King Jr. (1929–1968) thought about his leadership in the civil rights movement as well as his legacy. Ruth Tucker notes that in 1965 (three years before his death) he wrote to a friend: "I am many things to many people ... but ... I am fundamentally a clergyman, a Baptist preacher. This is my being and my heritage, for I am also a son of a Baptist preacher, the grandson of a Baptist preacher, and the great-grandson of a Baptist preacher."[16] His father traveled to Germany when King was five years old. So impressed was he of Martin Luther's legacy that when he returned, Mike King changed his name to Martin Luther King and changed his son's name as well. As Tucker comments, "Indeed living up to the legacy of Luther was daunting for a black youth in the American South."[17]

But King believed that the mission was bigger than himself and that God would grant him courage in the face of strong and violent opposition. On the night before he was assassinated, he spoke these words to a group in Memphis, Tennessee:

> We've got some difficult days ahead. But it doesn't really matter with me now. Because I've been to the mountaintop. I don't mind. Like anybody, I would like to live—a long life; longevity has its place. But I'm not concerned about that now. I just want to do God's will. And He's allowed me to go up to the mountain. And I've looked over. And I've seen the Promised Land. I may not get there with you. But I want you to know tonight, that we, as a people, will get to the Promised Land. So I'm happy, tonight. I'm not worried about anything. I'm not fearing any man. Mine eyes have seen the glory of the coming of the Lord.[18]

Earlier in this speech, King stressed the important of unity: "We've got to stay together and maintain unity." In like manner, Paul tied his vision of leadership with an insistence on unity among the believers in Philippi (see Phil 2:1–5). One aspect of this call to unity relates directly to our conversation on

---

15. This information was taken from a personal email exchange between the author and Rev. Dr. Chris Wright (9–10 January 2013). More information can be found at www.langhampartnership .org/about-us/lpi-leadership/chris-wright/.

16. Ruth A. Tucker, *Parade of Faith: A Biographical History of the Christian Church* (Grand Rapids: Zondervan, 2011), 488.

17. Ibid., 485.

18. For a copy of the speech, see www.americanrhetoric.com/speeches/mlkivebeentothemountain top.htm

leadership, namely, how the congregation can encourage healthy leadership. Paul points to the Philippians' united effort on his behalf. They supported consistently both his ministry as he worked in other cities and his collection for the Jewish Christians in Judea (Acts 18:5; 2 Cor 8:1–7; Phil 4:10, 15–18). The Philippians *owned* Paul's ministry as *their* own; they stayed the course with him, begging to be included in all that he was called to do. They did not flinch at his imprisonment; they did not waver when rivals sought to displace Paul (Phil 1:15–19). As Paul declares, they "shared with" him in his ministry (4:15); the noun cognate of the verb used here is the familiar term *koinōnia* or fellowship.

How might this look today? Financial support is front and center in Paul's letter to the Philippians, and it should probably be that way in our churches today. This need not take the form of a salary, for not all leaders are paid staff. But generous giving to ministries within the local and global church signals a unity between the leadership executing the ministries and the people who share in the ministries. Additionally, regular, open communication between leaders and their communities fosters the sense of ownership and unity exhibited by the Philippians and Paul. Moreover, the Philippians actually liked Paul and were worried about him. The emotional connections that enrich any relationship should be promoted between the leadership and the community. Casual get-togethers, shared meals, no-agenda outings — these all grow unity within the assembly and foster harmony among its members.

LISTEN to the Story

³I thank my God every time I remember you. ⁴In all my prayers for all of you, I always pray with joy ⁵because of your partnership in the gospel from the first day until now, ⁶being confident of this, that he who began a good work in you will carry it on to completion until the day of Christ Jesus.

⁷It is right for me to feel this way about all of you, since I have you in my heart and, whether I am in chains or defending and confirming the gospel, all of you share in God's grace with me. ⁸God can testify how I long for all of you with the affection of Christ Jesus.

⁹And this is my prayer: that your love may abound more and more in knowledge and depth of insight, ¹⁰so that you may be able to discern what is best and may be pure and blameless for the day of Christ, ¹¹filled with the fruit of righteousness that comes through Jesus Christ—to the glory and praise of God.

Listening to the text in the Story: Isaiah 5:1–7; 40:21–31; Jeremiah 9:23–25.

Most of Paul's letters begin with a thanksgiving, consistent with letter-writing practices of his day. Yet Paul's thanksgivings are expansive, hinting for the reader what he will address throughout his letter. Paul includes several key terms and themes in these verses, including (1) the unity within the church, (2) the second coming of Christ, (3) the partnership between Paul and the Philippians in the ministry of the gospel, (4) the importance of discipleship, and (5) the joy that is every believer's birthright.

Front and center is Paul's focus on unity within the Philippian church. He stresses that this unity silences opponents and models the servant attitude of Christ. He also emphasizes the unity of purpose he shares with the Philippians in the promotion of the gospel. Paul highlights the unity all believers share with Christ.

Second, the thanksgiving promotes the surety of Christ's second coming and our proper behavior until he returns. Throughout the epistle, Paul emphasizes Christ's exaltation, the believers' citizenship in heaven, and their bodily resurrection.

Third, Paul mentions sharing in the ministry of the gospel. We know from 2 Corinthians 8:1–4 that the Philippian church gave sacrificially to the gift for the Judean churches, and at several places in our letter Paul refers to their generous aid to him.

Fourth, Paul thanks them for their efforts in discipleship; throughout these four chapters he encourages them to press onward and upward, faithfully finishing strong. He mentions purity and blamelessness both in the thanksgiving and later when he distinguishes his blameless life in Judaism with the power of the gospel.

Finally, Paul emphasizes his own joy in his prayers for the Philippians, their love for him, and God's indescribable gift of salvation in Christ. He pleads with them to embrace that joy. The thanksgiving mentions his imprisonment and upcoming defense of the gospel only once, but it is enough so that later discussion of enemies does not come as any surprise. Paul's emphasis on unity is a key defense against the enemies who seek him harm.

EXPLAIN the Story

Every Time I Remember You (1:3–4)

If the first four words of the thanksgiving ("I thank my God") are easy to understand, though hard to live out, the next phrases have been interpreted in two very different ways. The more common understanding is that Paul joyfully remembers the Philippians (see NIV). The emphasis is on the temporal; Paul stresses that *every* time he remembers them, he *always* prays for them in *every* prayer (1:3–4). A better reading, I suggest, is that Paul thanks them for the fact that *they remember him*.[1]

What tips the reading in favor of seeing the Philippians remembering Paul is that this translation answers a puzzle that has confounded commentators. Virtually every expositor accepts that Philippians was written in part to thank the church for their financial gifts to Paul. Yet direct appreciation does not come until the end of the letter. That seems ungracious of Paul, so some have

---

1. The discussions about how to interpret prepositions and genitives end in a draw; both ways of translating the text stand up under normal grammar rules. The grammar questions include whether *epi* with dative should be translated "at" or "in" in a temporal sense. Usually *epi* is followed by a genitive to carry a temporal meaning. *Epi* with dative (as here) usually has a causal sense, indicating the basis for Paul's thanksgiving. A second issue surrounds *hymōn*, whether it is an objective (thoughts *of you*) or subjective genitive (*your* thoughts).

argued that our Philippians is made up of a number of letters of Paul stitched together at a later time: an early thank-you letter, and a later, longer letter (or several letters). Such historical reconstructions are unnecessary if we recognize that at the beginning, Paul expresses his deep appreciation for their care and concern. He stresses that he is *always* mindful of their gifts and is overflowing with gratitude.

Paul Is Thankful for the Philippians' Partnership (1:5–8)

Paul now gives two additional reasons for his thankfulness: because the Philippians share in the gospel with him (1:5), and because God will continue to shape and mold them as they grow into Christ's likeness (1:6). He stresses that his thanksgiving is well-placed because he loves them from the heart, for they have walked each step of his ministry with him (1:7).

A key term in these verses is *koinōnia*; the word carries the sense of "partnership," close fellowship, or participation with another. Paul uses the word in 1:5, and then repeats the word group in 1:7 with an added prefix that stresses their sharing *with* Paul. Some suggest that in 1:5 Paul is speaking to their salvation, that he is thankful they accepted the gospel message. But Paul probably uses "gospel" here in the active sense of preaching the message. The Philippians have staked their public honor on and offered their money to Paul's ministry. They even preached the message themselves in Philippi (1:27–28). They pray for Paul (1:19), likely during their weekly meetings, which would be open to anyone and audible from the street (cf. 1 Cor 14:23–25). As the saying goes, they "put their money where their mouth was." Paul sees their unflagging enthusiasm for the gospel and his own ministry as evidence of God's grace in much the same way as he senses God's grace uplifting him while in prison.

God Will Finish His Good Work in You (1:6)

Paul speaks confidently that God will finish the good work he began in the Philippians. God desires not only that people accept his free gift of salvation through Christ Jesus, but also that this gift includes the renunciation of our old self and the possibilities of a life free from sin. Paul knows without hesitation that God will complete and fulfill his purpose in the Philippians, because he raised Jesus from the dead and thus broke the chains of sin and death that bind all humans. Christ's resurrection proves sin's ultimate defeat, and God through Christ has established each believer as a new creation (2 Cor 5:17).

Note that Paul does not say that the Philippians have some time to complete or accomplish their salvation, as a teacher might say to the class that they have one hour to complete an exam. Rather, Paul stresses that it is God who brought them into fellowship with himself through Christ. Because he has established them, he will also maintain them until the end. Their continued participation with Paul in ministry serves as evidence of the steadfast loving-kindness of the Lord. These believers will fully realize what they were created to become.

What are believers made to do? Jesus describes such "completion" in Matthew 5:43–48 (where he uses a related word *teleios*, "perfect") as loving one's enemies and praying for those who persecute you. Paul declares that God will finish molding and shaping us into Christ's likeness, so that we will be fit for the day of Christ Jesus (see also Rom 8:29). Paul stresses later in this letter that he longs for this day (Phil 3:14, 20–21).

I Have You in My Heart (1:7–8)

Paul also underscores his own strong affections toward them. The Greek text literally reads that Paul's "affection" lies deep in the bowels—not the place most moderns locate their affections! But even if we use a different body part to locate our intense emotions, we can appreciate Paul's sentiment. He wants the Philippians to know that he is sincerely thankful for and appreciative of their unending generosity. This "affection" is the love "of Christ Jesus"; no deeper love can a person express than that demonstrated in and through Christ. Such affection creates in Paul a deep yearning for this church, and he is likely alluding to his hope to be reunited with them (1:25–26; 2:24).

Paul calls God as his witness in his claim (1:8), probably because in his day people were on the lookout for flatterers (cf. 2 Cor 2:17). In the ancient world, orators told you what you wanted to hear in order to get what they wanted from you: food, recommendations, and social advancement. But no one in Paul's day would have been as cavalier with God's name as to bring it forward as a witness if they were lying. Chrysostom asks: "Now had he been flattering them, he would not have called God to witness, for this cannot be done without peril."[2]

Paul's Prayer for the Philippians (1:9)

In 1:4 Paul indicated that he prays for them; now we discover the content of that prayer. He wants their love to grow to overflowing. In so doing, the Philippians will gain a more godly view of the world and a better discernment on how to live in a way that honors God. Paul connects love and intellect, a combination that is worth exploring a bit, since we tend not to make such connections today. We assume that knowledge should be coldly analytical,

2. Chrysostom, "Homily II on Philippians," *NPNF¹*, 13:188.

devoid of all emotional attachment. Paul sees love not as an emotion but as a state of being. God is love, Christ's incarnation demonstrates that love, and we who are in Christ share that love. This love captures the mind with a new view of the world: humans are not the center of the universe, God is. This love re-orients values: supreme good is self-giving, not self-aggrandizing.

This love refocuses the will: holiness and peace become the goals, not self-defense or self-assertion. Paul believes that as the Philippians' love grows more and more, they will *think* differently about God and the world. Thus when Paul connects love and wisdom here, we can safely assume that he takes for granted that this knowledge and insight flows from God, the source of all wisdom.[3]

When believers separate knowing from acting in love, they lose the connection to the one who made all things and knows all things. They imply that their view of the world is sufficient, satisfactory, and perhaps preferable to God's view. But knowledge without love is like facts without a narrative, like images with no context, like existing with no gravity. The absence of love makes any knower, even the most brilliant by human standards, *nothing*. Paul states this in no uncertain terms in 1 Corinthians 13:2; the one who can decipher deepest mysteries is but nothing without love. Love arranges knowledge so that it reflects God's wisdom and care for creation properly, and values life appropriately.

Paul imagines the Philippian believer on a journey; thus he speaks of their love growing in the present tense, a daily activity. Jesus describes something similar when he challenges his disciples to take up their cross and follow him. Neither Paul nor Jesus is speaking here of how one *becomes* forgiven of one's sins and joins the family of God; rather, they are speaking of what the Christian life looks like. For Paul, dying with Christ and rising to new life (Rom 6:3-4) opens vast avenues for developing the holy life, a life he had always desired to attain. Through Christ, believers can mature in godly wisdom and love.

Paul uses the term *agapē* for "love" in this context. When he speaks to reciprocal loving fellowship among believers, Paul usually uses this term. But its use here should include not only love of fellow human beings, but also love of God. Paul seems to genuinely avow that the Philippians have love, and indeed their steadfast concern for Paul supports that affirmation.

Moreover, Paul concentrates on the *source* of their love, not its object. The love he speaks of is only possible *through* Jesus Christ, and he notes that

---

3. Paul addresses the church in Rome with similar thoughts (Rom 12:2) as well as the church in Corinth (1 Cor 1:18-2:15).

believers through Christ will be filled with "the fruit of righteousness." Their fruit or harvest comes through Christ (see John 15:5); it is not generated through their own efforts. Said another way, believers do not create fruit; rather, they submit to God's will and allow God's love to overflow and their minds to be renewed.

Both Jesus in John 15 and Paul build on the well-known image of Israel as God's vineyard (Isa 5:1–7). In the Isaiah text, God is the vinedresser who plants and cares for his people, represented as his vine. The prophet condemns Israel for failing to uphold justice in their community and warns that God will judge them if they fail to yield fruit of righteousness. Paul states a similar sentiment in the positive: those who bear fruit of righteousness must be connected with the one who is righteous. Jesus (and Paul) add that good fruit is produced in community. Those who bear fruit that will last, fruit that is worthy, are those who obey his command to love one another (John 15:16–17). And Paul will soon declare to the Philippians that their status as members of Christ's fellowship and sharers of Christ's love should magnify their love for each other (Phil 2:1–5).

Prayer for Deeper Knowledge (1:9)

Paul prays that the Philippians' love will increase and that their knowledge will grow ever deeper. The Greek term Paul uses for knowledge has a prefix on it (*epignōsis*), stressing the idea of profound wisdom. Interestingly, only in the four Prison Epistles does Paul use this term in his thanksgiving (see Eph 1:17; Col 1:9–10; Phlm 6). In each case, he is praying for the congregation, asking that they might see the deep truths of God. Perhaps this should not surprise us, for Paul is facing possible martyrdom. He knows his situation has brought glory to God and the gospel to those who otherwise would have had no reason to hear the message (Phil 1:13). He desires that his fellow believers take the same view, namely, that his situation, whatever happens, should serve to honor God. This perspective calls for special insight and a sharper, firmer grasp on God's overarching plan to be accomplished in the day of Christ. Paul's prayer invites us today to pray likewise for our friends, fellow believers, and family who face situations that appear hopeless.

Prayer for Discernment (1:10)

It is not enough for a believer to know what is right; he or she must also act with social awareness and tact in expressing love. Paul prays for their discernment in determining what is the best approach. The term "discern" is used extensively in Proverbs (see, e.g., Prov 5:2; 14:6; 15:7). Some suggest this term means that Paul emphasizes here his concern for unity among believers. Yet the overall context is discerning appropriate behavior with an eye to Christ's return. Our obedience to God reveals our love of God. Chrysostom notes that Paul encourages believers to use reason and judgment so that heretical teachings or teachers do not beguile them, "for there is danger lest any one be spoiled by the love of the heretics ... that you receive no spurious doctrine under the pretense of love."[4]

Pure and Blameless (1:10–11)

This love that we extend with discernment results in believers being "pure and blameless" (1:10). "Pure" carries the sense of sincerity; it is the opposite of patronizing meddling that masquerades as kindness. Paul prays that as the believers' love overflows and their godly wisdom increases, their very self will be fashioned toward the genuine article, Christ himself.

Paul also prays that believers may be "blameless," which carries the sense of having a clear conscience (see Acts 24:16; 1 Cor 10:32). Paul points forward to Christ's second coming in the "day of Christ." Paul will say more about this at the end of chapter 3; for now, he concentrates on the preparedness of the believer for that day.

 LIVE the Story

Four simple words: "I thank my God." What rich theology and piety are captured in Paul's opening to the Philippians. The God whom Paul thanks is "God our Father," the one who redeemed us in and through the Lord Jesus Christ, as he has declared in his salutation.

Paul is thankful even while in chains for the gospel. This posture in the midst of extremely difficult circumstances challenges us today in a myriad of ways. At least three are worth a closer look. First, Paul's thankfulness is a public confession, not a private sentiment. Second, Paul is thankful for specific things, centering on God's faithfulness to his church. Third, Paul can be thankful in his deepest heart because he knows that God will redeem all suffering and rebuke all evil in the day of the Lord.

Public Confession of Thanksgiving to God

First, Paul probably prayed aloud,[5] following the typical practice in the ancient world.[6] Jesus' words to pray in private (Matt 6:6) suggests that normally Jews

---

4. Chrysostom, "Homily I on Philippians," in *NPNF¹*, 13:339.

5. See Pieter W. van der Horst, "Silent Prayer in Antiquity," *Numen* 41.1 (1994): 1–25.

6. Hannah's silent prayer (1 Sam 1:12–16) is heard by God, but Eli the priest misinterprets this act as being drunk. His reaction signals that silent prayers were not the norm. The first-century Jewish historian, Josephus, notes that when he was in dire straits and ready to surrender to the Romans, he prayed silently to God (*Jewish War* 3.353–4).

prayed aloud, so he advocates prayer in a private space.[7] Paul's prayers would have presented to any person in his room the gospel message, because Paul prayed in the Spirit, through Christ, to the Father. His public prayers testified that he *owned* the label "Jesus follower."

As a Jew, Paul's religious expressions would have been deemed odd, to say the least, to his Gentile guards. His comments about Jesus, the crucified Jew as the Savior of the world, would have sounded foolish (1 Cor 1:20–21). His personal prayers voiced aloud gave witness to his convictions and invited listeners to hold him accountable to his words of thankfulness. Today when we pray aloud in a Bible study or fellowship setting, we put ourselves on record, so to speak, before others as to our beliefs about God's power and love.

Thankfulness *to* God, not *for* Everything

Second, Paul is thankful for specific things that demonstrate the power of the gospel. He rejoices that the Philippians' renewed life in Christ is producing fruit. We will see in the rest of the letter that Paul does not say he is thankful for every specific event, thought, and attitude expressed in the world. Rather, he is thankful that nothing in this world can nullify God's grace. So everything will in the end serve God's purpose. If we cannot see that at present, we trust God's promise that evil, hardship, loss, and despair will not have the final word. Those very things make it a testimony of our faith to declare our thanksgiving to God.

The sentiment that you find out who your true friends are when the going gets tough rings true in these verses. Paul is chained to a Roman guard, but that does not stop the Philippians from standing with Paul, willing to join in his shame. They freely gave him their coins because they were committed to his ministry, they loved him, and they believed God had called them to support Paul. In spite of his present danger, Paul's ministry was not a "lost cause."

Paul mentions only in passing that he is in prison. He speaks of it as God's grace, which the Philippians share. With this aside, Paul invites us two thousand years later to pause and explore what would have been involved with the Philippians sharing Paul's sufferings in his incarceration. In some ways, prison is prison the world over: lack of personal freedom and choice, and potential for abuse by other inmates and guards. But in so many ways, the prison systems in the West are vastly different than those around the world today and those in Paul's time. Perhaps it can be summed up in one word: vulnerability. Many prisoners are at the mercy of their captors, without recourse to state their case or preserve their dignity. This is a fearful system.

---

7. A useful discussion of ancient prayer practices related to Matt 6:6 can be found in Craig S. Keener, *A Commentary on the Gospel of Matthew* (Grand Rapids: Eerdmans, 1999), 210–13.

One time during our three years in Kenya our car was commandeered by the local police. We lived in a rural area, and a young man, Paul, who helped in our house, was getting soda at the local *duka* or small shop. He used our old station wagon to bounce his way up the dirt road to return the glass bottles and get new ones. A short, ten-minute trip stretched to an hour; then I got a phone call from Paul saying that he was at the police station; they would not release him or our car. I asked Paul three times to put the local police on the phone, so I could assure them that Paul had not "stolen" the car and that they should release Paul to return home. "They refuse to talk with you," Paul said; "they will only speak with *Bwana Jim*" (my husband "Lord" Jim). Then he hung up the phone.

I stood for a moment in shock — did the police really refuse to speak with me? I was used to having the police on my side, not against me. A small fear gripped my heart, and honestly, it remained throughout my years in Kenya. Did the Philippians worry that the Roman authorities would commandeer their belongings, their means of livelihood, their very persons, all because they stood for the gospel of Jesus Christ? Did they pray daily for the strength and boldness to stand fast in the face of the oppression that came their way (1:28; cf. Eph 6:19)?

I have a much better appreciation for the vulnerability that some face within various "justice systems." And I hear with new urgency Christ's own words about visiting those in prison (Matt 25:31 – 46). Churches and parachurch groups do much to help those in prison and their children. Churches in low crime neighborhoods partner together with those in high crime areas. Believers who have legal education use their gifts to address the failures in the system at home and abroad. Those with skills in education or business help prepare inmates with skills for life outside prison walls. Those with God-sized compassion for the families of the incarcerated give them their time and love. The church around the globe speaks into the issue of justice by standing with prisoners, and strives for equitable society with an open press and independent judiciary.

These convictions stem from the strong biblical witness to the dignity of each human and the responsibility to show mercy and fairness in administering justice. The Philippians would have been astounded to see the ways in which their faithful partnership with Paul has challenged believers through two millennia to stand with those in prison, especially believers whose "crime" is their confession of faith. Their testimony of partnership encourages still.

Thankfulness in Our Future, Sure Hope

Paul is thankful because he knows how the story will end. He is deeply committed to the church *now* because he is so sure of its future glory in Christ.

One of the hardest things to do both in our personal lives and in the church is to walk in the tension of present demands and future concerns. We all recognize that what we do now greatly impacts our future, and so we take great care in making decisions that we know will impact what comes later.

Yet pulling against this truism is the siren call to immediate enrichment and personal satisfaction. Even the church is prone to pop psychology's promises of a happy, healthy, prosperous new you. Rick Warren challenges this sentiment in his best-selling book *The Purpose Driven Life*. He notes: "I have read many books that suggest ways to discover the purpose of my life. All of them could be classified as 'self-help' books because they approach the subject from a self-centered viewpoint. Self-help books, even Christian ones, usually offer the same predictable steps to finding your life's purpose: Consider your dreams.... Clarify your values."[8] But Warren notes that while worldly success is certainly possible following these guidelines, the results are hollow. We must begin with God, not with ourselves, if we want to find purpose and meaning. Paul does exactly that in his prayer—he thanks God, and all else falls into place.

---

8. Rick Warren, *The Purpose Driven Life* (Grand Rapids: Zondervan, 2002), 18–19.

CHAPTER 3

Philippians 1:12–18a

 LISTEN to the Story

> ¹²Now I want you to know, brothers and sisters, that what has happened to me has actually served to advance the gospel. ¹³As a result, it has become clear throughout the whole palace guard and to everyone else that I am in chains for Christ. ¹⁴And because of my chains, most of the brothers and sisters have become confident in the Lord and dare all the more to proclaim the gospel without fear.
>
> ¹⁵It is true that some preach Christ out of envy and rivalry, but others out of goodwill. ¹⁶The latter do so out of love, knowing that I am put here for the defense of the gospel. ¹⁷The former preach Christ out of selfish ambition, not sincerely, supposing that they can stir up trouble for me while I am in chains. ¹⁸But what does it matter? The important thing is that in every way, whether from false motives or true, Christ is preached. And because of this I rejoice. Yes, and I will continue to rejoice.

Listening to the text in the Story: Leviticus 19:18; Jeremiah 38:6–13.

Paul here informs the Philippians about his current situation in Rome, imprisoned but not silenced. Indeed, some believers are, ironically, made more confident to share the gospel because of Paul's chains. Sadly, others are using Paul's confinement to cast doubt on his ministry. Nevertheless, Paul declares that as long as the good news of Christ's redeeming love is proclaimed, he rejoices.

Paul explains here one of the ironies of the Christian life: what looks like utter defeat turns out to be victory — in God's hands. Common sense would dictate that Paul's influence is gone and his prospects washed up, for he has been languishing four years in prison (two years in Caesarea Maritima, two more in Rome). But "in Christ" (1:13) the impossible becomes possible and the gospel message spreads even more widely than if spoken only by Paul.

EXPLAIN the Story

Victory in Christ, Against All Odds (1:12–14)

In these three verses, Paul speaks of his imprisonment, but he does not describe his own mood or physical condition. Instead, he notes the contrast between his personal, restricted circumstances, about which the Philippians are well aware, and the public expansion of the gospel, a phenomenon they are not anticipating. Paul also speaks of the gospel's "progress" in 1:25, where the term refers to the advance of the gospel in the Philippians' own lives. Other than 1 Timothy 4:15, these are the only two places where Paul uses this term. The cognate verb describes a smith's hammering of metal to lengthen it or the passing of time, as in the phrase "the night is advancing." The verb carries the idea of progress and advancement.

What sort of progress might Paul be intending here? Of course, the gospel message is complete in itself; God's salvation plan for the world through Christ has been foretold in the prophets and enacted in history a few short decades before Paul wrote this letter. The progress is not with the gospel itself, but with the telling of the gospel. From Paul's statement that the whole Praetorian guard (NIV "palace guard") is now aware of the gospel, we can safely assume that Paul has in mind the numerical increase of those who have heard the gospel. But since he also speaks of many believers emboldened to speak, we can also understand this progress to indicate that within the church itself, there is growth as many believers take steps of faith, trusting God as they tell his story of redemption. Advancement of the gospel for Paul, then, is both the increased number of people hearing that message and the increased number of believers sharing it.

Content of the Gospel

It may be useful to pause and reflect here on the content of the gospel, which is spreading so surprisingly. Paul does not define the content here in bullet points, but a careful read of his letters suggests that a few central truths made up the message. First and foremost, the message is about Jesus Christ. He is the son of David and the Son of God (Rom 1:3–4). Christ died for humanity's redemption (Eph 1:7), and his death on the cross is shared by all believers (Gal. 6:14). Christ has been raised, according to Scripture (1 Cor 15:4), and he will return, having destroyed every ruler, authority, and power, including death itself (1 Cor 15:24–28). God's work in Christ is available to everyone—forgiveness of sins and new, abundant life in the Spirit. The believers' future is secure, because the hope is founded in Christ's resurrection, the firstfruits that indicate a complete harvest in the future (1 Cor 15:20). Most all of these ideas will be mentioned in the rest of Philippians.

Paul's Chains amidst the Praetorian Guard (1:13)

Paul informs the Philippians that his "chains" (a euphemism for imprisonment and also a literal description of his living conditions) are well-known among a group least likely to have any interest in the gospel, namely, the Praetorian guard. This elite force guarded the emperor; we might think of them as Secret Service and Navy Seals rolled into one. That such men would know a story about a crucified Jewish "Messiah" would seem an unlikely bit of conversation, but Paul states that "the whole palace guard" knows of his situation.

What precisely is that situation? Most likely the Roman guards have come to appreciate that Paul's present situation is on account of his testimony. This conclusion need not imply that Paul was arrested because he was a Christ follower, but only that his current circumstances are comprehensible when seen as part of God's redemptive plan in Christ for the world.

Imagine a Roman soldier's discussion with Paul and his subsequent astonishment when he hears Paul declare that his physical chains are not indicative of Caesar's hold on his life. Instead, those chains establish Christ's victory in spreading the gospel to all. Likely some guards shook their heads in disbelief, confident in the superior power of Caesar. Others laughed at Paul's "fairy tale." But perhaps a few went away pondering, seeing something in Paul that they had not seen in a prisoner before. Paul would identify that "something" as Christ.

Paul's Chains Encourage Proclamation (1:14)

Paul's chains have also served to greatly encourage Roman believers to preach the gospel. These believers see Paul's witness, and in that testimony they see the power of Christ. That power has raised their confidence to speak the word. Paul rightly notes that these Roman believers are not speaking because of Paul himself, but because their trust and confidence are firmly "in the Lord." Nothing makes Paul more pleased than that the gospel is being shared. He reminds his readers that all believers are equipped to talk about Christ's work, the gospel.

One does not need a seminary degree to speak about the death and resurrection of Christ, that work of grace accomplished by Christ and given to all who believe in his name. To some, Paul's words are a comfort, for they worry that they will not explain the gospel well or will not have enough knowledge to answer questions. Take heart—Paul notes that trust in the Lord will allow *anyone to speak the word.* They are fearless, for they trust that the same power that animates Paul will watch over them. To others, however, Paul's words represent an unwelcome conviction that they are responsible to speak. It is not their pastor's job, or their Sunday school teacher's job, or some other paid professional's job to speak the word. It is a responsibility shared by all.

These believers are bold and "without fear." Paul implies that any "sane" person would be frightened to speak. I am not bold when I speak about Christ to a group gathered in a public park, or from a pulpit here in the United States; I enjoy freedom of speech protection. But these Roman believers are speaking the word under a dark cloud of suspicion that perhaps their conduct will run afoul of Nero, and they will end up as Paul, or worse. Paul likely praises the Roman believers to the Philippians not only because they should be honored for their courage, but because the Philippians can follow their example as they face struggles in Philippi (as Paul enjoins them in 1:27–30).

Some Preach out of Envy and Rivalry (1:15–17)

Paul then qualifies his commendation with the note that some within that larger group in Rome have taken advantage of Paul's imprisonment to advance their own agenda, or perhaps diminish Paul's reputation. They preach "out of envy and rivalry." Of what are they envious? His chains? His personal confidence in the face of possible martyrdom? As we dig a bit deeper into Paul's vocabulary, we find that Paul uses a similar term for "rivalry" in the next chapter (Phil 2:3; cf. also Gal 5:20). His language there speaks to manipulating and maneuvering from selfish ambition. It seems their rivalry is about influence—specifically, wanting to gain influence over those who have previously sought Paul for understanding about the gospel.

Moreover, Paul explains that these believers speak "not sincerely," without pure motives (1:17). Later he encourages the Philippians to think about "whatever is pure" (4:8), using the same term without a negative, as here. Paul discusses these Roman believers as an implicit contrast to the expected behavior of the Philippians. Thus Paul's description here of the Roman believers is not an idle tale offered for local color; it serves as a warning to the Philippians.

These insincere believers hope to increase Paul's afflictions. Paul elsewhere speaks of afflictions or sufferings as a natural part of the church's life as it faces persecution (see 1 Thess 3:3) and as part of his ministry (2 Cor 4:17; Eph 3:3). Paul knows that the Philippians themselves are not strangers to affliction (see the reference to "severe trial" for the Macedonian believers in 2 Cor 8:2).

How did these Roman believers imagine they will increase Paul's afflictions? Do they think they can cause him mental anguish with their rival claims? Do they hope to cause him emotional disappointment at their barbed critique of his chains? Or is the affliction of a material nature? Have some approached the Philippians, asking that they throw their support behind them and leave Paul? Why throw their money to a prisoner? Or perhaps they target Paul's character, hinting that God had pulled Paul out of circulation based on some personal flaw. We do not know, for Paul does not explain the specific rationale for their behavior. His current circumstances make him an easy target, and some believers are attacking his defenses.

Some Preach Out of Love (1:15–17)

But not all; Paul points to others who preach Christ "out of goodwill" and "love." This may include love for Paul personally, but he primarily refers to these believers' espousal of God's work through Paul. The same term "goodwill" is found in 2:13, where Paul speaks of God working in the Philippians themselves to will and work his *goodwill* or purpose (see also Eph 1:5).

These Roman believers preach Christ because, like Paul, they embrace God's call on their lives to speak boldly. Paul describes their "love" using the term *agapē*, referring to a deep, unconditional love both for Paul and for God; it is the love that Christ extends to the church, that God extends to each sinner. This love is based on knowledge. They understand that Paul's situation is due entirely to his "defense [*apologia*] of the gospel." These Roman believers likely know that Paul's defense of the gospel includes declaring that male Gentile believers need not be circumcised to enjoy full membership in God's people. They know that Paul's chains are the outward evidence of his steadfast testimony to Christ's call on his life.

Paul uses the term *apologia* in its technical sense of offering a rational, logical argument. His primary focus, his searchlight that pinpoints the target, is the advancement of the gospel. Because of his absolute conviction that nothing can stand in the way of the gospel, he can say with total sincerity that it matters not a bit to him what may be a believer's attitude toward him or his imprisonment. If such believers are rightly speaking the word, Paul is happy (1:18). If they speak about Paul truthfully, fine. If they speak about Paul disingenuously, no problem. It is not about Paul; it is about Christ's gospel. So long as the latter is preached, all is well.

The reader should not assume, of course, that the disingenuous, envious, contentious speakers of the gospel will be praised for such character traits by God. Indeed not! Jesus has harsh words for hypocrites, and James warns those with selfish ambition that this reflects an earthly and unspiritual posture (Jas 3:14, 16). Paul notes that the fruit of the Spirit in one's life includes love and a pure heart and a charitable disposition (Gal 5:22). The lesson here is that Paul's detractors, while preaching the word of God, have failed to allow it to penetrate to their own relationships. They have taken advantage of a situation to the detriment of a fellow believer, even as they proclaim Christ's grace and love to the world. This "disconnect" between mouth and heart is what Paul wants the Philippians to avoid.

 **LIVE the Story**

Paul begins by stating that he wants the Philippians to know his situation. Surprisingly, he does not give much information about what has happened to him; instead, he minimizes his personal circumstances as he redirects attention to what really interests him, namely, the gospel's progress. Several lessons can be drawn from this posture. First, Paul is modeling the attitude he'd like to see in the Philippians, which is the posture of smallness. Second, Paul sees everything in relation to the work of the kingdom. Third, while Paul is not unwilling to tell of his dire circumstances (cf. 2 Cor. 1:8–11), his restraint here demonstrates his underlying emphasis on his present joy.

A Posture of "Smallness"

Imagine with me Paul writing this letter; would we paint him in the center of the canvas? Would we have the candlelight shining on his face, casting deep shadows into the corners of the tiny room? Would the Roman guard stand aggressively over him in an intimidating fashion? None of these details that would interest a modern reader (or painter) seem of any consequence to Paul. If he painted the picture, perhaps we'd see the Roman soldier in the spotlight, eagerly leaning toward Paul trying to catch his every word. Maybe the fourth wall of the room opens onto a teeming marketplace, showing clusters of people listening attentively to a speaker in their midst. Now what if I put myself in that picture?

When I lived in Kenya with my husband and two grade-school-aged children, I'd send news of our situation home to our supporters. I confess that these letters were usually filled with the struggles we faced, from natural calamities such as grasshopper infestations or mudslides, to physical concerns and illnesses, to business struggles as we managed a ministry. What I did not do, to my shame, is explain how those seeming limitations actually served to establish the "in Christ-ness" of our ministry. Instead, *I* was too much at the center of my circumstances.

By this I mean that while I prayed to God to bring all things to his good conclusion, I did not narrate my daily experiences in that reality. When I prayed, I thought like that, but when I talked with others, especially those back home, my story line was about me, not about God's work going on around me. Paul here shows a way forward from this self-absorption. He "resizes" the characters of the story, making himself small and Christ's gospel big and tall, worthy of full attention.

Seeing God's Work in One's Situation

Second, Paul has adjusted his spiritual glasses to see more acutely what events around him really indicate. He is open to irony, observant to subtlety, and able to comprehend progress when a quick glance at the situation suggests the opposite conclusion. This posture is the opposite of "positive thinking"; Paul is not humming under his breath "The Sun Will Come Out Tomorrow" from the musical *Annie*. He is not whitewashing his experience of imprisonment, waiting for a happier day. Instead, Paul's evaluation of his circumstances reveals a deep appreciation for the central truths of the gospel.

One of those truths that we miss today in the United States (but not in other parts of the global church) is the central role that suffering plays in God's redemption plan. Time and again, as Paul dreams of the day of Christ's return, the glorious resurrection of the saints, and our life with God eternally at peace enfolded in his love, he reflects that now is the time of suffering.

In a moving image of a mother giving birth, Paul in Romans 8:22–23 points to labor as symbolic of a believer's current situation. From the woman's perspective, her labor and delivery are the necessary transition for the life within her to be welcomed as a life on its own. The struggle in labor becomes a metaphor for Paul of our own lives now. Believers are as the mother laboring to give birth; they too suffer as the new life of the Spirit is formed in them and as God's kingdom is built through their faithful work. Paul sees in this everyday event a symbol of God's pattern — suffering brings new life. Suffering is not alien to the gospel; it enters into the gospel itself. (For more on this, see commentary on 3:10.)

Once we embrace this difficult but necessary truth that suffering is part of the believer's current lot and, even more, that such suffering connects us to Christ, we can begin to see our own circumstances with a similar subtlety. Paul was prevented (for at least four years) from moving freely to preach the gospel. This new situation seemed to have rendered his call as an apostle not doable. Yet Paul saw beyond his calling to the purpose of his calling and any other believer's calling, namely, the building up of the church and the growing of God's kingdom. Paul could embrace his new circumstances that reshaped and modified how he fulfilled his apostolic duties.

The church is full of believers who have similar stories. One such story is that of Eric Liddell (1902–1945). His story of ministry in China serves as a modern-day example of a person's ministry being expanded through the irony of imprisonment. Liddell's career as an Olympic athlete is immortalized in the award-winning movie *Chariots of Fire* (1981), when he stood firm in refusing to race on Sunday. But less is known of his later mission in China. Two situations serve to highlight Liddell's single-minded devotion to God's service. While in Tientsin, China, in 1929, Liddell raced the famous German track star Otto Peltzer; Liddell beat Peltzer in the 400 meters, but lost in the 800 meters. The German runner strongly urged Liddell to return to England to train for the 1932 Olympics, but as a friend of Eric's wrote, "Eric's diary had no room for that."[1] Instead, he remained in rural China, even after the outbreak of World War II.

In 1943, he was sent to the Weihsien internment camp. The Olympic goal medalist, well-known for his stirring sermons, now devoted most of his time to caring for the elderly and children in the camp, organizing lessons and games. Surely this was underutilizing the great man's capacities, right? Liddell gave no indication he thought so, but joyfully embraced the circumstances. The unanimous testimony of children from the camp indicates that "Uncle Eric" was their friend. He died of a brain tumor six months before the camp was liberated, but his smile of hope lived on in each of the children whose lives now testify to a man for whom no one was too small to care.[2]

Joy in the Moment

I noted above that Paul is not averse to explaining a life-threatening situation. It served his wider purpose in explaining his love for his readers and his hope of reconciliation. The fact that Paul does not tell the Philippians about his current situation is curious, but it may be no more than that he assumed when Epaphroditus returned, he would give them the details. Yet Paul invites the Philippians to model their behavior and thought patterns after his example (4:9), so we can take the opportunity to see what Paul's actions suggest. In this section, they show a man who is flexible in his own calling; he does not have a rigid expectation about how God will use him in his apostolic duties.

Second, Paul has re-calibrated "success" to be the advancement of the gospel, not his own personal fame. This is evident in two ways. First, he is happy to let others preach the word; second, he is unconcerned when his own person or ministry is attacked. How different would our towns look if all our pastors and church leaders modeled these convictions?

---

1. Dr. William Toop, "Recollections of Eric Liddell by People Who Knew Him," n.p.; see www .ericliddell.org/ericliddell/recollections-by-people-who-knew-him/dr-william-toop/. Toop notes that Liddell did practice on his own and eventually bested Peltzer's race-winning time.

2. For an in-depth comparison between Paul's ministry and Eric Liddell's work, see Lynn H. Cohick, "Citizenship and Empire: Paul's Letter to the Philippians and Eric Liddell's Work in China," *JSPHL* 1/2 (2011): 1–16.

CHAPTER 4

Philippians 1:18b–26

 LISTEN to the Story

Yes, and I will continue to rejoice, ¹⁹for I know that through your prayers and God's provision of the Spirit of Jesus Christ what has happened to me will turn out for my deliverance. ²⁰I eagerly expect and hope that I will in no way be ashamed, but will have sufficient courage so that now as always Christ will be exalted in my body, whether by life or by death. ²¹For to me, to live is Christ and to die is gain. ²²If I am to go on living in the body, this will mean fruitful labor for me. Yet what shall I choose? I do not know! ²³I am torn between the two: I desire to depart and be with Christ, which is better by far; ²⁴but it is more necessary for you that I remain in the body. ²⁵Convinced of this, I know that I will remain, and I will continue with all of you for your progress and joy in the faith, ²⁶so that through my being with you again your boasting in Christ Jesus will abound on account of me.

Listening to the text in the Story: Exodus 3:1–12; Book of Job.

With unsurpassed confidence, Paul declares that his fate is secure—he is in Christ. Thus life and death hold importance only as they shape his relationship with Christ. In this passage, he will trace out the two paths: one of continued ministry, the other death. In either case, he is sustained by Christ. He concludes that he will remain in ministry and even gain his freedom so that he can visit the Philippians once more.

 EXPLAIN the Story

Paul Rejoices (1:18b)

Paul continues to rejoice because the gospel goes forward. The gospel framework controls his entire vision of his work, his life, and his (eventual) death. To the Galatians Paul declares that he has been crucified with Christ; he no longer lives, but Christ lives in him (Gal 2:19–20). To the Romans Paul

51

declares that believers are buried with Christ in their baptism, and they are raised up to walk in newness of life (Rom 6:4). To the Corinthians, Paul declares that anyone in Christ is a "new creation" (2 Cor 5:17). Those words form Paul to his core, so he can thus declare to the Philippians that his life and his death are taken up in the promises of new life in Christ.

Paul's Deliverance through Prayer and the Holy Spirit (1:19)

Paul now discusses his views on his imprisonment. He reassures the Philippians that even in such dire straits as he now finds himself, he believes God will work for Paul's deliverance and the furtherance of the gospel. These two convictions are possible because of their prayers for Paul and the provision of the Holy Spirit. Paul rests on the sure hope that he will be bold to the end, whatever that end might be.

Paul speaks of his "deliverance" by using the word *sōtēria*, often translated as "salvation." Paul is likely speaking theologically here, claiming that God will vindicate his obedience and will further his plan even in the midst of what seems like a hopelessly failed situation—the apostle's imprisonment. Paul's use of *sōtēria* suggests he will get out of prison alive or be delivered from the Roman court system. However, it is wrong to think that Paul believes he will secure his eternal salvation by his faithfulness or potential martyrdom. Nowhere does the apostle indicate that we earn our salvation. Our obedience flows from our right standing before God; it does not create our right standing.

The key to understanding this verse correctly is to see salvation as broader than only the moment one "gets saved." G. B. Caird explains that the New Testament indicates "salvation is a threefold act of God: an accomplished fact, an experience continuing in the present, and a consummation still to come."[1] Caird continues, "The simplest way is to see the three tenses [past, present, future] as states in a process begun, continued, and ended."[2] Such progress occurs in the individual, as in Philippians 1:6, "He who began a good work in you will carry it on to completion until the day of Christ Jesus," and in the spreading of Christ's influence throughout the world and in the church (see Eph 4:13). Paul stresses that we are saved *from* the guilt of our sins and the final judgment, and are saved *to* a life freed from enslavement to sin, a life that *will be* consummated with a new, glorified body in the day of Christ (1 Cor 15:35–57).

Paul's imprisonment is another opportunity for God's grace to shine in his

---

1. G. B. Caird, *New Testament Theology* (ed. L. D. Hurst; Oxford: Oxford University Press, 1994), 118. He cites Rom 5:12; 6:22; Col 3:1–4; Titus 2:11–13; Heb 10:12.

2. Ibid., 122.

own heart and into a dark, blind world. His imprisonment and his potential freedom (either in life or by death) both serve as further evidence of God's redemptive plan working in Paul's life, and through Paul to the church and the world (see also Rom 8:28). For Paul, good is the only outcome, since God is at work; he has planned it that all who love him will be changed and be conformed to the image of the Son, Jesus Christ.

Paul's firm convictions about his salvation or deliverance are rooted in two things: the Philippians' prayers and the Holy Spirit. Paul does not tell us *how* their prayers are effective, nor does he indicate that had they not prayed, he would be in despair. Rather, Paul confirms the close ties he shares with them that with their prayers they show their commitment to the gospel and to Paul's ministry. In other words, Paul does not see himself as a "lone ranger"; rather, he embraces the help of his teammates, the Philippians, whose prayers make a difference.

Moreover, throughout his letters Paul mentions coworkers and fellow prisoners who have supported him and encouraged him. For example, Aris- tarchus, Mark (the cousin of Barnabas), and Justus are the "only Jews among my co-workers for the kingdom of God, and they have proved a comfort for me" (Col 4:10 - 11). He also speaks of Tychicus, Onesimus, and Luke (4:7, 9, 14). Romans 16 is filled with names of Paul's friends and coworkers, both Jewish and Gentile believers. In 1 Corinthians 16:15 - 18 he refers to Stephanas, Fortunatus, and Achaicus who brought news and encouragement from Corinth.

As Paul writes to the Philippians, perhaps in the back of his mind he recalls all these people and has in view the body of Christ with its different gifts. Paul writes to the Romans that some in the body have gifts of encouragement, some of service, some of generosity (Rom 12:6 - 8). Certainly the Philippians have demonstrated those gifts on behalf of Paul by sending Epaphroditus to minister to him, sending money to help him, and remembering him in prayer.

Paul also indicates that he has been provided the Holy Spirit (1:19). The phrase "provision of the Spirit" can be understood in two ways. On the one hand, "of the Spirit" can be interpreted as the subject who is doing the providing. Thus we would say that the Holy Spirit provides Paul's needs. On the other hand, the Spirit can be the object; Paul has been given the Holy Spirit as provided by God. The second option is preferable, because it follows Paul's use in Galatians 3:5 and retains the natural meaning of the noun ("provision").

Paul is not implying either here or in Galatians that the Holy Spirit comes and goes in a believer's life. Paul is firm in his insistence that a follower of Christ is sealed with the Spirit (Eph 1:13 - 14) and has received the Spirit of adoption (Rom 8:15 - 17). But Paul does indicate that the Spirit can be more or less active in a person's life. To the Romans he declares that the Spirit prays and intercedes for us when we run out of words (8:26). Paul encourages the Galatians to "keep in step with the Spirit" (Gal 5:25).

Paul adds another phrase to "Spirit": "of Jesus Christ." We face a similar interpretative dilemma—does Paul mean that Christ (subject) sends the Spirit? Or that the Spirit represents Jesus Christ in Paul's life? Once again we look to Romans 8. In 8:9–10, Paul speaks about both the Spirit of Christ and of Christ being in a believer. In 2 Corinthians 3:17, Paul explains that "the Lord [Christ] is the Spirit, and where the Spirit of the Lord is, there is freedom." The Holy Spirit is the "agent for manifesting Christ";[3] the Spirit is "the powerful presence of the risen and exalted Messiah."[4] Note that Paul ties together tightly the Philippians' prayers and the Spirit's presence with him in prison. It is through the one Spirit that the church experiences unity, as Paul declares to the Ephesians, "There is one body and one Spirit, just as you were called to the one hope of your calling, one Lord, one faith, one baptism, one God and Father of all" (Eph 4:4–6; see also 1 Cor 12:4).

Courage Sufficient unto the Task (1:20)

In 1:20, Paul speaks directly to an underlying concern of the Philippians, namely, his possible death. His statement matches his request in Ephesians 6:19–20 that the Ephesians pray that Paul will be bold and confident in his faith—to the end. Neither he nor the Philippians are under any illusions that possible torture and hideous death might await him. So how can Paul have any hope? Paul uses an interesting term along with hope, translated in the NIV as "eagerly expect." This term has the idea of watching something intently (see Rom 8:19). The picture Paul creates here is one of determined focus and firm conviction. Paul's hope is not wishful thinking but is based on the sure reality of Christ's glorification and honor.

What is Paul expecting and hoping? That, in the final hour, he will not fail in his testimony. Paul does not want to "be ashamed," to experience the public humiliation that would come with a denial of his faith. When we today hear the term "shame," we think of someone who feels bad for a wrong they did. But in Paul's day, to be ashamed was to be publicly humiliated. Thus when Hebrews declares that Jesus Christ ignored the shame of the cross (12:1–2), or when Paul announces that he is not ashamed of the gospel (Rom 1:16), the message is that the social stigma of the cross should not deter believers in their public testimony, any more than it deterred Christ from dying on

---

3. Reumann, *Philippians*, 244.
4. Bockmuehl, *Philippians*, 84.

a cross. Note Paul's own imitation of Christ's meekness in accepting public humiliation for the sake of the gospel.

Martyrdom (1:20 – 21)

His final phrase of 1:20 ("whether through life or through death") signals the possibility of martyrdom. Paul's martyrdom is not the focus of his letter, nor does he argue that such a death will bring him closer to Christ. Because this topic is germane to our interpretation of other passages in the letter (2:17; 3:10), it is important that we establish Paul's position on martyrdom here. First, Paul states clearly that he expects to visit the Philippians (1:25; 2:24); this firm conviction should carry its full weight in interpreting Paul's general comments about death. Second, he regards his struggles and the Philippians' struggles as the "same" (1:30), or closely related (2:17), and there is no evidence that Paul expects the Philippians to be martyred. Third, Paul's image of being a "drink offering" (2:17) is not a metaphor for his martyrdom (see comments). Fourth, Paul's "gain" is not in the type of his death, namely martyrdom, but that at his death, he is joined more fully to Christ.

To assume that Paul elevates the martyr's death as superior reads the ideals of the later church back onto Paul. Paul wants to be obedient unto death, whatever that death might be. A martyr does not choose to die in this manner; rather, a martyr accepts his or her type of death as God's choice for them. If martyrdom were the best way to know Christ, Paul would have explicitly encouraged it. Instead, what Paul does encourage, loudly and clearly, is preaching boldly the gospel of Christ. Beyond that, who can say how God will glorify himself in a believer's final seconds? Paul dies daily (1 Cor 15:31), as he suffers on behalf of the gospel.

Paul's Fruitful Ministry (1:21 – 26)

In the next few verses Paul explains his view of his ministry and his view of a believer's death. He openly processes his train of thought to the Philippians, including his desire to depart this life to be with Christ. He recognizes that his ministry bears fruit (1:22), but then he steps back and looks at the two ideas: "life with Christ" and "death to be fully with Christ." There is hardly a pause as Paul exclaims the great glory awaiting believers in the Lord (1:23). But after this spontaneous high note of joy, Paul returns to the matter at hand, namely, his own situation and the concern it raises among the Philippians (1:24 – 26).

Throughout this passage, Paul uses "I" extensively, which speaks to his intimate relationship with the Philippians. However, he also speaks as a representative believer, for every Christian can say that death is gain, for our hope of salvation is sure. Paul uses the representative "I" in 1 Corinthians 13:1 – 13, as he similarly includes all believers: "If I speak in human or angelic tongues, but do not have love, I am only a resounding gong or a clanging cymbal."[5]

To Live Is Christ (1:21)

In 1:21, Paul announces: "For to me, to live is Christ and to die is gain." The Greek sentence has no verbs, so in English we supply the verb "to be." Additionally, Christ is mentioned by name only in the first clause. Calvin and Luther (among others) read the verse, "To me Christ is gain in life and in death."[6] Here Christ, not Paul, is the subject. Rendering the statement this way certainly matches the sentiment that infuses Paul's letters and is behind his declaration that all things are now as rubbish compared to the surpassing greatness of knowing Christ (3:8). While the meaning of this translation is solidly Pauline (Gal 2:20; Col 3:4), it may not fully represent Paul's specific meaning in this context. Paul will go on in the next few verses to contrast the two possibilities, life in ministry and death, that join him fully to Christ. The Reformers' translation dulls the distinction between the gain in death and the necessity of Paul's continued ministry.[7]

The enigmatic phrase "to live is Christ" is further explained in 1:22 as life in a human body (lit., "the flesh") and life that produces fruit. Paul's grammar is ambiguous; at issue is the relationship between the first two clauses such that the sentence can read either (A) "but if living in the flesh — (if) this is fruit of toil to me, then what I shall choose I do not declare," or (B) "but if living in the flesh (is my lot), this is fruit of toil for me, and what I shall choose I do not declare."[8] In the former case, Paul is declaring that while his own preference is to die and be with Christ, he cannot allow that personal gain to outweigh God's fruitful work in his ministry. In the second case, Paul is acknowledging that as long as he is in the flesh, God will work in and through him.

Option A follows the Greek more closely and offers a better approach to understanding Paul's final clause in the verse: "Yet what shall I choose? I do not know!" God is working in Paul. He describes what living in the flesh is — namely, a life lived in total surrender to God who works in and through his people (see also 1:6; 2:13). In other words, option A is clearer in its emphasis

---

5. Paul also uses the representative "I" to refer to "we Jews" in Rom 7:7–25, see Douglas J. Moo, *The Epistle to the Romans* (NICNT; Grand Rapids: Eerdmans, 1996), 427–31.

6. Reumann, *Philippians*, 248–49.

7. Peter T. O'Brien, *The Epistle to the Philippians* (NIGTC; Grand Rapids: Eerdmans, 1991), 118–20. He notes that this position does not take full account of the Greek grammar, which includes a nominative article ("the") before "live" and "die."

8. Marvin R. Vincent, *A Critical and Exegetical Commentary on the Epistles to the Philippians and to Philemon* (ICC; Edinburgh: T&T Clark, 1897), 27.

that life in the flesh is synonymous with fruitful ministry. It is not that it will (or might) result in fruitful work, but that our life in Christ is God's good works working through and in us for the world. This is a word to all believers: labor is not limited to the apostles, pastors, or missionaries; fruitful labor is the birthright and responsibility of all those born anew in Christ.

Paul ends this thought with "I do not know!" Since the immediate context suggests Paul is happy to make everything known to the Philippians, this phrase intimates that Paul cannot say what he would do if he really had the choice between remaining in his ministry or departing to be with Christ. Either the choice has not been made known to him by God, or he cannot make it based solely on his (limited) human reasoning. Underneath Paul's words is his conviction that his personal choice is not the ultimate criterion in determining his future; rather, God is.

To Depart and Be with Christ (1:23 – 24)

In 1:23 Paul continues his train of thought, but now speaks more generally not only of his possible imminent death (which would be his gain), but the reality of any believer who both embraces God's work in their life as well as longs for the peace and rest received upon death. Paul is "torn" between the two options. The verb Paul uses creates the word picture of a road built between two walls that constrain the traveler. It carries strong emotional force. In other words, Paul is not describing choosing between chocolate and vanilla ice cream, but between the all-surpassing gain that each believer longs for in death, and the blessed reality of a fruitful ministry that also includes suffering for Christ.

Although he continues rhetorically as though he is dealing with the quandary posed in the previous verse, he is not in fact contemplating an actual situation wherein he gets to decide. Instead, he takes the opportunity to express theologically why any believer, when thinking only of a personal, individual relationship with God in Christ, desires to depart this life to enjoy God fully. The surpassing greatness of life with Christ unhindered by our flesh should excite all believers. Paul's language is clear in affirming death as a blessing for believers, but what is less clear is *how* Paul pictures what happens at death. Because he is not addressing this question in 1:23, we will explore the debates concerning Paul's view on life after death in the "Live the Story" section, orienting the reader in the wider discussion of this issue.

Paul's declaration that "to die is gain" must not be interpreted as denigrating our life in this world. Paul does not seek to escape the world. He speaks over and over that he is joyful because of the Lord's work. He joyfully and willingly embraces suffering as confirmation of God's activity in building his church and reaching out to the world. He declares that God's grace is magnified as he faces his afflictions (2 Cor 12:9–10).

Paul's hope is that this world will be made new when Christ returns. Christ's *bodily* resurrection stands as our own promise of resurrected life in the new heavens and new earth. Paul teaches that salvation includes becoming a member of Christ's body. No believer lives only unto himself or herself. So along with his exuberant outburst that to be with Christ is far and away the better option, he also knows that he is part of a community and is God's servant. Those realities in the end persuade Paul that he will gain his freedom from his Roman chains, so that he can continue his work among them (1:24–26).

Paul's Continuing Ministry (1:24–26)

Paul thus contrasts the personal "better" with the "necessity" or service-minded attitude characteristic of Jesus himself. How does he make this determination? Paul clearly wants to hang onto both realities — the importance of ministry for Christ and the ultimate reward of life forever with Christ. But over both of these truths stands Paul's ultimate conviction: that the gospel will go forward. To express these three beliefs, he notes several points: (1) his ministry is fruitful (God's work in and through Paul), (1:22); (2) his ultimate goal is the resurrected life with Christ (1:23); (3) the work of the gospel means that he will remain "in the flesh" for the continued progress and joy of the Philippians. Paul's argument as described, then, does not suggest Paul is vacillating. Moreover, this reading supports the basic fact that Paul is still alive, imprisoned by the Praetorian guard. In that real sense, he remains their apostle.

At bottom, Paul's so-called "dilemma" related to choice is imaginary, for God has called him into service. We might say today, this is a "win-win" situation for Paul, for "in Christ" he cannot lose. In these words the apostle carves out a path that we can follow, taking care to avoid sliding into complete immersion with the cares and triumphs of this world, or slipping into total disregard for the world's plight only to gaze with an unholy stubbornness toward heaven. Paul's hope of resurrection and the new heavens and earth do not distract him from his daily activities; rather, the vision energizes these duties and invests them with eternal significance. In short, Paul is willing to wait on God's timing in receiving his summons to depart and be with Christ.

Progress and Joy in the Faith (1:25)

Verses 25–26 offer further explanation of Paul's plans. He will assist the Philippians in their "progress" in the Lord; additionally, he will return to them and bring great boasting in God's goodness and power in Christ. He begins with the strong statement that he is "convinced" that he will remain in his ministry and come to visit them. He uses the same verb in 2:24 as he reiterates that he is "confident" in the Lord that he will visit the Philippians soon. Paul will not die in Rome now.

With this emphasis on an upcoming visit to "all of you," Paul is beginning to shift away from a discussion of his own circumstances to look closely at the Philippians' situation. He will insist on their unity in the remaining chapters, and here he offers a foretaste of this—and not only unity, but also their deepening walk with God and their growing joy in the Lord. These three convictions will permeate the remaining three chapters.

Thus 1:25–26 turns to look ahead in the letter. Yet these verses also serve to complete Paul's argument that began in 1:12, where he spoke of the "advance" or progress of the gospel, and here he speaks of the Philippians' "progress," repeating the same verb. In 1:12 the advancement is both the gospel being made known to many and the emboldening of believers in testifying to that message. The same meaning can be understood in 1:25, that the Philippians will boldly preach the gospel and live a life that matches the message they proclaim.

Thus, Paul defines "progress" relative to God's call on every believer's life to be obedient. In this Paul's message differs from the philosophers of the day, who stressed progress as working hard. Such people could boast in their own efforts. But Paul makes clear that believers' progress is grounded solely in God's work in and through them (cf. 2:13). Moreover, Paul's definition of progress frees believers from having to judge their own ministry's effectiveness. If it is God who gives the growth (1 Cor 3:6), then our progress is not based on the size or influence of our ministry. Indeed, Paul cautions the Corinthians not to judge his ministry by such standards, and Paul insists he does not do so either (4:2–5).

Not only does Paul have progress in view, but also he stresses that his remaining with them is for their "joy." This resounding note of joy chimes throughout this letter, for Paul knows the secret to a healthy spiritual life: joy. It is joy that allows one to have confident hope that all will be made right in the end through God's work in Christ (1 Cor 15:24–28). It is deep joy in the Lord that grows contentment, thus muting the siren calls to pursue passions, prestige, wealth, and fame. It is joy in the Lord that guards the heart from utter despair.

Paul qualifies their progress and joy as being "in the faith." "Faith" can mean the content of the gospel, that which is believed, or it can mean their personal faith, their trust in Christ (3:9). These ideas are not mutually exclusive. But since in 1:12 progress was related to the spread of the gospel's message, and since 1:27 also stresses the content of faith, on the whole, it seems more likely that Paul's point here is that the Philippians will progress in their understanding of the faith, and that their joy will be more solidly rooted in the truth of the gospel.

Boasting in Christ Jesus (1:26)

Finally, Paul believes they will "boast in Christ," as they see how Christ worked in their prayers and concern for Paul and in Paul himself, such that he was delivered from Rome and now is present with them. To our ears, "boasting" carries pejorative connotations because it is generally self-referential. But in the Bible, boasting reflects the issue of confidence. Does one have confidence in the Lord? Then one may boast in the Lord. Jeremiah 9:23–24 highlights types of boasting: one can boast in human effort or in the power of God. Paul distinguishes the two in Philippians 3:3–4, as he contrasts boasting in circumcision or boasting in Christ.

We might not use the phrase "boasting in the Lord" today, but when we say, "praise the Lord," we acknowledge publicly what God's power has done. In a sense, we are boasting as we praise, because we recognize God's work and remind ourselves it is not by our own strength that good is accomplished. The Philippians, Paul believes, will have the opportunity to glorify God as he answers their prayers (1:19). This too will be a cause for rejoicing.

 LIVE the Story

Paul declares to the Philippians that he is convinced that his situation (imprisonment) "will turn out for my deliverance" (1:19). These words mirror Job's declaration that "though he slay me, yet will I praise him; I will surely defend my ways to his face. *Indeed, this will turn out for my deliverance [salvation]*" (Job 13:15–16, italics added). Although Paul does not identify in his letter that he is quoting from Job, the words he uses are exactly the same in the Septuagint's rendering. Perhaps this verse circulated on its own within Judaism as a testimony to God's goodness in the face of potential martyrdom, much as God vindicated Job. Or perhaps Paul was thinking of the verse before, that though he may die, yet his dying breath will be one of praise to God. In either case, Paul's allusion invites us to look at Job and even more, God's response.

Job's Suffering

Suffering is one of the hardest issues for humans to understand and explain. Sometimes it is clear why one suffers—if I eat an entire pint of ice cream,

I will suffer pains in my stomach. If I fail to pay my electric bill, I will suffer darkness when the sun goes down. But suffering that seems arbitrary (an infant's cancer) or out of proportion (thousands dead from an earthquake or tsunami) raise questions about God's presence (or absence) and power. Paul invites believers to see suffering differently, that is, through Christ's grace. In this, he is following the book of Job's lead, as Job is directed by God not to ask for justice based on his righteousness, but humbly to seek wisdom, for God asks for a posture of faith.

In Job, two complaints are leveled at God: (1) the righteous do righteous deeds because they know that God will reward them, and (2) the righteous should not suffer, as suffering is punishment for sins. The first charge is leveled by the Adversary in 1:9–12; 2:4–6, and the first half of the book contains Job's correct refutation of that charge (e.g., Job 27). Job has lost everything, but he maintains his righteousness. But the second charge is challenged by God as too limited in scope and based on a false premise. It is too limited because it fails to appreciate God's unimaginably great wisdom. It is false in that it supposes that bad things happen to bad people, and thus good things must happen to good people.

Instead, God shows Job that suffering is part of the fabric of a creation that is not in its final form, for disorder still exists. God does not address suffering; instead, he addresses Job's assumptions about his situation and his claims of righteousness. God chooses not to explain suffering; instead, he shows himself to Job and asks Job to trust him. This trust is not based on the assumption that at some point suffering will make sense, for that is merely assuming a deeper justice by which God operates. It is not in the end justice, but wisdom, that God identifies as the explanation for how the world operates. Faced with God's wisdom, Job repents and worships.[9]

Christ, the Cross, and the Wisdom of God

Paul teaches that Christ is God's wisdom and power (1 Cor 1:24, 30), and God's wisdom is revealed in Christ's cross. Even more, Paul declares that believers "have the mind of Christ" (2:16) through the Holy Spirit, so that we can discern what is God's truth and reject the world's wisdom. Paul speaks of Christ's suffering similarly. He explains that suffering first by connecting sin to death (Rom 5:1–19; 1 Cor 15:20–28, 56–57) and then highlighting how Christ's death enters into our sin and death. As Hafemann explains, "Paul could thus interpret his suffering in terms of the cross of Christ, while his ability to endure it or God's action of deliverance from it, were an expression

---

9. I'm indebted to John Walton, my colleague at Wheaton College, for these insights. See John Walton, *Job* (NIVAC; Grand Rapids: Zondervan, 2012).

of the same divine power revealed in Christ's resurrection."[10] A similar call for believers to accept suffering with joy points to their testimony that God's wisdom is seen in the cross, and God's power is sufficient for any situation.

Paul sees even more clearly than did Job that suffering (illness, natural disaster, broken relationships, war) signals the disorder of this present age. But that is not the last word. Christ has been raised, and we now know that the end is closer than when we first believed (Rom 13:11). The deliverance that Job experienced was more than he could have imagined. He was freed from his small view of God and an inflated view of his own righteousness. He learned that God does not inflict suffering as payback for sin, nor is God *required* to bless the righteous. God's wisdom dictates his actions, and his character, while not arbitrary, is not completely comprehensible to the human mind.

Death Is Gain, Life Is Christ

For Paul, death is gain, and life is Christ. I've reversed the order of these biblical phrases because I think often believers today think about Paul's statement in this reverse order. We are prepared (at least we think we are) to die, because we rightly trust in Christ's righteousness and intercession on our behalf. But we do not have a real sense of what it means to live for Christ, as we have thought of Christianity basically as our "get out of jail free" card, our ticket to heaven. We might say that we live for Christ, but what we mean is that we live for Christ *and* for work, family, ministry, wealth, and so on. How can we get to Paul's place of living for Christ *period*?

It is not as though Paul did not have a ministry or friends. He knew what his ministry or call was — to preach Christ and not to baptize, for example (1 Cor 1:10–17). He submitted to God's teaching — he learned to be content (Phil 4:10–13), and he discovered that God's grace is sufficient (2 Cor 12:7–10). He actively critiqued the wider world's social and cultural definitions of success (Phil 3:4–14). He devoted himself to love (1 Cor 13) and never forgot that this present age is passing away.

Sometimes God reminds us of these truths in direct ways. In the mid–1990s, my husband, Jim, was drawn to join a new ministry that involved building and managing a pediatric rehabilitation hospital in Kenya. I had just completed my PhD and was eager to start looking for full-time work. During those long years of dissertation writing, I promised God that this degree was his to do with as he pleased. After much prayer, it was clear to both Jim and me that God was calling us to Kenya. However, I had no teaching job lined

---

10. S. J. Hafemann, "Suffering," *DPL*, 919–20.

up — in fact, no job at all. I realized then that when I thought I was giving my degree to God, what I was really saying was that I'd take (just about) any teaching job. I never expected that God might decide to closet the degree altogether. As it turned out, I did have teaching opportunities in Nairobi, but these emerged after we arrived in Kenya. It was an important lesson for me, challenging me as to whether God really has providential and wise authority over my life, work, and family.

Christ Will Be Exalted in My Body

Not only is Paul convinced "for me to live is Christ," but he also is confident that Christ will be exalted in his body. Lest we imagine that living for Christ in Paul's mind means grudgingly obeying or doing just enough to past muster, Paul declares that he desires Christ to be exalted in his body, in his life. What does that look like? Paul stresses that he is bold in proclaiming the gospel. Thus one important way to exalt Christ is to be bold in our conviction that the gospel is the truth. Such boldness can take many forms, but they all express the gospel truth in a loving manner. Some are bold at work when they refuse to gossip and instead speak words of healing and grace. Others are bold in their neighborhoods, looking for ways to extend God's blessings in practical, spontaneous ways. Some are bold as they obey God's call to engage in ministries that stretch them. Others are bold as they obey God's Word to wait patiently in their current situation. Exalting Christ in our lives happens as we boldly obey.

Paul exalts Christ as he focuses on the goal, the prize of life with Christ in his resurrected state. Exalting Christ means looking forward, driving onward, advancing with purpose, having an eschatological frame of reference. Like a hound with his nose on the scent, Paul runs with a dedicated goal and singular purpose. Paul never loses sight of the reality that Christ will return, that the dead will be raised, and those whose names are written in the book of life (Phil 4:3) will enjoy God's company forever. That picture never slips from his mind.

No Case Made by Paul for His Martyrdom

I noted above that Paul is not presenting a case for his impending martyrdom. I now would like to examine why the topic is more than academic. It is not so much that Paul's martyrdom in general is problematic. Church tradition teaches that Paul was beheaded under Nero, and there is no reason to doubt this. Rather, the problem with interpreting Philippians as Paul's statements about his martyrdom is that the position can be articulated in such a way as to elevate martyrs above "ordinary" believers. The second- and third-century church fell at times to this temptation. A martyr should not boast in his or her martyrdom, for it was God who called them to this death. It is God's decision not to call other believers to such a death. In both cases, the believer is judged on their faithfulness, not on the manner in which they died.

The Martyrdom of Perpetua and Felicity

One of the most well-known martyrs in the early church is Perpetua, who was killed in AD 203 in Carthage, North Africa.[11] The account of her martyrdom is drawn in large part from her personal writings from prison shortly before her death, making this work one of the earliest Christian testimonies written by a woman.[12] At her arrest, her father (a non-Christian) begs her to recant, to which she boldly responds, "Father, said I, do you see ... this vessel lying here to be a little pitcher or something else? ... Can it be called by any other name than what it is? ... Neither can I call myself anything else than that which I am, a Christian" (*Passion* 1.2).

As the day of her death approaches, she describes visions or dreams that encourage her to hold fast to her faith. The day before her death, she has a vision of herself facing wild beasts in the amphitheater, and she realizes her fate is sealed. Yet the vision continues in a most remarkable way. She sees herself becoming a man, facing down a large Egyptian gladiator. Another figure dominates the ring, a person of great height wearing a purple robe. The fight commences, and Perpetua struck the gladiator's face with her feet and trod upon his head. At this, the purple-robed figure awarded her the victory and kissed her and said, "Daughter, peace be with you" (*Passion* 3.2). Perpetua realizes that her vision showed she would not be fighting beasts but the devil, and that victory awaits her. As she and Felicity enter the arena, their appearance shocks the audience, for Felicity had just given birth two days earlier and Perpetua had recently weaned her young son. The other martyrs with them fall, and Perpetua is left to guide the young gladiator's sword to her throat, for his first blow did not finish the job.

Perpetua's reflections indicate that over the many days of her imprisonment, she grew to understand what was to be her fate and to strengthen her resolve. She mourns the fracturing of her relationship with her father, she aches for her young son, and she wonders about having strength for the final

---

11. Translations and commentaries on the *Martyrdom of Perpetua and Felicity* include Joyce E. Salisbury, *Perpetua's Passion: The Death and Memory of a Young Roman Woman* (New York: Routledge, 1997), and Thomas J. Heffernan, *The Passion of Perpetua and Felicity* (Oxford: Oxford University Press, 2012).

12. See the online translation of the *Passion of Perpetua and Felicity*: www.newadvent.org/fathers/0324.htm; the reader should distinguish between the *Passion* and a later work known as the *Acts of Perpetua*.

battle. But throughout her last weeks, she testifies to the companionship of her fellow martyrs and to the empowering presence of God.

Later generations rightly praise her courage. Augustine comments years later that she and the slave, Felicity, modeled Christian courage and virtue: "In the power of these virtues, they turn their backs on the world's promises and threats, and stretch out to what lies ahead (Phil 3:13). These virtues climb up to heaven by trampling on the head of the serpent, as it hisses and whispers its various suggestions."[13] Augustine ends this homily with this encouragement: "So we too are the fruit of their toil.... At least we are all in attendance upon the same Lord, all following the same teacher, accompanying the same leader, joined to the same head, wending our way to the same Jerusalem, pursuing the same charity, and embracing the same unity."[14] Augustine rightly connects the martyrs with the entire church in their singular pursuit of Christ.

Missionaries and the "Average" Believer—Two-Tiered Configuration?

The two-tiered system of martyrs and "average" believers exists in the American church in a different guise today. Now we place missionaries or pastors above other believers, creating a privileged class that does the church no good. Paul felt compelled to speak the gospel (1 Cor 9:16); God had called him for this task, and he was only being obedient in carrying out that task—God gives the growth (3:6). Paul cannot boast in anything, just as the man washing dishes is obeying the call to be a cleaner of the restaurant kitchen, or the woman performing surgery on an infant's heart is obediently using the gifts of healing given her by God.

And the missionary is no more obedient to God's call than the housewife and stay-at-home mother. I've been both—I know. In each case, obedience is the operating factor. That means that missionaries cannot boast that they are doing more for the kingdom or are somehow gifted with a higher calling. Sadly, not all missionaries I have met would agree with me. Moreover, many like to exalt missionaries because as they build them up, they can rationalize that since they are not such strong Christians, God could never call them into mission work. The two-tiered system thus meets both needs—that of the missionary who wants to feel privileged, and that of the "average" believer who does not want God to call them to missions.

---

13. Augustine, *Sermons: III/8 (2730305A) on the Saints* (ed. John E. Rotelle; trans. Edmund Hill; *The Works of Saint Augustine: A Translation for the 21st Century* (Hyde Park, NY: New City Press, 1994): 74; for a copy of the homily, see www02.homepage.villanova.edu/allan.fitzgerald/Ser280-2.htm.

14. Ibid., 280.6.

This God-dishonoring dance needs to stop. It also means that the house-wife has as much responsibility to live into God's kingdom, to step outside her comfort zone and obey God as he asks her to risk for the sake of the gospel. The point is not *what* we do; the point is that we are doing what God asks us to do.

Life after Death

Let us return to Paul's declaration "for to me, to live is Christ and to die is gain." Paul expands on death's gain a few verses later, writing of his desire to depart and be with Christ. These statements are not meant to establish doctrine about what life after death looks like, but bringing up the subject invites us to probe into the big picture as presented in Paul's letters. Paul notes that when he departs (dies), he will be with Christ, which implies that he will be with the Lord immediately upon death (see 2 Cor 5:6–8; cf. Acts 7:59). This suggests a conscious, bodiless existence in an intermediate state before the resurrection. Paul also uses the word "sleep" when describing a believer's death, indicating perhaps a semiconscious existence or soul sleep (1 Cor 15:51–2; 1 Thess 4:14, 16; 5:10). Paul may want to stress here as well the different sort of death believers face because their life is now hidden in Christ. They died with Christ (Gal 2:20), and they need not fear physical death; it is no more frightful than falling asleep.

The matter is made more complex because Paul also insists (rightly) on Christ's second coming, his parousia. When that happens, those believers currently alive on earth will meet the Lord in the air and escort him down to earth (1 Thess 4:17; cf. Col 3:4). The believers receive their resurrected bodies at the end, at the final judgment (or at the millennium, depending on one's reading of Revelation). They are then fit for life in the new heavens and new earth, a life of blessing and full fellowship with the Son.

Since the end has not yet occurred, we might assume that those who are "asleep" in Christ do not have their resurrected bodies. However, we are trapped in a linear, time-based view of the world. Could it be that the instance any believer dies, for them it is as though the end is now here? And that for believers left to mourn their passing, time continues? In the end one thing we can be sure of: "neither death nor life, nor angels nor demons, neither the present nor the future, nor any powers, neither height nor depth, nor anything else in all creation, will be able to separate us from the love of God in Christ Jesus our Lord" (Rom 8:38). At the graveside, no one should doubt that those loved by God are safe in their Father's arms.

Philippians 1:27–30

 LISTEN to the Story

> ²⁷Whatever happens, conduct yourselves in a manner worthy of the gospel of Christ. Then, whether I come and see you or only hear about you in my absence, I will know that you stand firm in the one Spirit, striving together as one for the faith of the gospel ²⁸without being frightened in any way by those who oppose you. This is a sign to them that they will be destroyed, but that you will be saved—and that by God. ²⁹For it has been granted to you on behalf of Christ not only to believe in him, but also to suffer for him, ³⁰since you are going through the same struggle you saw I had, and now hear that I still have.

Listening to the text in the Story: Job 1:1–2:10; Acts 16:19–40.

"I am the Lord's servant.... May your word to me be fulfilled" (Luke 1:38). With those words to the angel Gabriel, Mary the mother of Jesus Christ began a new journey, one that would stretch her faith almost to the breaking point. Opposition from other Jews, and eventually from the Romans, pierced her soul.[1] Yet Mary was privileged to witness the birth of the Messiah and the beginning of the church at Pentecost (Acts 1:14). In a similar sense, Paul sums up for the Philippians the realities of their journey with the Lord. They were the first ones in Macedonia to hear the gospel, and they had remained steadfast ever since. Paul commands them to live into the faith that is theirs, clinging to their sure salvation with one hand and grasping the cup of suffering with the other. By publicly standing fast against opponents, the Philippians live out their faith and reveal the coming condemnation of their enemies.

---

1. The prophet Simeon foretold to Mary that "a sword will pierce your own soul too" (Luke 2:35).

EXPLAIN the Story

Paul's Insistence That the Philippians *Politeuesthe* the Gospel of Christ (1:27)

Having assured the Philippians that he intends to visit them after his imprisonment, Paul focuses attention back on their situation. Verse 27 has created various interpretations because Paul uses *politeuesthe,* a verb unknown in the rest of his writings. I have written the term in transliterated Greek because it is almost impossible to translate into English without having already decided on its meaning. But before we examine this unusual word more closely, I will look briefly at the first two words in the verse.

The first word is the adverb "only" (NIV "whatever happens"), which alerts his readers that he is making only one request or command. As we unpack Paul's command, we find many layers of application. The demand itself is singular, but it encompasses all of life; in this way Paul gives his readers an organizing principle against which to make decisions and judgments.

His second term, translated in the NIV as "worthy manner," sets the standard for how believers are to implement Paul's request. Paul is not given to sentimentality, but focuses on the responsibilities and obligations taken up by those who proclaim the gospel of Christ. When we use the word "worthy" today, we often do so in a comparative sense. A parent might say that a boyfriend is not worthy to date their daughter, or a coworker was not worthy of a promotion. Underneath such statements is the sense that the deficiency is based on actions, and we might say that a truly worthy person has earned their accolades. Paul gives no hint here or anywhere else that a person is ever determined worthy by God to be saved. Entirely the opposite—Paul is clear that God's salvation is a free gift, an unearned gesture on his part toward humanity.

Paul's point in raising the call of worthiness is that believers, in claiming the grace of God in Christ, also now represent Christ and his teachings to the wider public. As such, their worldview, behaviors, and attitudes are all shaped by the cross and resurrection of Christ. We live worthy of the gospel when we embrace the song sung around the throne of God, "You [Christ the Lamb] are worthy to take the scroll and to open its seals, because you were slain, and with your blood you purchased for God persons from every tribe and language and people and nation. You have made them to be a kingdom and priests to serve our God, and they will reign on the earth" (Rev 5:9–10). Worthy living is kingdom living.

One final note before delving into the meaning of *politeuesthe*: Paul indicates that he may or may not be coming to see them. Since he just finished stating directly that he is coming to them (1:26), what does he mean by this conditional statement? The reader finds echoes here from his earlier discussion about living or dying (1:20 – 25). Paul is not referring to his possible release from prison, but rather the possible unexpected crisis necessitating his travel elsewhere than Philippi. Paul expresses his desire to see them, but he also leaves open the possibility that events might dictate otherwise. Nonetheless, Paul desires to keep in communication.

We turn now to analyze *politeuesthe*. The root of the term is related to *polis*, the Greek term for "city." The verb signals a person's actions in the *polis*, namely, being a citizen.[2] Combining these elements, it suggests living one's life especially as it relates to public or civic affairs. This verb also occurs in Acts 23:1 in Paul's defense of his behavior: "*I have fulfilled my duty* to God in all good conscience." The related noun *politeia*, used in Acts 22:28 and Ephesians 2:12, indicates citizenship, the body politic, or civil polity. A second noun, *politeuma*, used in Philippians 3:20, has the sense of commonwealth status and often describes a group of foreigners within a city. It also can indicate the business of government.

Two basic theories have emerged as to the meaning of this verb. One argues that Paul intends political overtones; a second contends that Paul references the Jewish context and religious identity within the scope of the verb's meaning.

(1) *Stand fast against pagan leaders in Philippi.* The political argument takes its cue from several pieces of data. First, when Paul wants to describe a believer's behavior, he generally uses the verb "walk," and the English translations often use "live" to capture the meaning of that verb (see, e.g., Phil 3:17 – 18; also Gal 5:16; 1 Thess 2:12 and Eph 4:1 [the latter two also use "worthily"]). That Paul does *not* use "walk" here suggests he wants to emphasize a politically or civically nuanced message to the Philippians.

This argument is strengthened because Philippi was a Roman colony with rights granted to cities on Italian soil, the only city with this elite status visited by Paul. Roman citizenship and civic duty played a key part in the city's own narrative, and this theory suggests Paul draws on that usage but nuances it to focus not (only) on Philippi and Rome, but (also) on Jesus Christ and his gospel. Paul could be suggesting a dual allegiance, where Philippians carry out their civic duties, but set their hearts beyond the kingdom of Rome to the kingdom of God. If so, what might those civic duties include? Clearly it cannot mean participating in pagan festivals or trade guild celebrations of the patron deity. It might include more generally the civic duty of acting responsibly toward one's patrons or clients and paying taxes. In the case of the

---

2. Reumann, *Philippians*, 262.

Philippian jailer, for example (Acts 16:27–34), he would continue at his post, but now with Christ as his master.

Many commentators identify the antagonists as perhaps government officials who harass believers, or city and trade guild leaders who provoke public outcry and damage reputations. Acts 16:19–24, which tells of Paul and Silas's beating, arrest, and imprisonment, is also cited as representative of Christians' treatment in Philippi by city magistrates and civic leaders. Looking closely at 16:35–40, we find that the officials released Paul and Silas *before* they were made aware of Paul's Roman citizenship, suggesting that their release was not related to Paul's citizenship. Would this also suggest that the mob action against Paul and Silas the day before had no definitive or lasting implications for believers? The charges brought by the angry owners of the slave girl did not stick, nor did the charges by the crowd, namely, that Paul and his group were Jews and were promoting customs contrary to the Roman way of life. Thus, Paul's experience may suggest sporadic attacks against individual believers that were not ultimately supported by official ruling.

(2) *Stand fast against those who promote circumcision.* The second theory argues that if Paul had intended political overtones, he would not have asked them to act worthy of the gospel, but would have spoken of "the city." Rather than direct Roman political overtones, this theory argues for a Jewish backdrop to the term's use here. First, Jewish authors use the verb to describe living as a Jew. For example, Josephus uses it to describe his life as a Pharisee (*Life* 2), and most believe he is referring to his acceptance of the Pharisaic way of life. Similarly, 2 Maccabees 6:1 speaks of Jews who have turned from their ancestral laws and are not obeying the laws of God. The term communicated the sense of living out one's identity as a person of God in public life (cf. Acts 23:1).

Second, the larger vision of the community of believers living in a city made by God for God's people rings loudly in New Testament writings (see, e.g., Heb 11:10, 16). Underneath these statements is a conviction that doing God's will, being faithful to one's calling as a member of God's people, is a public act having social or community consequences; a believer's beliefs naturally flow into acts of faithfulness. Paul explains the larger concept in Ephesians 2:10, that believers will do good works prepared by God for them to do, as a result of God's work in their salvation. In the case of the verb in Philippians 1:27, then, this second interpretation argues that Paul is challenging the Philippians to be publicly faithful in witnessing to the reality of their new life in Christ.

In the case of the cognate noun *politeuma* (citizenship), used in 3:20, Paul intends to distinguish the Philippian believers as citizens of heaven over against those who are enemies of the cross of Christ (3:18). Against these enemies the church is to stand firm in their resurrection hope (4:1). I will later discuss these enemies (called "dogs ... mutilators of the flesh," 3:2), but to anticipate my argument, I suggest tentatively that the enemies of 3:18–19 are Jewish or Gentile believers intent on persuading the Philippians to circumcise. These teachings blended Christ's gospel with traditional Jewish practices and imposed those practices on Gentile believers.

By using a similar noun and verb in 1:27 and 3:20, Paul implies a link between the opponents of chapter 1 and the enemies of chapter 3. These strong verbal connections lead to the conclusion that Paul's frame of reference in using *politeuomai* is both Roman and Jewish.[3] The rhetorical force of *politeuomai* and *politeuma* is located more distantly in the Roman context, and more directly in Paul's contemporary Jewish milieu. But this does not mean that Paul's message lacks political nuance. Paul's kingdom focus, if you will, is rooted in Israel's history and the Davidic kingdom. Paul describes Jesus as one "who as to his earthly life was a descendant of David, and who through the Spirit of holiness was appointed the Son of God in power by his resurrection from the dead: Jesus Christ our Lord" (Rom 1:3–4). Paul emphasizes living out of the gospel message, the testimony of God's work in Christ.

To conclude, I believe that Paul has two different though related groups of opponents in mind. Those destined for destruction in chapter 1, are, in a limited way, in *the same general category* as those who promote circumcision in chapter 3; both groups must be strongly resisted. Both of these groups represent the present age, without the Savior Jesus Christ and without the hope of resurrection.

With the little information we have from Acts and Paul's letters, we can tentatively reconstruct various possible situations faced by the Philippian believers. They may have faced a general offensive from some in the wider Jewish community against Paul's message, and then within the believers' community itself, perhaps a group of Jewish believers who speak against Paul's gospel. Members of these groups might carry influence with the Roman city council since they represented their ethnic (Jewish) group, and thus they could cause pressure to be put on Jewish and Gentile believers.

From Colossians and Galatians, we find the churches struggling with distinguishing Paul's gospel from those who preached a gospel linked with circumcision and advocating other aspects of Jewish life to Gentile believers. In Acts 16 and 17, strong opposition to Paul by both Jews and Gentiles

---

3. Gordon Fee, *Philippians*, 31–34, argues for two sorts of suffering: an external tension with the citizens of Philippi (1:27–30; 3:20) and internal unrest characterized by a call for Gentile believers to take shelter in the Jewish community, a legitimate religion under Rome.

punctuate Paul's short visits to Philippi and Thessalonica. Additionally, in 1 Thessalonians 2:2, Paul refers to the shameful treatment he received both in Philippi and in Thessalonica, and in 2:14, Paul praises the Thessalonians for enduring hardship from their countrymen, as did Judean churches from some Jews in Judea.[4]

Stand Firm, Striving Together (1:27)

Paul defines how the Philippians are to live worthy of the gospel by asking that the Philippians "stand firm"—a verb also used in 4:1 as he encourages believers to "stand firm in the Lord" (see also 1 Cor 16:13; Gal 5:1). This verb controls two participles, "striving together" and "[not] being frightened." Does he imagine a static pose, standing still in the face of strong winds or high waves? Or does he imagine an active posture, meeting the enemy in battle?

To answer this, we must look at the corresponding phrase "in one Spirit." This phrase could mean that the Philippians are to stand as a single person, a unified human "spirit" or the Philippians' esprit de corps (see NIV note). But more likely Paul speaks of the Holy Spirit's action here. In 1 Corinthians 6:17, Paul notes that individual believers are united to the Spirit when they are in Christ. In Galatians 6:1 Paul encourages the believers to help each other to refrain from sinning, by relying on the Spirit within them to restore gently one who is heading toward transgressions. The unity Paul calls for is rooted in the Spirit, the Spirit of the living God.

If we return to my earlier question, Paul seems to enjoin believers to be solidly planted on the deck of a rolling ship. That is, believers cannot know whether calm seas or high weather await, but their security is maintained by the Spirit's grip, locking them tightly to the ship's deck.

As they stand firm in the Holy Spirit, Paul asks believers to "strive together" (*synathloutes*) in unity, going forward (lit.) "with a single mind." Paul uses the word *psychē*, sometimes translated as "mind," but can also mean "soul, life"—that part of the human person distinguished from body. The NIV writes "as one" (see also Acts 4:32). To have one purpose/soul is to experience unity among friends. In this we find an important theological distinction: All believers share in the same Holy Spirit, but believers do not have the same opinions. Unity implies diversity or difference. Paul emphasizes unity increasingly in this letter; here he notes the foundational point that unity is created only as each believer stands firm in the Holy Spirit. As they do so, they also exhibit a singularity of purpose, namely, the advancement of the gospel.

---

4. It is not clear whether 2:14 signals persecution from both Jewish and Gentile antagonists, but G. K. Beale suggests this is the case (*1–2 Thessalonians* [IVPNTC; Downers Grove, IL: InterVarsity Press, 2003], 81).

Here and in 4:3, Paul stresses the importance of the church working together for a common end. It brings to mind the three-legged races so popular at picnics. To win the race, the pair needed to stride together in unity. Perhaps my race analogy is not far afield. The word family for "striving" (*athleō*) draws on images of competing in athletic contests (see their use in 2 Tim 2:5; Heb 10:32). In our own passage, Philippians 1:30 includes a similar term, *agōn* ("struggle"), which can refer to an athletic or gladiatorial contest, and metaphorically in philosophical texts to the striving against passions.[5]

Paul is emphasizing here, then, the discipline of behavior and singleness of purpose as believers move in one accord for the advance of the gospel (3:10–14; 4:11). The verb "striving together" calls to mind team work. His concern is that the Philippians help each other face the struggles that match Paul's struggles to present the gospel clearly and boldly. Additionally, Paul speaks more broadly here about the nature of the believer's experience with suffering. In 1:30, "struggle" carries the general meaning of suffering, as Paul focuses on Christ's suffering and our own invitation to suffer in his name. Paul's message parallels both his statement in Colossians 1:24 about accepting afflictions for the sake of Christ's body, the church, and his conclusion concerning the thorn in his side (2 Cor 12:6–10). God has granted each believer the opportunity to share Christ's life of service and suffering so that Paul can declare that the Philippians have the *same* suffering as does Paul (1:30). While they are not in prison or perhaps have not been beaten, shipwrecked, or flogged, their own hardships resulting from obeying the call of God are as important and valuable to the advance of the gospel as Paul's witness from prison.

For Paul, it is always and only about the gospel of Christ. The gospel message works its will within Paul and within the church. This gospel of Christ is powerful against foes, strong to unite believers, and redemptive to save. The gospel includes both the truth of Jesus Christ's redemption and the Spirit-led way of life, flowing from the reality that believers belong to God's kingdom. We have a saying today, "When in Rome, do as the Romans do." Paul, with much more sense of urgency, says to the Philippians, "In Christ, you are not destined for Philippi; therefore, you must act as befits one whose allegiance is with Christ."

Stand Firm, without Being Frightened (1:28)

Paul offers a second way the Philippians can think about standing firm, that is, to not fear their opponents. The verb "to fear" can be used to describe a

---

5. Note too Paul's extended use of arena imagery in 1 Cor 9:24–27 and 15:30–32.

herd of stampeding horses, wild and out of control in their panic. While horses are created with the "flight, not fight" instinct, Paul indicates that believers need not run blindly or anxiously from those who harbor ill will toward them.

The Believer's Hope of Salvation and Deliverance (1:28)

Why should the Philippians bravely stand firm? Because God has accomplished their salvation. The term "salvation" in Paul generally means one's eternal life with God, but it also carries a more mundane meaning in Greek: deliverance from trouble. Paul has both meanings in view, as he is convinced that the Philippians' steadfast declaration of the gospel will prevail against any forces of evil. In this Paul reveals a mystery of the faith, namely, that a believer's steadfastness in the face of opposition has spiritual ramifications greater than the immediate situation. For example, in the beginning of Job, God and the Adversary discuss Job's potential reaction to suffering. What Job does not realize is that his subsequent faithfulness in the face of dreadful circumstances has ramifications in the spiritual realm; Job helps defeat the Adversary's plan and advance the larger cause of righteousness through his own obedience.

In a similar manner, Paul shows the Philippians that their lack of fear in the face of suffering carries with it greater spiritual ramifications than their personal maturity in the faith. It also signals the ultimate overthrow of evil and the victory of God in Christ. The guilt of the oppressors is displayed in their persecution of the righteous, and their ultimate destruction comforts those afflicted now. Paul reminds the Philippians that God's victory in Christ is sure. He is not arguing that believers chase down suffering and oppression as though to prove their faith, only that they stand fast when waves of suffering and struggle threaten to knock them over.

Believing in and Suffering for Christ (1:29–30)

Paul writes here that God gave to the Philippians two things: belief in Christ and suffering for Christ. Both of these infinitives are in the present tense, indicating a current and continuing situation. Looking at the first phrase, "to believe in him [Christ]," Paul uses this phrase when speaking to the Galatians: "we have come *to believe in* Christ Jesus" (2:16; see also Rom 10:10, 14). In Galatians, Paul stresses the distinction between works of the law and belief in Christ in terms of justification. In Philippians, Paul emphasizes the present and ongoing action of believing in Christ, parallel with the current and ongoing suffering experienced by the Philippians. This is the only place in Philippians where Paul uses the verb "to believe," but its cognate noun "faith, belief" is used several times (e.g., 1:25, 27). In 1:27, "the faith of the gospel" is a unique phrase in Paul and likely carries both the sense of faith as the content of the gospel message and the act of faith that the gospel message generates in believers.

Lest we imagine that faith in Christ is merely intellectual acceptance of cold facts, Paul conjoins faith and suffering in his picture of the Christian life. For Paul, suffering only makes sense and is bearable because of the immeasurably rich faith—our belief in the sure, faithful work of Christ—that is the gift God gives to every believer. Paul reassures the Philippians that suffering is redemptive inasmuch as it testifies to Christ's work on the cross. Suffering is an expected aspect of the end of the current age dominated by sin and oppression. But suffering does not have the final word; God will gain the victory, as evidenced already in Christ's resurrection, which is the gospel that the Philippians confess.

Paul uses the verb *paschō* here in describing suffering; the cognate noun is "Passover." In 1 Corinthians 5:7, Paul describes Jesus as the "Passover Lamb" (*pascha*). With this term, Paul sets the stage for the Christ hymn in the next chapter, a poem that marvels at Christ's death on the cross. In Philippians 3:10, Paul uses a related term for suffering (*pathēma*; cf. also Rom 8:18, where Paul declares that our current circumstances of suffering are but a mere speck on the screen when compared to the all-surpassing grace experienced by believers).

To be sure, Paul is not minimizing the reality or difficulty of suffering; he does not encourage a stoic demeanor that learns how to avoid pain in the future or a naïve denial of the deep pain and sorrow that scar so many lives. Rather, he sees all of this in the light of God's glory, the glory that believers will enjoy in the new heavens and new earth, with resurrected, glorified bodies. This is why Paul can repeatedly encourage the Philippians to rejoice in the Lord.

Suffering for God in Jewish and Gentile Communities

How would such a claim—that God would grant believers the opportunity to suffer for Christ—have sounded to the Philippians' ears? If there were Jewish believers in the group, they could easily recall their recent history, for example, the Maccabean martyrs who died for the sake of God's law (2 Macc 7). The Jews in Paul's day honored martyrs' memories, believing that their suffering was a testimony to God's ultimate victory for Israel.

The Gentiles among the believers, however, would have no similar history to draw on. They understood suffering in relation to the gods, who manipulated the planets, which then influenced the course of human life. "Astrology provided the ultimate justification for an absolute determinism,"[6] such that people often surrendered to fate.[7] The solution to suffering, then, was to either pursue *apatheia* (i.e., freedom from passions) or to use charms and magic spells that ward off demons and evil spirits.[8]

People today still turn to astrology for comfort, for a sense of control over their lives, and especially for a glimpse into the future. Christians might be tempted to read their horoscope just for fun, but behind the seemingly harmless act is an underlying assumption that the world (or at least your life) is determined by forces that can perhaps be manipulated. These forces are not benign, but stand against God. Christians should not be drawn into their orbit.

To make any sense of suffering, people need a God's-eye view, and that is precisely what Paul provides (see also ch. 3). Perhaps added to Paul's voice was that of Jesus in his Beatitudes: "Blessed are those who mourn, for they will be comforted," and "blessed are those who are persecuted because of righteousness, for theirs is the kingdom of heaven" (Matt 5:4, 10).

Paul declares that the Philippians are experiencing the same suffering he underwent in Philippi and now endures in Rome. While their experiences might be different, the suffering in both cases is rooted in their testimony for the gospel. Their sufferings may be of an economic sort. Tradesmen and craftsmen were usually part of guilds. These guilds honored their patron god or goddess regularly, but a believer would no longer partake in the pagan festivals. This could lead to expulsion from the guild, effectively ending their employment possibilities.[9] Again, day laborers depended on their good reputation to get work, and the new believer could be seen as abandoning their ancestral customs — a terrible deed in the ancient world. Perhaps a spouse decided that they did not want to be married now that their husband or wife followed a new, foreign religion. The economic hardships would put an added strain on the small community, threatening their unity and steadfastness. It is all too easy, then and now, to cry "every man for himself" when the situation gets tough. Paul had higher goals for the Philippians and believed they could reach them if they stood firm, together, in their faith.

---

6. Everett Ferguson, *Backgrounds of Early Christianity* (3rd ed.; Grand Rapids: Eerdmans, 2003), 241.

7. Note Suetonius's statement about Emperor Tiberius, who, because he was "fully convinced that everything is ruled by Fate, neglected the practice of religion"; Suetonius, *Life of Tiberius* 69, as quoted in ibid.

8. See Clint E. Arnold, "Magic," in *DPL*, 581.

9. Oakes, *Philippians*, 89–96.

LIVE the Story

Walking Your Faith

Paul asks the Philippians to live a life worthy of the gospel, to walk in such a way that its message is embodied and actualized in their everyday activities. To the Philippians, this encouragement would have made sense, as any Gentile knew that following a philosophy called for a changed life, and any Jew accepted the law as a guiding light for their life. Yet Paul also turns on its head the Aristotelian view that doing makes being—that repeated acts of kindness, for example, makes you into a kind person. Paul does not share such a robust confidence in human ability; rather, he is convinced that sin is more powerful and deceptive than humans acknowledge. For Paul, being precedes doing; a believer's actions grow from their new life in Christ.

Today, however, some Christians resist any notion that confessing the gospel obligates them to walk within moral boundaries established in Christ. However, Christ's death ought to silence any claims that God is soft on sin. As the psalmist declares, "You [God] love righteousness and hate wickedness" (Ps 45:7).

The believer's focus is better placed on how he or she can live in the righteousness of God, how she or he can be salt and light (Matt. 5:13–16). Stott suggests that Jesus' declaration that his followers are salt and light indicate important truths about believers, including that they are "*radically different from non-Christians*";[10] they are elements, salt and light, which work in their environment for change. "The influence of Christians on society is intended by Jesus to be both negative (checking the spread of evil) and positive (promoting the spread of truth and goodness, and especially of the gospel)."[11]

Salt and Light in Ethiopia

Dr. Larry Thomas is salt and light in Ethiopia. An emergency room doctor by training, Larry works in Loma Linda, California, but his heart is in Ethiopia. In 2009, he worked alongside ministries to prevent and cure podoconiosis, a disease of the feet caused by silica crystals in the volcanic soil. Feet swell, smell, and take on the appearance of "horrible, rotting cauliflower."[12] "Podo" affects an estimated one million Ethiopians, and those most at risk are the poor, who cannot purchase shoes. The treatment is basic and simple: wash

---

10. John Stott, *The Living Church: Convictions of a Lifelong Pastor* (Downers Grove, IL: InterVarsity Press, 2007), 130, italics original.

11. Ibid., 133.

12. Tim Stafford, "The Foot-Washers of Ethiopia," *Christianity Today* (May 31, 2011); see christianitytoday.com/ct/2011/may/footwashers.html?paging=off.

feet with bleach, and apply lotion and pressure bandages. Larry watched nuns bathe the patients' smelly, grotesque feet and was challenged by their joy in that service. So he now works with Adventist and Catholic churches, and through his own Tropical Health Alliance Foundation, in raising support and awareness of podo.

But as he looked around the towns of Ethiopia, he noticed other under-served health conditions. So he has taken on the challenge of cataracts, a condition that affects not only the patient but also often a young girl who functions as a "seeing eye dog." Larry commented that a simple surgery not only cures the patient, but releases a young child to join school and play with her friends. Larry works with a Catholic nun and an Ethiopian ophthalmologist to bring sight to the blind and freedom to the captive.[13]

Newness in Christ

Paul's command to live worthy of the gospel is sometimes confused with a call to earn, or at least influence, one's salvation. This position suffers from a small view of salvation. It is absolutely true that only Christ can forgive sins. Yet our salvation is more than forgiveness of sin, it is also the creation of a new being, for now the person is one with Christ.

Think of salvation in relation to a wedding day and a marriage. The wedding day is to be joy-filled, and months of planning go into making it special. For our wedding, my husband wrote all the music, including the processional and recessional. When he sang to me at the altar, there was not a dry eye in the church! Photos and videos capture the events; I remember smiling so much my jaw hurt the next day! The bride and groom exchange rings and vow to love and cherish the other forever. Yearly anniversaries mark the happy occasion, for we want to celebrate and remember the beginning of a new relationship.

So too when a new believer experiences the beginning of his or her faith, the joy of forgiveness fills to overflowing; I distinctly recall my own heart "warmed" as I prayed in my father's study one late afternoon during my high school years. John Wesley testifies to such an experience. On May 24, 1738, he attended a meeting where Martin Luther's "Preface to Romans" was read. Wesley writes that while the speaker "was describing the change which God works in the heart through faith in Christ, I felt my heart strangely warmed. I felt I did trust in Christ, Christ alone for salvation."[14] Today we might take photos or videos to commemorate that day, or the day of baptism. We declare

---

13. Dr. Larry Thomas has a facebook page for his Tropical Health Alliance Foundation: www.facebook.com/pages/Tropical-Health-Alliance-Foundation-THAF/121519251207003.

14. See www.ccel.org/ccel/wesley/journal.vi.ii.xvi.html.

vows that Jesus is Lord (Rom 10:9–10), and we are challenged to take up our cross (Luke 9:23).

But just as a wedding leads to a married life for the bride and groom, so too a believer's forgiveness of sins leads to freedom to live a holy life (Rom 6:17–18). Said another way, just as a marriage is more than the wedding day, so too salvation is not only about the day you "got saved." The wedding day begins a lifelong journey of learning what it means to be *one* with the person to whom you have pledged your life. It opens doors to pray for and serve another who is yet, mysteriously, also part of you (Eph 5:31–32). In an analogous manner, the believer has a moment when he or she heeds God's call and accepts Christ's work on his or her behalf. Then begins the "married life" of learning about the Beloved. In this picture, there is no question of works or keeping score; rather, the spouse seeks ways to show his or her love.

To continue the analogy, we know within a marriage, loving deeds are essential to its health. Saying "I love you" once at the altar is not enough to last throughout the marriage. Instead, we expect loving words and actions, gifts of flowers, hugs, a listening ear. Paul imagines this sort of relationship with Christ[15] — one governed by a fidelity that judges all attitudes and deeds from the standpoint of how they reflect on God's truth and character. We can give a listening ear to Christ as we read Scripture and hear his words of encouragement or challenge. We can give a hug to a lonely fellow believer or send flowers to celebrate a believer's new job; in so doing, we give a hug or flowers to Christ (Matt 25:34–40).

To Those Who Refuse to Walk Worthily, What Happens?

This raises the question: What happens if a Christian does not walk worthily? Perhaps the example of Peter will help us sort out what "worthily" means. Because Christ forgave Peter after his denial, we can be sure that God is always, *always*, ready to forgive. Christ sought Peter; he did not wait for Peter to act. So walking worthily does *not* mean walking sinlessly. It means walking forward (see also 3:13). It means walking with open eyes. Jesus commends those who fed him, clothed him, and visited him in prison (Matt 25:34–40). Surprisingly, they did not realize they were feeding Christ when they were caring for those in need among them. Yet their hearts were tuned to God's wavelength; they perceived his compassion and love and sought out those who needed it.

---

15. Jesus refers to himself as the bridegroom in Matt 9:15; Mark 2:19; Luke 5:34; John the Baptist speaks of Jesus as the bridegroom (John 3:29); see also Rev 19:7; 21:2, 9–10; 22:17.

Walking Together

Walking in a worthy manner is best done in community. Paul wants the Philippians to be of one mind, having a single purpose. This does not mean that
they all think the same way on specific points of doctrine, but it does require
that they hold a singular passion for the advancement of the gospel. For this
to work, Christians must trust each other and be trustworthy; they must think
charitably toward other believers and be faithful and grace-filled. And over
all this, they must put on love. Maybe it's a lot like many families' Christmas
holiday. They agree on a single purpose—that Christmas be special, warm,
and loving. But within that unity of purpose and goal, we find lots of diversity. One family makes small, handmade gifts; another family buys expensive
gadgets. One member bakes homemade desserts; another buys frozen veg-
etables for the feast. When certain actions are judged to be morally superior
(or inferior), unity breaks down. But when each contribution is welcomed,
unity is restored and community is strengthened.

Sometimes our worthy acts can heal fractured communities. Dr. Sunday
Agang is a pastor and the president of the Theological Seminary Kagoro, a
school located in the heart of the sectarian tension in northern Nigeria. The
local church has experienced violent massacres at the hands of radical Muslims, the Boko Haram, and the temptation is strong to respond in kind. Sunday's ministry includes the role of community leader who serves as a mentor
to the youth, teaching them to strive for justice through nonviolent means.

Sunday has seen such efforts work in the past. He tells the following story.
A river near his home area of Moro'aland (Southern Kaduna State) flooded
regularly, separating the Christian community who lived on either side of it.
People drowned, but the Muslim government officials did nothing. In 2001,
Sunday cofounded Gawon Ministries to aid widows and orphans, including
Muslims. The governor took notice; "he was deeply moved, and he decided
to award a contract to build a bridge that would prevent the drowning. This
was not just any bridge—it was a world-class structure that went above and
beyond their [Christians'] expectations!"[16] Sunday continues his work for
peace between Muslims and Christians in this battered region, to break the
cycle of violence. "We need to remember that we are there not just for the
church, but also for the whole society . . . we need to be engaged with what is
happening."[17]

---

16. Interview with Dr. Sunday Agang, Langham Partnership International, August 21, 2011.
http://articles.langhampartnership.org/category/impact-news/scholars-impact/.

17. Ibid. For further reading, see Sunday Agang, *The Impact of Ethnic, Political, and Religious
Violence on Northern Nigeria, and a Theological Reflection on Its Healing* (London: Langham Mono-
graphs, 2011).

Suffering: God's Gift?

Have you ever received a gift you wanted to return to the store for credit? Christians may sometimes feel like that when they hear that God has granted or gifted them with belief in Christ *and suffering for his sake*. We like the first part of the gift, but not the second part. How does a loving God give such a gift? To answer this question fairly, we need to view our situation from an eschatological perspective — we need to see the full scope of our eternal salvation and God's kingdom building activities.

Moreover, we might do well to think of different sorts of suffering. On the one hand, we may experience suffering that directly results from our Christian confession. This sort of suffering tests our resolve and reveals our authenticity. It allows us to count the cost of following Christ. John Stott identifies this sort of suffering as a "weapon" in the Christian's armory that works for the social good: "Those who defend God's law and God's gospel are bound to suffer opposition."[18]

On the other hand, we have suffering that seems unrelated to any actions, suffering that attacks the innocent. Famine, floods, disease, accidents — all fall into this category. Jerry Sittser experienced such a loss when a car accident caused by a drunk driver claimed the lives of his wife, mother, and daughter. His book *A Grace Disguised*[19] stresses the inevitability of grief and the deep pain of catastrophic loss, but it also offers a way forward. He does not promise recovery from such trauma, if by that one means that one can pick up where one left off before the accident. Instead, he makes several observations that acknowledge both the continuing struggle with catastrophic loss and incurable disease, and the God who is present in and with him.

Sittser notes that loss is loss, and we do well not to compare who has suffered most. Second, he stresses the importance of making choices. He felt himself living in terrible darkness, and he decided "to walk into the darkness rather than try to outrun it, to let my experience of loss take me on a journey wherever it would lead, and to allow myself to be transformed by my suffering rather than to think I could somehow avoid it."[20] And *in* this darkness, Jerry experienced life; he discovered that being alive was a holy thing.[21] Third, he came to realize that he could not suppress or ignore the pain, and he could not make it go away by venting anger or moving to a new house. Pain signals a deeper issue, our mortality. Facing our mortality gives us the opportunity to ask what matters most, and often our answers end up simplifying our life.

---

18. Stott, *The Living Church*, 138.
19. Jerry Sittser, *A Grace Disguised* (expanded ed.; Grand Rapids: Zondervan, 2004).
20. Ibid., 42.
21. Ibid., 45, 49.

"Suffering can lead to a simpler life, less cluttered with nonessentials.... That is why many people who suffer sudden and severe loss often become different people."[22] Suffering can make us alive to the present moment.[23]

Sittser writes: "Catastrophic loss is like undergoing an amputation."[24] I resonate personally with his image of amputation, as I felt that a hole had been dug into my side when my sister, at age twenty-six, was killed in an accident. I wondered how no one else could see this obvious wound, as I felt cut in two. Waves of grief would wash over me, and as in an angry ocean, knock me off my feet and send me thrashing and gasping for air. But Sittser goes on with his sentence, "catastrophic loss is like undergoing an amputation *of our identity* ... of the self from the self" (italics added). He observes that we are cut off *from ourselves*, which moves us to see the transformative power of suffering. It gets to the heart of Paul's claim that participating in Christ's suffering is transformative (3:10–11). When we are cut off from who we think we are, when we come to the end of ourselves, "we have come to the beginning of our true and deepest selves. We have found the One whose love gives shape to our being."[25]

Nicholas Wolterstorff experienced something similar at the death of his twenty-five-year-old son. He too changed; "the suffering of the world has worked its way deeper inside me."[26] He added that more suffering is accessible to him, because he sees it from the inside. And he knows about helplessness, "of what to do when there is nothing to do."[27] This helplessness can manifest itself in fear — fear that another catastrophe will strike and the pain would be unbearable. Four years after my sister's death, my husband and I felt called to work in Kenya, at a mission station about one hour from Nairobi. For months I wrestled with the call, and it boiled down to one main question: Did God love my children as much as I did? You see, my sister died overseas, in an accident in Thailand that may have been preventable (humanly speaking). In moving to Kenya, I was placing my children outside first world medical care. Fear of losing a child, going through such massive pain again — I could not manage. In the months of honest questioning, an answer emerged. "Yes, I love them more than you do, because I love more." Wolterstorff explains that God's love is powerful, but this power is shown in the Son's suffering "*like* us, through his suffering to redeem us from suffering and evil."[28]

---

22. Ibid.. 74.
23. Ibid., 76.
24. Ibid., 81.
25. Ibid., 91.
26. Wolterstorff, *Lament for a Son* (Grand Rapids: Eerdmans, 1987), 72.
27. Ibid., 72.
28. Ibid., 81 (italics original).

Suffering and Hope

Sittser speaks of failing in his mind as a parent, failing to achieve his potential at work. But he rejoices that he also knows now how small and limited is his life and how great are God's provisions. He encourages readers to be hopeful and to expect new enjoyments, ones that do not replace the loss, but that bring different joys. An innocent question asked by acquaintances at a dinner party brought home to me the wisdom of his words and the difficulty in living them out. My parents and my husband and I traveled to Australia in December 2012, and the pastor of a local Sydney church where I spoke invited us and another couple to dinner. During the conversation, we talked about Christmas traditions. I am from Pennsylvania, and we dream of a white Christmas. Our Sydney hosts plan a barbeque in the backyard!

Someone asked my mother what Christmas traditions we have, and she froze. When my sister died, we gave up our one big family tradition—decorating the Christmas tree with ornaments that my mother had bought for us every year since our birth. Now, instead, we often travel over Christmas, or put poinsettias and wreaths and red ribbons around the house—but no tree. A loss, but in that loss there is also gain, including meeting believers in Sydney with whom to share the Christmas season.

CHAPTER 6

Philippians 2:1–5

 LISTEN to the Story

> ¹Therefore if you have any encouragement from being united with Christ, if any comfort from his love, if any common sharing in the Spirit, if any tenderness and compassion, ²then make my joy complete by being like-minded, having the same love, being one in spirit and of one mind. ³Do nothing out of selfish ambition or vain conceit. Rather, in humility value others above yourselves, ⁴not looking to your own interests but each of you to the interests of the others.
>
> ⁵In your relationships with one another, have the same mindset as Christ Jesus:

> *Listening to the text in the Story*: Leviticus 26:11–13; Nehemiah 8:10; Isaiah 53:2–3; Habakkuk 3:17–19; John 15:12–18.

Paul pulls out all the rhetorical stops in these few verses (2:1–4 is a single sentence) to galvanize the Philippians' heart, soul, and mind toward a vision of unity within their church. He alludes to the Trinity, to their salvation in Christ, and to their membership in the community of the faithful (2:1) — all with the purpose of exciting their imagination to the surpassing joy that such unity brings. Paul pulls the rug from under the prevailing honor-based culture with his call to humility (2:3) and the active establishment of another person's honor.[1] All this is with an eye to offering a hymn to Christ, the one to whom every knee will bow.

Paul finished chapter 1 by stressing the importance of faithful suffering for Christ. He is not unaware that in the face of adversity, fear and selfishness tend to rule conduct. Thus the apostle exhorted the church to be of a single purpose and to exercise their Christian witness in the face of strong enemies. He roused them not to fear those whose end is destruction, but to embrace their suffering for Christ in hope. At the time of the Revolutionary War, Ben-

---

1. For a discussion of honor/shame cultures, see pp. 29–30.

jamin Franklin declared, "We must all hang together, or assuredly we shall all hang separately." Paul might have resonated with this sentiment as he wrote to the Philippians. He recognized, however, that not every enemy is without; often the real dangers are power grabs, prima donnas, and prestige-seeking believers who weaken the body of Christ from within (2:3–4). It is to this potentially lethal danger that Paul turns in the beginning of chapter 2.

EXPLAIN the Story

Call to Unity (2:1–2)

Paul's opening clauses in 2:1 are often rendered in English with "if," perhaps suggesting that Paul is not certain of his statement. In fact, these "if" clauses are Paul's way of getting the Philippians to recognize what they all know to be true. The NIV adds the word "therefore," because it conveys a sense of certainty that is clearly evident in Paul's thought. Paul wants his listeners/readers to be nodding their heads with him, agreeing with his implied questions. He wants them to be thinking deeply about each clause, allowing the truth to settle deep within.

The opening clause suggests that there is great "encouragement" in Christ. While the Greek noun (*paraklēsis*) can indicate exhortation, its meaning here is closer to the sense of comfort or consolation. The previous chapter ended with the profound reality that believers are called not only to Christ, but also to suffer for Christ. Both the Philippians and Paul have undergone hardship and suffering because they identified themselves as followers of Christ.

Paul expresses similar sentiments to the Corinthians in 2 Corinthians 1. There he connects the reality of suffering for Christ with the expansive encouragement that envelopes believers in their times of struggle (2 Cor 1:3). Here Paul declares that the God of compassion[2] is the one who encourages both them and Paul each step of the way. Even more, Paul declares that the encouragement received from God is so abundant that one believer can pass it along to another who is going through a difficult time. The riches of God's compassion overflow; they are powerful in believers' testimony to God's steadfastness in their troubles.

Comfort from His Love (2:1b)

The second clause can be understood as either focused on the "comfort" of Christ's love or on the comfort of Love, a euphemism for God the Father.

---

2. The same term translated "compassion" (*oiktirmos*) is used in Phil 2:1 and 2 Cor 1:3.

Paul may be stressing the believers' sure support from Christ, but I think more likely he is pointing to the all-sufficient power of the Godhead to meet both their struggles (as noted in ch. 1) and their internal divisions, as will be discussed in these verses and in 4:2–3.

One of Paul's own experiences of this "comfort" is a near-death experience wherein he faced his mortality head-on (see 2 Cor 1:8–10). It is hard to pin down exactly what this traumatic experience was. Suggestions include facing wild beasts in Ephesus, though this is unlikely.[3] Perhaps Paul faced severe opposition by human opponents, but if so, how was it different in degree than what he had experienced in Lystra (Acts 14:8–20) or the various beatings and imprisonments he mentions in 2 Corinthians 11:23–28? Some target the riot instigated by Demetrius the silversmith (see Acts 19:23–41), but Paul notes in 2 Corinthians 1:8 that this crisis occurred in Asia, not specifically in Ephesus. Moreover, Acts does not present Paul in immediate danger or miraculously rescued in that riot.

The best option, perhaps, is to understand Paul's perilous experience as a severe illness. The theory of illness (malaria, perhaps) does justice to Paul's implication that his near-death experience might reoccur. And recovery from a severe illness can be understood in terms of getting a new lease on life (Isa 38:16 records Hezekiah thanking God for healing him and bringing him back to life). In any case, in that desperate moment, God rescued Paul and comforted him. It is the power of God that makes secure our hope in Christ — that is the "comfort" Paul speaks of here.

Common Sharing in the Spirit (2:1c)

Paul's third clause emphasizes the "sharing" or partnership in the Holy Spirit. Of the nineteen times that *koinōnia* occurs in the New Testament, thirteen are in Paul's letters. And of those thirteen, three are in our short letter. The word carries a sense of partnership, common sharing, or ownership, as in the case of inheritance where each heir owns all of the property.[4] The Holy Spirit is both the gift and the giver; the Spirit is the means of fellowship with other believers even as each believer is also in fellowship with the Holy Spirit.

Might Paul in these three clauses be reminding the Philippians of the trinitarian truth of the Godhead?[5] While Paul never used the term "Trinity," the concept itself would not be foreign to him. He declared Jesus as Lord and worshiped him. Since he was a monotheistic Jew and not a polytheist,

---

3. See the arguments of Murray J. Harris, *The Second Epistle to the Corinthians* (NIGTC; Grand Rapids: Eerdmans, 2005), 164–72.

4. Hansen, *Philippians*, 109–10.

5. Fee, *Philippians*, 179.

we must conclude that he understood God the Father and God the Son as having a relationship that both distinguished them but also recognized their essential sameness of essence. Offering another trinitarian allusion, Paul appeals to the Romans that "by our Lord Jesus Christ and by the love of the Spirit … join me in my struggle by praying to God for me" (Rom 15:30). Similarly, in 2 Corinthians 13:14, Paul writes: "May the grace of the Lord Jesus Christ, the love of God, and the fellowship of the Holy Spirit be with you all." Here the Philippians hear of union with Christ, love from God, and a sharing in the Holy Spirit.

Tenderness and Compassion (2:1d)

After laying out the importance of Christ's encouragement, love's consolation, and the fellowship of the Holy Spirit, Paul speaks of the affections of the heart and of mercy. He asks the Philippians if they have "any tenderness and compassion" (the latter term can be translated "mercy"). Is Paul referring to the Philippians' attitudes toward him? Or toward each other? Or God's tenderness and compassion directed toward his people? The answer to this set of questions is tightly tied to whether the reader understands the previous three clauses to speak primarily to the community's concern for each other and Paul, or to God's love and compassion directed to the church.

Support for the former theory comes from Colossians 3:12, "Therefore, as God's chosen people, holy and dearly loved, clothe yourselves with compassion, kindness, humility, gentleness and patience." Paul charges the Colossians with demonstrating a "heart of mercy."[6] Support for the latter understanding comes from Paul's use of "mercy" found in his appeal to God's "mercy" (Rom 12:1) and to "the Father of mercies" (2 Cor 1:3 ESV).[7] The latter suggestion carries more weight, considering the overall tone of the previous clauses stressing God's sure encouragement, compassion, and fellowship granted to believers.

Unity Brings Paul Joy (2:2a)

The imperative verb governing verses 2:1–4 is Paul's call to the Philippians to "make … complete" his joy. This is an interesting exhortation at several levels. First, Paul assumes that his joy is an important motivator for the Philippians. Second, he speaks about joy as a marker of ministry "achievement." Third, he encourages them to work toward unity in spirit and mind.

(1) Paul assumes that his disposition is of great importance to the Philippian church. His comment about joy reveals a bit of historical nuance to

---

6. Ibid., 182.
7. O'Brien, *Philippians*, 175–76.

our reconstruction of the biblical world's understanding of teachers and their disciples. We see it with Jesus' training of disciples. The master-teacher pours his life into the disciples, living among them, being transparent in his actions, forthcoming with his thoughts. The disciple sees the entire person from when they wake to when they turn in for the night. Such deep engagement develops the character of the disciples, shaping their perception of the world.

Paul describes himself as a nurse caring for the Thessalonians (1 Thess 3:7), or as a woman birthing the newly formed church in Galatia (Gal 4:19). He tells the Corinthians that he is their father in Christ (1 Cor 4:15). These familial images fit nicely alongside the master-teacher images in highlighting the intense closeness between the one who brings the gospel and the one who receives the gospel. Thus both Paul and the Philippians would agree that the teacher's joy is of utmost concern to the student. A joyful apostle is one whose coworkers and churches have mastered the message and have grown to maturity. To our modern ears, it might sound like Paul is on an ego trip. This false impression is based on a failure to appreciate the scope of investment the master-teacher gives to one's disciples.

(2) A word to pastors and lay leaders: notice Paul's personal goal in ministry—joy. What does ministry look like if one's goal is joy? It means, at least, that numbers don't matter. It means that the "other" is always in view. It means that achievements have to be understood in light of the congregation's maturing in Christ. It means that the focus of ministry, the orientation of one's goals, actions, and purposes, is to increasingly rejoice. Nehemiah says that "the joy of the LORD is your strength" (Neh 8:10); Paul lived that reality (see below, Phil 3:1).

(3) A modern reader might be a bit perplexed that Paul values internal unity over external witness. In the American church today, I venture to say that more focus is put on outreach of some sort in the local community, on national issues, or on world missions. We put a low premium on community, or at least deep community. We all want friends, but the hard work of building community cuts into our "rights" of individual choice and self-expression. So we are happier when we have a project to serve the community or combat a social ill, and trust that such a project will create unity. But this is not the level Paul is speaking to, as we will soon see.

Paul's call here to put the unity of the body of Christ on the local church level as of first importance cuts as well to the heart of the American value of efficiency. It takes lots of work to be united at the deep level of gospel. This is the really hard work of putting someone else's wishes and honor above your own. It means in Paul's world that the owner will serve the slave. It means the patron will take a lesson from her client. In the American context, it means at the very least socioeconomic and racial/ethnic divides are openly addressed. We must practice personal inventory taking, allowing God to challenge us, especially with everyday interactions.

Paul's emphasis on unity is not a promotion of navel gazing or self-preening that passes for unity in some churches. But it signals to us today that all our social programs and the incredible good they do are a truncated view of what the church is. The church's public witness must be secured by its internal vitality and strength. The church's life force is the breath of the Spirit, the blood of Jesus, the mind of Christ, the will of the Father. That is, the church manifests the life of God in its unity of believers in Christ's body.

Often the experience of unity occurs in the fellowship of small groups. John Stott noted the increase of the house church movement around the globe, an apparent spontaneous movement of the Holy Spirit that also was perhaps a "protest against the dehumanizing processes of secular society and the superficial formalism of much church life."[8] In his church's fellowship groups, he looked for *koinōnia*, which included a threefold focus on reading Scripture and prayer, serving the community, and caring for each other in love.[9]

Like-mindedness and Unity in Mind and Soul (2:2b)

Paul lists several phrases explaining what his joy looks like. He asks that they be "like-minded," hold "the same love," and be "one in spirit and of one mind." Twice he uses the verb "to think" (*phroneō*), in the first and last of his clauses. This suggests the importance of having the same outlook on the world, on the work of God in the world, and on one's responsibilities in light of those truths. This verb is not easy to translate because our term "think" suggests theoretical knowledge. The Greek verb, by contrast, carries the idea of wise behavior.

For example, Paul elsewhere distinguishes between the behavior of those led by their "flesh" and those led by the Spirit by stating that each group has their minds set on things that lead in one or the other direction (Rom 8:5). He cautions Gentiles not to "think" proud thoughts but to stand awestruck by God's work grafting them onto the olive tree of salvation (11:20). The phrase "be like-minded" is also found in Romans 15:5 and 2 Corinthians 13:11, which suggests that this call to frame the community's vision about who they are in Christ and in the world is a recurrent theme in Paul's churches. The effort to live in harmony is so crucial that Paul repeats it twice in one verse.

Paul also asks that they "have the same love" (cf. also "love" in 2:1). His

---

8. Stott, *The Living Church*, 90.
9. Ibid., 95–96.

meaning is likely twofold. First, since he alludes to the love of God the Father in 2:1, that reference likely shapes his meaning here. The type of love he advocates is the sort of love lavished by the Father. Paul speaks of this love in Romans 5:5, where he describes the believers' hope realized in God's love, which is poured into our hearts through the Holy Spirit. And in 8:35–38, Paul eloquently expresses the power of God's love in Christ, which overtakes and overwhelms all that life throws at us; it even conquers death. This is the love Paul imagines available to the Philippians, namely, the Father's love exhibited through the giving of his Son, Christ's love demonstrated on the cross, and the Spirit's love invigorating a believer's heart.

Second, this love is to be enjoyed not only individually but also corporately. Paul acknowledged in 1:9 that the Philippians have love for each other, and he prayed for that love to overflow. Perhaps no more eloquent vision of such love is presented than in 1 Corinthians 13:4–8a: "Love is patient, love is kind. It does not envy, it does not boast, it is not proud. It does not dishonor others, it is not self-seeking, it is not easily angered, it keeps no record of wrongs. Love does not delight in evil but rejoices with the truth. It always protects, always trusts, always hopes, always perseveres. Love never fails" (1 Cor 13:4–8a). Though often read at weddings, Paul's focus to the Corinthians is life in the church, using the gifts of the Holy Spirit in love rather than in competition with each other. The call to the Philippians is similar; nothing matters except that we act in love, the sort expressed by God.

Paul's use of "same" suggests that this love comes from the same source, namely, God. Love's expression within the community will not always look the same—the community does not put on love as schoolchildren put on their school uniform. Rather, this love generates a proactive self-giving and a consistent, humbling self-denial. Perhaps for some in our highly individualized society, the term "same" has a negative cast. Who wants to show up at the prom with the "same" dress as another girl? Who wants to have the same bike as a playmate? We stress individuality and promote celebrity-ism that thrives on shock value and newness.

But Paul's world was highly stratified according to class, wealth, and social rank. Sameness was horrifying to them as well, though for different reasons. Could an owner and her slave be the same? Could a Roman citizen and a Jewish immigrant be the same? "Same" cut across the social and cultural boundaries. It was great news to those on the bottom of the social pile, but unsettling to those who rode the crest of the social wave. Then or now, "same" is scary and freeing, all at the same time. Paul's injunction to have the same love was a call to have the same view of humanity as God the Father, who is no respecter of persons (Eph 6:9), and God the Son, who died to redeem the fallen world.

Being One in Spirit (2:2c)

The next phrase of verse 2 is actually a single word that translates literally as "one-souled" and carries the idea of living in harmony. This term factors in Aristotle's description of friends having one soul between them: "Friends have one soul between them; friends' goods are common property; friendship is equality."[10] Paul speaks similarly in 1:27, when he asks the Philippians to have "one soul" or "one mind." In 2:2, the term probably stands with the final phrase, "of one mind." Paul's overarching idea is that the Philippians act in accordance with the wisdom of God and demonstrate friendship at the level of treating each other equally and sharing resources. Said another way, the terms "same" and "one" reflect singleness of heart and mind, actualized in community through sharing of resources, honor, and life.

How is this call different from 1:27? Is Paul repeating himself here? More likely, Paul is building on his call to stand against threats from the outside by asking them to not neglect the source of their strength, which is their oneness in Christ, their fellowship with the Holy Spirit, and their access to the wellspring of God's love — that this might overflow among them.

Call to Resist Selfish Striving (2:3a)

Having sketched the believers' proper focus and attitude, Paul makes clear what concerns him. He pushes against any self-seeking behavior that elevates self at the expense of others. Paul warns against all "selfish ambition," using the same term as in 1:17 to describe those who preach out of envy. The term carries the sense of having evil or malicious intentions.[11]

Is Paul suggesting that a similar faction exists in Philippi that stands against Paul's ministry? Evidence within the letter for this hypothesis is lacking; indeed, the warmth and love extended to Paul by the Philippians suggests entirely the opposite. However, this term and the term translated "vain conceit" (discussed below) are also used in Galatians 5:20–26, wherein Paul describes the works of the flesh and the discord, strife, and envy that characterize such behavior. The Galatian churches were pulling away from Paul (4:12–20); could it be that such is happening with a faction in Philippi (cf. also 2 Cor 13:20)?

This hypothesis of discord between the Philippians and Paul cannot be sustained on the thin support of these two terms. Nevertheless, the fact that in Galatians 5 Paul lists fifteen attitudes and actions characteristic of the flesh, of which eight relate to issues of social discord, suggests that Paul believes

---

10. Aristotle, *Eth. Nic.* 9.8.2.
11. Carolyn Osiek, *Philippians, Philemon* (ANTC; Nashville: Abingdon, 2000), 53.

such behavior is anathema—it is a curse on the church.[12] Paul's description of the envious faction in Rome (Phil 1:17), then, is not only a snapshot of his current situation taken for the Philippians' benefit, but it serves as a warning about the dangers of ignoring strife in a community.

The second noun, "vainglory" or "vain conceit" (*kenodoxia*), is found only here in Paul, but a cognate adjective is found in Galatians 5:26, where Paul warns the Galatians against competing with each other and notes that their conceit leads to envy and strife. The word is a combination of the Greek terms "empty" and "opinion, honor." Interestingly, in the next few verses, Paul will speak of Christ "emptying" himself and receiving "glory."[13] Paul implies a sharp contrast between the vacuous assertions of self-promotion and the releasing or giving up of what is rightfully one's own to lift up others. In the honor-seeking Roman world, Paul's words cut deep. In Philippi, people stressed not your character, but what was *thought* about your character. Perception is reality—a truism in the first century, and perhaps today as well.

Identifying True Virtue from False Humility (2:3b)

The believer should not care a whit about social prestige; for Paul the goal is humility. Several points bear mentioning, including Paul's radical critique of the wider culture, the culture's distance from our own, and Paul's insistence on humility as a virtue in and of itself.

To the first point, the Greek term translated "humility" (*tapeinophrosynē*) is not found before the Christian era, although classical Greek did have a similar term that meant "meanness of condition."[14] The word is a combination of the Greek word "lowly" and the verb "to think"—the same verb Paul used twice in 2:2 and used again in 2:5 (a total of ten times in this short letter). Recall that "to think" involves actions and attitudes. The same emphasis carries here—believers are called to imagine (or re-imagine) themselves as of lowly stature.

A parallel idea occurs in Romans 12:3, where Paul enjoins the Roman believers to carry a solid, realistic view of themselves. Imagine Jesus himself holding up a hand mirror for you. Would you preen? Or feel awkward that you even care about how coworkers, classmates, or neighbors might evaluate your appearance? With Jesus holding the mirror, would we be as inclined to think ourselves hotshots in the workplace or church social? True humility starts with the believer, knowing we are beloved children of God, joint heirs with Christ based *only* on his work.

---

12. Gordon Fee, *God's Empowering Presence: The Holy Spirit in the Letters of Paul* (2nd ed.; Peabody, MA: Hendrickson, 2009), 440–43.

13. Fee, *Philippians*, 186, n 68.

14. Vincent, *Philippians*, 56.

Today Christians, and many others, praise humility as a virtue. This was not the case in the Roman world; there was virtually no difference between humility and humiliation—both ended with the reality of low status. Paul's call for humility is unprecedented in the ethics of his day; no self-respecting Gentile would concede that humility is a virtue. Deeds were to be done where people could see them and thus praise the one doing those actions. Personal self-worth and value were determined in the public sphere, not in the private reflections of the individual.

In the Jewish context, humility played a more prominent role, but not to the extent we find in Jesus' teachings. For example, Josephus (*Ant.* 3.212) explains humility by pointing to Moses:

> Having declined every honor that he saw that the multitude was ready to bestow upon him, [Moses] devoted himself exclusively to the veneration of God. He refrained from ascents to Sinai. Going into the Tent, he received responses from God concerning those matters that he asked, behaving as a ordinary person and conducting himself both in dress and in all other respects just like a common man and desiring to seem to be different from the majority in no respect other than this alone, to be seen caring for them.

Feldman comments that "an indication of Moses' humility is the fact that in an era in which clothing was even more important than it is today as a sign of one's societal standing, Moses, in Josephus's extra-biblical comment, dresses like any ordinary person and bears himself like a simple commoner."[15] The rabbis believed humble servanthood was due those who held power, yet the latter should not abuse their authority.[16] However, no one taught humility as Jesus did by using a child as an example (Matt 18:1–5). In our context today, humility is generally valued positively and is thought to be self-imposed, while humiliation carries with it a suggestion of an outside force or opponent. We decry the bully who humiliates another, and we praise people who do the right thing regardless of whether anyone notices their actions.

Humility as a Key Christian Virtue (2:4)

To Paul humility is a key virtue. Why? Because God is no respecter of persons. He shows no partiality. Christ is the measure of all things, and all believers are in Christ. Paul continues to explain humility by stating that the Philippians

---

15. Louis H. Feldman, ed., Flavius Josephus, *Judean Antiquities 1–4: Translation and Commentary* (Leiden: Brill, 1999), vol. 3, n 563. Greek terms omitted from quotation.
16. Keener, *Matthew*, 447.

should look "to the interests of the others." His point is not that humility is the means to the end of caring for others. That might leave open the door that one could use another, equally satisfactory, means to care for others. Indeed, one might argue that humility is an inefficient means to care for and be considerate of others.

If the only goal was the physical care of others, perhaps any means would be satisfactory. But the goal is far greater — namely, the obedience of each believer to the will of God (2:12 – 14). A prideful attitude cannot bow to God's good purposes and might confuse one's selfish desires with God's will. Only from a posture of humility can one see clearly both God's good works laid out for them and their own need for God's strength in doing those works. The Old Testament is replete with examples of Israel challenged not to rely on its own strength, but on God's mighty right arm to deliver (Num 11:23; Deut 4:32 – 35; Pss 44:3; 77:15). Paul continues this thread, now locating the power to do God's will in the indwelling Holy Spirit.

This humility is that which considers others as surpassing oneself.[17] Other believers' needs should be of primary importance, not one's own needs. This begs the question: What is a need? Paul most likely has in mind here the economic and social needs of the community.[18] The Philippian believers likely struggled financially from their stand for Christ before their pagan neighbors. Their refusal to honor the pagan gods and the imperial cult insulted the townspeople, who then took their business elsewhere.[19] Moreover, Paul asks the Philippian believers to forego any public honor or honor within their church community for the sake of raising up others.

This does not mean, of course, that some believers should be emotionally starved while pouring their hearts into others. Such a stance would imply that others are more deserving of love and affection. Paul is not addressing this level of human need. Rather, he is tackling the difficult situation wherein some believers conclude that others' financial help and social care are not worth the trouble, for to offer aid would not boost their own standing in the community.

Paul clearly advocates humility; what is less certain is his call for believers to care for others. Is Paul saying that believers should not (always) look out for their own interests but *also* look to other believers' interests as well? Or is it more radical? Is Paul declaring that we are *not* to look to our own interests at all but to the interests of others? Perhaps even asking the question in this

---

17. Fee, *Philippians*, 189, n 78.

18. Fee, ibid., 190, notes the tension in Paul between the individual and the community and suggests that the accent falls on community here.

19. Oakes, *Philippians*, 89 – 102.

way signals a failure to appreciate Paul's point. The verse aims to de-center the self, not to set up guidelines that establish when enough is enough and when you can focus on yourself. The point is that just as people work to feed themselves and their families, Paul asks that they think now of their family as much larger than those who reside in their home.

Jesus noted that the second great command is to love one's neighbor as oneself (Matt 22:39; Mark 12:31). The assumption here is that people naturally look out for themselves. They know they must feed their bodies and keep themselves dry, warm, and hydrated. Such self-interest is not selfish; it is basic to life. The Christian is to take that basic trait and enlarge the focus to include other believers in that circle of need. We should not be surprised at this teaching because Paul taught his churches that they were the body of Christ, members of Christ's body, the temple of the Holy Spirit (1 Cor 3:16–17; 12:12–27; 2 Cor 6:16; Eph 2:21). I might be an eye, needing my brother "ear" and my sister "hand" to complete the body, being Christ to the world.

The Link between Exhortation and Hymn (2:5)

This bridge verse joins Paul's call for unity and his description of Christ. It reads (lit.): "This think in you (pl.), which also in Christ Jesus." A verb must be supplied in the second half of the verse; options include the verbs "to think" (taken from the first half of the sentence), "to have," or "to be." The NIV renders the verse, "In your relationships with one another, have the same mindset as Christ Jesus."

In interpreting this verse, then, "the choice ... is between a command to have the attitude that was in Christ Jesus and a command to have an attitude that belongs to those who are in him."[20] It comes down to whether the reader (1) sees the following verses as primarily stressing Christ as the church's example, or (2) understands the Christ hymn as speaking doctrinally to the nature and person of Jesus Christ. In this case, believers are enjoined to hold an attitude that characterizes those who are in Christ.

Those who hold to the first reading generally see the phrase "in you" as meaning *within* each believer and insert "was" or "is" in the second clause ("which was/is in Christ Jesus"). In other words, Paul wants believers to show the same attitude as demonstrated by Jesus Christ. A weakness with this explanation is that 2:9–11 becomes in a sense irrelevant, as no one suggests that believers model Christ's exaltation.

The second theory argues that "to think" should be repeated in the second

---

20. Morna D. Hooker, "The Letter to the Philippians," in *NIB*, 11:507.

clause, which suggests that the verse instructs the Philippians to think among themselves the way they also think as believers united with Christ. The phrase "in Christ" then refers to their salvation in him. Later in the letter, Paul speaks to Euodia and Syntyche to "think in the Lord," using the same verb and preposition "in" (4:2). A similar use of verb and preposition occurs in Romans 15:5, suggesting to Silva that Philippians 2:5 could be translated, "Be so disposed toward one another as is proper for those who are united in Christ Jesus."[21] Following Silva's translation, one can draw a tight connection between 2:5 and 2:12, wherein Paul commands the Philippians to work out their salvation. The hymn is thus framed with pleas to behave as befitting a believer in Christ; believers do not think as Christ, but think as those who are "in Christ." The community that is in Christ will seek to act as Christ did, and they will desire to study Christ's actions in full confidence that their participation in his death and suffering will also mean their participation in his eternal life (see Rom 8:17).

What is at stake in interpreting this verse? Basically, it serves to introduce the Christ hymn, and it signals to the reader whether he or she should see Christ primarily as their example or as their Redeemer. Of course, Christ is both, but the point is where the accent lies. In the end, it is probably best not to push too hard one option over the other. The gospel message that Christ redeems sinful humanity for a life of holiness and service means that believers embrace both the humanity/divinity of Jesus Christ exalted in the hymn, as well as the demands of discipleship incumbent on those who are in Christ. "The best translation of the verse, therefore, is one that conveys the whole extent to Paul's appeal, which is *both* to the attitude shown by Christ Jesus *and* to the attitude that is therefore appropriate to those who are 'in him.' "[22]

To argue that Paul strongly stresses Christ as model is too limited an interpretation, but for our ears today, to focus the interpretation on Christ as the incarnate and glorified second person of the Trinity seems too abstract. Both dissolve when we emphasize participation or union with Christ, our Redeemer, who redeems us that we might be an example of his holiness to the world.

LIVE the Story

Vanishing Unity within the Church

Why was unity so important for the church? Before addressing that question, we must think more deeply about the nature of the unity called for. As

---

21. Moisés Silva, *Philippians* (BECNT; Grand Rapids: Baker, 2005), 97.
22. Hooker, "Philippians," 11:507, italics original.

described by Paul it seems to have two layers, the local and the global. At the local level, the church must care for every member of the community, uphold each member's dignity and worth, and work actively to seek the others' good. At the global level, such immediate care is not possible, but the general sense of responsibility should be evident.

The demand is not that the church interprets particular doctrines the same way or organizes church polity the same way. These things, though important, are part of a believer's conscience (see Rom 14:1–23). Rather, the unity is at the place of participation in Christ, being a member of his body. Thus it is not the soup kitchens or other public services that mark the church, nor is it the glorious worship music composed throughout the centuries, or even the missionaries who risk life and limb to bring the good news to those who have not heard, that testifies to the reality of Christ in the church. It is the unity in the body, the oneness that results when everyone is seen as a participant in Christ.

To discover why unity is so important, we turn to Jesus' words in John 17:20–23. Keener notes, "Just as the unity of Father and Son was central to John's apologetic (one thus dare not oppose the Son while claiming loyalty to the Father, 10:30), the unity of believers is at the heart of John's vision for believers (10:16; 11:52; 17:11, 21–23)."[23] Keener observes that Jesus' prayer in John 17, with its emphasis on believers' unity, and his prayer earlier in 11:42 at the raising of Lazarus, both speak to Jesus' origin and relation to the Father.[24] Jesus states clearly that his own relationship with the Father is testified to in a tangible way in the oneness of the believing community. Jesus reoriented the focus from the temple and the law to himself as the full revelation of God and the complete witness to reconciliation with God.

Paul brought that message of reconciliation to urban communities around the Mediterranean, a society highly stratified with various ethnic groups jostling for position and staking claim over limited resources. Overlaying that was a strong separation between Jew and Gentile. This meant that crossing boundaries into another community could even be seen as treasonous, as one's identity and livelihood were intimately tied to his or her community identity. Against this reality, Paul calls for Jews and Gentiles to live out their new status as members of the same community (Eph 2:14–22); his claims were radical and difficult to actualize.

As a way to make this unity tangible, Paul took up a collection from his churches, predominantly Gentile, for the Jewish churches in Judea. He notes that the Philippians were in the forefront of this effort; they gave sacrificially,

---

23. Craig S. Keener, *The Gospel of John: A Commentary* (Peabody, MA: Hendrickson, 2003), 2:1061.

24. Ibid.

as Paul indicates, "in the midst of a very severe trial, their overflowing joy and their extreme poverty welled up in rich generosity.... Entirely on their own, they urgently pleaded with us for the privilege of sharing in this service to the Lord's people" (2 Cor 8:2–4).

A critical piece of this history is the equal worth of the Jewish and Gentile communities in Paul's eyes. He recognizes that some Gentile churches, such as the Corinthians, were in a better financial situation. But he does not translate that into a position of power over the Judean churches. Instead, he reminds his churches that they need the theological history and understanding of their Jewish brothers and sisters in Christ (Rom 15:26–27; 2 Cor 8:13–15).

Strengthening Unity in the Global Church

A similar situation faces the global church today, as Western Christians have a surplus of wealth and Christians in the global South have great financial needs. A problem is that some Western Christians also believe that they bring superior theological perspective to the South. Fortunately this is changing, as more American churches and mission societies are forming true partnerships with churches in Africa, Latin America, and the East. These relationships are a two-way street, with both communities learning from each other and each group taking stock of their own weakness and blind spots.

For example, the African church holds up a mirror to the American church that shows the pervasiveness of its individualism. And the American church holds up a mirror to the African church that highlights the damage that corruption and bribes create in their midst. This give-and-take requires humility and sacrifice, which leads to the unity Paul describes as a unity that can only be explained by God's power. It supersedes social norms of ethnic and social separatism. It is gained by vulnerability, humility, and seeking first the other's good.

Carrie Boren experienced this power of partnership during a Mission Africa[25] trip in September 2010, an outreach connected with Cape Town 2010. She was part of a four-member team that included a Presbyterian and an Anglican, both from Texas, and a nondenominational evangelist from England. They worked with a Zimbabwean evangelist named Orpheus, who organized events with forty churches from various denominations. Throughout the week, this group joined with local African churches to preach the

---

25. Mission Africa worked with Cape Town 2010, the Third Lausanne Congress on World Evangelism (www.lausanne.org/en/gatherings/cape-town–2010.html), to invite twenty-one international evangelists to work in various African countries, partnering with local African evangelists. Carrie Boren serves as missioner for evangelism for the Episcopal Diocese of Dallas. Her essay, "Partnership in Zimbabwe: A U.S. Perspective" appeared in *Lausanne World Pulse*, Jan/Feb 2011, pp. 8–9: www.lausanneworldpulse.com/pdf/issues/Jan2011PDF.pdf.

gospel in schools, in hospitals, and in the streets. Boren concludes that this sort of partnership is essential for the cause of Christ, for two reasons. First, the testimony of different voices coming together "demonstrated that the gospel of Jesus Christ is for *all* people." This created a visual example of the gospel reality that God "desires to transform the lives of each and every person on earth." Second, the partnership embodied the theological truth that all believers make up the body of Christ. "Our love and unity serve as a visible testimony to God."

The World Is Waiting and Watching

What is interesting is that the wider world gets it; people expect the church to be unified. In the ground-breaking book *Half the Sky*, the authors Nicolas Kristof and Sheryl WuDunn (a husband/wife team) challenge the American church to care for the women in Africa as much as it does for the unborn fetuses in the United States (a reference to the abortion lobby).[26] Underlying the argument is the sense that if the church is really global, Christians with means (as in the West) should be supporting in meaningful ways their brothers and sisters in need. The unity of the church, in other words, should have a tangible presence.

Carolyn Custis James takes up that challenge in her book *Half the Church*. She notes that Christians are quick to volunteer in emergencies, but they "miss the chronic, systemic tragedies that are snatching one anonymous life at a time."[27] Moreover, the American church is caught up in drawing lines about where and when women can serve within the local church. Yet James reminds us that the Bible's vision of women differs sharply from the views that allow women to be discarded, objectified, trafficked, silenced, and degraded because it declares in the opening scene that women and men have equal value: "He gives *both* male and female the exact same identity — to be his image bearers."[28] She notes that believers have the obligation to demonstrate to those who have not heard the good news that "every human being is God's image bearer.... Every human being possesses a derived significance — grounded in God himself."[29]

Carolyn James relates an example of such demonstration. A four-year-old girl in India had been legally married to a much older man, although she still lived at home. Her husband suddenly died, and she was destined for *sati* or the

---

26. Nicolas Kristof and Sheryl WuDunn, *Half the Sky* (New York: Vintage, 2009).
27. Carolyn Custis James, *Half the Church: Recapturing God's Global Vision for Women* (Grand Rapids: Zondervan: 2010), 26.
28. Ibid., 50.
29. Ibid., 53.

funeral pyre of her husband.[30] But before this could happen, her older brother wakened her in the middle of the night and secreted her out of the house to a missionary couple's care. This girl grew up to be a godly grandmother, whose granddaughter testifies to God's great work.[31] Yet the wounds of life can be deep; this little girl experienced a wrenching away from her family. Without succumbing to pessimism or minimizing tragedy, James encourages readers that "conflict reinforces our need for God, drives us to him, forces us to look at him more closely, and deepens our trust."[32] From this place of deepened trust, local churches, missions, and parachurch groups model the reality of God's love and care for all humans.

Dietrich Bonhoeffer's Call to Unity

During the rise of Nazism in Germany, the young German theologian Dietrich Bonhoeffer discovered afresh the supreme importance of church unity. He established a Preachers' Seminary, located in Finkenwalde, Germany, in 1935. It was closed by the Gestapo two years later, but during the two years it was open, Bonhoeffer sought to live out the gospel's call for unity. In 1939, he published *Life Together*, a reflection of his experience at the seminary. In it he declares: "Christianity means community through Jesus Christ and in Jesus Christ. No Christian community is more or less than this."[33] Bonhoeffer's community was tested severely in the coming years as Nazism grew and the Confessing Church was persecuted. But in these increasingly dangerous times, he wrote about the unique power of Christian community:

> Worldly wisdom knows what distress and weakness and failure are, but it does not know the godlessness of man. And so it also does not know that man is destroyed only by his sin and can be healed only by forgiveness. Only the Christian knows this. In the presence of a psychiatrist I can only be a sick man; in the presence of a Christian brother I can dare to be a sinner. The psychiatrist must first search my heart and yet he never plumbs its ultimate depth. The Christian brother knows when I come to him: here is a sinner like myself, a godless man who wants to confess and yearns for God's forgiveness. The psychiatrist views me as if there were no God. The brother views me as I am before the judging and merciful God in the Cross of Jesus Christ.[34]

---

30. The traditional funeral in India includes burning the body on a structure or a stack of wood called a pyre.

31. James, *Half the Church*, 79, 95–96.

32. Ibid., 96.

33. Dietrich Bonhoeffer, *Life Together: The Classic Exploration of Faith in Community* (New York: Harper & Row, 1954), 21.

34. Ibid., 119.

Hubris Masquerading as Humility

True humility is a rare find, and often what passes for humility is really gluttony or self-centeredness cloaked in apparent self-denial. C. S. Lewis captures the latter brilliantly in his *Screwtape Letters*.[35] In this imaginative letter exchange between a minor demon, sent to trip up a new believer, and his mentor, the latter mentions to his charge that the believer's mother should be encouraged in her belief of her humility—for she is anything but humble. Rather than accept tea and toast at friend's house, she will "humbly" state that she can't eat toast, only muffins, but that she does not want the friend to trouble herself to get her muffins. And of course she can't drink tea on its own, so she just won't have anything. Of course, the friend ends up doing twice as much work for the "humble" woman who nevertheless thinks she is humble. We've all been around those who are demanding and require lots of work to make happy—while these folks maintain they are just simple and easy natured.

"Look not to your own interests but each of you to the interests of others." Simple words, but hard to follow. The point of networking is so that you might gain a friend who can help you in work—very calculating, and at bottom driven by self-interest. We make decisions about "investing" in people with an eye to "return"—perhaps in referrals, or jobs for our kids, or introductions to clients. Church members not socially connected or with any apparent skills that we might at some point draw on are not befriended for they are judged not to be a good use of our time. Such an arrogant posture assumes that we know what we need and can control our future.

Babysitting and Tattoos

Looking to others' interests is often no more than seeing a need and thinking creatively. A friend told me this story about his son's girlfriend. While in middle school, her parents led a ministry for young couples involved extensively in ministry. She observed marriage crises and the sense of "burnout" that intense ministry can bring on a family and a church. From that experience, she became convinced that couples need time to connect with each other as a way to cope with the pressures of intense ministry. So when she started college, she committed herself to offer free babysitting to couples of her college church who were deep in ministry, including the pastoral staff, counselors, and certain church members. She did this faithfully during her time in college and now has four other young women doing the same volunteer work.

Sometimes we wonder if there is really anything we can do to alleviate

---

35. C. S. Lewis, *The Screwtape Letters* (New York: Macmillan, 1980), 76–78.

suffering; the problems seem so big, and our capabilities so small. But seeking God and allowing for some creative possibilities often lead to surprising results. Chris Baker, a tattoo artist, came to faith as an adult. Desiring to use his talents for Christ, Chris began praying how he might serve. He discovered that gang members often marked their bodies, making it difficult to leave the gang. He decided to volunteer to remake or cover up those body-inscribed indications of gang activity.

As he worked with law enforcement and ex-gang members, he learned of another group of people who are tattooed—victims of human sex trafficking. They have an image, or even a bar code, tattooed on the neck, back, or buttocks. Chris designs beautiful flowers or shooting stars to cover the marks of human slavery, redeeming the ugly mark of sex slavery with an image of beauty and color.[36] This free gift of artwork changes a symbol of bondage to a statement of new life, free from the past. Baker's work represents in a physical sense the spiritual reality that a believer is a new creature in Christ (2 Cor 5:17) and is sealed with the Holy Spirit (Eph 1:13–14).

Examples of Serving the Interests of Others

Paul would encourage those who have little in the world's eyes not to despise what they have, but to use that to help fellow believers. In other words, no act of service is too small to be unimportant. An example of such service recently came to my attention. One of my husband's colleagues has a severely handicapped daughter who suffers from seizures, necessitating sudden trips to the hospital. Their neighbor, a retired man with no medical skills, discovered that this family has a dog. This neighbor loves dogs and enjoys walking them. So he offered to walk the dog morning and evening every day. It was his way of saying, "I'm here; I want to help." I include this example because I think it was just this sort of "little" thing that Paul is thinking about here. He wanted the church in Philippi to embrace the needs of others in their midst, even the seemingly minor things, rather than think their efforts might be too insignificant.

Sometimes small acts of kindness become life-changing events. On February 18, 1942, the US Navy destroyer *Truxtun* was escorting the *USS Pollux*, which carried supplies for the Allies in Europe. A terrible winter storm blew up, rendering the navigational equipment useless. Both the *Truxtun* and the *Pollux* ran aground off the coast of Newfoundland and were torn apart by the high waves and savage wind. Few reached land alive. One fortunate soldier was an African-American mess attendant, Lanier Philipps, from Georgia. He

---

36. Annie Sweeney, "Tattoo Removal Helping a 'Branding' Victim Break from Her Past," *Chicago Tribune*, December 27, 2012. See also www.ink180ministry.com/the-ink–180-story.html.

was covered in oil, soaking wet and freezing, as he began to walk toward a village. He fainted on his journey but was found, put on a sled, and brought to town, where a group of women were cleaning and bandaging the soldiers.

As Mr. Phillips tells the story, he awoke to find the women cleaning his now naked body — he a black man, naked in the presence of white women. Back in Georgia, simply talking to a white woman could lead to a beating or even hanging. Yet these women kept up their massaging of his limbs, trying to restore circulation and prevent permanent damage from the cold. They were rubbing his arms and legs not only to keep them warm, but also to remove the oil that had spilled from the sinking vessel and covered his wet body. Soon Mr. Phillips realized that they had never seen a black man, because they kept trying to get the dark color off his skin. Later, one of the women, Violet Pike, took Mr. Philips to her house to continue his convalescence until the Navy could collect him the following day. She fed him, clothed him, and treated him as if he was her own son. Such generosity overwhelmed Mr. Phillips, whose boyhood school had been burned by the KKK. Her kindness offered to him a new vision of racial relations and a new conviction to work for civil rights. Mr. Phillips became the first African American in the Navy's history to hold the post of sonar technician (1957). He endured the difficult journey for equal rights and reconciliation in large part because of the vision cast by Violet Pike, a vision created not by eloquent words but by the simple acts of cleaning and feeding a dirty, half-frozen sailor.[37]

In the case of the dog-walking neighbor, we see that simple jobs done with faithfulness can yield a rich harvest of blessing for the recipient. But what happens to the one giving? He or she learns the hard, yet rewarding virtue of perseverance. What of the WWII veteran and his life-saving friend, Violet? The life-threatening emergency became a life-changing event that shattered prejudices and fears. Racial stereotypes could not stand against ordinary human acts of kindness. Everyone can be that neighbor who walks the dog, the Violet who extends simple meals and basic necessities to those others forgot or despise. Neither act requires lots of money, time, or skilled talent — only the willingness to see another's needs and the willingness to help.

Why We Resist Giving Praise

How often do we feel less valuable or honored, even slighted, when we hear someone else praised? We are reluctant to give honor to another, or praise another from our heart, because we imagine that honor is a set quantity — it is

---

37. Matt Sampson, "Disaster at Sea: The Story of the USS *Truxtun* and USS *Pollux*," www .weather.com/outlook/weather-news/news/articles/truxton-pollux-maritime-disaster_2012-02-16.

like a glass full of water or a bucket full of sand. As we sip the water or shovel out the sand, the amount grows less. In the same way, we imagine that if we give a bit of praise here and a bit of praise there, we will soon be left with no praise. Or we think that in any given day or particular event, there is only so much praise and honor to go around. So if on this day the boss praises your coworker, then he or she must implicitly be removing praise from your "inbox." But this is entirely the wrong way to see honor and praise in the kingdom. Praise for one person's good efforts, attitudes, and heart does not pull from some heavenly storehouse, thereby reducing the overall amount of praise left to dole out. Rather, praise from God springs from an unending source of love.

Perhaps an analogy will help. When my firstborn son was born, I thought my heart would burst of love for him. Two years later we had our daughter. I wondered while pregnant how I could possibly love another child as much as I love our son, for I love him 100 percent. But I discovered that "love arithmetic" is not like earthly math, for I love our daughter 100 percent, with that same overwhelming joy. That same "heavenly math" works in the praise department; one believer's honor does not diminish the other believers' honor. This means that believers can be free with their praise, not clinging to it out of fear of their own loss of face.

LISTEN to the Story

⁶Who, being in very nature God,
   did not consider equality with God something to be used to his
      own advantage;
⁷rather, he made himself nothing
   by taking the very nature of a servant,
   being made in human likeness.
⁸And being found in appearance as a man,
   he humbled himself
   by becoming obedient to death—
      even death on a cross!
⁹Therefore God exalted him to the highest place
   and gave him the name that is above every name,
¹⁰that at the name of Jesus every knee should bow,
   in heaven and on earth and under the earth,
¹¹and every tongue acknowledge that Jesus Christ is Lord,
   to the glory of God the Father.

Listening to the text in the Story: Genesis 1:1–3:24; Leviticus 26:11–13;
   Psalm 8; 97:9; Proverbs 8:22–31; Isaiah 40–55 (esp. 45:23).

In Kenya, our house sat on the edge of an escarpment overlooking the Great Rift Valley. One could see for miles, the flat plain stretching to the extinct volcanoes in the distance. In the morning, the sun would climb over the escarpment behind me and cast its rays across the valley. This, I often thought, is a suitable place for all the nations to gather, bowing their knee and raising their voice, proclaiming Jesus is Lord.

Paul packs lofty theology into these two Greek sentences and sets up this passage with an enigmatic opening line (2:5). I suggested above that this verse enjoins the Philippian church to have a singular goal and passion, namely, serving each other in the name of Christ. This verse should be read as a restatement of 2:1–2, wherein Paul calls to mind the Trinity as foundational for appreciating the importance of unity in the body. Paul says, in essence, "You believers can say that you are in Christ, which means that you are forgiven, changed, made new, and made whole. Translate that newness to your relationships within the body of Christ; let the church be a place of grace, newness, and wholeness."

 EXPLAIN the Story

Exploring the Mystery of the Incarnation (2:6–11)

Philippians 2:6–11 speaks with great economy of words about mysteries no human mind can fully comprehend—the character of the Godhead, the incarnation of Jesus, the glorification of Christ. But if we cannot know all, we can at least claim some things as true for our lives now and in eternity. This "Christ hymn" describes the person of Jesus Christ and, in so doing, develops a vision for what it means to be fully human before God.

The question is often posed as to whether this passage describes doctrine or sets Jesus as an example for believers to imitate. Such a query, however, begins at the wrong spot and offers an incomplete set of choices. The key is to recognize the believers' *participation* in Christ. Then Jesus is not set up as an ideal, whose perfection we strive to reach but of course never can. Nor is Jesus understood merely through a doctrinal lens divorced from our personal experience. But understanding that each believer is even now seated with Christ (Eph 2:6; Col 3:1), having been crucified with him and thus no longer living on one's own (Gal 2:19–20), allows for this hymn to celebrate the nature of Christ and also connect personally and practically to our own experience.

Additionally, if we say that the hymn is on the whole about Christ modeling ethical behavior and sees Jesus primarily as an example, we run into interpretive issues in 2:12–14, for in these verses Paul states that the Philippians should work out their salvation and that God is working in them. Are they working out their salvation just as Jesus did his through obedience to God? Impossible! Instead, 2:12–14 offers the picture of our sanctification in Christ and thus encourages the Philippians to live into their salvation, to grab hold of it, even as God has grabbed hold of them. God is at work within each believer and within the church because of what Christ did through the incarnation, passion, resurrection, and glorification. The hymn puts front and center the magnificence of God's salvation plan (see Eph 1:3–14, one sentence in Greek!).

The social implications of this theological tour de force are serious and compelling. For the Philippians, the Christ hymn announces that their worship of Jesus Christ as God has the concomitant position that Caesar is not

Lord (cf. Acts 25:26). The imperial family, including Augustus, his wife Livia, and her grandson Claudius were all worshiped in the imperial cult in Philippi when Paul wrote this letter. Each member of the imperial family mentioned was granted an apotheosis; that is, they were understood at their death to be changed into a god. Suetonius draws on the hope of apotheosis as he illustrates Vespasian's sense of humor when he quotes the emperor in an illness late in his life, "methinks I am becoming a god."[1] But the hymn of Christ speaks of kenosis (emptying), not apotheosis; the hymn declares humiliation/death rather than earthly glorification/divination.

This difference is important because even today, and even in the church, we too often model ourselves based on the imperial family, not on Christ. The imperial family was expected to act generously, but this service was in fact self-serving, for it would result in adulation by the crowds. So how is their behavior different from Christ's actions? Christ accepted humiliation, while the emperor acted kindly but not humbly. The imperial family's self-giving was part of the expected package that reinforced their social status; Christ's humiliation was bewildering, and it cut across the social grain and upended expectations. Said another way, Caesar always had the choice to act selflessly, and it was immediately praised; moreover, his so-called selflessness flowed from a position of strength. But Christ did not speak up, he did not call down angels to defend him in the end, and he did not expect human praise.

Some church people and leaders might model Caesar more than they think: they retain control, determine just how much they will serve, and never own humiliation. Their "humble" service only serves to support their high social standing, because to qualify as "humble" the deed has to be beneath them. Thus their actions are not humble, nor do they embrace the example of Christ's humiliation. We define humble as that which is beneath us, and as long as we continue to see ourselves as better than our "humble" actions, we are not modeling Christ. Only when we embrace the reality that our status as believers removes any claims to define our deeds as humble can we know the slave-humiliation of Christ. This is far from the emperor's self-understanding, and certainly of our world's today.

Passage Structure and Story
As we dive into the deep exegetical waters of 2:6–11, remember to surface occasionally and appreciate the overarching vision given here. This vision is Grand Canyon grand; it is oceans deep, and as high as the moon and stars. It should take our breath away and cause us to wonder, ponder, imagine, and

---

1. Suetonius, *Vespasian* 23.4.

sing with the angels, "Worthy is the Lamb, who was slain, to receive power and wealth and wisdom and strength and honor and glory and praise!" (Rev 5:12).

The passage is known as the "Christ hymn" because its structure has a poetic rhythm and flow to it. "Everyone agrees on the fact that exalted, lyrical, quasi-credal language is employed in these verses."[2] The tension emerges in defining "hymn," for we have no evidence one way or another that this passage was sung or recited in Pauline churches. We do know that Christians sang hymns in their gatherings (Eph 5:19), so it is not impossible that this passage also was integrated into church worship. Yet the lack of specific evidence has led some to suggest that "poem" is a better description of the lyrical passage.[3] In general, five criteria are used to establish a hymn: (1) a disruption in the flow of the prose, (2) stylistic and terminology differences, (3) use of introductory phrases, (4) antithetic style that highlights a contrast, and (5) use of rare and ceremonial terms.[4] While we should resist reading back into Paul's day our own use of hymns, I think the passage fits the five criteria. Moreover, the label "hymn" fittingly accounts for the passage's lyrical elements.

Christ Hymn, Part 1: Philippians 2:6–8

The Christ hymn's structure can be separated into two halves, the first looking at the incarnation and passion (2:6–8), the second focusing on Christ's exaltation (2:9–11). We will analyze the first section by asking three primary questions: (1) Did Paul write this hymn, or is it pre-Pauline? (2) Does 2:6–11 presuppose a Greek or a Jewish backdrop? (3) Does 2:6 speak of Christ's preexistence? The answers to these questions rely on interpretations of four especially difficult terms: *morphē* (used 2x), *harpagmos,* and *homoiōma,* as well as the theological impact of the verb *kenoō,* "emptied (himself)" or "made himself nothing."

While it might seem beneficial to begin with the bricks and mortar—the vocabulary and syntax of the passage—I suggest, because the terms' meanings are contested, it is more helpful to begin by examining the architectural plans presupposed by scholars. That is, we must establish the underlying story into which interpreters place this hymn.

(1) *Author question.* Generally speaking, this hymn is said to have either a Hellenistic backdrop or an Old Testament/Jewish heritage. Of course, background story is related to authorship; thus, those who believe the hymn reflects a pagan backdrop do not argue for Pauline authorship. Claims about non-Pauline authorship go in two, opposite directions. (a) If Paul did not

---

2. Bockmuehl, *Philippians,* 116.
3. Fee, *Philippians,* 193, n 4.
4. R. P. Martin, "Hymns, Hymn Fragments, Songs, Spiritual Songs" in *DPL,* 421.

write it, then we cannot interpret the hymn in its Philippian context, or (b) even if Paul did not write it, he is using it within his letter and thus supports its context; moreover, we must understand the meaning of the hymn based on its present context in Philippians.

The argument for non-Pauline or pre-Pauline authorship is usually based on the passage's presumed non-Pauline theology or vocabulary. However, such an evaluation is overconfident. We simply do not have the necessary volume of writing by Paul to draw conclusions about what sort of words and syntax he would use. The arguments based on theology likewise flounder, for Paul is capable of speaking of the preexisting Christ in 2 Corinthians 8:9[5] and can speak about the cross without noting the resurrection (Rom 10:6–15; Gal 2:20). In the end, Bockmuehl offers wise advice, "The exegete is duty-bound to accept that Paul uses all his material because in his opinion it says what he wants, and that he means what he says."[6]

(2) *Backdrop.* The background of the hymn is generally brought to the fore in attempting to discern whether Christ is understood as preexistent and what might be meant by that term. For much of this passage's interpretive history, it was believed to proclaim Christ's preexistence as the divine Son of the Father. The story line was that of Israel's God bringing salvation to the world through Christ, the Son. But in the modern era, another argument developed about the Hellenistic hero-gods who through apotheosis gained the status of deity. In this scenario, Gentile believers produced the hymn, using symbols from their own pagan background to interpret the man/god Christ. This heavenly redeemer is not God, but is a divine *Urmensch*. In this case, Paul is not the author, and thus the letter in which we find the hymn should not be used to determine the passage's meaning.[7]

Today, few hold to the Hellenistic Greek heavenly redeemer man/god as the model for Christ in this hymn; however, the idea that Christ might be "extramortal" and not divine is supported by some who draw on Old Testament images. In a general sense, J. Murphy-O'Connor suggests that the overarching story of the fall is behind 2:6. He argues that Jesus was viewed as the sinless or perfect human, and as such, could claim as his right to be treated as god.[8] But would a first-century Jew imagine that any human, however godly, might *attain* the rights and privileges of God? Would not they think that such a being always was God? Moreover, the hymn does not say "he had the right

---

5. Bockmuehl, *Philippians*, 118.
6. Ibid., 119.
7. N. T. Wright, *Climax of the Covenant: Christ and the Law in Pauline Theology* (Edinburgh: T&T Clark, 1993), 70; he cites Käsemann and Bornkamm as examples of this view.
8. Jerome Murphy O'Connor, "Christological Anthropology in Philippians 2:6–11," *RB* 83 (1976): 25–50.

to be considered equal to God," an emendation required with this interpretation. Finally, this interpretation has no place for 2:7, for Christ taking the form of a human being.[9]

A more specific example from the Old Testament is drawn by Osiek, who suggests that the preexistence implied by 2:6 is best understood as existing outside of space and time, but not necessarily as God. She points to Proverbs 8 and the figure of Wisdom as that which existed before time, but was not divine.[10] I suggest the opposite interpretation of Proverbs 8 in the following section, Live the Story.

(3) *Adam and Christ.* A more common argument put forward is that the hymn serves as a comparison between Adam and Christ. Dunn suggests that this hymn replays the fall, but this time, Christ got it right. Rather than grasp at God, which Adam did, Christ humbled himself. The implication of this comparison is that Christ, like Adam, did not in fact share equality with God. Dunn argues that the hymn is not about preexistence but about the human Jesus, who restores humanity as the second Adam and who takes up the glory that the first Adam lost.[11]

Wright also holds that Paul had as a story line for the hymn a limited comparison between the first and second Adam, but he parts company with Dunn's conviction that preexistence is not at issue. For Wright, the Adam-Christology is tied to Israel-Christology, which points to Christ's incarnation and subsequent work of redemption.[12] Thus seeing a comparison with Adam in the hymn does not automatically indicate that the interpreter discounts Christ's preexistence as a theme in the hymn.

Finally, many point to the Isaiah 45:23 quotation in 2:10 as a signal that Paul is drawing on the Servant passages of Isaiah 40–55 to inform the entire hymn.

This quick survey of interpretations for the hymn's underlying story has demonstrated that the predominant view throughout the ages has been that the hymn highlights the incarnation of the Son of God, who in the later creeds was explained in explicit trinitarian language.[13] In the mid-fourth century, Athanasius argued against the Arians and held that there was never a

---

9. Wright, *Climax of the Covenant,* 75, offers these three critiques.

10. Osiek, *Philippians, Philemon,* 58.

11. James D. G. Dunn, *Christology in the Making* (2nd ed.; Grand Rapids: Eerdmans, 1996), 114–21. Dunn declares, "it seems to me that Phil. 2.6–11 is best understood as an expression of Adam christology, one of the fullest expressions that we still possess" (114). For summary of this argument, see Bockmuehl, *Philippians,* 132–33.

12. Wright, *The Climax of the Covenant,* 61.

13. John Webster offers a cogent discussion of Christology; see "Jesus Christ," in *Cambridge Companion to Evangelical Theology* (ed. Timothy Larsen and Daniel J. Treier; Cambridge: Cambridge University Press, 2007), 51–61.

time when the Son was not.[14] The incarnation grounds our redemption, and the deity of Christ assures our salvation.

Vocabulary and Syntax of Philippians 2:6–8

As we now examine the specific terms, phrases, and syntax of 2:6–8, we will see that the choice of definitions is tied to the interpreter's predisposition about the nature of the hymn and its purpose, its story line, and its function in Paul's argument to the Philippians. We must keep in mind the general literary structure of this passage. To anticipate my conclusions, in the following I will note that the phrase "in very nature God" (1) is parallel to "equality with God" (2:6) and (2) is contrasted with "form of a slave"[15] (2:7). Whether the phrase "form of a slave" is paralleled by the phrase "in human likeness" (2:7) remains a debate.[16]

"Being" or "existing" (2:6). Verse 6 begins with the phrase "who, being [existing] in very nature God." The participle translated as "existing" is related to the main verb in the next clause, "did [not] consider." The relationship has been understood in at least three different ways: (1) concessive, *"although* in the form of God"; (2) causal, *"precisely because* [he] exists in the form of God"; or (3) circumstantial, "who being *in the circumstance of being* in the form of God."[17] The participle probably carries a causal sense, suggesting the idea of existing in one's essence or expressing the reality of the situation. The concessive meaning is also possible, if the point is to drive home the contrast between our own expectations of God (God would never act as a slave) and God's actual character, which embraces absolute humility and service. This participle is in the present tense, which contrasts with the aorist participles in 2:7–8 that describe Christ's taking the form of a slave; the former was the reality (2:6) when the latter happened (2:7–8).[18]

Morphē ("form" or "nature") (2:6). The term "form" or "nature" translates the Greek word *morphē*. This term invites the question: Does *morphē* suggest

---

14. Athanasius, *Discourses against the Arians* 1.14.

15. Note that I will use "slave" instead of "servant," as used in the NIV.

16. Bockmuehl, *Philippians*, 126.

17. Fee, *Philippians*, 202, n 40; see also Bruce N. Fisk, "The Odyssey of Christ" in *Exploring Kenotic Christology: The Self-Emptying of God* (ed. C. Stephen Evans; Oxford: Oxford University Press, 2006), 45–73.

18. Fee, *Philippians*, 203, writes, "the participle also stands in temporal contrast with the two aorist participles at the end of the sentence. That is, prior to his 'having taken the "form" of a slave' he was already 'in the form' of God.'" Debate continues on the best way to understand tense in Greek; does it indicate the time of the action, or the verb's aspect? The latter approach insists that Greek verb tenses highlight how the author understood the actions to take place or chose to represent those actions. A summary and evaluation of the discussion can be found in Constantine R. Campbell, *Verbal Aspect, the Indicative Mood, and Narrative: Soundings in the Greek of the New Testament* (SBG 13; New York: Peter Lang, 2007).

Jesus' preexistent state? I argue that it does, when viewed in the wider context of "equality with God." The term *morphē* carries the sense of external shape and characteristics of the object. The difficulty in interpreting this term is that we find it only here and in Mark 16:12, and in both places it can signal visible, outward appearance or "distinguishing characteristics that correspond to this appearance."[19]

In Classical Greek, *morphē* was synonymous with *ousia* or "essence," but we cannot assume that this inference carried through to Paul's day. A Jewish parallel might be in Philo's *Life of Moses*, which uses *morphē* to describe what Moses saw in the burning bush: "a most beautiful form [*morphē*], not like any visible object, an image supremely divine in appearance, shining with a light more brilliant than that of fire. One might suppose this to be the image of Him Who Is [*eikona tou ontos*]; but let us call it an angel."[20] Bockmuehl suggests that Paul reflects an interest in a "well-established Jewish mystical tradition which could speak of God and heavenly beings in unabashedly visual and even anthropomorphic terms."[21] Paul speaks in such a way to the Ephesians, that they grow into maturity, "to the measure of the full stature of Christ" (Eph 4:13). Indeed, *morphē* is an elastic term that gains nuance from its context.

In our case, that context is the phrase "equality with God." To what is Paul referring here? Most likely he points to Christ's nature or metaphysical essence, to his "god-ness." Support for this claim comes mainly from the context, which stresses the distinction with becoming a slave (*doulos*). Paul is stressing that the character of God, seen in Christ, is that of selfless giving. Barth argues that Jesus Christ's humility and his obedience are essential to God, "the humility in which He dwells and acts in Jesus Christ is not alien to Him, but proper to Him.... He is amongst us in humility, our God, God for us, as that which He is in Himself, in the most inward depth of His Godhead."[22]

After two thousand years, we might be comfortable with that picture of God, but the Philippians would not have been. Their gods/goddesses used their power to advance themselves, to subdue others into submission, and to take advantage of weakness.[23] For example, Artemis (Diana to the Romans) had a reputation of being hot-tempered. Actaeon, an unsuspecting hunter,

---

19. Bockmuehl, *Philippians*, 126.
20. Philo, *Life of Moses* 1.66.
21. Bockmuehl, *Philippians*, 129.
22. Karl Barth, *Church Dogmatics* (4 vols.; trans. G. W. Bromiley; London: Continuum, 2004), IV/1, 193.
23. For a general discussion of Greco-Roman religion, see D. E. Aune, "Religions, Greco-Roman," *DPL*, 786–96.

came upon her as she was bathing. In her outrage, she turned him into a stag, and his own dogs tore him apart.[24] Again, in Phrygia, Asia Minor, local tradition held that Zeus and Hermes visited the area and only an old married couple, Baucis and Philemon, showed them hospitality. After receiving a meal, the gods sent a flood that destroyed everyone else in the town.[25] We can understand the people of Lystra in their eagerness to welcome Paul and Barnabas as Hermes and Zeus; they would not want to make the same mistake as did their ancestors and experience the wrath of the gods (Acts 14:8 – 13).

But this is not the sort of God about which Paul speaks. God's form, God's character, is demonstrated, Paul says, by seeing Christ — whose form shows us God. And what did Christ do? He did not selfishly demand his due; he did not take advantage of what another would think he was owed. But it goes deeper. Christ shows us what God's character is like. Though the world might believe that gods have the right to throw their weight around, the one true God, seen in Jesus Christ, demonstrates that the true God is the self-giving God.

Challenging the argument that *morphē* points to preexistence, Dunn argues that *morphē* should be viewed as a synonym to *eikōn* ("image"), and the phrase "image of God" in Genesis 1:27 is the backdrop for our passage. Dunn concludes that Paul is proclaiming Jesus as the new Adam; "the case for hearing a deliberate allusion to and contrast with Adam in Philippians 2.6 – 11 remains strong."[26] In critiquing Dunn's position and similar arguments, Jowers addresses the claim that Daniel 3:24 is a useful link between the Genesis passage and the Christ hymn. In the Septuagint of this text, the Hebrew term for "image" is translated with the Greek *morphē*, thus providing another link between the terms "image" and "form." One weakness of Dunn's argument is that 3:19 – 24 speaks of Nebuchadnezzar watching three men thrown into the furnace. He then sees a fourth man among them, who has the *morphē* of a god. Paul is not suggesting we see Christ with the same blurry, vague image that the pagan king saw in the unnamed fourth figure.[27] Moreover, to see Philippians 2:6 – 8 as presenting Christ only as human, as the best Adam, seems to confuse the issue of what exactly Christ is emptying himself (2:7).

In sum, the better way forward in looking at these two clauses, "in very

---

24. Richard Woff, *A Pocket Dictionary of Greek and Roman Gods and Goddesses* (London: British Museum, 2003), 11.

25. Ovid, *Metamorphoses* 8:611 – 724; Craig S. Keener, *The IVP Bible Background Commentary: New Testament* (Downers Grove, IL: InterVarsity Press, 1993), 362.

26. James D. G. Dunn, *The Theology of Paul the Apostle* (Grand Rapids: Eerdmans, 1998), 286.

27. Dennis W. Jowers, "The Meaning of *morphē* in Philippians 2:6 – 7," *JETS* 49.4 (2006): 739 – 66.

nature God" and "equality with God," is to see a claim about Christ's person as a member of the Trinity. The Nicene Creed, embraced by most Christian churches (Catholic, Orthodox, and Protestant) conveys such a portrait of Jesus Christ:

> We believe in one Lord, Jesus Christ,
> the only-begotten Son of God,
> eternally begotten of the Father before all worlds,
> God from God, Light from Light,
> very God from very God,
> begotten, not made,
> being of one substance with the Father
> by whom all things were made.[28]

Harpagmos ("something to be used to his own advantage") (2:6). Philippians 2:6 includes another complicated term, *harpagmos*, found nowhere else in the New Testament. It can mean (1) the *act* of robbery, or (2) grasping at an *object*, either as (a) something one does not have, or (b) something one rightly possesses. It has also been understood to refer to (3) an *attitude* that one has toward that which one has and continues to have.

These options have led to a variety of interpretations. It could mean that Christ did not grasp at equality with God, an equality he did not share to begin with. In this case, Christ, who is in the form of God, gains glory and equality with God by being obedient to death on the cross.[29] Or Christ, as the perfect, sinless man, was due the honor of equality with God but did not grasp at it. This position stumbles over the historically implausible claim that a Jew would think a sinless person (could there be one?) would thereby deserve the honor reserved for God. Additionally, one would have to add the phrase "the right to be considered" before "equality with God." Finally, this interpretation leaves no place for 2:7, becoming a slave.[30] On the whole, interpretations that insist on this verse as having as its subject the human Jesus do not give full credit to the language used or to the sharp contrast made between 2:6 and 2:7.

Other interpretations of *harpagmos* include that Christ did not gain his equality with God by grasping at it, with the implication that Christ was always equal with God. Conversely, some have decided the issue was not gaining divinity but keeping it by clinging to it. In this case, Christ did not

---

28. The Nicene Creed was approved in the First Ecumenical Council, AD 325.
29. For a discussion and critique of this position, see Wright, *Climax of the Covenant*, 67–69.
30. For a discussion and critique of this position, see ibid., 74–75.

cling to the privileges entailed with divinity or Christ abandoned his status of equality with God, which he held in his preexistent state.[31]

More recently, a way forward has been suggested that looks not at the individual terms but at the phrase as a whole: "did not consider … *harpagmos*." This idiom in its wider Greek usage refers to the attitude the person has toward something they have and will continue to have, but which they will not use to their advantage. In viewing the clause this way, many problems are dissolved. The questions about how or whether Christ clings to his equality with God become moot, for it is not his preexistence and equality that are at issue, but how Christ understands that reality relative to his incarnation. Thus the passage points forward, and Christ's "grasping" begins from his equality with God, it does not aim toward it.[32] Said another way, Christ's equality with God is embodied in selflessness, in refusing to use the power and glory that are due God's majesty for his own advantage.[33]

Verse 2:6 is only half the equation, while 2:7 provides the full picture of Christ's work. Paul begins this verse with a contrast, "rather," and then states that Jesus "emptied himself" or "made himself nothing." The verb *kenoō* ("to make empty") is rarely used in the Septuagint or the New Testament. In four of the five places the term occurs in the New Testament (Rom 4:14; 1 Cor 1:17; 2 Cor 9:3 [all passive]; 1 Cor 9:15 [active]), it is arguably used metaphorically. Thus we might expect Paul would also nuance the term here in Philippians 2:7 metaphorically. The meaning is captured in the idea that Christ embraced humiliation and powerlessness.[34]

The question is often asked: Of what did Christ divest himself? Kenotic Christology suggests that in his incarnation, Christ emptied himself of his omnipresence, omniscience, and omnipotence, but he retained his holiness, love, and righteousness. This theory, however, runs ahead of the specific evidence in our hymn. The term "empty" likely does not refer to an emptying of divine attributes. Such a reading seems to assume that 2:6 reads, *although* Christ was in the form of God, he took the form of a slave, "*despite* his status of equality with God."[35] However, the overall sense of the hymn is that Christ "*manifested* the form of God in the form of a slave."[36] T. F. Torrance asserts

---

31. For a discussion of these various views, see Wright, *Climax of the Covenant*, 69 – 70.

32. Ibid., 79. See also Thielman, *Philippians*, 116.

33. Denny Burk, "On the Articular Infinitive in Philippians 2:6: A Grammatical Note with Christological Implications" *TynBul* 55.2 (2004): 253 – 74, argues for the following translation: "who though he existed in the form of God, did not consider equality with God as something he could grasp for," concluding that "form of God" and "equality with God" carry different meanings.

34. O'Brien, *Philippians*, 217.

35. Bockmuehl, *Philippians*, 133 (italics original).

36. Ibid., 134.

that this hymn does not speak to a metaphysical change such that God the Son lost divine powers. Rather, Christ, in the form of God, did not empty anything out of himself; "he emptied *himself* out of a heavenly and glorious *morphē* into an earthly and inglorious *morphē*, that is, he made himself of no reputation."[37]

Another way to answer the question concerning the meaning of "emptying" is to outline 2:6–8. As the reader can imagine by now, there are almost an infinite number of suggested arrangements for the hymn overall. As Morna Hooker declared, "I myself have produced six or seven different analyses — and found each of them convincing at the time!"[38] I will suggest only two as a way to illustrate the best options for understanding 2:7.[39] One option is to arrange the stanzas thus:

> Who in the form of God existing
> Not an advantage considered
> His being equal with God
>
> But nothing he made himself
> The form of a servant adopting
> In likeness of men becoming
>
> And in appearance being found as man
> He humbled himself
> Becoming obedient to death —
> And death of a cross

In this arrangement, the emphasis falls on understanding Jesus' incarnation as becoming human and becoming a slave/servant. The two inform each other and are both equally in contrast to his preexistence discussed in 2:6.

A second possible arrangement focuses on the repeated term *morphē* and the participle *genomenos* (translated as "being made" in 2:7 and "by becoming [obedient]" in 2:8), which suggests an inclusio or unit of thought. Moreover, the first line in each includes a participle, which controls the prepositional phrase, and the third line of each stanza describes Jesus' action (emptied, humbled).

---

37. Thomas F. Torrance, *Incarnation: The Person and Life of Christ* (ed. Robert T. Walker; Downers Grove, IL: InterVarsity Press, 2008): 74–75. Kevin Vanhoozer notes that for Torrance, the incarnation as well as the cross and resurrection accomplish atonement. Kevin Vanhoozer, "Atonement," in *Mapping Modern Theology: A Thematic and Historical Introduction* (ed. Kelly M. Kapic and Bruce L. McCormack; Grand Rapids: Baker Academic, 2012): 183–84.

38. Morna Hooker, "Philippians 2:6–11," in *Jesus und Paulus: Festschrift für Werner Georg Kümmel zum 70. Geburtstag* (ed. E. E. Ellis and E. Grasser; Göttingen: Vandenhoeck & Ruprecht, 1975), 157.

39. Silva, *Philippians*, 93–94, 99.

Who in the **form** of God existing
Not an advantage considered his being equal with God
But *nothing* he *made* himself
The **form** of a slave adopting

In the likeness of men **becoming**
And in appearance being found as man
He *humbled* himself
becoming obedient to death

The key point to note for our purposes is the different ways the relationship between the terms "servant/slave" and "human" are treated relative to the verb's meaning. In the first outline, the hymn emphasizes the distinction between the divinity and humanity of Jesus, with both nouns emphasizing the depth to which Jesus descended from his preexistence with God. Said another way, "servant" and "man/*anthropos*" are synonyms. The verbal phrases are seen as parallel, so that "emptied himself" is further explained as taking the form of a servant and the form of a human.[40] This reading commends itself in its emphasis on the debasement Jesus experienced relative to his preexistence, but it has a fatal flaw. Treating "slave" and "human" as synonyms presents an inaccurate picture that minimizes the reality that humans are made in the image of God; it suggests that in itself, being human is similar to slavery.

In the second arrangement, the contrast is drawn sharply: "form of God" with "form of a slave." The incarnation is introduced not with the idea of "slave/servant" but in the next line, "being made in human likeness." The point of this passage, then, is to show the character of God. From our human wisdom vantage point, we might think Christ would seek his own power, yet Christ shows that God does not grasp; rather, God gives himself. In this reading, the verb "emptied" or "made himself nothing" (2:7) is understood as further explaining what "being in the form of God" entails. It is both a rejection of taking advantage of his equality with God and an acceptance of or embracing of servanthood.

Suffering Servant of Isaiah 53. A final way to think about "emptied" and "slave/servant" is by reading them through the lens of Isaiah 53, a Suffering Servant passage, including perhaps a direct allusion to 53:12, "he poured out his life unto death." While this specific text does not use the term *doulos*, elsewhere in the Suffering Servant section, the Servant is identified as a slave (42:19; 48:20; 49:3, 5), and the important second-century Greek translation by Aquila includes *morphē* when speaking of the servant/slave in 52:14 and 53:2.[41] The

---

40. Bockmuehl, *Philippians*, 133.
41. Ibid., 135.

Old Testament elsewhere speaks of God as seeing, hearing, and knowing the distress of his people in slavery and coming down to their aid (Exod 3:7–8). Again, God promises, "I will put my dwelling among you.... I am the LORD your God, who brought you out of Egypt so that you would no longer be slaves to the Egyptians" (Lev 26:11–13).

Other connections are made between the Suffering Servant motif and our hymn, particularly in the concept of humility and obedience. In the Greek translation of Isaiah 53:8 the term "humiliation" describes the failure of justice for the Servant, and his death is mentioned specifically. In both cases, his death is understood to be part of God's plan and to be redemptive for others. Of course, unlike the Suffering Servant, Christ humbled *himself*; he was not humbled by those around him. In the end, it seems reasonable to read the picture of Christ in Philippians 2:7 with one eye trained on the Suffering Servant of Isaiah.

This focus ties in well with Jesus' own comment: "The Son of Man came not to be served, but to serve, and to give his life as a ransom for many" (Mark 10:45). This theological truth was played out in the church in at least two interesting ways. First, leaders of the church, including Paul, Peter, and James, identified themselves as slaves of Christ Jesus and God (Rom 1:1; Phil 1:1; Titus 1:1; 2 Pet. 1:1; Jas 1:1). Since these men were also apostles, we get a sense of what they thought their leadership was to look like. Paul states it more explicitly in 2 Corinthians 4:5: "For what we preach is not ourselves, but Jesus Christ as Lord, and ourselves as your servants [slaves] for Jesus' sake." Second, Paul describes believers as "slaves to righteousness" (Rom 6:16–20). He encourages the Romans to understand their new life in Christ as free from sin's tyranny, free to live holy lives under the protective care of their Lord, Jesus Christ.

Summary of 2:6–7. In the end, the best way of seeing "emptied" or "made himself nothing" is to understand that Christ did not give up anything; instead, Paul is explaining the nature of Christ, reinterpreting the common understanding of glory to mean self-negation.[42] "Divine equality meant sacrificial self-giving."[43] The equality between Christ the Son and God the Father is not maintained or expressed by grabbing and grasping. Indeed, the nature and character of God, seen in Jesus Christ, seeks not advantage but slave-like service.

In Human Likeness: The Incarnation of Christ (2:7–8)

Paul continues in 2:7 to stress that Jesus took the likeness of humanity. Paul

---

42. Wright, *Climax of the Covenant*, 83.
43. O'Brien, *Philippians*, 216.

writes "in the likeness of men becoming" and uses the plural "humanity" (*anthropoi*); he does not use the specific term for man/male (*anēr*). At this point in the discussion, we must again ask where this line fits within the context of 2:6–8. If this passage is the final line of the second stanza, then the hymn tightly connects "form of slave" and "humanity." Thus "form of slave" is nuanced and expanded to include that Christ "humbled himself" and "became obedient" [to God].

Several concerns should be raised with this interpretation. First, this close correspondence might inadvertently dull the contrast between slave and God. That is, it might reduce our perception of the social status and functional emphasis that such a contrast between God and slave would bring to bear. Second, it might also suggest that the proper way to see humanity is as enslaved. Now it is true that Paul uses such a metaphor when discussing humans' captivity to sin (Rom 6:11–18). But here the point is not humanity's slavery to sin; rather, it is Christ's representative existence as a member of humanity.

What is involved with Jesus taking on humanity, assuming a human body, being born a human? Does he have a sinful nature as have all children of Adam? Not according to 2 Corinthians 5:21, which states that Jesus knew no sin. Is Jesus then not really like us? Does he not know our struggles or temptations? Indeed he does (Heb 2:14–18; 4:15). The hymn is drawing attention to the fact that Jesus embraced mortality in taking up a body. He who was immortal, preexistent with God, took up corruptible flesh, a body that would decay and putrefy if it remained in the grave. Not only did he take up mortality, but also he was obedient to the very end, to actually die. Athanasius, a fourth century church father, declared: "For he [Jesus] was incarnate that we might be made god."[44] Jesus, the Son of God, identifies with us and participates in humanity, and thus we may identify with him and participate in his death and new life.[45]

If the phrase in question ("being made in human likeness") is the start of the second stanza, the description of humanity is not that of slavery, and it opens the possibility to two specific contrasts made in these verses: (1) form of God and form of slave, and (2) human, and obedient, humiliated human death on a cross. In both cases, the irony is palpable. God a slave? Free man, choosing crucifixion? In this analysis, the hymn stresses that the form of God does not take advantage; rather, God's character is defined as self-giving service.

---

44. Athanasius, *On the Incarnation*, 54 (Yonkers, NY: St. Vladimir's Seminary Press, 2011): 167. See also http://www.ccel.org/ccel/athanasius/incarnation.pdf.

45. Scot McKnight, *A Community Called Atonement* (Nashville: Abingdon, 2007), 108–9.

In Paul's day, it was natural and normal for a slave to do all manner of humiliating tasks—and for a slave they were not so much humiliating as expected of one's status. But if a free man would, for example, wash another free man's feet—that was humiliating (see John 13:3–17). You see, sometimes it is not the task itself that is humiliating, but it becomes such if it is "beneath" the status of the person. By separating slave and human and focusing on humanity itself, the hymn suggests what Christ did in his obedience was not something expected in the regular course of things, as it would if humanity was portrayed as slavery. The shocking point of the hymn is that Christ stood on its head the common understanding of free man as one who sought honor and avoided at all costs what society viewed as humiliating.

A true human is one who embraces obedience, even if that path leads to humiliation. It is not that God delights in humiliation; it is that in God's eyes, what humans consider worthy of exaltation is vainglorious, and he cannot be a part of such status seeking. What we consider humiliation, in other words, is only so because we exist in a world that privileges self, not God.

Christ Humbled Himself (2:8)

The finite verb guiding these two participles "being made" and "being found" is "humbled (himself)" (2:8). The participle "being made" points to his voluntary actions, while "being found" has the sense of the circumstances wherein one finds oneself.[46] The hymn thus stresses the willingness of Christ to embrace his humanity, even unto death. While Christ could not climb up onto the cross himself, he accepted and submitted to this form of execution.

Fisk examines the story line of Christ's incarnation side by side with ancient novels. These stories often begin with the hero or heroine at the heights of fame, success, and status. They trace the rapid descent to the depths of humiliation brought about by Fate. Then, with surprising brevity, the stories recount the main characters' vindication by the gods, who rescue them from death. Our Philippian reader might initially assume a similar story for Christ, but would quickly be brought up short on two points. First, Christ initiates his own humiliation; second, God does not act to save Christ from death on the cross.[47] These distinctions are crucial in distinguishing Christ as Lord and critiquing the pagan view of earthly status and seemingly appropriate actions for the gods.

The power of the hymn is precisely in its critique of the world's picture of humanity and of deity. Christ's actions suggest that all acts of obedience are worth the same, and all humans are called to act obediently. For example, who

---

46. Bockmuehl, *Philippians*, 138.
47. Fisk, "The Odyssey of Christ," 72–73.

should change the baby's diapers? Is it a job *naturally* suited for an immigrant woman? If her high-income employers change the diapers, do they deserve credit for being humble—like Christ—because such work is beneath their dignity? There are no tasks of obedience and service suited to one status, ethnic group, or sex. To think otherwise is to invite sexism and racism into our midst.

Christ's Exaltation (2:9–11)

If the hymn ended here ("death on a cross"), we would still be in our sins. But in fact, God raised Christ from the dead, and with that extended forgiveness to all who call on the name of Jesus Christ (Rom 10:9–13). The hymn's final verses, however, do not celebrate Christ's victory over death as much as his humble obedience and suffering unto death. Harris distinguishes between exaltation and resurrection, "The Resurrection proclaims 'He lives—and that for ever', [*sic*] the Exaltation proclaims 'He reigns—and that for ever.'"[48]

The hymn declares that God exalted Christ, and with Paul's quotation of Isaiah 45:23, we see the magnitude and magnificence of Christ's obedience. After a brief discussion of the structure, we will turn to the three critical questions raised in this section: (1) Is Jesus rewarded by God for his obedience? (2) What is the "name"? (3) Is the homage paid to Christ (knees bowing, tongues confessing) voluntary?

Syntax and vocabulary of 2:9–11. In Greek, 2:9–11 is one sentence, with God as the subject, two finite verbs ("exalted," "gave"), and a purpose clause that includes two subjunctive tense verbs ("bow," "acknowledge"). No difficult syntax, grammar, or vocabulary here—a welcome change from 2:6–8. In the hymn's first three verses, its rhythm moves in short, staccato steps, but in the second half, the movement slows and expands in "grammatically and thematically rich descriptions."[49] The first finite verb, "[highly] exalted," is a compound verb found only here in the New Testament. Paul often uses the prefix *hyper* in the superlative sense; that is, Paul is not saying Christ is more of something now than he was before his death on a cross. This verb is used in Psalm 97:9: "For you, LORD, are the Most High over all the earth; you are exalted far above all gods." Perhaps Paul was thinking of this passage when he wrote, for its sentiment fits nicely with this passage.

God exalts Christ (2:9). Several important theological ideas about the nature of the Godhead are presented and must be explored. Paul begins 2:9 with the conjunction "therefore," which has led to two basic

---

48. Murray J. Harris, *Raised Immortal: Resurrection and Immortality in the New Testament* (London: Marshalls, 1983), 85, cited in O'Brien, *Philippians*, 236.

49. Bockmuehl, *Philippians*, 140.

interpretations: one argument contends that God rewarded Christ for his obedience; a second theory suggests that God vindicated Christ's actions.

The first interpretation was roundly criticized by Calvin, who saw in it a nod to the system of merit that plagued the church in his day. It is in large part to this issue that the Reformers responded with the loud chorus of God's bestowing on believers unmerited grace. Calvin insists the verse indicates that Christ's exaltation by the Father was a consequence, not a reward, of Christ's obedience. He scoffs at those who suggest that Christ gained merit for himself first, as though Christ needed something he did not already possess. Calvin worries that if one believes that Christ gained merit here, two terrible consequences follow. First, believers will not see the amazing love of Christ, who devoted himself to us. "In every instance in which the Scriptures speak of the death of Christ, they assign to us its advantage and price: — that by means of it we are redeemed — reconciled to God — restored to righteousness — cleansed from our pollutions — life is procured for us, and the gate of life opened." Second, people might embrace the falsehood that a human could merit divine reward, as though the glory spoken of in Isaiah 45 might somehow accrue to a human being.[50]

Calvin rightly points to the problem and corrects it. But it may be that such a problem can be avoided altogether if we see that the hymn was not focused on Christ's vicarious sacrifice on our behalf. Thus we need not ask the question of merit in terms of our justification. Instead, the hymn points us to connect Christ's exaltation as a counterbalance to his humiliation[51] and by extension, connect our suffering with our sanctification, which will lead to glorification.

Some nuance the idea of reward, suggesting that while Christ did not obey to earn a reward, nevertheless, if we see Christ's reward as vindication, we can appreciate it as God's gracious gift accepting Christ's work of obedience.[52] The reward is not something added to Christ's character or person; he does not gain a new identity or become more "God-filled" after his death. Instead, a focus on God's gracious giving is understood as a signal that Christ's actions reveal the true nature of the self-giving God. "As God's 'yes' to *this* expression of 'equality with God,' God the Father" exalted Jesus Christ.[53]

Such an understanding helps prevent seeing Christ as passive in the divine plan of salvation. But does such an interpretation do full justice to the "there-

---

50. John Calvin, *The Epistles of Paul the Apostle to the Galatians, Ephesians, Philippians, and Colossians* (ed. David W. Torrance and Thomas F. Torrance; trans. T. H. L. Parker; Grand Rapids: Eerdmans, 1965), 250 (discussed in Hansen, *Philippians*, 160).

51. Bockmuehl, *Philippians*, 140.

52. Hansen, *Philippians*, 161.

53. Fee, *Philippians*, 220.

fore"? Bockmuehl suggests that while Christ did not gain a new identity or change in his essence as God, the incarnation and exaltation are a recognition of Jesus Christ's new name (Lord) and function.[54] Romans 1:3–4 speaks to a similar point, as Christ was declared the Son of God with power at his resurrection. Christ did not gain a higher status than what he had as the preexistent Son; rather, he celebrates the accomplishment of salvation, experienced now by God's people, and with more to come in the new heavens and new earth. He became the firstborn from among the dead and is the firstfruits of those who have died, and he has with his resurrection become coheirs with those who through him are now God's children. Christ's exaltation highlights the nature of the triune God's character as self-giving, as well as Christ's particular function as the Incarnate and Exalted One. To use a limited analogy, in God's "new math," Incarnation + Humiliation = Exaltation.

Jesus is Lord (Isa 45). At the name of Jesus, our hymn continues, every knee will bow and every tongue will confess that Jesus Christ is Lord (2:10–11). This remarkable claim draws on Isaiah 45:22–24, with a significant difference: in our hymn, Paul identifies Jesus as Lord. In doing so, he indicates both that Jesus Christ and God the Father have the same nature and that they are not the same person.

The majority opinion understands Paul as identifying "name" with Lord, who is the ultimate ruler, authority, and power over all creation. The term "Lord" (*kyrios*) is the Greek Bible's way of writing the special name of God, YHWH. So to speak of Jesus as Lord is to indicate Christ's unity with the Father (and Holy Spirit) in the Godhead (see also Eph 1:21; Heb 1:4). Paul could be thinking here of Psalm 8, which begins and ends with the glorious chorus, "LORD, our Lord, how majestic is your name in all the earth!" Hebrews 2:9 explains this psalm as celebrating the Son of Man, who was made a little lower than the angels but was crowned with glory and honor. The point is that Jesus is and will be worshiped.

Acknowledging Jesus as Lord (2:11). The hymn pictures every knee bowing and every tongue confessing, but it does not say whether these actions will be given willingly or not. The verb "acknowledge" suggests an admission of a truth without a concomitant honoring of the victor. Returning to Isaiah 45:22–24, God calls to the ends of the earth, inviting all to worship him, but also speaks of those whose shame will be exposed when every knee bows to God's greatness. In Romans 14:10–14, Paul quotes Isaiah 45:23 in the context of believers' work being judged in the end, whether they have regarded a fellow believer harshly or contemptuously. He calls the Roman church to avoid judging each other on matters of food and drink, which likely reflects a

---

54. Bockmuehl, *Philippians*, 144.

church context where Jewish concerns over unclean foods bumped up against Gentile table fellowship. Paul stresses that each believer must focus not on the believer next to them, but should keep their eyes squarely on Christ their Lord, to whom they owe absolute submission.

Paul is not reflecting on unbelievers' behavior in Romans, so we are still without conclusive proof as to whether unbelievers will bow unwillingly or under coercion. The question is important because it touches not only on human salvation but also on God's character. It reveals the tension within the New Testament itself, expressed in the firm convictions that God is not willing that any should perish and that each person should call on the name of the Lord to be saved. God's will cannot be thwarted, but God has also determined not to impose his love when and where it is unwelcome.

Two points are worth noting. First, James explains that demons believe God is one, and they shudder (Jas 2:19). The supremacy of God does not soften them; it only brings fear and obstinacy. Second, some humans will confuse their use of the name and the miracles they do in its power with their own obedience. In this case, Jesus will say to them, "I never knew you. Away from me, you evildoers" (Matt 7:23). In both cases, the underlying issue is lack of obedience—the same focus on obedience is made in our hymn. Every knee bowing is another ramification of God's plan for the end of time. The picture is not focused on the attitude of those bowing and acknowledging, but on the inevitability of the verdict—Jesus Christ is Lord.

God's glory (2:11). The final clause, "to the glory of God the Father," suggests to some that Paul is protecting the ultimate honor of the Father and implying the subordinate status of the Son. But the quotation from Isaiah points to their one essence, their God-ness. Hill argues that the hymn is not commenting here on the different functions of the Son and the Father. This final phrase is not making gradations of honor between Father and Son; instead, it insists that Son and Father are of the same essence—both God.[55]

Implications of the Hymn Today

The Christ hymn smashes human arrogance even as it affirms the worth of the human body and creation. Christ's incarnation is not a mere vehicle used by the Godhead to rescue human souls; it serves to pull back the curtain that had separated a human vision of God. Christ became human, but his behavior was counterintuitive; rather than demand rights appropriate to a king, he demonstrated God's character of self-giving. His humiliation in obedience

---

55. Wesley A. Hill, " 'Redoublement' and Relationality in Philippians 2.9–11: A Reconsideration of the Function of 2.11b in the Construction of the Christ-Hymn's Christology," paper delivered at the 2011 annual meeting of Society of Biblical Literature, in San Francisco.

changed forever the course of humanity, forward throughout eternity. The last word in the story is not "and he breathed his last" (Luke 23:46), but "Jesus Christ is Lord" (Phil 2:11).

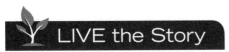
LIVE the Story

History or Theology? That Is the Question

There is a revolution going on in evangelical biblical studies. The issues revolve around the place of doctrine vis-à-vis historical context and which approach should have pride of place. A story might help illustrate what I'm talking about. A few years ago at the annual meeting of the Society of Biblical Literature, a man gave a paper on the hymn of Christ. He looked specifically at the issue of the relationship of the Son to the Father as expressed by the term "glory" in Philippians 2:11. To answer this question, he used the discussions of the patristic church about the Trinity and the person of Jesus Christ. After making his case, the speaker took questions. A man in the audience raised his hand: What do you think is lost when you use later church writings to explain Paul's message? The speaker tossed the question back to the questioner, who responded passionately that the speaker missed the social world of Paul, specifically Paul's direct engagement with the imperial cult. The meaning in the original context was buried under later theology.

This short vignette typifies my point that biblical exegesis is in a perpetual dance with theological claims. They are not mutually exclusive, but they have been set at odds with each other in critical scholarship. Some worry about imposing later, perhaps alien beliefs back onto the Bible. Others wonder whether a keen focus on historical context leaves any room to explore application for today. And many readers now recognize that their perspective or situation shapes the way they read the text.

My own convictions in reading Paul's letters lean toward understanding theology as a useful conversation partner, not an uninvited gatecrasher. Doctrines serve as "clarifying agent[s], an enduring tradition of theological judgments."[56] Irenaeus speaks of the "rule of faith" (*Against Heresies* 9.4) as those central beliefs about God's salvific work in Christ that form the central narrative of our belief claims. "He also who retains unchangeable in his heart the rule of the truth which he received by means of baptism," Irenaeus notes, will examine the ideas used in heretical explanations of biblical events and figures and will reassemble these ideas to their proper narrative shape. His point is

---

56. Daniel Treier, "Series Preface," in *Proverbs and Ecclesiastes* (BTCB; Grand Rapids: Brazos, 2011), xi.

that it is not enough to know the name Jesus, but one must also know his story properly.

The dogma established in the early church creeds concerning the Trinity and the full deity/humanity of Christ help us today to understand the full narrative of the gospel. Augustine explains further that the rule of faith cannot be boiled down to simple truisms (we might say today bumper stickers). Instead, the rule of faith is a habit of mind, a posture of humility and desire for understanding that every Bible reader should take as he or she reads as a member of the community of faith. Drawing from Jeremiah 31:33, Augustine writes to those preparing to join the church that "the creed is learned by listening; it is written, not on stone tablets nor on any material, but on the heart."[57]

The Genevan Confession, written by John Calvin and William Farel in 1536, includes the teaching, "We confess then that it is Jesus Christ who is given to us by the Father, in order that in him we should recover all of which in ourselves we are deficient. Now all that Jesus Christ has done and suffered for our redemption, we veritably hold without any doubt, as it is contained in the Creed." The Confession then writes out the Nicene Creed. Thus a consistent thread of teaching down through history reiterates the rule of faith, the dogma of the church concerning the nature of the God revealed in Scripture, as the foundation on which to build exegesis.

What does this mean for the study of the Christ hymn? The short answer is that readers can be confident and comfortable including theological reflection in their exegesis. Also, we can include Paul's theological claims, and that of the entire canon, in the interpretation.

The Christ Hymn and Lady Wisdom (Proverbs 8)

The enigmatic figure of Lady Wisdom in Proverbs 8 offers an interesting vantage point from which to study the Christ hymn. The two passages work synergistically in revealing God's work in creation and redemption. Proverbs 8:22–31 reads:

> The LORD brought me forth as the first of his works,
> before his deeds of old;
> I was formed long ages ago,
> at the very beginning, when the world came to be.
> When there were no watery depths, I was given birth,
> when there were no springs overflowing with water;
> before the mountains were settled in place,
> before the hills, I was given birth,

---

57. Augustine, *Sermon* 212.2.

before he made the world or its fields
or any of the dust of the earth.
I was there when he set the heavens in place,
when he marked out the horizon on the face of the deep,
when he established the clouds above
and fixed securely the fountains of the deep,
when he gave the sea its boundary
so the waters would not overstep his command,
and when he marked out the foundations of the earth.
Then I was constantly at his side.
I was filled with delight day after day,
rejoicing always in his presence,
rejoicing in his whole world
and delighting in mankind.

Who is Wisdom? Weaving together Proverbs 8 and Philippians 2, we begin to discern the pattern. Negatively, Wisdom is not a creature, even the best or first creature. Wisdom is distinct from creation, yet deeply involved in creation. Second, Wisdom is not merely a divine attribute; it is not something God created. Said another way, there was not a time when God was not wise. Third, Wisdom is not merely an aspect of creation, a created intermediary between God and humans to bridge the chasm between the unreachable, unapproachable God. If that were the case, we would need an intermediary to bridge the gap between Wisdom and God, and then another intermediary to help the first one, and so on ad infinitum. Instead we see that God is not absent from his creation; God is deeply engaged with his creation and creatures. In Proverbs 8:22–31 we see a hint of the grand condescension that becomes clear in Philippians 2:6–11, that Wisdom is for all, the king and the serf. Everyone can be wise by learning from God.

Christ the Wisdom of God. What can we say in the positive sense that Proverbs 8:22–31 teaches in relation to the Christ hymn? Most important, Wisdom does more than mediate; Wisdom reveals. Using the language of "brought forth," Proverbs 8:22–31 signals continuity between God and Wisdom (or Father and Son). "The begetting metaphor, far from subordinating the Son to the Father as creature to Creator, actually indicates continuity of divine life and character."[58] What is revealed? Proverbs 8:22–31 cautions humans that our understanding is limited and should be shaped by the divine perspective. We as creatures see only to the horizon; Wisdom shines from beyond the horizon and directs those who seek understanding. The Christ

---

58. Treier, *Proverbs and Ecclesiastes*, 50.

hymn acknowledges this crucial aspect of human existence and thus begins the hymn with a call to *phroneō*, to have a way of thinking, an attitude or posture, a disposition consistent with the person of Christ.

But the Christ hymn goes a step further to address a second human limitation, sin, in relation to the Wisdom of God. The Wisdom of God is shown not only in the surpassing beauty and intricacy of creation, but also in the condescension of God in the incarnation. God did not create the world as an experiment — bubbling and boiling away in a pot left unattended — but to enjoy. Proverbs 8:30–31 declares that God is continuing to rejoice and delight in his creation. The supreme proof of such enjoyment is the incarnation. John 3:16 says it plainly, "For God so loved the world that he gave his one and only Son, that whoever believes in him shall not perish but have eternal life." Philippians 2:6–11 spells out the mysterious, amazing truth of the incarnation and exaltation of Christ. Even more, 2:1–11 declares that as believers participate in Christ, they too can share in Christ's wisdom and ultimately share in his victory over sin and death.

Said another way, it is precisely because Jesus Christ is divine that believers can imitate him. It is because Jesus is the one and only Son that any human can be a child of God the Father by grace. Jesus Christ is by nature the only Son of the Father, but we who are in Christ are children of the Father, by grace. Paul writes along these lines to the Colossians: Christ is "the image of the invisible God, the firstborn over all creation ... he is the beginning and the firstborn from among the dead ... and through him [God was pleased] to reconcile to himself all things, whether things on earth or things in heaven, by making peace through his blood, shed on the cross" (Col 1:15–20). Paul speaks of a similar matter to the Corinthians when he exclaims that Christ is the wisdom of God, and that this wisdom is lived out on the cross (1 Cor 1:21–25, 30).

Christ's Humiliation Lived Out Today in His People

The importance of knowing who Christ is cannot be underestimated, but it can be underutilized. The grand words of mystery and praise can become the stuff of idle theory rather than deep reflection. We must ask not only what these words *meant*, but also what such words would have *done* in the first-century Roman empire. From there, we can suggest how such words might ring out in our own context.

Briefly, Paul's declaration of Christ's humiliation would have cut to the heart of the social code of the day, which emphasized status and distributing honor based on status. Additionally, Paul's confidence of Christ's exaltation would have put a stake through the heart of paganism, including the imperial cult's claims. Both these ramifications have resonance with our situation today, even if the United States is not an honor-based culture and we do not fight overt paganism. Today, Christ's humiliation is resisted in our Western fascination with individualism, often expressed in our celebration of celebrity.

Obedience to Christ

Paul's hymn challenges to the core a common mind-set today, the resistance to obedience. Americans pride themselves in not taking directions, not following tradition, making their own way, and dancing to the beat of their own drum. Even our description of salvation falls into this trap of independence. We say we have asked Jesus into our lives, but in the Christ hymn Christ did not invite God into his life to bless it and help it along. Rather, the hymn shows the human Christ's absolute obedience to God the Father. The self is kicked off the throne of the heart, and God is placed rightfully in his place.

A corollary to this is the attitude displayed by Christ in his obedience, namely, his voluntary humility. We like the celebrity, the flashy, the bold and brash. We like the blogger who takes on his or her opponents with gloves removed, and our culture rewards such boldness. Within the Christian subculture, we baptized the secular "servant leadership" model invented by Greenleaf in the 1970s, but used it to paper over a continuing model of leadership that promoted power and being served. I suggest that Paul's picture of Christ would stand up well beside Jesus' teachings in Mark 8–10. There we see "servant leadership" beside servants and slaves. There is no call to reject one's pride (always hard to do the negative), but rather a call, a command, to embrace humility.

I'll try to distinguish what I mean here. Striving to avoid pride is like telling a softball player, "Don't strike out." Our minds don't process the "not"; we can't both swing the bat and not swing the bat. We need a clear picture of what to do, and then we imagine ourselves doing it. Not having pride is something difficult to imagine doing, because it is framed in a "not doing" sort of way. But being humble is an action, and we can imagine acts of humility.

A True Volunteer

What might these acts look like? In broad strokes, it challenges the volunteerism mentality. Let me explain. We can construct a model of volunteering whereby we "give of our time" as though it is ours to give, and those to whom we give are somehow in our debt. We go to the soup kitchen to help, but we know we are only there for a time, and then we return to our "regular" life. The volunteer label is just that, a sticky nametag that we wear when we are at an event, only to peel off when we get home. Our real lives lie outside the volunteer arena.

We do this in our homes as well. We establish roles for wives and husbands, and when a wife or husband does "the job" of the other, they get bonus points for their humility. For example, the husband who gets the kids ready for church is praised for going above and beyond what he should do, because he's doing his wife's task of caring for the regular needs of the children. The point is that these volunteer jobs are seen as such because they are beneath our capabilities or "pay grade," but we do them to be nice or to show how humble we are.

Christ's lesson to us, demonstrated in the hymn, is that no job is below our pay grade, no task is "beneath us," and no service is so outstanding that it is worthy of God's special praise. We must work to avoid the separation of *our* life and the volunteer (grunt work) activities that we do to feel better about ourselves. The point is that cleaning up after a baby or an elderly parent is exactly who we are in Christ, even if we also run a company or are senior pastor of a church. The former is not window dressing on the latter; it should not serve as an illustration of lack of pride.

Henri Nouwen, a Servant of Christ

Henri Nouwen exemplified my point. A Harvard Divinity School professor, he grew increasingly unhappy with his life. A chance meeting with Jean Vanier, the founder of L'Arche (communities for developmentally disabled people), led him to join a group home in Toronto. At this home, four caregivers looked after six mentally and physically handicapped people — or at least that was what it looked like at first glance. Nouwen describes it differently.

> Recently, I moved from Harvard to a place near Toronto called Daybreak. That is, from an institution for the best and brightest to a community where mentally handicapped people and their assistants try to live together in the spirit of the beatitudes. In my house ten of us form a family. Gradually, I'm forgetting who is handicapped and who is not. We are simply John, Bill, Trevor, Raymond, Rose, Steve, Jane, Naomi, Henri, and Adam.
>
> I want to tell you Adam's story. After a month of working with Adam, something started to happen to me that had never happened before. This severely handicapped young man whom outsiders sometimes describe with very hurtful words started to become my dearest companion. As I carried him into his bath and made waves to let the water run fast around him and told him all sorts of stories, I knew that two friends were communicating far beyond the realm of thought.
>
> Before this I had come to believe that what makes us human is our minds, but Adam keeps showing me that what makes us human is our

heart, the center of our being where God has hidden trust, hope and love. Whoever sees in Adam merely a burden to society misses the sacred mystery that Adam is fully capable of receiving and giving love. He is fully human—not half human, not nearly human, but fully, completely human because he is all heart. The longer I stay with Adam, the more clearly I see him as a gentle teacher, teaching me what no book or professor ever could.[59]

This is the attitude enjoined by Christ in Mark 9:33–37, that "anyone who wants to be first must be the very last, and the servant of all." The example Christ gave to illustrate his meaning was to choose a child from the crowd and state that in welcoming such a one—one who cannot repay kindness, who might not even realize kindness being offered, and whose care is seen as menial by most—the disciple demonstrates the posture of service that characterizes the child of God. Because this teaching is so hard and so uncharacteristic of the human existence, the disciples resisted. Jesus stated the same teaching again in Mark 10:35–45, concluding that "the Son of Man did not come to be served, but to serve, and to give his life as a ransom for many." Philippians 2:6–8 puts such claims in poetic verse, to be sung in each believer's heart.

---

59. Taken from the following website: http://speakingoffaith.gather.com/viewArticle.action ?articleId=281474976713391 (accessed June 3, 2013). This summary of Henri Nouwen's relationship with Adam is adapted from his book *Adam: God's Beloved* (Maryknoll, NY: Orbis, 1997).

CHAPTER 8

Philippians 2:12–18

LISTEN to the Story

¹²Therefore, my dear friends, as you have always obeyed—not only in my presence, but now much more in my absence—continue to work out your salvation with fear and trembling, ¹³for it is God who works in you to will and to act in order to fulfill his good purpose.

¹⁴Do everything without grumbling or arguing, ¹⁵so that you may become blameless and pure, "children of God without fault in a warped and crooked generation." Then you will shine among them like stars in the sky ¹⁶as you hold firmly to the word of life. And then I will be able to boast on the day of Christ that I did not run or labor in vain. ¹⁷But even if I am being poured out like a drink offering on the sacrifice and service coming from your faith, I am glad and rejoice with all of you. ¹⁸So you too should be glad and rejoice with me.

Listening to the text in the Story: Exodus 15:16; Numbers 14:1–36; 20:1–5; 21:4–9; Deuteronomy 1:27; 32:5; Psalm 55:5; Daniel 12:3.

After the incredible scene in 2:9–11, where Paul pulls back the heavenly curtain to let us peek into God's awesome display of righteousness, justice, and holiness that will one day define all life in the cosmos, the curtain falls back into place, and Paul asks believers to live in light of that glorious foretaste of glory divine. The magnificent vision presented in the Christ hymn should not only make our hearts sing, but also give new energy to our arms and legs in service. In the hymn, we saw Christ's humility and obedience stressed. It presented God's character as seen in Christ; Christ did not take any advantage for himself; rather, he embraced selfless service. In his incarnation Jesus portrays what it is to be fully human—humility and obedience.

In 2:12–18 Paul completes the call to steadfastness and holy living that he made in 1:27–30, and he continues to stress both obedience to God and humility toward all believers (2:1–5). For example, in 1:27–30, Paul requested that the Philippians walk faithfully, whether or not he was with them. Moreover, he admitted that the wider community of Philippi stands against the believers. Third, he nudged the Philippians to cast their spiritual eyes beyond the present horizon, to see into the eschatological future that awaits them. Finally, he stressed perseverance, standing firm against the onslaught of evil. Each of these ideas comes into play in 2:12 – 18, suggesting a unit of ethical instruction rooted in theological reflection.

 EXPLAIN the Story

Work Out Your Salvation (2:12 – 16)

Luther's clarion call, "justification by faith alone," rings from pulpits across the U.S. and around the world. Thus Paul's statement here that believers work out their salvation registers a 9.0 on the theological Richter scale. But before we imagine Luther's insight reduced to rubble, we must closely examine the intent of these verses. Briefly, Paul is not speaking about salvation here as synonymous to the doctrine of justification by faith alone. Additionally, Paul does not see justification only as a past event, but as having future reference (Rom 2:13; 8:33; Gal 5:4 – 5). Moreover, Paul speaks of God judging believers based on their works (Rom 14:10 – 12; 1 Cor 3:15; 2 Cor 5:10). McGrath suggests that "believers are justified by faith, and judged by its fruit."[1]

But here, in 2:12 – 16 Paul looks at that part of salvation that happens once a believer steps through the gate and onto the path of being "conformed to the image of [God's] Son" (Rom 8:29). God's salvation plan stretches back before the world's creation (Eph 1:4) and forward to the creation of the new heavens and new earth, with believers sharing eternal life in Christ (1:14). To the Philippians, Paul continually encourages them to understand their position in Christ based on the day of Christ, when Paul hopes to boast in their faith (2:16; see also 1:10, 3:20 – 21).

Often we focus so much on 2:12 – 13 that we lose sight of the imperative in 2:14, that we do all things without grumbling. To our Western ears, this sounds like a second order command, an illustration of right living. But I suggest that nothing in the Greek text, or in Paul's letters as a whole, should lull us into thinking that community relationships, the fellowship of the saints, is a "second order" business. Indeed, in 1 Corinthians 11:17 – 22, Paul decries the Corinthians' communion celebrations not because they lacked solid theology, but because the poor were left hungry while the rich exalted themselves in their presence. Such behavior puts the congregation in a situation we might call today "code blue," possibly leading to the need for "life support." As we dig deeply into Philippians 2:12 – 13, we will proceed with half an eye toward

---

1. A. E. McGrath, "Justification," *DPL*, 522.

2:14 – 16 and its focus on avoiding arguments on the way to being blameless beacons of light.

God Works Out Your Salvation (2:12 – 13)

Paul calls to the Philippians in 2:12 to "work out" their own salvation with fear and trembling, and he connects two dependent clauses to this thought, "as you have always obeyed" and "not only in my presence, but now much more in my absence."[2] Paul places the verb "work out" last in the sentence, so we will start there and work toward the front of the verse. The verb "work out" is an imperative. Fee points to the opening conjunction ("therefore"), which, when followed by an imperative, often indicates a locally focused argument geared at the church body.[3] Paul uses this verb twenty times (including Romans 7:13, 15, 17 18, 20) as he describes sin's hold on those still living in the flesh. In Romans 7, he highlights how important it is not only to agree that God's will is good, but also to actually do that will. Romans 8:2 – 14 highlights the law of the Spirit of life in Christ Jesus (8:2) that makes possible the doing of God's good will. Thus working out one's salvation is another way of saying, "Live in the Spirit" (8:12 – 14). But only in Philippians is the object of this verb "salvation."

Paul wants believers to work out their *own* salvation. Each believer must listen closely to Paul's admonition. The word "salvation" (*sōtēria*) carries two general meanings across the New Testament: (1) deliverance from danger, such as being saved from one's enemies, and (2) forgiveness of sin and eternal redemption. *Sōtēria* "carries the general sense of health, welfare, and well-being, and especially protection and deliverance from danger."[4] While Luke uses "salvation" in both senses, Paul typically uses it only in the latter connotation, emphasizing its eschatological and soteriological aspects. That is, Paul speaks of one's eternal and present status as God's child, redeemed in Christ, when speaking about salvation.

Does Paul speak here in 2:12 about how someone gets saved? Some point to the plural verb as indicating that Paul has a corporate sense in mind, suggesting Paul is not speaking about getting saved from sin. But this will not hold water, for Paul can use a plural verb to speak to the action of a group of individuals. "The challenge is both to 'each of them' and to 'all of them.'"[5] Moreover, we have here a "both/and" scenario; just as one is not a member of God's family unless his/her sins are forgiven in Christ, so too anyone whose

---

2. Bockmuehl, *Philippians*, 149.
3. Fee, *Philippians*, 231.
4. Osiek, *Philippians, Philemon*, 70.
5. Bockmuehl, *Philippians*, 151.

sins are forgiven in Christ is automatically a member of the body of Christ. "From Paul's perspective ethical behavior is motivated and empowered by the eschatological reality of salvation."[6]

Elsewhere, Paul stresses both the present (1 Cor 1:18; 15:2) and the future aspects of salvation (Rom 13:11; 1 Thess 1:9–10).[7] In Philippians 1:19, Paul testifies that in his current imprisonment, God is working in Paul to speak the gospel, and in the final judgment Paul's trust in God's faithfulness will be vindicated. We should expect that same tension between the present and the future aspects of salvation to hold here in chapter 2. Thus Paul enjoins the Philippians to live into the promises of God in Christ, so that their testimony on the day of Christ will be that God's good work (1:6) has been lived out in their lives (2:13).

The manner in which one should work out one's salvation is described by two phrases: "fear and trembling" and "not only in my presence but now much more in my absence." The former phrase occurs in the Old Testament, where the focus is most often on reactions to the supernatural powers of God (or of Satan). For example, Exodus 15:16 reads: "Terror and dread will fall on them. By the power of your arm they will be as still as a stone" (see also Deut 11:25; Ps 2:11). Yet at times attention is given to a human enemy, as in Psalm 55:5, wherein the psalmist writes concerning his enemies, "Fear and trembling have beset me; horror has overwhelmed me" (see also Deut 2:25). Interestingly, Paul is the only New Testament author to use this phrase (in addition to Phil 2:12, see 1 Cor 2:3; 2 Cor 7:15; Eph 6:5). He expects the Philippians to obey him and his call to unity and holiness as they stand in awe in the presence of the Lord, their God.

Paul also asks that they work out their salvation "not only in my presence but now much more in my absence." Paul uses this same theme in 1:27 as he encourages the Philippians to live worthy of the gospel whether he comes to them or only hears of their progress. This phrase is best understood as related to the main verb "work out," though some connect it with the earlier clause "as you have always obeyed," a statement of Paul's appreciation of the Philippians' obedience. The specific word used for "not" here is generally used with imperatives ("work out" here) rather than indicatives ("obey"). Paul's point is that the Philippians are to focus on living out their calling as believers irrespective of his presence in their midst. He insists that they are capable of embracing their own salvation and growing deeper into the life God has called them to, regardless of Paul's circumstances.

---

6. Hansen, *Philippians*, 174.
7. Bockmuehl, *Philippians*, 151.

Obedience and Obeying (2:12)

Paul begins 2:12 by affirming how his "dear friends" have always obeyed. Yet Paul does not provide an object detailing their obedience. The same was true in 2:8; Christ's obedience did not include an object. In this latter case, most assume that the object is God; thus most conclude that Paul intends in 2:12 the Philippians' obedience to God. Moreover, note how Paul does not stress his authority as apostle to the Philippians, so it does not seem likely that he is suddenly referring here to obedience to his apostolic authority. In other words, Paul praises the Philippians for obeying Christ, revealed in the gospel (see 2 Cor 2:9; 7:15; 2 Thess 3:15). They obeyed the call of God and have continued to embrace their mission of sharing the gospel through supporting Paul's ministry.

While Christians in the West today would say that they want to obey God, the wider society does not always encourage the notion of obeying another person.[8] This was also the case in the ancient world, at least for those who believed in the autonomous, virtuous person.[9] But for many in the ancient world, one's livelihood and social status depended on obeying someone else; slaves to owners, women to men, clients to patrons, sons to fathers — all needed an obedient attitude and were praised for demonstrating it. Paul is not asserting the hierarchical, class-conscious structure of his world, but is merely drawing on one value that is laudable when it is placed in service of the gospel, namely, obedience to God and the gospel.

God Works in You (2:13)

For Paul, any human obedience, goodness, righteousness, joy, or love has at its root the goodness, righteousness, joy, and love of God. So in 2:13, Paul stresses God's activity underpinning and empowering his people toward greater holiness. In fact, the verse begins with the word *theos*, "God," placing it in the emphatic position. Interestingly, the term does not have an article with it, which signals that it is the predicate noun connected to the subject of the sentence — in this case the participle *ho energōn* (lit., "the one working").[10]

Paul insists that God empowers the believers both in their will to do and in their actual doing of those acts that fulfill his good purpose. Ephesians 2:10 similarly promises that God has prepared good works for his people to do. Paul learned for himself that his strength comes from the Lord, who

---

8. Exceptions to this can be found in the military, in sport teams, and other tightly structured, hierarchical organizations.

9. Bockmuehl, *Philippians*, 150.

10. This is called Colwell's rule: "a definite predicate noun which precedes the copulative [the verb "is" that connects the subject and predicate] lacks the definite article with the noun." See Fee, *Philippians*, 230, n 4; the most celebrated case of the application of this rule occurs in John 1:1c.

said, "My grace is sufficient for you, for power is made perfect in weakness" (2 Cor 12:9). Elsewhere he admits that he is the least of the apostles because he persecuted the church, but he goes on to say that God's grace to him has not been in vain, for he worked harder than all of the other apostles—and then he pauses and states, "yet not I, but the grace of God that is with me" (1 Cor 15:10).

Perhaps a mundane example will serve to illustrate my point. God is not doing the good works for the Philippian believers, as a parent might do a child's homework. Instead, God is making it possible for them to work by giving them access to the power to accomplish what he has asked. Parents give their child a good supper, a quiet place free of distractions, and encouraging comments about their previous good work. Thus well fortified and encouraged, and with the proper tools and environment, the student can do his or her homework.

Work and Reward for God's Good Purpose/Pleasure (2:13)

Christians often have a hard time parsing the difference between God working in them and working themselves to earn points with God. We think any effort we make falls into the latter category. Paul's experience taught him otherwise. He knew the struggle to accept—even embrace—the perils of travel, the dangers of speaking the gospel, and the anxiety tied to leading fledging churches. The Spirit of Christ was with Paul, but it was also very much Paul who was hungry, cold, sore, and tired. Paul does not count those experiences as works that might persuade God to love him more; rather, he sees his ministry as participation in kingdom work. His full-hearted and submissive joy embracing God's purpose is what gains his reward. This reward is the result of Paul's actions done in the power of the Holy Spirit according to God's plan that "work done in one's life has remained a condition of some established effect in the new world order of 'what abides' as the fruit of the Spirit or as the work of God's kingdom (1 Cor 13:8–13)."[11]

God's work has a good purpose to fulfill. The word "purpose" (*eudoxia*) can also be translated "pleasure" (see ESV). Why does God find pleasure in our works, which he strengthens us to do? As I was working on this passage, our daughter called me with news that she was accepted into medical school. Did she do the work to get in? Certainly. Did I find immense pleasure in seeing her achieve her dream? You bet. Was she excited to have earned a spot? Undoubtedly. Now what if I had paid off the admissions committee (not possible on my professor's salary!), would she have the same sense of victory, and

---

11. Anthony C. Thiselton, *The First Epistle to the Corinthians* (NIGTC; Grand Rapids: Eerdmans, 2000), 304–5.

would I have the same feelings of deep joy? Not a bit. So too God could, with a snap of his fingers, so to speak, create all goodness and complete obedience in his people. But even as parents take great joy in their children's hard work and successes, so too in a mysterious way, God also delights in our obedience. As Fee notes, "it delights God to delight his people."[12]

Be Blameless Children of God (2:14–16)

Turning to 2:14–16, Paul builds his argument from the Old Testament story, interpreting its trajectory in important ways in response to Christ's work and the gospel message. Several terms and phrases warrant special mention, including "grumbling" (2:14), "blameless," "warped and crooked generation," and "shine . . . like stars" (2:15). Paul uses the wilderness experience of the Israelites, draws on priestly sacrificial practices, and highlights Deuteronomy 32:5 and Daniel 12:3. Underneath these examples and descriptions lies the story of Israel's wanderings in the desert and their pursuit of the holy life, including the times when God's people failed to serve him fully. Paul weaves the Philippians' story into Israel's story, for they are all part of the story of the children of God. Knowledge of past failings might prevent the present generation from repeating them — at least that is Paul's hope (read also 1 Cor 10:1–13).

The admonition to "do everything without grumbling or arguing" might get lost in the shuffle of theological dialogues on merit and grace (2:12–13) and sanctification and transformation (2:15–16). But to relegate this verse to the minor leagues is to miss a key component in Paul's argument. Verse 14 provides a concrete application of working out one's salvation (2:12) and living blameless, innocent lives (2:15). The call to cease grumbling and stop arguing defines for Paul the nature of unity and community in the church.

If we were writing this letter today, many of us would put at the top of our list describing blameless living: "stop committing fornication," "stop cheating/stealing," or even "stop watching porn." Few would put gossip and grumbling at the top of the list of sins to be avoided in church. Is it because the Philippians scored a perfect mark in avoiding sexual and financial temptations that Paul had to move farther down the list of bad sins, to pinpoint one that fit their context? More likely, Paul was deeply troubled at the serious problems that dissension caused. Sadly today many churches have relabeled gossip as "prayer requests." We can hardly shine like stars (2:15) if we are rolling in the mud and muck of spite, rumor, and innuendo.

Paul might be speaking even more specifically here about grumblings against leaders. This suggestion arises from the pointed allusions to Israel's wilderness experience in verses 15–16. Several times while the Israelites were

---

12. Fee, *Philippians*, 240.

wandering in the wilderness, the people grumbled. For example, when the Israelite spies reported that the land promised to them was inhabited by powerful groups with well-fortified cities, the people grumbled against Moses and Aaron, lamenting that it would have been better to have died in Egypt (Num 14:2–3). Again, lack of water brought complaints against Moses and Aaron (20:2–13).

Wilderness Lessons

Our letter hints at the possibility that tensions surrounded leaders and perhaps their supporters. For example, in 1:1, Paul addresses all the saints in Philippi and then adds, "with the overseers and deacons," a curious phrase in Paul's opening addresses. Does this signal an issue with the leadership, that perhaps the congregation is not walking with the leaders? Again, in 4:2, Paul speaks directly to two leaders, coworkers with Paul in the gospel effort, Euodia and Syntyche. They are urged to "be of the same mind in the Lord," the same phrase we saw in 2:2.

It is unusual for Paul to identify particular congregants as he does in 4:2, so one must suppose the situation was serious. Were these leaders competing, much as Aaron and Miriam did in their grumbling against Moses? In Numbers 12, Aaron and Miriam become frustrated with Moses for marrying a Cushite woman and spoke against him, while building up themselves by saying that God would also speak through them. God responded by declaring that though he spoke to prophets in visions, with Moses he spoke face to face. Aaron and Miriam were chastised, and Aaron confessed their foolishness and apologized to Moses (12:10–12). Moses also reminded the Israelites that they had grumbled against God by refusing to enter the Promised Land (Deut 1:27). When the people grew impatient and grumbled again against God and Moses, God sent snakes in their midst. The people repented, and Moses made a bronze snake and fitted it to a pole; all who looked on it were healed (Num 21:4–9).[13]

Whatever the case in Philippi, churches today underestimate the gravity of grumbling to their peril. Our sanctification, our growth in godliness, is linked with our willingness to control our tongue. James says that directly: "Everyone should be quick to listen, slow to speak and slow to become angry" (Jas 1:19); "with the tongue we praise our Lord and Father, and with it we curse human beings, who have been made in God's likeness. . . . My brothers and sisters, this should not be" (3:9–10). The admonition against grumbling has personal and community ramifications; Paul's call to unity and his injunction against grumbling are two sides of the same coin. Just as fire destroys everything in

---

13. See John 3:13–15.

its path, so too gossip gobbles up reputations and friendships, leaving a path of charred ruin and destruction (see Jas 3:5–6).

Wilderness living is hard. It stretches you, and it calls for faith. As Fowl notes, "life in the desert calls for a particular sort of practical wisdom."[14] The demands of the nomadic life were far different from those required of Israel during its slavery in Egypt. The psalmist urges the people to faithfulness, to learn from their past disobedience in the wilderness (Ps 95:6–11). The author of Hebrews draws on this psalm in exhorting believers to strengthen their faith and turn away from sin (Heb 3:7–19). Those who fell in the desert had rebelled against God, Hebrews notes, but we have a high priest, Jesus, who empathizes with us and who will extend mercy and grace for our journey of obedience (4:14–16). Could not the same implication be hinted at here for the Philippians, namely, that their Christian stance requires a different wisdom, a distinct mind-set from that which informed their lives as pagans?

Even more, is Paul suggesting that believers reckon themselves to be on a journey? Most likely. Earlier in this chapter, the Christ hymn ended with the triumphal promise that all the world will proclaim Jesus is Lord. In the next chapter, Paul stresses his pursuit of the heavenly calling (3:14) and reminds the Philippians that they are waiting for the Savior from heaven (3:20–21). Both these passages suggest that the current situation is not the final one. For the Philippian believers, many of whom struggled to fill their bellies, clothe their bodies, fight off illnesses—such news was welcome. The danger today is for affluent churches and believers to settle for their (short term) comforts, even as Israel longed to return to the security of Egypt. It is tempting to park permanently at a rest stop on God's highway. We are not interested in a journey, for we are comfortable with life as it is.

Blameless and Pure Walk (2:15)

The call to be "blameless" draws on the Old Testament instructions in choosing a spotless sacrificial animal, but it was also used to describe faithful and sincere Israelites. The psalmist writes, "LORD, who may dwell in your sacred tent? Who may live on your holy mountain? The one whose walk is blameless, who does what is righteous, and who speaks the truth from their hearts" (Ps 15:1–2). Paul makes similar comments to the Colossians, to whom he stresses that their reconciliation with God is "to present you holy in his sight, without blemish and free from accusation" (Col 1:21–22). Paul does not promote a "holier than thou" attitude, as though believers have achieved something on their own. Indeed, Paul hopes this blameless walk will attract others to God and stand as a witness against the evil that hurts so many people.

---

14. Fowl, *Philippians*, 126.

Purity is not a weapon to beat down others or to build up individual pride. Purity stands against sin that destroys lives, often the lives of the weakest among us, such as the poor, the widow, and the orphan. An African proverb says it well: "When elephants fight, the grass gets trampled." "Blameless and pure" believers, however, shine their godly light on the "elephants," who grab power and wealth, and send a beacon of hope to the "grass," those trampled down by life and needing God's powerful mercy and gentle love. If we think of purity as primarily a matter of our private life, we rationalize impurity as something that hurts only us. Yet as the epidemic of pornography has shown, such rationalization is far from the truth. The porn industry exploits, objectifies, and humiliates those caught in its web. Thus when someone uses porn, they "trample" on others.

Warped and Crooked Generation (2:15)

The phrase "warped and crooked generation" is found in Deuteronomy 32:5, 20, as Moses chastised Israel for its faithlessness. But Paul uses the phrase here to refer, not to Israel, but to the culture around the church in Philippi. Some have suggested that Paul intends to highlight believers over against Judaism, to declare that the church has superseded Judaism or replaced the Jews as God's chosen people.[15] This position is then tied to Philippians 3:2,[16] wherein Paul warns the Philippian believers to watch out for those who teach that following the Jewish law (including circumcision) is incumbent on all Christians. This theory, however, places too much weight on the phrase "warped and crooked generation."

Paul's primary emphasis is that believers grow in Christlikeness before a watching world — Jew and pagan alike. Jesus uses the phrase himself when answering a man whose son had not been healed by the disciples: "You unbelieving and perverse generation ... how much longer shall I stay with you? How long shall I put up with you?" (Matt 17:17). Jesus healed the boy, and the disciples later asked him why they were unable to do so. Jesus answered that they lacked the faith: "Truly I tell you, if you have faith as small as a mustard seed, you can say to this mountain, 'Move from here to there,' and it will move. Nothing will be impossible for you" (17:20). Some have suggested that Jesus' reference to the mountain was an oblique reference to the Temple Mount and the sacrificial system and law, which Jesus fulfilled in his death and resurrection. If so, Paul may be thinking of not only his fellow Jews (as did Jesus), but also the Gentile listeners, both of whom failed to see God's work.

---

15. See O'Brien, *Philippians*, 294, 358.

16. Gerald F. Hawthorne, *Philippians* (WBC; Waco, TX: Word, 1983), 102: "the church now has the privilege of replacing Israel as God's children."

Shine Like Stars in the Sky (2:15)

Paul declares that believers "shine ... like stars/lights," a phrase found in Daniel 12:3. In the latter passage, Daniel promises the righteous that they *will* shine, a promise awaiting its fulfillment. Paul uses the present tense, indicating that the Philippian believer enjoys that reality now, at least in part. The term translated "stars" (*phōstēr*) can include any heavenly luminary, such as the moon (see Gen 1:14, 16; Sir 43:7). Paul's specific use of the word found in Daniel reinforces the interpretation that he is thinking of this Scripture (Rev 21:11 is the only other use of this term in the New Testament). Paul excites the imagination of his Philippian readers as he describes the grand entrance of Jesus the Savior (Phil 3:20). In that great moment of victory, believers realize their longed-for hope of a transformed, new body, capable of living in the new heavens and new earth. The thread of eschatological hope, the victory of God over evil, energizes Paul's understanding of the church and informs his present hope in the midst of suffering.

Hold Firmly to the Word of Life (2:16)

With verse 16 Paul turns again to the Philippians' situation. In 2:12, he praised them for their pattern of obedience; now he remarks that their steadfastness will have the added benefit of providing a boast for him on "the day of Christ." This verse is linked grammatically to the preceding verse because the participle "hold firmly" refers back to the previous phrase, "so that you may become blameless." The Philippians' blameless and pure behavior is expressed not only as shining like stars in their pagan universe, but also as clinging to the Word of life.

The verb can be translated as "hold firmly" or "hold out." Either meaning would fit Paul's understanding of the gospel task: believers are to *hold fast* to their convictions, and to *hold out* those convictions (i.e., the gospel) to those around them. Fee argues for the latter meaning, in part because the phrase "word of life" suggests an evangelistic posture.[17] However, the scales tip toward "hold fast to their convictions" because Paul repeatedly encourages the church to remain steadfast (see 1:27; 4:1), even as he praises their faithfulness to his ministry and the gospel (cf. 1:7; 4:10–18, where Paul highlights their sharing in his ministry).

The nuance "hold firm" also fits with the intertextual echo with Daniel 12:3 (LXX), where the righteous ones are called to hold fast to the words of Daniel. The believers are enjoined to hold fast "the word of life," a phrase

---

17. Fee, *Philippians*, 247.

found only here in Paul, though similar phrases occur elsewhere in the New Testament (see, e.g., 1 John 1:1).

Boasting: A Social Convention in Paul's Day (2:16)

If the first half of the verse offers only minor questions about its meaning, the second half, with its reference to Paul's boasting, raises concerns for the modern reader. Specifically, Paul sounds arrogant, manipulative, or at least self-serving. It is unlikely that the Philippians would have viewed his message that way, however, because the lens through which they saw his claim was that of the honor/shame code.[18] Osiek notes that Paul is pulling out the rhetorical stops here, using common persuasive techniques to influence his readers.[19] The key to understanding the argument is appreciating the convention of "boasting" and understanding the importance of Paul's allusions to the grumblings of Israel in the wilderness.

First, the social convention of boasting.[20] Leading philosophers and rhetoricians of the day have much to say about boasting.[21] Self-boasting was as obnoxious then as it is now; however, it was allowed if one sought to defend oneself against accusations. Self-praise with the goal of encouraging the audience to better, nobler deeds was also deemed acceptable. It was also understood that one should pepper one's self-praise with some stories of misfortune, so that one does not incite envy in the listeners.

Paul uses these social conventions to his advantage, but he fills the rhetoric with new, gospel-truth content: all boasting must be done to and in the Lord. Such a move—taking pride in one's weakness, or in one's lowly status—was incomprehensible to the Greco-Roman system.[22] But for Paul, it is the essence of the gospel. Paul tells the Corinthians, for example, that he boasts about his weaknesses, because then it is clear that it is Christ's power that brings good (2 Cor 11:30; 12:9). This fits neatly with his earlier statements to this church that God chose the lowly and despised and thus turned on its head the "wisdom of the world." Paul declares God did so "so that no one might boast before [God]" (1 Cor 1:29). He concludes with a quotation from Jeremiah, "Let the one who boasts boast in the Lord" (1 Cor 1:31; see Jer 9:23). Paul promotes the same motif of humility in the face of God's grandeur in his

---

18. See introduction for a discussion (pp. 29–30).

19. Osiek, *Philippians, Philemon,* 72.

20. Paul uses the noun *kauchēma,* which means "boast, object of boasting, pride." The verb *kauchaomai* means "to boast or glory in or about something or someone."

21. Plutarch, *Mor* 539e–f; Quintilian, *Institutes* 11.1.15–28.

22. Duane F. Watson, "Paul and Boasting," in *Paul in the Greco-Roman World: A Handbook* (ed. J. Paul Sampley; Harrisburg, PA: Trinity Press International, 2003), 86.

communication with the Philippians, who, with all believers, "boast in Christ Jesus, and who put no confidence in the flesh" (Phil 3:3).

We should note that Paul's boasting here will happen "on the day of Christ," a phrase found only in this letter (see also 1:10). More typically Paul speaks of "the day of the Lord," as in 2 Corinthians 1:14: "you can boast of us as we will boast of you on the day of the Lord Jesus"; Paul had just written that he had always been sincere and transparent (1:12). Ethical behavior is a key theme in Philippians 1:10 as well, as Paul speaks of believers being "pure and blameless for the day of Christ." While the Greek words do not match between the two letters, the meanings are similar. Paul's phrase "day of Christ" pushes the Philippian community to make connections between their ethical decisions now and the coming return of Christ.

Laboring or Running in Vain (2:16)

Paul's statement that he does not want to have run his ministry race in vain is related to the Philippians living blameless and pure lives until the day of Christ. On the one hand, Paul speaks hypothetically here, inasmuch as he is confident that "he who began a good work in you will carry it on to completion" (1:6). God will achieve his goals. On the other hand, Paul's understanding of his ministry's effectiveness is related to the Philippians' steadfast faith and witness. Note again his use of a traveling image (running) on the way to our final destination (cf. Paul's use of running also in 1 Cor 9:24, 26; Gal 5:7). If we lose sight of the eschatological dimension of Paul's thought, we might find his "interference" with the church overbearing. But when we realize that both he and the Philippians are on a journey and must rely on each other to succeed, 2:16 makes sense.

We can focus so much on Paul's boasting that we fail to appreciate fully his description of his ministry as running and working so hard as to result in weariness of the flesh. The verb "labor" implies heavy work. Today we might say "bone tired" to describe such weariness from great exertion. Paul uses this same verb to describe local leaders in several churches (see Rom 16:6, 12; 1 Cor 16:16; 1 Thess 5:12).

This verse presents a strong challenge to our Western individualism, especially in our understanding of the church. "Am I my brother's keeper?" (Gen 4:9). It seems that since the beginning of time, humans have sought to answer that question in the negative. Paul's comments in 2:16 make clear that he is his brother's (and sister's) keeper. Fowl laments, "for most American Christians, it is inconceivable that we might be held accountable before God for the lives of our fellow believers."[23] Yet in the images of boasting in 1:26 and

---

23. Fowl, *Philippians*, 128.

2:16, we find that "Paul and the Philippians are engaged in each other's lives to such a degree that they can bear each other's burdens and rejoice in each other's successes."[24]

The Old Testament Use in the New Testament

Paul presents a picture of God's people to the Philippians that is steeped in Old Testament allusions. He warns against grumbling, calling to mind the numerous times the Israelites grumbled in the wilderness. He spotlights the Philippians' calling to shine like stars, an image drawn from Daniel 12. At the very least, Paul demonstrates the importance of the Old Testament for believers. In Philippians 2:14–18, the Old Testament emphasis highlights God's concern for (1) holy living at the personal and community levels, (2) strong witness to and for the world, and (3) steadfastness until the day of Christ. Paul saw the world through the prism of God's Word. The same rereading, deeper exploration, and reconfigured worldview should be instinctual for believers today in the U.S., where literacy rates and leisure time for reading provide abundant opportunities that the Philippians could not have imagined.

One might ask whether the Philippians, most of whom are Gentile, would have connected the dots between Paul's statements and the Old Testament. A solid historical case can be made that both the Jewish community in Philippi and the Gentile God-fearers, such as Lydia, were few in number. That means that some at least in the church would be unfamiliar with the full story of God's people in Scripture. True enough, but Paul sees their potential lack of knowledge as an opportunity to inform them. As the Philippians read and reread, and listened again and again to this letter, more and more of the gospel story would become clearer.[25] On the fourth or fifth reading, perhaps with Epaphroditus's commentary or Timothy's additional teaching, one can easily imagine the community being brought up to speed, so to speak. We can assume that these letters prompted believers to reexamine the Scriptures, as the apostles encouraged people to do (Acts 2:17–35; 7:2–50; 8:32–35; 13:16–41).

Rejoicing in Your Offering of Faith (2:17–18)

Paul's final sentence in 2:14–18 features one of his key terms in Philippians: rejoice! Moreover, he continues his Old Testament allusions, this time drawing on images of sacrifice. Paul focuses on the Levitical priesthood (Exod 29:38–42; Num 28:1–8), thinking of sacrifice at the Jerusalem temple (or the earlier tabernacle). Gentile believers in Philippi would have participated

---

24. Ibid.
25. Ibid., 125.

in animal sacrifice and drink offerings of wine in their previous pagan rituals. But with Paul's strong statements against idolatry (1 Cor 10:14–22; 2 Cor 6:14–17), it is hardly likely that he encourages his congregation to reflect on their past pagan practices.

The Gentile believers in Philippi undoubtedly knew of Jesus' death as a sacrifice for their sins as they celebrated the Lord's Supper, which interpreted the wine as "the new covenant in my [Jesus'] blood" (1 Cor 11:25). Both Paul *and* the Philippians offered gifts to God. Fowl notes the "three-way nature of his [Paul's] relationship with the Philippians" and with God, to whom Paul offers himself as a living sacrifice.[26] The Philippians give a sacrifice and "service." The word "service" (*leitourgia*) is used infrequently by Paul, but it is found in this letter again in 2:30 to describe Epaphroditus's work (see also 2:25), and in 3:3 to distinguish the believers' worship from the circumcision party's worship (see also Rom 15:16).

Paul states that he is as a drink offering (2:17), and their service to the Lord is as a sacrifice and an offering to God. The picture is of complementary acts of worship, a sacrifice and a drink offering poured out—both having in view the praise of God. The language is not common in Paul (Rom 15:27; 2 Cor 9:12), but the images are. Paul speaks of believers being "living sacrifices" (Rom 12:1–2) or Christ as a sacrifice to God on our behalf (Eph 5:2).

Paul is not hinting at his martyrdom here, for a drink offering is not an offering of blood (though in 2 Tim 4:6 he uses the same language to refer to his own death; see also Ignatius, *Romans* 2.2).[27] Nevertheless, the grammar of this passage suggests not that Paul is wondering if he might actually be martyred —rather, "if indeed, as is the case, I am currently being poured out."[28] Even more, Paul is confident he will be released (Phil 1:19–20, 24–26; 2:24). And he speaks of his own suffering as similar to that of the Philippians, but there is no hint that the latter are facing martyrdom (1:30).

More intriguing is the possibility that Paul thinks of his ministry as representing the Servant of Isaiah. Paul may be referring to (1) Isaiah 49:4, which speaks of a fear that the Servant labored in vain; (2) Isaiah 49:6, which emphasizes that he brings light and salvation to the Gentiles, and (3) Isaiah 53:12, wherein the Servant pours himself out unto death.[29] Of course, the salvific aspects of Christ's death are exclusive to him; Paul speaks of the Suffering Servant's obedience in bringing God's message despite personal travail. To the

---

26. Ibid., 129.

27. Ignatius, *Romans* 2.2, "Grant me no more than that you [Roman believers] let my blood be spilled in sacrifice to God, while yet there is an altar ready." The Bishop of Antioch was martyred in Rome in the early part of the second century.

28. Fee, *Philippians*, 253.

29. Bockmuehl, *Philippians*, 159.

Colossians, Paul remarks that he rejoices in his current sufferings "for you, and I fill up in my flesh what is still lacking in regard to Christ's afflictions, for the sake of his body, which is the church" (Col 1:24). Paul does not include his own actions as in any way salvific on another's behalf, unlike Christ's death, which brought life to all (Rom 5:18).

Two major alternatives rise to the surface.[30] On the one hand, Paul could understand his struggles as part of the messianic tribulations in the last days before the day of the Lord (Matt 24:4–8). On the other hand, he may see his union with Christ to include any of Paul's own suffering and current imprisonment on behalf of the gospel as part of Christ's own afflictions (2 Cor 1:5–7). Recall Christ's question to Paul on the Damascus Road, "Saul, Saul, why do you persecute *me*?" (Acts 9:4). In attacking believers, Paul was assaulting Christ. In either case, the *imitatio Christi* calls all believers to embrace the call of God, including any attendant suffering.

Paul's Joy (2:17)

Paul finishes this section of his letter by using the term "rejoice" four times. In 2:17, he uses the verb "rejoice" (translated in the NIV as "I am glad") and "with-rejoice," and in 2:18 he implores the Philippians to "be glad" and to "with-rejoice" with him. I've chosen this awkward rendering in English to show that Paul uses the core verb "rejoice" twice, and then uses the same verb with a prefix meaning "with" or "co-" to stress the point that would have been obvious to any Greek listener. The joy Paul experiences is far deeper than happiness, for the latter is based on circumstances. The joy of the Lord is grounded in the sure sufficiency of Christ's work and the solid hope of our redemption. To rejoice in the midst of suffering, imprisonment, and affliction is to declare boldly that this present age does not have the last word. Christ the Savior will return, transform our bodies into conformity to his glorious body, and be declared Lord.

LIVE the Story

As You Have Always Obeyed Me

During communion one Sunday, a little boy, perhaps four years old, stood beside me at the altar. We had already received the bread and the wine/juice, and after a moment he stage-whispered to his father, "Can I have another?" So much theology packed into that question, whose literal meaning was apparent

---

30. Murray J. Harris, *Colossians and Philemon* (Exegetical Guide to the Greek New Testament 12; Grand Rapids: Eerdmans, 1991), 65–67.

as well. The boy's question made me think: Do I ask for more of Christ? Do I wish for more participation in Christ? Do I long for such intimacy? If I answer "yes" to these questions, another question immediately follows: Am I willing to be transformed as I grow in Christ? Paul paints a picture of sanctification with words that sound a bit old-fashioned today. Blameless, innocent, without blemish—these terms could be construed as elitist, exclusivist, "holier than thou." At times Christians have acted haughtily and self-righteously; indeed, that is a human failing. But the call to holiness, to resist evil and pursue the good, is part of the salvation "package," if you will.

Evangelicals have (unwittingly) shrunk the meaning of salvation to equal only justification or forgiveness of sins. Dietrich Bonhoeffer speaks of "cheap grace" and "costly grace," and that distinction works well as an exegesis of our passage. Bonhoeffer's story is compelling. Born to affluent German parents, the family lost a son two weeks after he enlisted in WWI. That tragedy shaped the younger Bonhoeffer, and he determined to study theology, earning his doctorate at age 21.[31] But it was his year in New York City in 1930, and specifically his worship at the Abyssinian Baptist church, an all-black church in Harlem, that heightened his lifelong interest in church as the communion of saints (*sanctorum communio*); this was to be foundational in his thinking as anti-Semitism rose in his home country.

In 1937, he wrote *Nachfolge*, translated into English as *Discipleship*.[32] In this work he laid out his concern that the Protestant church, specifically his beloved Lutheran church, had substituted the "costly grace" that Luther himself taught for the crowd-pleasing "cheap grace" on which malnourished congregants grew ever weaker. The only way to be obedient to Christ, declared Bonhoeffer, was by living in the world and protesting against the claims of this world.[33] This was Luther's insight, forgotten by his heirs. Luther declared that the *sinner* is forgiven, justified to live an obedient life, but quickly the church began to teach that God forgives or justifies the *sin* and does not require obedience. "The justification of the sinner in the world became the justification of sin and the world. Without discipleship, costly grace would become cheap grace."[34] The turning point, according to Bonhoeffer, was in imagining that self-will was acceptable to God. He explained that for Luther, it was God's

---

31. Dietrich Bonhoeffer, *Sanctorum Communio: A Theological Study of the Sociology of the Church*, in *Dietrich Bonhoeffer Works*, Vol. 1 (English ed.; Minneapolis: Fortress, 1998).

32. Dietrich Bonhoeffer, *Discipleship*, in *Dietrich Bonhoeffer Works*, Vol. 4 (English ed.; Minneapolis: Augsburg Fortress, 2001). Published in 1948 as *The Cost of Discipleship*.

33. Bonhoeffer notes that Luther realized in the monastery that his apparent self-denial was really a form of self-affirmation, "the monk's escape from the world [was] really a subtle love for the world" (*Discipleship*, 48).

34. Ibid., 50.

grace that allowed him to make that final break with his self-love and thus opened the doors to full happy fellowship and obedience.[35]

Unfortunately, the church turned the answer into data points, doctrinal decrees that were added together to achieve an altogether different answer, namely, that grace is available no matter what; thus, nothing matters in terms of my behavior because I've already been forgiven anyway. Rather than grace being the key that unlocks the chains of self-direction, grace becomes the "get out of jail free" card used to excuse any and all behaviors and attitudes. Grace becomes, ironically, the implicit stamp of approval on anything I decide to do. Bonhoeffer concludes: "Only those who in following Christ leave everything they have can stand and say that they are justified solely by grace."[36]

Not only in Bonhoeffer's generation, but also in our own, the temptation of the church is to offer grace at the cheapest cost. He astutely notes that the church in Germany, in seeking for humanitarian reasons to make grace available, ended up draining all grace from the gospel. He writes, "Cheap grace is that grace which we bestow on ourselves."[37] It is grace without the cross, confession of sin, and the call to discipleship. But costly grace is grace because it comes from God, and costly because it cost God the Father his Son, and "nothing can be cheap to us which is costly to God."[38] Paul says it this way: "Christ did not send me to baptize, but to proclaim the gospel — not with wisdom and eloquence, lest the cross of Christ be emptied of its power" (1 Cor 1:17). And what is the gospel? "We preach Christ crucified, a stumbling block to Jews and foolishness to Gentiles, but to those who are called, both Jews and Greeks, Christ the power of God and the wisdom of God" (1:23–24).

So what must we do to obey? Bonhoeffer declares that one learns obedience by obeying. Frustratingly vague, perhaps, but absolutely spot on. Obedience is not a list to accomplish but a relationship to deepen. So pray, using the prayers written in Scripture as a start, and build your conversation with God. And listen; practice listening to the Spirit who whispers while you read Scripture or listen to sacred music or visit with friends. And then be bold. Obedience is not for the faint of heart.

Bonhoeffer points to Peter's experience with Christ and the rough seas as an example. Peter asked Christ to call him to make that first step. Once the call was given, Peter had the choice whether to obey. He stepped out of the boat, an act of obedience that grew his faith. "Faith is only faith in deeds of

---

35. Ibid.
36. Ibid., 51.
37. Ibid., 44.
38. Ibid., 45.

obedience."[39] This was not a "work" on Peter's part; that type of assessment is just the sort of analysis that Bonhoeffer is trying to resist. To obey Christ is to walk in your salvation. It is not to earn your salvation, but to enjoy the possibility that grace now affords. It is in taking the step of obedience that your faith is proved real. "Show me your faith without deeds, and I will show you my faith by my deeds. You believe that there is one God. Good! Even the demons believe that—and shudder" (James 2:18–19).

There is only self-deception in excusing your lack of trust in God and rationalizing your failure to obey. It comes down to this: Can God be trusted to work in you as he said? Is he as strong as he said he is? Is he as good as he said he is? And most important, does he really love you and want your best, as he said? Here is the crux of discipleship. God promises to conform us to the image of the Son (Rom 8:29). Do we really want this?

Without Grumbling or Arguing

Paul's injunction to the Philippians against grumbling is backlit by the story of the Israelites in the wilderness, specifically their grumbling. Time and again Moses pleaded with the people to trust God, and with God to forgive the people. Their grumbling revealed their lack of faith in God's plan, their questioning of God's wisdom in directing them as he did, and their resistance to God's expectations of holiness for them (Exod 15:24; 16:2; 17:2–3). God repeatedly warned the Israelites that their words have consequences.

Leviticus 19:16 puts it bluntly: "Do not go about spreading slander among your people. Do not do anything that endangers your neighbor's life. I am the LORD." Proverbs 16:28 warns that "a perverse person stirs up conflict, and a gossip separates close friends" (see also 26:20). The psalmist laments that his enemies gather mischief in their hearts to tell others: "All my enemies whisper together against me; they imagine the worst for me" (Ps 41:6–7). Paul picks up this thread in his description of human depravity: "They have become filled with every kind of wickedness, evil, greed and depravity. They are full of envy, murder, strife, deceit and malice. They are gossips, slanderers, God-haters, insolent, arrogant and boastful" (Rom 1:29–30).

The damage done when people grumble and spread rumors—when they use their tongue to wound, not heal—is not easily repaired. A popular Hasidic story (attributed to Levi Yitzhak of Berditchev) neatly sums up this truth. A man told nasty lies about the local rabbi throughout the town. After a bit, he was filled with remorse over his deeds and asked the rabbi's forgiveness. He also wanted to make things right. The rabbi told him to get a feather

---

39. Ibid., 64. See Matt 14:22–33.

pillow, cut it open, and scatter the feathers to the wind. This the man did and returned to the rabbi. Then the rabbi said, "Now, go and collect the feathers." The man's heart sank, for the feathers had flown far and wide. So too, the rabbi declared, did his rumors and lies fly, and there is no getting them back. Charles Haddon Spurgeon noted, "If you want the truth to go round the world you must hire an express train to pull it; but if you want a lie to go round the world, it will fly; it is as light as a feather, and a breath will carry it. It is well said in an old proverb, 'a lie will go round the world while truth is putting its boots on.' "[40]

Gossip in the Church

The church too struggles with gossip. Pastor Jim Cymbala addresses the problem head on. About twenty-five years ago, in his public welcome address to new members, he felt prompted by the Holy Spirit to add this charge: "And now, I charge you that if you ever hear another member speak an unkind word of criticism or slander against anyone ... that you stop that person in mid-sentence and say, 'Excuse me—who hurt you? Who ignored you? Who slighted you? Was it Pastor Cymbala? Let's go to his office right now. He'll apologize to you.' ... I'm serious about this, I want to help you resolve this kind of thing immediately. And know this: If you are ever the one doing the loose talking, we'll confront you."[41]

Pastor Cymbala's message has not changed; he stands by his words that gossip and slander are the most dangerous threats to the church today. Why? Because it grieves the Holy Spirit, and a house divided against itself cannot stand (Mark 3:23–27). "Crack cocaine, alcohol, and sexual temptation have slain their thousands, but bickering, quarreling, and criticism in the church have slain their ten thousands."[42] How tempting to tear another down; we feel a bit taller if they are now shorter than we think we are. How subtly delicious to nibble on another's good reputation and eat away at it; we feel our own self nourished. Yet in fact we are ingesting poison. The strength we feel after cutting down another person is vanity's adrenaline; it does not last long, and it leaves in its wake a terrible hollowness.

Instead, to fill up and restore our sense of self-worth, we must look to the one who knows us fully (1 Cor 13:12) and fully loves us (1 John 4:10, 15–16).

---

40. Charles Haddon Spurgeon, *Sermons Delivered in Exeter Hall, Strand, During the Enlargement of New Park Street Chapel, Southmark* (London: Alabaster & Passmore, 1855), 180. See also "Joseph Attacked by the Archers," www.spurgeon.org/sermons/0017.htm.

41. As told by Dave Burkett, www.christianity.com/Home/Christian%20Living%20Features/11542440/. See also *Current Thoughts and Trends* (October 2000).

42. Jim Cymbala, with Dean Merrill, *Fresh Power: Experiencing the Vast Resources of the Spirit of God* (Grand Rapids: Zondervan, 2001), 99.

Alan Redpath, former pastor of Moody Church in Chicago (1953–1962), offers the following THINK test:

> **T** —Is it True?
> **H** —Is it Helpful?
> **I** —Is it Inspiring?
> **N** —Is it Necessary?
> **K** —Is it Kind?

He adds, "If what I'm about to say does not pass those tests, I will keep my mouth shut!"[43]

---

43. Alan Redpath, quoted by Melvin Tinker, http://www.e-n.org.uk/p-770-Proverbs-and-the-power-of-words.htm; see also Father Funston at http://thefunstons.com/?p=3455; see also http://dailychristianquote.com/dcqredpath.html.

CHAPTER 9

Philippians 2:19–30

¹⁹I hope in the Lord Jesus to send Timothy to you soon, that I also may be cheered when I receive news about you. ²⁰I have no one else like him, who will show genuine concern for your welfare. ²¹For everyone looks out for their own interests, not those of Jesus Christ. ²²But you know that Timothy has proved himself, because as a son with his father he has served with me in the work of the gospel. ²³I hope, therefore, to send him as soon as I see how things go with me. ²⁴And I am confident in the Lord that I myself will come soon.

²⁵But I think it is necessary to send back to you Epaphroditus, my brother, co-worker and fellow soldier, who is also your messenger, whom you sent to take care of my needs. ²⁶For he longs for all of you and is distressed because you heard he was ill. ²⁷Indeed he was ill, and almost died. But God had mercy on him, and not on him only but also on me, to spare me sorrow upon sorrow. ²⁸Therefore I am all the more eager to send him, so that when you see him again you may be glad and I may have less anxiety. ²⁹So then, welcome him in the Lord with great joy, and honor people like him, ³⁰because he almost died for the work of Christ. He risked his life to make up for the help you yourselves could not give me.

Listening to the text in the Story: Numbers 25:1–9; 1 Samuel 3:1–14; Jeremiah 31:33–34

When I was little, I loved to see new places, but I disliked the long car rides to get there. It was boring—miles and miles of grass and trees or long stretches of nameless buildings (the days before portable electronics!). Today, more people are able to fly to their destinations. I enjoy seeing the excitement on the children's faces as they explore all the new gadgets on the plane and peek into the cockpit as they move to take their seats. For me, flying can often mean long lines and lackluster meals. For children, it is an adventure!

In Philippians 2:19–30, Paul speaks about the travel plans of Timothy and Epaphroditus. After the excitingly rich teachings we have explored thus far, this section could appear to be the equivalent of waiting in security lines at an airport—boring. I suggest, however, that as we encounter the "who," the "where," and especially the "why," we will find, in the mundane patterns of earthly life, Paul's application of his soaring theological teachings. We will note three significant teachings in these verses: (1) the character traits of these two men, which serve as models for believers today; (2) Paul's approach to ministry "failure"; and (3) most important, Paul's own main focus, namely, "the work of the gospel."[1]

 EXPLAIN the Story

Timothy's Visit (2:19–24)

Paul speaks highly of two believers, both well-known to the Philippians: Epaphroditus and Timothy. The latter is mentioned in several other New Testament works, and in every case he is highly praised by Paul. Indeed, he seems to have been Paul's stand-in when the apostle to the Gentiles was unable to be present himself. We meet Timothy on Paul's second missionary journey, a son and grandson of godly women, but whose father was a Gentile (Acts 16:1–5). He becomes as a son to Paul (2:22), indispensable to Paul's ministry. He is known in Macedonia, Corinth, and Ephesus (Acts 17:14; 18:5; 19:22; 1 Cor 4:17; 16:10; 1 Thess 3:2; 1 Tim 1:2; see also Eusebius, *Church History* 3.4). He coauthored with Paul not only Philippians, but also 2 Corinthians, 1 Thessalonians, and Philemon. Here in Philippians, Paul describes Timothy as one (lit.) "equal in soul" (Phil 2:20), which is further explained as one who shares Paul's devotion to evangelism. It seems that Paul was fond of Timothy personally, and he believed it best "in the Lord Jesus" (2:19) that Timothy serve among them in Paul's absence.

Timothy exhibited the characteristics Paul notes in 2:3–5, namely, looking toward others' interests and focusing on Christ and his gospel. Paul provides a negative example in his rather sharp comments in 2:21 against those who, in contrast to Timothy, look to their own interests. Most likely this verse is a second reference to the believers noted in 1:15–17, who were seeking to damage Paul's reputation and were preaching the gospel with a heart of envy and strife. For Paul, Timothy represents that singular focus so admirable in any follower of Christ—the joyful delight in building up believers, encouraging them into further and deeper devotion to Christ.

Timothy is currently with Paul in Rome, but he will be traveling to Philippi

---

1. Reumann, *Philippians*, 439.

soon. Paul wants Timothy to be able to report on his situation, which should be sorted out in a few months. Interestingly, Timothy is not carrying this letter to the Philippians. This raises the question as to why Paul would think it necessary to send Epaphroditus back quickly rather than have both men remain with him for a few months. This question will be examined below, but the upshot for Timothy is that he will head to Philippi a few months after the Philippians receive Paul's letter, and then after a brief visit, will return to Paul to report on how the letter was received (2:19).

At one level, this is typical of Paul; he tries to keep in contact with all his churches, and he often sends coworkers ahead of him to smooth out any possible misunderstandings before he himself arrives (on Titus, see 2 Cor 7:6–7). But the fact that Paul is doing so with the Philippians raises the possibility that he is at least a bit concerned about the possible reception he might receive. Why this concern? Paul's call to unity, with its attendant challenging of social and rank hierarchy, could be a steep climb for at least some believers. And the issue concerning Euodia and Syntyche, whether a disagreement between these women or a disagreement they shared against Paul, could also have created a flashpoint of contention that concerned Paul as it might jeopardize his warm relationship with the congregation. Paul hopes that his message in the letter will prompt positive changes in the community; thus, he will "be cheered" at this news that Timothy will bring back to him (Phil 2:19).

Epaphroditus's Return (2:25–30)

Epaphroditus, mentioned only in this letter, is less well-known. He was the Philippians' emissary, sent to help Paul in his imprisonment and to deliver a financial gift. The details of his mission are tantalizingly vague, and thus several scenarios about his ministry have been drawn.

Paul describes Epaphroditus in glowing terms: my "brother, co-worker … fellow soldier," "your messenger," one sent "to take care of my needs." "Brother" is a generic term Paul uses to speak of other believers in the Lord. But to add "my" is distinctive and suggests affection and personal commendation. "Co-worker" is also a designation shared by several New Testament figures, including Euodia and Syntyche in 4:2–3.[2] "Fellow soldier" is used to praise Archippus in Philemon 2. Paul uses such military language to describe his ministry as a campaign (2 Cor 10:3–4; see also 1 Cor 9:7).

Paul next describes Epaphroditus as "your *apostolos*," a term that carries the meaning of a messenger. At issue is whether Epaphroditus is commissioned

---

2. For other examples, see Timothy (2 Cor 1:24; 1 Thess 3:2), Apollos (1 Cor 3:9), Titus (2 Cor 8:23), Prisca and Aquila (Rom 16:3), Urbanus (16:9), Philemon (Phlm 2), and Luke, Mark, Aristarchus, and Demas (Phlm 24).

by Christ himself as an apostle to the church, or whether the Philippian church commissioned him as its emissary to Paul. Paul refers to himself as an apostle sent by Christ and uses the label "apostle" to refer to Silvanus/Silas (1 Thess 2:7), Apollos (1 Cor 4:9), Barnabas (1 Cor 9:1, 6), Andronicus and Junia (Rom 16:7), and a group sent to Judea with funds (2 Cor 8:23), plus those "super-apostles" who claim power from the Spirit (2 Cor 11:5; 12:11).

It is difficult to reach a definitive conclusion on Epaphroditus's apostleship, whether it was a commissioning by Christ or by the Philippians. If commissioned by the Philippians, was this commissioning to be lifelong service to Paul? If so, one could say that he did not "make the grade" because Paul sends him back to Philippi.[3] If the commissioning was by Christ, we then have an example of an apostle who ministers primarily in one location, as some believe Timothy and Titus did in their final years (Ephesus and Crete, respectively).

A final descriptive term for Epaphroditus is *leitourgos*, a well-known label from Greek culture meaning "civic official."[4] He was sent by the Philippians "to take care of" Paul's needs. The root word carries a sense of religious ministering, which should not surprise us, as we know the ancient world did not divide church and state as we do today. Ancient civic authorities supervised pagan festivals and offerings as part of their city duties. Moreover, Paul explains in chapter 4 that their partnership and giving is as a fragrant offering and acceptable sacrifice (4:18).

We know that Epaphroditus was ill, either as he journeyed to Rome or once he arrived. He did not die, but we are not told that he recovered full strength. We know he was quite distressed or agitated that the Philippian church learned of his illness. Finally, we know that he was sent by the church not only with financial help for Paul, but also to render service to him. Up to this point, everything makes sense, and there is nothing unusual. But then we read that Paul makes the decision to send him back, and he asks that the Philippians receive him "with great joy." This begs the question — *why* would Paul need to say this?

The puzzle presented by Epaphroditus is not in his coming to Paul, but in his leaving Paul. Did he fail in his mission? Or said more neutrally, did he fail to fulfill the goals the Philippian church set when they commissioned him? At the very least, apparently Epaphroditus returns to Philippi sooner than expected, and thus Paul must explain what led to this change in plans. Reumann suggests that he is "invalided home."[5] If that is the case, why would we think the Philippian church would do anything else than be joyful and

---

3. Osiek, *Philippians, Philemon*, 79.
4. Reumann, *Philippians*, 426.
5. Ibid., 439.

grateful at his return? Paul seems to be saying one thing (honoring Epaphroditus because he risked his life for the church) and doing another (sending him home so that he will not die). If this is all we knew, we might conclude that it was not so much his illness as his ineffectiveness as a minister that lies behind Paul sending him back to Philippi. But Paul sincerely praises his efforts, so we must conclude that Paul thinks Epaphroditus did a good job. Thus it is his general weakness or physical condition that cannot bear up under the demands of the job. Does Paul imagine that Epaphroditus will have a fruitful ministry among the Philippians, implied by his request that the latter honor him (2:29)?

A possible scenario of Epaphroditus's situation could look like this. The Philippian church set apart Epaphroditus to serve alongside Paul long term, and they contributed much financially toward Paul's ministry, including Epaphroditus's participation. But the rigors of this life ultimately prevented Epaphroditus from fulfilling that mission. Paul decides to send him back. Mission accomplished? No. However, was Christ honored? Yes, and that is the point Paul drives home in requesting the Philippians to honor Epaphroditus.

 LIVE the Story

Boldly Minister without Burnout

Does Paul expect every disciple to be A-level, that is, one who faces danger or works himself or herself to exhaustion? O'Brien sees a pattern of discipleship that involves facing death — Jesus, Paul, and Epaphroditus.[6] Some argue that Epaphroditus got sick on the way to Rome, and despite this, finished the journey even though it almost killed him — such was his dedication. However, it seems that Epaphroditus was not destined to be a long-term companion to Paul, even though his church thought as much.

On the one hand, I'm sympathetic to the claims that discipleship requires each person to pick up his or her cross and follow Jesus (Matt 16:24; Luke 9:24). On the other hand, I worry that we create a muscular Christianity or a heroic Christianity if we elevate risk-taking and near-death experiences as the best sign of true or dedicated discipleship. For example, should American missionaries forgo malaria preventative medicines? Should they resist coming back to the United States for cancer surgery? Is a modern-day missionary a failure if he or she ends up unable to remain in the place where God called them to work?

I suggest it takes much courage to be an Epaphroditus today — one who

---

6. O'Brien, *Philippians*, 342–43. Thielman (*Philippians*, 153) rightly points to Paul's compassion in releasing Epaphroditus from caring for Paul's needs.

trusts that God is leading all the time, even though the plan turns out different than expected. Do we give God the flexibility to move us, challenge us in one direction for a time, and then shift us in a different direction? Or do we so value and cling to the label "pastor" or "missionary" that we stop our ears to God's redirections? Paul warns the Corinthians not to judge another person's ministry in terms of its effectiveness (1 Cor 4:3–5), but leave it to the Lord to judge. Epaphroditus offers us an example of this teaching, one that should ring as loudly today as Paul intended in his day.

Incarnational Ministry Model

Jesus is the example par excellence of obedience and self-sacrifice held up to the church, but Paul also uses his experiences, and those of his coworker Timothy and his friend Epaphroditus, as examples of selfless service. In recent years, an attempt to connect the Christ hymn with the modern church's responsibility toward missions has given rise to a movement known as "incarnational ministry." As with any movement, there is a range of views, but essentially this approach to evangelism, pastoral work, and cross-cultural ministry focuses on being *incarnate* to the group to which you are called to minister. By this is meant learning the language and customs of the new group's culture in order to represent the gospel to them.

The Christ hymn becomes paradigmatic for missions in the following way: just as Jesus lived among to the Jewish people and learned Aramaic and their customs, so too missionaries today must live among the people they are called to serve. Alan Hirsch, a proponent of incarnational ministry explains, "The Incarnation not only qualifies God's acts in the world, but must also qualify ours. If God's central way of reaching his world was to incarnate himself in Jesus, then our way of reaching the world should likewise be *incarnational*."[7]

The incarnational approach is right to critique patterns of missionary behavior that sequestered the missionary from the wider culture, sheltering their mission station with greater privileges than those to whom they taught the gospel. It is important that missionaries acculturate themselves into their new surroundings. Again, the approach rightly stresses relationships above programs. Much of the movement's strengths come from its belief that the gospel must touch people where they live. Thus no single culture or language is privileged, for every communication of the gospel is expressed from a culture and in a culture.

But is the best descriptor for this concept "incarnational ministry"? Several

---

7. Alan Hirsch, *The Forgotten Ways: Reactivating the Missional Church* (Grand Rapids: Brazos, 2006), 133, italics original. He adds that incarnational ministry is "also *revelatory*—that they [nonbelievers] may come to know God through Jesus" (ibid.).

problems surface with this terminology. To begin with the theological issues, union with Christ does not make a human divine in the same way Jesus Christ is divine, because even "in Christ" the human remains a creature utterly distinct from his or her Creator. The creeds declare Jesus Christ is one person with two natures, fully divine and fully human. The incarnate Christ is the same subject as the preexistent Son. Humanity has but one nature, even when united with Christ (1 Tim 2:5).

Schnabel suggests that "the use of the term 'incarnational' is not helpful to describe the task of authentic Christian missionary work."[8] He puts forward "inculturation" or "contextualization" as better options. Another recent term that expresses the idea of the church being in and for the world is "missional." Ross Hastings offers a definition: "a theology of the church that is, in a nutshell, *participational*, that its missional identity is an organic consequence of union in and participation with the missional God, who is bidirectional in His missional nature. He *both sends and brings*."[9]

The theological point I'm driving at this: as humans, we cannot repeat the incarnation of Christ, for we are not preexistent and we are not both fully human and fully divine. However, Christ's acts of emptying and serving —these can be imitated and emulated in relinquishing our own rights and serving others. We can emulate the act of foregoing the rights granted us by our position (e.g., apostle) or social standing (e.g., patron), so that we might serve. Paul does as much in 1 Corinthians when he declares that he has not made use of his apostolic rights for financial support (1 Cor 9:15). He releases his claims on his rights so that he might better serve: "Though I am free and belong to no one, I have made myself a slave to everyone, to win as many as possible" (9:19). Paul's attitude of being all things to all people, both Jews and non-Jews, is not claiming a similarity to the unique event of the Word becoming flesh, but is better understood as reflecting the call to obedience and total surrender to God's service (9:19–23).

On a more practical level I also suggest the incarnational ministry approach runs into problems. Is it possible for one person to become fully a member of another's culture? One is what one is, culturally speaking. Every culture has both laudable and shameful qualities, and every person carries with them their culture, their mother tongue, and their instincts and reflexes, which from birth have helped them sort out culture and society. A related question follows: Should the missionary aim to become as closely aligned to

---

8. Eckhard J. Schnabel, *Early Christian Mission*, Volume 2: *Paul and the Early Church* (Downers Grove, IL: InterVarsity Press, 2004), 1574–75.

9. Ross Hastings, *Missional God, Missional Church: Hope for Re-evangelizing the West* (Downers Grove, IL: InterVarsity Press, 2012), 15, italics original.

the new culture as possible? Potentially, this focus could lead to unwelcome entailments.

For example, missionaries do not bring a "pure" gospel, but their own inculturated gospel. That is, a missionary has heard and knows a gospel that is peculiarly related to their own cultural setting. It works like this: (1) the missionary thinks about the gospel and forms an opinion about what it means; then (2) moves into the new culture and attempts to become incarnate in that culture, as well as translate his or her inculturated gospel into the new host culture, and thereby (3) can elevate an ethnocentric definition of the gospel to the status of divine Word.[10]

Ironically, the acquisition of the language or cultural practices may serve as a way for the missionary to retain a sense of control or power over the host culture or people whom they serve. During my three years in rural Kenya, this was brought home to me in one incident that illustrates my point. I was visiting with a few Kenyan women from the surrounding areas when another white missionary came on the porch. She spoke in Kikuyu (the mother tongue of the villages around us), but the women did not understand what she was saying. After several more failed attempts, with exasperation she spoke in Kiswahili, "It's cold this evening!" and all the Kenyan women nodded in understanding and agreement. But the missionary went on her way with a parting comment in Kiswahili, "See, I know." It suddenly hit me—she uses language to maintain control; ironically, learning the language keeps her from the very women she professes to serve.

Additionally, the Christ hymn does not present Jesus, the preexistent one, as having a culture prior to being born of the Virgin Mary. Said another way, the Trinity does not have a culture, for cultures are human constructions. Thus, Jesus did not leave one culture to learn a new one. Jesus Christ never forsook his deity; he never was merely human. He was always the second person of the Trinity, God's Son. The incarnation is a unique event unrepeated in history and unrepeatable because there is only one Son. That is why our redemption is secure in his work alone. Though many men (and a few women) died on crosses down through the centuries, only Jesus' death on the cross was efficacious for humanity's sins and offered forgiveness and eternal life in resurrected, glorified bodies for those who are in Christ.

Union with Christ as Missional Model

Christ's incarnation, death, resurrection, and sending of the Spirit testify that union with him is possible. It is this union that makes a crossing of cultural

---

10. J. Todd Billings, *Union with Christ: Reframing Theology and Ministry for the Church* (Grand Rapids: Baker Academic, 2011), 131.

divides achievable. Said another way, the missionary starts first with union with Christ and then shares the gospel, becoming united to the new believers within the body of Christ (the church). Thus, he or she better understands the new culture. An added benefit of this approach is that both cultures are critiqued by the gospel, as the host culture speaks into the life of the missionary, even as the missionary shares his or her story. Both are spoken under the umbrella of union with Christ; neither culture is inherently privileged.

Union with Christ not only allows for effective cross-cultural ministry, but it also speaks to unity among factions in the same village. A friend of mine was working with Food for the Hungry in Uganda in 2003. As he tells the story, he "sat with a group of about 40 parents and grandparents in a village about 10 kilometers south of the town of Lira in northern Uganda. Our chairs were gathered under a huge tree canopy — and the people represented five different church congregations (Anglican, Baptist, Methodist, Pentecostal and Presbyterian). Twenty yards away was a newly dedicated school building. According to their testimony, the churches had never before cooperated on a project. Yet when presented with the opportunity to improve the futures of their children, they banded together and acted as one. The new school gave testimony to the "success" of their unity in Christ for the better future of their children.[11]

---

11. Ben Homan, President, Langham Partnership USA; formerly President, Food for the Hungry. Email correspondence, March 2012.

CHAPTER 10

Philippians 3:1–14

 LISTEN to the Story

¹Further, my brothers and sisters, rejoice in the Lord! It is no trouble for me to write the same things to you again, and it is a safeguard for you. ²Watch out for those dogs, those evildoers, those mutilators of the flesh. ³For it is we who are the circumcision, we who serve God by his Spirit, who boast in Christ Jesus, and who put no confidence in the flesh — ⁴though I myself have reasons for such confidence.

If someone else thinks they have reasons to put confidence in the flesh, I have more: ⁵circumcised on the eighth day, of the people of Israel, of the tribe of Benjamin, a Hebrew of Hebrews; in regard to the law, a Pharisee; ⁶as for zeal, persecuting the church; as for righteousness based on the law, faultless.

⁷But whatever were gains to me I now consider loss for the sake of Christ. ⁸What is more, I consider everything a loss because of the surpassing worth of knowing Christ Jesus my Lord, for whose sake I have lost all things. I consider them garbage, that I may gain Christ ⁹and be found in him, not having a righteousness of my own that comes from the law, but that which is through faith in Christ — the righteousness that comes from God on the basis of faith. ¹⁰I want to know Christ — yes, to know the power of his resurrection and participation in his sufferings, becoming like him in his death, ¹¹and so, somehow, attaining to the resurrection from the dead.

¹²Not that I have already obtained all this, or have already arrived at my goal, but I press on to take hold of that for which Christ Jesus took hold of me. ¹³Brothers and sisters, I do not consider myself yet to have taken hold of it. But one thing I do: Forgetting what is behind and straining toward what is ahead, ¹⁴I press on toward the goal to win the prize for which God has called me heavenward in Christ Jesus.

Listening to the text in the Story: Numbers 25:1–9; Ezekiel 36:22–36; 1 Maccabees 2:23–26; 2 Maccabees 2:21; 4:13.

In the 1986 movie *The Mission*, a poignant tale about the slave trade along the Paraguay River in the eighteenth century, one of the most powerful scenes involves a former slave trader, Mendoza (Robert DeNiro), climbing a rocky cliff beside a cascading waterfall, with a bulky, heavy load on his back. He finally reaches the top, to find the rest of his party, made up of Jesuit priests, waiting with the indigenous tribesmen they've come to serve. As he stumbles up to the group, one of the tribesman walks over, and without a word, cuts loose the pack, sending it tumbling down the mountain. After his initial shock, DeNiro begins to cry, even to sob—with gratitude. Carrying the pack was his penance for killing his brother in a duel years earlier; its removal symbolized that his sins were forgiven, his burden cast away forever.

Often we imagine Paul in a similar way, trudging alone under the burden of the law, bent double under the weight of his sin. Yet such an image would be inconsistent with his own telling of his story in 3:1 – 11. Paul emphasizes here his journey from his Jewish boyhood home until his call to be an apostle to the Gentiles and his new life in Christ. He offers the story as a corrective to the alternative "gospel" given by his Jewish Christian opponents, who demanded that Gentile believers take up the ethnic markers of Judaism: circumcision, food laws, and Sabbath observance. Paul stands opposed to the proposal that Gentiles must first become Jews to be full citizens in the church. His personal example serves as additional evidence as to the rightness of his gospel, namely, righteousness by faith in the work of Christ alone, open to all people, Jew and Gentile, slave and free, through the gracious gift of God.

In this chapter we will explore several key points: (1) the historical identity of the "mutilator" group; (2) what Paul reveals about himself; and (3) the theological impact of his teaching on (a) the righteousness of God, (b) the works of the law, (c) faith in Christ, and (d) knowing Christ in his suffering and resurrection.

 EXPLAIN the Story

Rejoice (3:1)

As Paul transitions from his discussion about Timothy and Epaphroditus, he again encourages the Philippians to rejoice (3:1). This silver note of joy rings throughout the letter and is a constant refrain amidst the struggles faced by Paul in prison and by his congregation. His next statement, "it is no trouble for me to write the same things to you again, and it is a safeguard for you," is less clear in its reference. Is Paul looking ahead to his discussion about his opponents, or is he looking back to his concluding remarks about Timothy and Epaphroditus? What are these "same things" he is writing? Given the brief description of his opponents in verse 2, Paul has probably already in his earlier visits to the city spoken about those who promote circumcision (and perhaps Sabbath and food laws) for Gentile believers. Yet he indicates here that he *wrote* to them about these things, likely pointing to Philippians 1 and 2.

When this letter was read aloud to the congregation, as it would be on numerous occasions, the verbal reminder to be joyful would reinforce previous injunctions of the same. Listening believers would think back to Paul's claim that he prays with joy for them (1:4), that he rejoices even in his chains (1:18), that he encourages them to make him joyful in their community's unity (2:2), that they should rejoice together (2:17–18), and that he exhorts them to joyfully welcome Epaphroditus (2:29).

But what does Paul mean that his words are "a safeguard" to the Philippians? This term carries the idea of steadfast or safe and is found in the Greek version of Proverbs 3:18 describing the Lord's wisdom. Paul builds on an Old Testament idea that "the joy of the LORD is [one's] strength" (Neh 8:10). The psalmist declares, "The righteous will rejoice in the LORD and take refuge in him" (Ps 64:10), while the Chronicler writes, "Splendor and majesty are before him; strength and joy are in his dwelling place" (1 Chr 16:27).

Unfortunately we have diluted the term "joy" so that it often means "be happy" or "have fun." As we will see in the next few verses, nothing is further from Paul's definition. His joy is one with eschatological content, not fleeting emotion. The Philippian believers have almost no say in the course of their lives: they don't have political power or the option to vote for leaders; they have no government social safety nets, no thriving economy to explore new jobs or educational opportunities to "re-tool" their job skills. They live hand-to-mouth under imperial rule, with famine and war looking over their shoulders. Strength is found in the surety of God's provision, with Christ's resurrection as the assurance for their own life after death. This truth is what safeguards them and brings deep and lasting joy unaffected by their dismal circumstances.

Paul's Opponents: Their Historical Identity

Paul writes one of his strongest rhetorical statements in 3:2, repeating the verb "watch out" three times. He describes the people whom the Philippians should avoid as "dogs," "evildoers," and "mutilators of the flesh." Most likely these dangerous people are believers who hold that Gentiles should become Jewish to participate fully as members of God's people, the church (see Acts 15:1, 5). But as we look at their identity, we cannot do so in isolation from the rest of the letter.

Several pieces of evidence must be considered in forming an opinion, not least of which is the thread of similar vocabulary that runs between sections of the letter. First, we find the unique term *polisteuesthe* ("walk/live in a properly civic way") in 1:27 and the noun *politeuma* in 3:20, describing the believers as citizens of heaven. Second, we have the call by Paul to "stand firm" against opposing forces in 1:27 and 4:1, suggesting by implication a similar threat against which the same counterpunch is required. Third, Paul speaks of the Philippians working together with the unusual term translated as "striving together" (1:27) and "contended" (4:3). Finally, the end of the enemies is destruction (1:28; 3:19). Added together, this suggests that the forces working against the Philippians fall under a single umbrella, namely, those who represent the present age over against believers, who are destined to be transformed on the day of Christ (1:10; 3:21).

Paul makes a similar argument to the Galatian believers, most of whom are Gentile. These churches were bombarded with a counter-message to the gospel that promoted circumcision as the necessary step for Gentiles to be fully members of God's family in Christ. Paul reminds them that they did not formerly know God and thus were slaves to the weak and miserable principles of this world (Gal 4:8 – 11). The reader immediately thinks Paul is referring to pagan idolatry, and in part he is. But a close reading reveals that Paul equates the results of paganism with the circumcision of Gentile believers. That is, in turning to circumcision as a necessary expression of the Gentiles' faith in Christ, these believers were in essence returning to their former pagan days. In both cases, they were falling back to a worldview centered on this "present evil age" (1:4). Paul is not equating Judaism and paganism wholesale; rather, he stresses a single, vital commonality, namely, that either system must be understood as part of this present age. As such, neither is an acceptable alternative to life in Christ, life in the Spirit.

Those promoting circumcision of Gentile believers noted in 3:2 are the "enemies of the cross" noted in 3:18; they may already have some community presence in the city and thus present themselves with the political terminology (*politeuma*). Standing against them puts the Philippians in the crosshairs of the wider community in Philippi, with the resulting economic hardships and vulnerability that follows. The economic element of the church's struggle is important, and Oakes carefully demonstrates how joining a new religious group would likely have negative economic implications.[1] Paul's approach is to focus on why the Philippian believers must resist the pull to move into an established and legally sanctioned social group, Judaism, through circumcision.

---

1. Oakes, *Philippians*, 77 – 102.

What does this mean for our understanding of the letter? First, it means that the imperial cult is not the main challenge alluded to in 1:27–30.[2] Second, it recognizes that tensions would mount between the new believers and their pagan family and friends because of the former's refusal to participate in imperial cult worship and other pagan festivals. The temptation to receive the sanction from leaders of the synagogue (or more accurately, *proseuchē*)[3] would be strong. Third, this interpretation recognizes that a main issue for Paul around the Aegean and in the interior of Asia Minor was the internal struggle with Jewish Christ-believers, who might have had the political cover of the synagogue.

Paul's rhetoric sends a fiery blast against his opponents. In both Jewish and Greek literature, dogs were seen as scavengers, exhibiting behavior unfit for human society. Proverbs 26:11 uses a dog returning to its vomit as an image for the fool who returns to foolish behaviors. Even more in the Jewish context, dogs ate anything; they did not distinguish between clean and unclean. Paul's contention drips with irony — those who would make Gentiles "clean" through circumcision are themselves unclean like dogs. Moreover, they are "evildoers." This phrase is found nowhere else in Paul, but similar language is used in 2 Corinthians 11:13 in describing the "deceitful workers" who were "masquerading as apostles of Christ."

Finally, Paul labels them "mutilators," which in Greek sounds similar to the term "circumcision." Circumcision served as the identity marker for Jewish men throughout the Roman empire; it signaled their status as members of God's family. Paul argues with his play on words that Gentiles can be full members of God's people if they are in Christ. He is not contrasting Christianity and Judaism here; rather, he is arguing with other believers about the proper way Gentiles are to live out their faith in Christ. To the opponents, a proper lifestyle for them includes the ethnic Jewish marker of circumcision. They maintain that the Messiah would want Gentile believers to be pure and clean, to be circumcised, and thus to eat kosher food and rest on the Sabbath. Paul made his case against such understanding in almost all of his churches (Gal 2:12; Eph 2:11; Col 4:11; Titus 1:10). He is not arguing against opponents who say that Gentiles must earn their salvation; he is combating the view that holy, righteous living can happen outside of faith in Christ. The law is not the vehicle for knowing Christ; faith is. The Torah will not empower a person for holy living; the resurrection power is the only force capable of that.

---

2. See Introduction for discussion of the imperial cult.
3. See p. 16 for a discussion of synagogue and *proseuchē*.

Paul's Opponents and the Use of Strong Rhetoric Today

Paul's use of strong rhetoric raises the question as to when it is appropriate to label one's opponents with such forceful language. How do we know when the stakes are high enough to warrant the use of such language? Such questions are especially important in the age of the Internet and social media, when a tweet can circle the globe in less time than it takes me to write this sentence. If we examine Jesus' preaching, it shows that he did not attack individuals by name, with the exception of Herod Antipas, whose rule Jesus condemns (Luke 13:32). Otherwise, Jesus speaks broadly about the abuse of power, the failure to teach correctly, and the lack of concern for others demonstrated by the Jewish leadership of his day. He speaks with broad-brush strokes, addressing issues and the resulting character flaws that accompany such behavior ("hypocrites" is a common charge, see Matt 23:13 – 32). Jesus speaks directly and pointedly to the disciples when they fail to see his purposes.

What Jesus refused to do was defend his person against attack. So too Paul, as he notes in Philippians 1:15 – 17, refuses to take on enemies that seek personal advantage over him. He pays no attention to the attack on his personal honor. A lesson for us today might be to stick close to the topic of debate and resist venturing into personal comments or presumption of motives. Fiery language should be reserved for the short list of ideas that speak directly against the heart of the gospel — in Paul's case, those who would necessitate that Gentiles become circumcised as a second requirement of salvation.

A second lesson is about praying for our enemies and blessing those who persecute us. Paul laments his enemies' choices "with tears" (3:18); he does not gloat over their ultimate demise. In this he follows his Lord's example, who, when he entered Jerusalem on what we now call Palm Sunday, wept over the city: "If you, even you, had only known on this day the things that make for peace" (Luke 19:42).

The Religious Identity of the Followers of Christ (3:3)

Paul claims the title "the circumcision" as descriptive of all the people of God in Christ — a bold rhetorical thrust. He does not take on Judaism here; rather, he speaks to those who imagine the Messiah community as one that continues certain Torah practices. Luke tells us about such a group: "Certain people came down from Judea to Antioch and were teaching the believers: 'Unless you are circumcised, according to the custom taught by Moses, you cannot be saved' " (Acts 15:1). When Paul and Barnabas reached Jerusalem to talk with the apostles and elders, "some of the believers who belonged to the party of the Pharisees stood up and said, 'The Gentiles must be circumcised and required to keep the law of Moses' " (15:5). The Jerusalem Council debated the issue and concluded that Gentiles did not need to be circumcised to be full members of God's people.[4] This decision allowed Jewish believers to continue their practices without mandating such on Gentile believers. The significance of the pronouncement was not in restricting Jewish practices for Jews, but in allowing Gentile believers the freedom not to practice circumcision and other Jewish laws.[5]

Paul translates the council's decision for the immediate situation faced in Philippi. He reminds the Philippians that they "serve God by his Spirit," trusting in Christ's new life granted to each believer. Paul contrasts the old way, that of relying on one's Jewish heritage (flesh) to live a holy life, and the new way forged by Christ. He does not ask Jewish believers to work on the Sabbath or to eat a pork sandwich (see Rom 14:2–18). What he asks is that no one demand that one group change to become like another group, that no group establish their ethnic practices as a standard of holiness. Importantly, the early church differentiated practices that distinguished clean and unclean regulations from moral issues such as sexual immorality and idolatry. In the latter category, there was no debate—sexual immorality and idolatry were unacceptable practices for God's people.

Paul's Life before Being Called by Christ (3:4–6)

Paul identifies seven characteristics about himself as he contrasts the position of "the mutilators" with his own qualifications to present the gospel:

- circumcised on the eighth day
- of the people of Israel
- of the tribe of Benjamin
- a Hebrew
- a Pharisee
- a zealous persecutor of the church
- a blameless doer of the law

The first three are accidents of birth, while the last four mark out Paul's choices in expressing his birthright. Paul's claim to be a "Hebrew of Hebrews" is a way of saying: I'm strongly committed to my Jewish heritage (see 2 Cor 11:22). Paul may also be referring his knowledge of Aramaic and (probably)

---

4. The council did add that Gentile believers should "abstain from food polluted by idols, from sexual immorality, from the meat of strangled animals and from blood" (15:20; 21:25). Several interpretations of this passage have been offered, including (1) that the council draws on Leviticus 17 and 18 for these codes, (2) that they are speaking against pagan practices related to idolatry, and (3) they are ad hoc conclusions addressing the specific tensions in Antioch, Syria, and Cilicia (15:23).

5. In Acts 21:20–26, Paul fulfills a vow in the temple, demonstrating his own obedience to the law. Paul sought to give believers freedom to decide on these practices (see Rom 14:1–15:9).

Hebrew with this remark. Paul would have learned Greek, whether he spent most of his early years in Tarsus or in Jerusalem, for he quotes from the Greek Old Testament throughout his letters. Less clear is whether he could write in all three languages. At this time, writing was a special craft, primarily the domain of scribes. Paul used a scribe or secretary (amanuensis) in writing his letters (Rom. 16:22).

Paul indicates that he had "zeal," evidenced by his persecution of the church. This term carried strong overtones of support of God's law. Drawing on Paul's autobiographical sketch in Galatians 1:13 – 15, we find that he uses the term "Judaism" to describe his religious orientation. This term suggests he saw himself in opposition to the Greek thought and lifestyle that swept through Galilee and Judea during the triumph of Alexander the Great and continued to swell over the next 400 years. In 167 BC, zealous Jews revolted against their Syrian Hellenistic overlords who outlawed circumcision, forbade rest on the Sabbath, and insisted that Jews show loyalty to their pagan leaders by taking a bit of pork as a sign of fealty. Second Maccabees tells the story of uprising and describes Judea's national religion as "Judaism," the patriotic expression of their national identity (2 Macc 2:21; 8:1; 14:38) and the opposite of Hellenism (4:13; see also 1 Macc 2:23 – 26). Paul's zeal manifested itself in the mob violence against Stephen (Acts 7:54 – 58).

Paul also declares himself "faultless" when judged by the Jewish law. It is important that we hear what Paul did *not* say: he did not claim to be sinless or perfect. Instead, he only indicates that given the guidelines set out by the Pharisaic interpretation of the Torah, he followed those to the letter. As an analogy, I might say I am blameless in my driving if I follow all the traffic and speed laws. That would not make me a perfect driver, just a blameless one.

The Religious Identity of Paul in Christ (3:7 – 14)

These verses are arguably some of the most theologically rich in all of the New Testament. In dramatic fashion based on his personal commitment and apostolic authority, Paul sets out the pattern and goal of every believer's life. He responds to the charge he gave the Philippians in 2:12, "work out your salvation with fear and trembling." He encouraged them to be "blameless" (2:15) — and now he distinguishes blamelessness in Christ from a blamelessness based on Torah observance. Paul is not here describing *how* someone gets saved, nor is he contrasting Judaism as a works-based religion with Christianity as a faith-based religion. Paul explains, in vivid colors and enticing detail, the journey of the believer from their valley of sufferings to the heights of glory in the resurrection. Paul admits in 3:12 that he has not attained such knowledge of Christ yet, but he is eager to drink deeply of the well of living water.

Not only does Paul paint a vision of breathtaking devotion to know Christ, but he also draws a compelling portrait of Christ, who is referred to almost as frequently as Paul in this section. Christ is knowable—something that pagans could not declare with confidence about their deities. Christ opens himself to a relationship with believers through his faithfulness and our response of faith. Christ invites believers to enter with him into his death, a gift that assures resurrection life (Rom 6:4–5) and life abundantly now in the Spirit (Gal 2:20; 3:1–2). Christ demonstrated power over death by his resurrection. Christ shares his sufferings with us as well, that we "may share in his glory" (Rom 8:17). Read alongside the Christ hymn of 2:6–11, this provides a stunning picture of the Son of God becoming incarnate, and serving, suffering, dying, rising, and reigning—and Paul wants to *know* this one. Amazingly, Christ gives an open invitation for all to know him—the great and the lowly, the rich and the poor, the Jew and the Greek. Those who embrace the invitation are changed forever, as Paul goes on to describe.

Gains and Losses (3:7–8)

Paul uses the language of business and accounting when speaking of "gain" and "loss." The business connotation is important because in business, a gain is often context specific. "The value of assets is always assessed in the light of business objectives."[6] Thus what was once important or of supreme value to Paul, such as his Pharisee lifestyle, his zeal, his Jewish heritage, is reevaluated and reassessed based on different criteria and goals. If one wants to know Christ, the common currency of Jewish ancestry and practice is of no value. Indeed, holding onto all such things is detrimental to achieving the new goal of knowing Christ. Why is that the case, given that God established the Torah and commanded the Jewish people to obey it?

The answer is found in the resurrection of Christ, whose new life believers share and whose resurrected life believers long to realize. The resurrection condemned this present age as at best limited, and at worst evil. Thus Paul could say earlier to the Philippians, "For to me to live is Christ and to die is gain" (1:21). Ethnic claims, education assets, economic, social, political advantages—all are judged as virtues based on earthly standards. But when placed beside Christ, the one who reigns over death, all advantages pale. In fact, advantages become toxic, germ-carrying, rotten trash when they are not properly valued in light of Christ. Sabbath, circumcision, food laws, Jewish ancestry, commitment to Pharisaism—all use worldly currency. They are of secondary importance, and if they remain secondary, they hold no danger to

---

6. Bockmuehl, *Philippians*, 204.

a believer's health. But if they take center stage, if they become the basis on which believers build their relationship with God, the believers will end up with a pile of garbage.

Knowing Christ Is Gain (3:8–11)

Paul's lengthy sentence here carries a central theme — knowing Christ. In 3:8, he contrasts knowing Christ and the worthlessness of all other things. Knowing Christ includes gaining Christ and being found in him (3:9). These two verbs point forward to the final resurrection. They make a lie out of today's assumption that being a Christian is all about holding a "get out of jail free" card, and not thinking too much about God until you stand before the pearly gates with your card in hand. Paul is not talking here about hedging your bets when you die; he is speaking to the fullness of our salvation in Christ, which includes a lifelong deepening relationship. And just so that the Philippians hear him clearly, Paul reiterates his desire to know him (Christ) in 3:10.

Jeremiah prophesied that when God restored the exiles, he would "make a new covenant with the people of Israel and the people of Judah.... No longer will they teach their neighbors, or say to one another, 'Know the LORD,' because they will all know me, from the least of them to the greatest" (Jer 31:31, 34). Paul recognizes the fulfillment of this hope in Christ, that every believer will *know* him directly, not through an intermediary teacher or neighbor. In 3:10 Paul uses the same verb "to know" (*ginōskō*) as in 1 Samuel 3:1–14, the story in which Samuel first hears God's voice. Initially, the lad believes Eli is calling to him, but eventually Eli realizes that Samuel is hearing God's voice. The narrator tells us that Samuel was confused because he "did not yet know the LORD: The word of the LORD had not yet been revealed to him."

Paul is like Samuel. On his fateful journey to Damascus, when a bright light blinded him and a voice rang out from heaven, Paul did not recognize the Lord's voice (Acts 9:3–6). But since that moment, when Christ took hold of him, Paul sought to say, with Samuel, "Speak, LORD, for your servant is listening" (1 Sam 3:9). The message Paul relays here is profoundly pertinent to the Philippians: no earthly love, worldly passion, time-bound desire, or acquired privilege can begin to compare to the ongoing relationship that is ours in Christ to enjoy.

Through Faith (3:9)

Paul explains further what being found in Christ means with a brief statement in which he distinguishes a righteousness based on the law and a righteousness that comes from God. I will speak in depth about the contested meaning of righteousness below. Here I want to focus on the possible meanings of the two phrases "through faith in Christ" and "on the basis of faith" (3:9). "Through faith in Christ" can also be translated "through the faithfulness of Christ"; the ambiguity centers on whether Christ is the subject or the object of the noun "faith" (*pistis*). Of course, both meanings are true theologically; the question is what Paul accents here.

To answer this, we need to turn to the second occurrence of "faith": "by/on the basis of faith." This phrase can be linked with the preceding discussion about righteousness, or it can introduce Paul's declaration in the next verse that he wants to know Christ. If the former, then Paul is either (1) reiterating the believer's response of faith by stating it twice, or, (2) more likely speaking first of Christ's faithfulness and then a believer's response of faith. If the latter option is chosen, Paul is stressing that he knows Christ by faith, and he declares that the power of the resurrection and participation in the sufferings are likewise lived out by faith. Any of the above options is theologically correct, and the exegete's choice is based on establishing the overall message Paul conveys here. Perhaps we do not need to make a hard distinction among these options, for Paul may be deliberately ambiguous, reinforcing that all life in God—the knowing, the doing, the gaining, the suffering—all is through faith.

Knowing Christ Is Resurrection Power and Suffering (3:10–14)

Paul circles back to his central theme of this passage in the opening words of 3:10—knowing Christ. Paul established that his knowing Christ included gaining and being found in him, which reinforced his contention that a life lived outside of Christ is no better than garbage when stacked alongside Christ's greatness. But knowing Christ is not just about avoiding what is worthless; it is also about embracing what is glorious. In 3:10–11 Paul highlights the paradox of knowing Christ, the power that overcomes death, and the suffering that submits unto death.

At first glance it seems backward for Paul to put resurrection before suffering, but he uses a chiastic construction that connects 3:10 and 3:11. Thus he stresses the power of Christ's resurrection (A) and his own hope to attain such resurrection (A^1), and sandwiched between these statements, his desire for "participation in sufferings" (B) is elaborated upon with "becoming like him in his death" (B^1). Paul connects grammatically the terms "power" and "participation," suggesting that resurrection power and suffering are two sides of the same Christ coin. These three key terms—power, participation, and suffering—deserve closer attention.

Power. The term "power" (*dynamis*) is important in Paul. He speaks of the gospel as the "power of God" (Rom 1:16; 1 Cor 1:18), of Christ being both the power of God (1 Cor 1:24) and the Son of God with power (Rom 1:4), and of the kingdom of God revealing God's power (1 Cor 4:20). Paul also speaks of the power of the Holy Spirit (Rom 15:13, 19; Eph 3:16–20; 2 Tim 1:7), and several times God's power is expressed in raising the dead (1 Cor 6:14; 15:43; 2 Cor 13:4; Eph 1:19).

All this emphasis on power might suggest that Paul taught a triumphal message, but nothing is further from the truth. Although Paul declares that he demonstrated the power of signs and wonders to the Corinthians (2 Cor 12:12), he stresses that God's power is made perfect in weakness (12:9). He will state as much to the Philippians in 4:13, that it is the Lord who strengthens or empowers him. Indeed, Jesus Christ in his ministry did many "acts of power," which we translate as "miracles." Revelation pulls back the curtain for us to see the celebrations in heaven: "Now have come the salvation and the power and the kingdom of our God, and the authority of his Messiah" (Rev 12:10); and the roaring of the great multitude, "Hallelujah! Salvation and glory and power belong to our God" (19:1). Paul echoes this exaltation of God's power by desiring to know it more deeply.

Participation in Christ's sufferings. Suffering is lived out through participation in Christ. Paul uses the term *koinōnia* to describe participation in sufferings, which likely shocked the Philippians. Usually the term *koinōnia* indicated human relationships within the church, as when he spoke of their "partnership" in community (1:5; see also Acts 2:42; Gal 2:9). He also uses the term when defining the Corinthians' participation in Christ's death when they drink the cup of blessing and eat the bread (1 Cor 10:16). Believers experience in a tangible way a fellowship in Christ's death by taking communion and by refusing to accept any substitute festival that paganism offered them. Paul speaks of becoming like Christ in his death, using a term that combines the prefix "with" and the root "form" (*morphē*) (Phil 3:10). That is, we take Christ's form as we fellowship in his sufferings. Paul used a similar term to describe Christ as in the form of God and taking the form of a slave in 2:6–7, and he will speak about the transformation of our bodies with using another cognate in 3:21. For Paul, then, fellowship in suffering involves changing our very nature in conforming to Christ.

Paul's suffering and believers' sufferings. What does Paul include in his term "suffering" (*pathēma*)? Most likely it is those hardships experienced by believers as a direct result of their testimony for Christ. This suffering will be like Christ's at his death. As a Roman citizen, Paul would not face execution by crucifixion, but he probably has in mind the humility with which Christ faced his accusers, the forgiveness he extended to those who beat him, and the gentleness with which he extended love to his mother and the grieving women along the road to Golgatha. We become like Jesus in his death when we turn the other cheek, walk the extra mile, and bravely trust that God will vindicate his work in us so we need not justify ourselves to others.

In other parts of the world and in other contexts, sometimes becoming like Christ in his death does mean martyrdom. In the early 1990s a young Cambodian woman whose family had survived the Pol Pot genocide came to believe in Christ and attend a Christian college. Her family viewed her public stand for Christ as a complete rejection of their Buddhist culture and disowned her. They mailed her their only family photo, symbolic of their removal of any trace of her existence in their family. She was a living martyr, dead to her family but alive to God. Such stories can be multiplied around the world and throughout generations.

Few in the United States have such dramatic stories of suffering for Christ, and we might be tempted to exaggerate our own discomforts to compensate for feeling guilty that we are blessed. Perhaps a better option would be to actively reach out to suffering Christian minorities around the globe. Join hands with them in their suffering, as Paul instructs the Galatians: "Carry each other's burdens, and in this way you will fulfill the law of Christ" (Gal 6:2).

Paul's deep desire to know Christ, the power of resurrection, and participation in suffering runs like electricity through 3:12–14 as he elaborates on his passionate focus. While the general tone and direction of these verses are not in dispute, different interpretations arise over whether Paul is speaking with reference to Judaism, Christianity, or Jewish Christians. Additionally, questions revolve around the meaning of the verb "to perfect," what Paul has not attained, and what he is now forgetting.

Paul Presses On (3:12)

This verse has five verbs, including two that are compounds of a third. Paul writes that he has not already "obtained" all this (what is mentioned in 3:8–11), but he presses on to "take hold" of that for which Christ Jesus "took hold" of him. The verb translated "obtained" occurs twice in the compound verb "take hold." By adding a prefix, the compound verb carries an intensification of meaning and also can refer to grasping something with the mind.

The verb "take hold of" should have a direct object connected with it, but Paul does not supply one. This leaves interpreters wondering if Paul intended the reader to recall his mention of the resurrection in the previous verse to stand as the object. Since the resurrection of the saints has not happened and the full measure of Paul's participation in Christ is yet unfinished, it seems best to assume that Paul is putting to rest here any speculation that he believes himself to have arrived at some sort of complete, experiential oneness with Christ.

Paul desires this deep level of understanding of Christ, and then, with a lovely play on words, he uses the passive form of the verb to indicate that he was grasped by Christ. Paul is ever reaching out for a greater understanding, even as he has been taken up by Christ himself. One way to picture this is to think of a mother picking up her toddler, even as the little one reaches out to wrap his tiny arms around her neck. From the mother's perspective, she has already grasped the child, and from the child's viewpoint, he is reaching for his mother. So too with Christ who grasps us, even as we lean forward to wrap our arms around him.

Perfection or Meeting the Goal (3:12)

Not only has Paul not attained full power of resurrection or full participation in sufferings, but he also is not "perfected" or "arrived at his goal" (*teleioō*). What does this verb mean? Some suggest that Paul polemically counters his opponents (Jews or Jewish believers), who claim they can become perfect or sinless through law keeping.[7] Others believe Paul uses his opponents' own words here, for ideas of attaining and perfection are rooted in a thought system based on the law and human achievement.[8] However, Paul never claimed to have been perfect even when he was a Pharisee, nor does he say that about his opponents. Another possibility is that Paul is countering those who believe that Christians can achieve eschatological perfection in this lifetime,[9] and certainly Paul holds that believers still wait for the final consummation, the last day (2 Thess 2:1 – 3). A final possibility is that Paul uses "perfection" to emphasize completion of a goal.[10] This option stresses the verb "press on" in 3:12, which means to pursue, as in a race. It is unclear whether Paul intends a racing motif here, but the idea of pressing forward is clearly emphasized.

Since Paul does not use the verb *teleioō* elsewhere in his writings, we will examine perhaps the most famous passage on the topic of perfection, Matthew 5:48, where Jesus instructs his listeners to "be perfect ... as your heavenly Father is perfect." In this section of the Sermon on the Mount, Jesus draws on Leviticus 19:18 ("love your neighbor as yourself") to stress the foundational place of love in any understanding of perfection (Matt 5:43). This perfection is not an inner feeling or an ascetically rigorous life; rather,

---

7. O'Brien, *Philippians*, 418.
8. Reumann, *Philippians*, 554.
9. O'Brien, *Philippians*, 423.
10. Osiek, *Philippians, Philemon*, 96.

it is a walk of obedience. McKnight writes, "the notion [of perfection], then, is not the rigor of sinlessness but the rigor of utter devotion."[11] Luke records Jesus as saying, "Be merciful, just as your Father is merciful" in stressing love of enemy (Luke 6:36). Being perfect, therefore, includes forgiveness and love of one's enemies.

Paul applies Jesus' teachings in his letter to the Ephesians, encouraging the church to "reach unity in the faith and in the knowledge of the Son of God and become mature [perfect]" (Eph 4:13), and to "be kind and compassionate to one another, forgiving each other, just as in Christ God forgave you. Follow God's example, therefore, as dearly loved children, and walk in the way of love" (4:32–5:2). Just as Jesus called his followers to be perfect as our heavenly Father is perfect, so too Paul puts forward God's example that we must follow. And what is that example? Forgiving others as we have been forgiven, showing mercy, and blessing those who hate us.

Paul takes Jesus' teachings about being perfect, loving enemies, and redefining the identity of my neighbor and applies them to the Philippians' situation of mixed, Jew/Gentile churches. The Jewish identity markers of circumcision, noble ancestry as God's people, and knowledge of God's law all tended in Paul's day to reinforce a love of one's own people, not a love of all people. Thus these qualities of Jewish culture, while neutral in themselves, become traps because they mute God's message in Christ of love for Jew and Gentile.

Perfection in the sense Jesus means it refers to that attitude of service, forgiveness, and love of others. Paul strives after an ever-deepening experiential knowledge of this life. This raises the question: Do believers today share that passion? Often, at least in the U.S., Christianity is peddled as getting to know more about who you are, what your skills and talents are, and how you can actualize them. We want to know Christ only as it enhances what we already love about ourselves. Being conformed to Christ, becoming like him in his death (humble, obedient) — is this really, in my deepest parts, what I want?

Typically, I want to be humble on my own terms and to be obedient when God's plans line up with my own vision. The perfection called for by Christ (and Paul) is a complete restructuring of what we often think it means to be Christian and what it means to be fully human and a fulfilled human. This sort of perfection is antithetical to what our culture tells us to be — authentic, autonomous beings. Instead, Paul presents a vision of humanity as obedient to another, Christ, and ready to be molded in ways that might feel unauthentic or nonfulfilling.

---

11. Scot McKnight, *Sermon on the Mount* (SGBC; Grand Rapids: Zondervan, 2013).

The reader might form the impression that my understanding of discipleship implies a "one size fits all" sort of model. That is not my point; rather, I suggest that authenticity is not about autonomy but about service. A friend who worked as an intern for John Stott years ago recently remarked at the number of testimonials that emphasized his service to people who had no claims on him (Stott died in July 2011). In particular, my friend noted, "servanthood looks different in differing personalities." He added a story he heard about Stott's distinctive service. At a large gathering sponsored by Billy Graham, Stott "greeted so many by name that someone asked him about it, and he replied that they were people on his prayer list."[12]

A quick glance through the memorial stories bears witness to this form of service. Kedrick Mapalo met Stott in 1988 at a conference in South Africa, where Stott challenged the apartheid policies publicly on TV. Ten years later, the two met in Seoul, South Korea. As Mapalo writes, "to my surprised [*sic*] he remembered that he'd met me ... in South Africa about 10 years before. When Dr. Stott remembers you that way, you feel great!"[13] In another example, Daniel Devadatta met Dr. Stott only once when the latter spoke at Calvin College in the 1990s. After introducing himself to Dr. Stott, he was asked, "Who is Sam Devadatta?" Daniel answered that Sam was his father, who had died in 1973. Stott "with a smile, looked at me and said: "Your dad was responsible for my first trip to India, where I have gone each single year since then." Devadatta remarked on Stott's memory, which focused on knowing people.[14]

Stott's life of faithful service touched people around the world. Most of us will never get as many stamps in our passports as Dr. Stott. But we each have areas of service that invite our response. For some, it might be faithful, focused prayer; for others, consistent communication through letters and acknowledged birthdays and anniversaries. Still others might serve by snow-blowing a neighbor's sidewalk (I have just such a wonderful neighbor!), or by watching a neighbor's child after school. These seemingly little, and at times inconvenient, acts of service open us to the reality of life lived as Christ did, a humble servant. They open for believers a vision of the world as it really is, a view of who we really are, and a hope of what we will be in our resurrected bodies in the new heavens and new earth, always with Christ.

---

12. Personal communication in January 2013 with Greg Scharf, professor of pastoral theology at Trinity Evangelical Divinity School.

13. Kedrick Mapalo, Walvis Bay, Erongo, Namibia; see www.johnstottmemorial.org/remembrance-book.

14. Daniel Devadatta, Bangalore, Kar/India; see ibid.

Focus Forward (3:13–14)

It is precisely that vision that motivated Paul to such unrelenting devotion to know Christ. In 3:13–14 he states unequivocally that he believes himself not to have attained the full measure of his salvation, his resurrected body. But such knowledge does not disappoint him; rather, it spurs him to action. He determines to focus ahead; he looks neither back nor to either side, nor down at his feet, nor up at the stars. He looks straight ahead, at a goal, at a prize. To further cement this image in his readers' minds, he repeats the verb *diōkō* ("to pursue"), with the verb's attending nuance of racing. If a runner looks at his feet, his entire posture changes, and he fails to maximize his stride. If another runner looks back, her body shifts from its straight-arrow momentum, again slowing her down. Looking side to side from the corner of the eye might help the runner keep a good distance from other runners, but turning the head knocks the stride off. It is the forward focus that keeps a runner going.

In my first of two half-marathons, when I was in the twelfth mile, every muscle begged loudly to walk (or stop!), and when I bent my head to stare at my feet, my pace slowed and my resolve flagged. But when I kept my eye on the distant building that marked the race's end, I was able to stay mentally tough and eventually cross the finish line. That last mile was a pivotal lesson on the importance of focus.

Paul kept his focus, not simply in standing firm in his witness before his Roman prison guards or before his Jewish compatriots in the Sanhedrin. He also zeroed in on God's specific call on his life. He emphasizes to the Corinthians that God called him as an apostle, and thus he did not baptize many (1 Cor 1:17), nor did he remain long in a community to disciple and train believers (3:5–10). Instead, he journeyed to cities around the Mediterranean, taking advantage of his natural affinity for the city (after all, he was born and raised in Tarsus, a good-sized Roman city). There he preached to Jew and Gentile alike in Greek, the *lingua franca* of the day.

These two aspects of Paul's focus—his unrelenting determination to be faithful in every situation and his conviction that God called him to specific tasks—we must imitate if we are to rein in our frenetic-paced lives. Paul's caution for us is to stay focused in three areas. First, keep your eye on the finish line; that will encourage your weary feet. Second, participate in sufferings in the name of Christ; this is the work of your hands today. Third, stand firm in your calling, your specific tasks in building and caring for God's kingdom now.

This final caution serves as an added reminder that we do not race alone; we are not called as isolated adventurers charting a new path. Instead, we are connected and unified, in Christ, each of us together focusing on the prize, running together like a great marathon snaking through the streets of time. Otherwise stated, the pursuit of holiness and perfection is not one done in isolation from our brothers and sisters in Christ. It is done in concert with them.

Forget What Is Past, Look to the Future (3:13)

Paul indicates that he forgets his past in his efforts to move forward. Psychologists rightly note that a fixation on the past, feelings of guilt or shame, can pull down a person's self-esteem and lead to depression. But Paul is not speaking here in a generic sense about the past; rather, he has in mind his previous actions as a Pharisee bent on destroying the church. In 1 Corinthians 15:9 – 10, Paul acknowledges his persecution of the church: "I am the least of the apostles and do not even deserve to be called an apostle, because I persecuted the church of God" (15:9; cf. Gal 1:13 – 17). But he does not remain in this state of frustrated guilt; instead, he "worked harder than all of them — yet not I, but the grace of God that was with me" (1 Cor 15:10).

Paul forgets his failure, seeing only God and his grace at work in Jesus the Messiah. He pays no attention to the privileges he enjoyed as a member of the educated elite Jewish leaders. Paul may also be including here his activities since being called as an apostle. He seems uninterested in evaluating his efforts, as he notes in 1 Corinthians 4:3 – 4, "I do not even judge myself. My conscience is clear, but that does not make me innocent. It is the Lord who judges me." It is not a matter of success or failure for Paul, but of obedience. Thus the past is useful only as it instructs the present. In his next chapter, Paul says to the Philippians that he has *learned* to be content — his past experiences have added up to a character-building lesson (Phil 4:11 – 12).

We only have the present; we cannot remake the past, and the future is yet to be. However, for Paul, the future resurrection hope must shape believers' present reality. Paul speaks of the target or "goal" (*skopos*), the "prize" (*brabeion*), and the upward calling of God as part of his stretching forward toward the future. The noun *skopos* does not appear elsewhere in the New Testament, but Paul uses the corresponding verb in 2:4, when he enjoins the Philippians to look out for the needs of others. He will use the verb again in 3:17 to encourage them to watch closely those who model Christ. In 3:14, he speaks of the finish line, the goal to which each competitor runs. Paul connects the prize that awaits each finisher with the call of God.

The prize itself is not God's call (i.e., his invitation to conversion), for Paul says he has not yet received the prize. But if we understand God's call more broadly as the salvation brought by Christ and accomplished in the final judgment, the prize is eternal life with God, with resurrected bodies in the new heavens and new earth. With this vision firmly in mind, the believer presses on joyfully, together with all the saints, until that day when "every knee [will] bow ... and every tongue acknowledge that Jesus Christ is Lord, to the glory of God the Father" (2:10–11).

The Theological Impact of Paul's Teachings (3:1–14)

I deferred talking about key phrases above because they deserve to be treated in the larger theological conversation. To appreciate where we are now, we need to understand the history of the theological debate surrounding Paul's teachings, especially on the matter of justification by faith. Historically, Paul was thought to teach that Jews sought salvation through human works and effort (known as the anthropological view). Two important historical events changed forever the status quo in Pauline theology: the discovery of the Dead Sea Scrolls and the Holocaust. The former provided a window into sectarian Judaism of Paul's day, giving scholars examples of term usage and theological exchanges among contemporaries of Paul. The latter exposed underlying anti-Semitic beliefs supported, even justified, in the name of Christ.

The new perspective on Paul. Scholars have revisited common assumptions about Paul's teachings and the Judaism of his day.[15] In 1963, Krister Stendahl, a Swedish Lutheran, wrote an article wherein he argued for Paul's "robust conscience."[16] He challenged the prevailing notion that Paul was consumed with his own guilt under Judaism, from which Christ set him free. A decade later, E. P. Sanders wrote *Paul and Palestinian Judaism,* in which he concluded that Second Temple Judaism was not legalistic; that is, Jews in Paul's day did not do good deeds in order to get to heaven or become saved. Instead, Jews obeyed the Torah because they were *already* God's people. Sanders coined the phrase "covenantal nomism," by which he meant that Jews were God's people because of his covenant in creating and calling them through Abraham. They obeyed the law (*nomos* in Greek) to demonstrate their status as God's people.[17]

These ideas have been grouped under the label "New Perspective on Paul,"[18] a theory that stresses that Jews in the first century AD did not seek to earn their salvation.[19] Instead, Jews understood obedience to God's law as

---

15. An early example of this is G. F. Moore, "Christian Writers on Judaism," *HTR* 14 (1921): 197–254.

16. Krister Stendahl, "The Apostle Paul and the Introspective Conscience of the West," *HTR* 56 (1963): 199–215.

17. E. P. Sanders, *Paul and Palestinian Judaism* (Philadelphia: Fortress, 1977).

18. James D. G. Dunn, *The New Perspective on Paul* (Grand Rapids: Eerdmans, 2008). See also Kent L. Yinger, *The New Perspective on Paul: An Introduction* (Eugene, OR: Wipf & Stock, 2011).

19. For a work that challenges the New Perspective in some of its claims, see *Justification and Variegated Nomism: The Paradoxes of Paul* (ed., D. A. Carson, Peter T. O'Brien, Mark A. Seifrid; Grand Rapids: Baker Academic, 2004).

their response to God's choosing them as his people. Therefore, when Paul speaks of a "righteousness of my own that comes from the law" (3:9), he is not explaining that he tried to earn his salvation; rather he was following Torah in light of his identity as a Jew. Interpreters of Paul continue to wrestle with the new evidence from Jewish sources such as the Dead Sea Scrolls in order to understand Paul more accurately.

"Righteousness" and "to justify" in Paul (3:9). A key Pauline term in discussing his life as a Pharisee and his life in Christ is "righteousness" (*dikaiosynē*). We find this noun fifty-seven times in Paul (thirty-three in Romans alone), out of ninety-one occurrences in the New Testament. The cognate verb "justify" (*dikaioō*) occurs twenty-seven times in Paul (fifteen in Romans) out of thirty-nine times in the New Testament.[20] While in English the terms "righteousness" and "to justify" carry different nuances, the terms share a common Greek root. For the Greek speaker, the term righteousness indicated an ideal measure whereby to gauge one's actions. But in Hebrew, the corresponding term (*ṣᵉdāqâ*) carries the sense of obligation of someone in a relationship. For example, in 1 Samuel 24:17, David is declared more righteous than Saul because the former did not act violently against the king when he had the chance (see also Gen 38:26; Pss 51:14; 65:5; 71:15; Isa 46:13; 51:5 – 8; 62:1 – 2). The Dead Sea Scrolls include this testimony:

> As for me, (12) if I stumble, the mercies of God shall be my eternal salvation. If I stagger because of the sin of the flesh, my justification shall be by the righteousness of God which endures for ever. (13) ... He will draw me near by his grace, and by his mercy will he bring (14) my justification.... Through his righteousness he will cleanse me of all the uncleanness of (15) man and of the sins of the children of men.[21]

Using this conceptual backdrop, we would expect Paul in Romans 1:16 – 17 to be saying that the "righteousness of God" describes God making good on his promises when he created humanity, and especially when he established his covenant with Abraham and Israel. If we follow this line of reasoning, the dilemma of the Reformation concerning the proper definition of the verb "to justify" takes on a different complexion. Instead of having to choose between "make righteous" or "reckon as righteous," the term indicates both realities, for it is God who draws people to himself (reckons as righteous) and enters a relationship with them, which leads to their transformation (make righteous).

Righteousness in Philippians 3:9. Looking specifically at 3:9, we find the

---

20. James D. G. Dunn, *The Theology of Paul the Apostle* (Grand Rapids: Eerdmans, 1998), 340.
21. 1QS 11:11 – 15; see ibid., 343.

parallel phrases "from the law" and "from God." Are there two types of righteousness discussed here, or two ways of gaining righteousness? One could say that there are two types of righteousness, if by righteousness one means the daily, faithful obedience to God. Under the law, righteousness includes Sabbath observance, food laws, circumcision of male infants, and other markers of Jewish practice. The hope in this sort of righteousness is to touch in some small way the perfect holiness of God as witnessed in the temple services and sacrifices. The law stipulates sacrifices, and God can accept them and render the person forgiven. Now Christ has come and given his life as a ransom for many (Mark 10:45), a sacrifice once for all (Heb 10:10). In him, righteousness is by faith; it distinguishes sinful from holy, moral from immoral, but not clean and unclean. In Christ, righteousness is rooted in life in the Holy Spirit and in the body of Christ, the church.

One might also say that there are two sources of righteousness imagined here, human and divine. The righteousness that is from the law is empowered by human effort and energy. We need not conclude that effort springs from arrogance or boasting; rather, it is just that the law has no power unto itself to make new or overcome sin (Rom 7:7–14). The righteousness from God is established through Christ's death and resurrection and thus has the power of life itself to change and make new everyone who believes in him. I contend that the contrast is between Paul's obedience/faithfulness that draws its sense of righteousness from following the law, and Christ's obedience/faithfulness that overcame the power of sin and fulfilled the law. The contrast is between Paul and Christ, not two activities of Paul—blameless law-keeping and faith.

Works of the law (3:9). Paul emphasizes the righteousness from God based on faith (3:9). This is contrasted with a righteousness under the law (3:6). The specific phrase "works of the law," at the center of the debate, is known outside Paul in a Dead Sea Scrolls document, 4QMMT, *Miqsat Maʿase Ha-Torah.* The title means "Some of the Works of the Law," and the text indicates that these works separate the sectarians (probably Essenes) from other Jews. The authors of this text expressed frustration at other Jews for their implementation or interpretation of aspects of the law. In this case, the issue is not distinguishing Jews from Gentiles or pagans, but discriminating between different factions of Jews.

What does Paul mean by the phrase "works of the law"? Paul believes the law defines sin (Rom 7:7–13), and sin brings divine judgment (3:19–20; Gal 3:10). The law also instructs Israel (Gal 3:24). The phrase "works of the law" means, broadly speaking, doing all the law requires and avoiding all it cautions against. Yet in Paul's day, it seems also to have had a nuanced meaning that focused on particular laws that distinguished between groups. In the case of the Essenes, they had special works of the law or special emphases surrounding certain laws, which marked them as different from other Jews. For Paul, the phrase "works of the law" would include (but not be limited to) a list of specific laws that symbolized ethnic or religious Judaism, most notably circumcision, Sabbath, and food laws (Gal 5:2 – 6).

In other words, "works of the law" for Paul includes those laws that have been pushed to the forefront of the gospel proclamation with the express purpose of enjoining Gentiles to take on the identity of Jews, as they also testify to faith in Christ. Let me emphasize that "works of the law" are not the same thing as "works" in Paul. The latter are encouraged and applauded by Paul, as he states to the Galatians, "Carry each other's burdens, and in this way you will fulfill the law of Christ," and "Let us not become weary in doing good, for at the proper time we will reap a harvest if we do not give up" (Gal 6:2, 9). We have already discussed the importance of work in our analysis of Philippians 2:12 – 14.

A righteousness of my own (3:9). The New Perspective explains that it is not the law per se that is problematic, for the law is holy (Rom 7:12) and Jews knew that they were not earning salvation by following the law. Rather, Paul speaks against the additional belief that the law encourages or mandates a nationalistic or exclusivist posture against the nations. The law was understood to represent and uphold Israel's privilege; God chose Israel, and God's righteousness was *only* for Israel.

If this is the case, then what does Paul mean by the phrase, "my own [righteousness]," contrasted with his claims about the righteousness from God based on faith (3:9)? Does the pronoun "my" convey that Paul has attained his own merit from doing the law (argued in the anthropological view)? The New Perspective insists that Jews at this time did not think that doing the law earned their salvation; thus, Paul would not suggest here that "my righteousness" was based on human effort or merit. Instead, Paul understands "my righteousness" to indicate that upright behavior shown by obedience to the law. Luke describes Elizabeth and Zechariah as righteous (*dikaioi*) before God, walking in his ways and following his commandments (Luke 1:6), and Matthew speaks of Joseph as a righteous (*dikaios*) man (Matt 1:19).

In Paul's case, when he speaks of his righteousness as "faultless" (3:6), he uses as his reference point the general terms of the covenant between God and Israel. And when he explains his past as a Pharisee (3:5), we "catch an unmistakable whiff of the factionalism of late Second Temple Judaism."[22] The point he makes in 3:9 concerns his covenant standing before God, that

---

22. Dunn, *Theology*, 349.

he now stands righteous because of the righteousness from God accessed by faith through the faithfulness of Christ. Those aspects of the law that served in Paul's day to separate Jews and Gentiles at the level of ethnic and nationalistic boundaries are now rendered obsolete because of Christ's work. Paul uses a visual picture of this reality in Ephesians 2:14–18. There he says that Christ has torn down the dividing wall of hostility between Jews and Gentiles. Now both groups can approach the throne of grace by the blood of Christ (see Heb 10:19–23).

Summary of the anthropological view and the New Perspective. In sum, the anthropological view holds that Paul's language suggests Jews in his day sought to achieve salvation by works of the law. Once Paul was saved in Christ, he abandoned his efforts of human striving, although aspects of the law, particularly the moral injunctions concerning loving one's neighbor and avoiding immorality, remained central. This view is consistent with the Reformers' reconstruction of Second Temple Judaism, which they drew as similar to their contemporary church's insistence on human merit as essential in a person's ultimate salvation. The anthropological view sees humans as proud, rebellious, and self-justifying.

The New Perspective position holds that Jews in Paul's day believed they were members of God's family by birth, and they took up obedience to the law in grateful response to God's calling. Jews did not do the law to "get saved." Rather, the law was to guide their lives of faithful service and worship. The New Perspective argues that the phrase "works of the law" does not denote self-effort to win God's favor or earn salvation. Rather, only Gentiles (those born pagans) needed to convert to the one true God. The law of God provided guidance on how to live as faithful members of his family. Jews who failed to follow the law might be considered apostate, that is, no longer members of the Jewish people.

These two views exist on a continuum, with scholars planting their flags more or less within the boundaries of one or the other camp. The complexity of the evidence means that scholars nuance their views, and new angles of inquiry continue to provide further discernment and explanation of the complicated reality that is Second Temple Judaism.

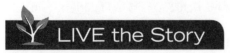 LIVE the Story

Joy and Rejoicing

For those of us weaned on the inalienable rights of life, liberty, and the pursuit of happiness, we can read Paul's call as affirmation to pursue what makes us happy. But Paul is not condoning hedonism or even self-actualization in his call to rejoice. He is not saying "be happy," but "be joyful." Recall that he is writing this letter from prison, under attack personally by other Christians who seek advantage over him, and he has just gone through deep waters with Epaphroditus's serious illness. The apparent disconnect between the charge to rejoice and his circumstances invites us to dig more deeply into the meaning of joy. In the New Testament, words meaning "joy" occur 326 times, with about 40 percent of those in Paul's letters.[23] In Philippians 3:1, Paul uses the verb "to rejoice," which is related to the noun "joy." Both terms share the same root as the term "grace." The linguistic connections support the theological ties between God's grace extended freely through Christ and the believer's resulting joy in Christ.

Paul's insistence on rejoicing recalls another prison experience, one in which he and Silas were imprisoned in a Philippian jail (Acts 16:22–34). After being beaten, the men were put in stocks. Amazingly, a few hours later these two were singing hymns and praying! We cannot say with certainty what they were praying for, but it may have been for the salvation of the fellow prisoners and the jailer. Whatever the case, a sudden earthquake opened the cell doors and broke the prisoners' chains. The jailer came running, only to find all the prisoners still in the jail. He was dumbfounded but realized that God was at work. He asked Paul, "What must I do to be saved?" In accepting the gospel proclaimed, his first act as a believer was to clean their wounds. After he and his household were baptized, Acts notes that the entire household rejoiced.

This posture of rejoicing springs from Jesus' own life. Luke's gospel uses the term "joy" more than the other gospels, and we see that even before Jesus was born, the angel told John the Baptist's father, Zechariah, that his son will bring joy not only to his family, but rejoicing to many (Luke 1:14). While still in Elizabeth's womb, John the Baptist "leaped for joy" (1:44) upon hearing the voice of Mary, the mother of Jesus. So too Mary proclaimed her own rejoicing at God's work (1:47), and the angel announced "good news that will cause great joy for all the people" at the birth of Jesus (2:10). Such joy reflects God's own joy at the repentance of a single sinner (15:1–32). Luke's final picture of the disciples is one of worshiping God "with great joy" (24:52). So too Paul invites the Philippians to continue to rejoice in the Lord (Phil 4:4).

Paul discovered that joy comes from people, not from things. Joy comes from relationships, not from circumstances or experiences. Societies and cultures have tended to reverse that order; while they may tout love and family as central, in actual practice, personal honor or wealth are more highly prized.

_____

23. W. G. Morrice, "Joy" *DPL*, 511.

Our modern consumer culture, tied to capitalism, is especially susceptible to this reversal of priorities. Although the first century did not wrestle with the ramifications of capitalism, the people then, as now, struggled with desire for financial security, wealth, and honor. Jews were not exempt from these social temptations, although they had God's law to guide them.

The Story of Rabbi Shimon bar Yohai

A later rabbinic story sums up nicely the particular temptation that Jews faced in elevating the law above love and relationships.[24] The study of Torah can be the spice of life or a poison pill, as these rabbis discover.

The story begins during the later Roman imperial period. Three rabbis sit down, discussing their daily lives, and one Jew, a convert (Yehuda b. Gerim), stands with them. R. Shimon rejects R. Yehuda's positive assessment of Roman influence and instead postulates that the Romans seek to enrich themselves and practice immorality. When the Romans discover this seditious attitude, they seek to kill R. Shimon. To avoid capture, R. Shimon and his son hide first in the yeshiva (academy) and are cared for by his wife. But he still fears for his life, and so he escapes with his son to the wilderness to hide in a cave. Thus he remains for thirteen years, fed by a carob tree and a spring. The father and son do no work other than study; they study naked, covering themselves with the sand of the cave's floor. Their nakedness symbolizes their connection to Adam, the newborn human in his pristine state. Their study makes them powerful, but ironically blind to true wisdom.

When they venture from their cave, they despise their embodiment and the world of family and work. They sharply contrast the eternal, seen in their study of the law, and the temporal, families and farming. They extol the life of the mind, the life focused only and solely on the eternal. Their abhorrence for work and play is seen in their violent rejection, and the story says that their eyes burn, indicating they destroy all that they look on. But the Voice from heaven rejects their assessment and sends them back to the cave, where they stay another twelve months.

This time frame is significant, as another tradition has it that Jews who do wrong will spend up to twelve months in hell before gaining heaven. Thus the story indicates God's strong disapproval, not merely of a life of study, but of a life that mocks and devalues the community, the family, and the joyous necessities of hard (sometimes tedious) labor. When they are released to go back to the world, R. Shimon shows that he understands God's chastisement; sadly his son, R. Eleazar, has not. The latter has known nothing but isolated

---

24. *B. Šabbat* 33b–34a, often called "The Education of R. Shimon bar Yohai."

study and so continues to use his acquired power to destroy. It is only when they come upon great joy in hard work that they both begin to rest easy, and the father embraces the goodness of family and work.

The real hero of the story is not R. Shimon, the learned miracle worker. The wisest man is an old character rushing home to celebrate Shabbat with his family. He carries two bunches of sweet-smelling myrtle to make the meal beautiful. He brings great joy to the doing of the law, which promotes the celebration of God and family. His example of simple piety and overflowing joy cut to the heart of R. Shimon and his son and change the former's course. When he returns to his town, he seeks ways to bless the community, such as making decisions on what ground is pure and what is impure. This enables the community to avoid what might be impure, giving them peace of mind and easing their burdens.

The story makes three points relevant to our topic. First, note the joy of the old man bringing flowers to the Shabbat dinner. The rabbi and his son fail to see, while living in the cave, the worthiness of labor: the importance of crops and making bread and celebrating as a family around the dinner table. The man overflows with joy; he brings not one but two bunches of myrtle to grace the family table. His joy includes sharing a meal, made possible by the labor of farmers, grain grinders, and bread makers. He rejoices in the goodness of sowing and reaping. Perhaps it is harder today in some occupations to see directly the fruit of our labors, but the man's joy is not only tied to eating a meal but also with sharing that meal with his family.

Today, our society struggles with fractured and fragmented families, and many carry around the wounds inflicted by those who should have loved them. But this man's joy prods us today to look for ways to be the healing balm for broken people, to be infectious carriers of joy to our coworkers and fellow volunteers, our neighbors and friends. This old fellow would have been a familiar character in Jesus' village, as fathers and other family members hurried home for Shabbat meal. Jesus would have experienced the joy of breaking bread amidst the sweet-smelling flowers that graced Mary's table. Jesus invites every believer to his table; can you smell the sweetness of grace that lingers in the air?

Second, R. Shimon's story begins with zealous vigor to embrace fully the law of God, but gradually shifts into utter sadness and blindness as the son and his father dwell in the cave. It becomes for them a hell, because it separates their life of the mind from what is true about being human — namely, that we are embodied creatures meant to be in relationship. They see the study of the law as an end in itself rather than as a way to bless those around them. They gain knowledge and power, but they use it to condemn, not to bless.

Christians often have a knowledge of the Bible, but they use that knowledge to tear down others, not to bring them hope and joy. Paul knew such believers—the Corinthians had knowledge, but they only grew arrogant. Paul explains, "Knowledge puffs up while love builds up" (1 Cor 8:1). Knowledge without love is worse than ignorance: "If I have the gift of prophecy and can fathom all mysteries and all knowledge, and if I have a faith that can move mountains, but do not have love, I am nothing" (13:2). Jesus speaks harsh words to those teachers who have themselves the key of knowledge but hinder others from entering the kingdom of God. He chastises those who use their knowledge of the law to burden others while at the same time elevating themselves in public (Luke 11:45–52). Instead, Jesus calls his disciples to obey God's Word (11:28).

Third, we see in R. Shimon's story that study combined with active social engagement reflects the ideal balance. From his time of study R. Shimon gained much knowledge and thus could provide more answers to questions than ever before. But he grew wise once he realized that knowledge of the law alone breeds contempt for others and for the embodied life of relationships. Sadly, not all the rabbis and elders embraced R. Shimon's changed life. The story ends with a warning. An old man who knew R. Shimon's testimony criticized the latter's new engagement with society. He argued that R. Shimon's efforts to ease the trouble for Jews concerned with purity issues were a false and misguided mission. Better to learn the law than to worry about the daily lives of people. Seeing a vision of his earlier self, R. Shimon "cast his eyes at him," and the old man was no more. R. Shimon learned that fleeing the world, decrying hard work and family relationships, does not develop holiness or understanding; quite the reverse, it makes one ignorant of the value of human life and blind to true human joy.

"Him I Want" as the Plea of Thomas Cooper

"I want to know him [Christ]" (3:10). Paul's words ring down through the ages, a plea, a defiant shake of the fist against the world that drags us further into its vortex of sin and self. Often we start out well, fervent in our faith and dedicated in our devotions; then time and troubles soften our resolve and weaken our commitment. In the Victorian period, Thomas Cooper made a winding journey from professing faith at age fourteen, extensive schooling, then becoming schoolmaster and pastor, next a journalist. In this last post, he became influenced by the political radicalism of the Chartist movement, a working-class movement that called for reforms, such as the right to vote for everyone and a secret ballot. He was arrested and jailed for two years, during which time he became increasingly disillusioned with Christianity. In 1845 he was released from prison and joined the ranks of the skeptics. He took up speaking against the Bible's historicity.

But after about a decade, he began to feel uneasy about the ramifications of his skepticism, especially as he believed it offered no grounding for morality. His doubts increased, and he sought the advice of his friend, Anglican clergyman Charles Kingsley. In one of Cooper's letters to Kingsley, he pours out his frustrations: "Can you tell me what to do—anything that will help me to Christ. *Him* I want. If the Four Gospels be half legends I still want him."[25] His worries about the veracity of human wisdom and knowledge grew, and a sense of personal sin deepened. After a two-year struggle, he confessed he was a Christian.

A momentous event served as the final catalyst in his turn to preach Christ. He and a friend were boarding a train when a conductor motioned them into another car. Shortly thereafter, several others joined them, but then one of those men left to ride in another car with a friend. About an hour into the journey, the train hit a cow, and several cars flipped off the track. None in Cooper's car was injured, but the man who left the car and his friend were both killed. They were riding the car originally assigned to Cooper. It was a miraculous rescue, Cooper declared, and he devoted himself to God's service thereafter. The following year he was baptized, on Pentecost Sunday in a Baptist church. He continued his lectures and writing, but with a new song in his heart and a new script defending Christianity.

An Inspired Song; Hannah More

About a generation earlier in England, Hannah More (1745 – 1833) recognized the responsibility that came with her advanced education and book knowledge.[26] More was a celebrated poet and playwright, but when she met William Wilberforce in 1787, her writing took on new energy in works such as the poem *The Slave Trade: A Poem*. In this lengthy poem she attacks the racism that supported the slave trade and challenged her countrymen to end this horrible practice. Her poem reads in part:

No fictitious ills these numbers flow,
But living anguish, and substantial woe;
No individual griefs my bosom melt,
For millions feel what Oroonoko felt:[27]

25. T. Larsen, " Cooper, Thomas," in *Biographical Dictionary of Evangelicals* (ed. Timothy Larsen; Downers Grove, IL: InterVarsity Press, 2003), 159.

26. M. Jones, "More, Hannah," ibid., 437 – 40.

27. Oroonoko is the name of the lead character in a book by Aphra Behn, *Oroonoko: The Royal Slave* (1688).

Fir'd by no single wrongs, the countless host
I mourn, by rapine dragg'd from Afric's coast.
Perish th'illiberal thought which wou'd debase
The native genius of the sable race!
Perish the proud philosophy, which sought
To rob them of the pow'rs of equal thought!
Does then th' immortal principle within
Change with the casual colour of a skin?
Does matter govern spirit? or is mind
Degraded by the form to which 'tis join'd?
No: they have heads to think, and hearts to feel,
And souls to act, with firm, tho' erring, zeal;
For they have keen affections, kind desires,
Love strong as death, and active patriot fires...

Hannah More looked, not only to the distant social horizon, but also in her immediate backyard in her desire to use her knowledge for good purpose. With the encouragement of Wilberforce, Hannah More established education for the poor, against the strong resistance of both farmers, who believed it would harm agriculture, and absentee clergy, who knew her efforts exposed their failures to help their parishes. Students were taught to read Scripture and were given domestic and agriculture training. Reading classes held at night were offered for adults. The schools were a great success, with church attendance in the town of Cheddar moving from fifty to seven hundred in ten years, and crime decreased in all the towns under the influence of her education system. Her success and evangelical faith created some enemies, but all agreed that her efforts to aid the poor were motivated by sincere faith.

R. Shimon gained much knowledge, but needed to learn wisdom. Thomas Cooper confused his skepticism and limited human knowledge with real wisdom, until he saw the power of God in his life. Hannah More rested not on her laurels and the praise of others for her erudite poems and plays, but rolled up her sleeves to give opportunities to know and read Scripture to those ignored by many leaders in the church. Cooper and More understood Paul's cry to know Christ. R. Shimon experienced the vacuity of knowledge without love and joy. Jesus calls each person to know him, and thus to know eternal life, a life of love and obedience.

Philippians 3:15-21

LISTEN to the Story

¹⁵All of us, then, who are mature should take such a view of things. And if on some point you think differently, that too God will make clear to you. ¹⁶Only let us live up to what we have already attained.

¹⁷Join together in following my example, brothers and sisters, and just as you have us as a model, keep your eyes on those who live as we do. ¹⁸For, as I have often told you before and now tell you again even with tears, many live as enemies of the cross of Christ. ¹⁹Their destiny is destruction, their god is their stomach, and their glory is in their shame. Their mind is set on earthly things. ²⁰But our citizenship is in heaven. And we eagerly await a Savior from there, the Lord Jesus Christ, ²¹who, by the power that enables him to bring everything under his control, will transform our lowly bodies so that they will be like his glorious body.

Listening to the text in the Story: Septuagint of: Deuteronomy 18:13; 1 Kings 11:4; 1 Chronicles 28:9.

Paul now pauses to catch his breath after reaching such heights of expression in the previous verses. He draws the readers together with him and then launches into his final salvo against the opponents described in 3:2–3. He finishes with a strong contrast between the fate of those enemies of the cross and the Philippian believers, who belong to God's kingdom.

EXPLAIN the Story

Hold Fast and Keep Growing (3:15a)

These two verses contain interesting puzzles and questions about Paul's intentions and the Philippians' situation. Verse 15 is one of those verses that interpreters wish was preserved on audio! Is Paul speaking sarcastically when he mentions the *teleioi* ("mature")? Does he mean "the mature" or "the perfect ones"? Again, does Paul expect dissent from his convictions expressed in the previous verses and so makes room for disagreements? Or does he put a slight note of disapproval on the term "differently"? What sort of revelation does Paul expect God to provide to the Philippians? Judging from 3:16, Paul expects the revelation, if and when it comes, will support the direction and teachings he has presented to the Philippians. These few verses offer us a glimpse at Paul's expectations for churches to be accountable to their spiritual growth.

Paul gave an autobiographical sketch in 3:4–14, and he now builds on that. Should his personal experiences be normative? In fact, in highlighting his own experiences, Paul draws on a common philosophical assumption of his time. Most philosophies, including the predominant Stoicism, believed that true knowledge moved beyond the subjective sensory level and one's personal perspective to speak in a fully rational, transcultural sense. The one with knowledge overcomes one's own identity as a single human and can speak for humanity as a whole and thereby can come to objective truth, shared by all who cultivate rationality.

This is not to say that Paul is a Stoic; rather, it acknowledges that in his day, people recognized that true knowledge of universal thought could be gained by rational thinking. The Philippians would not read these verses as merely private musings of Paul. Rather, they would understand them as representative of any Christian's journey into knowing Christ, because Paul is not conveying a personal mystical encounter, but an objective knowledge that rational thought could ascertain.[1]

How, then, should we understand the adjective *teleioi*: as "perfect ones," or as "mature"? The latter option, taken by the NIV, focuses on keeping Paul consistent with his previous declaration in 3:12, namely, that he has not yet arrived at his goal. Some add that Paul is taking a swing at those in Philippi who identify themselves as "perfect."[2] According to this theory, Paul challenges those who claim perfection to listen to his words; if they did, they would see the error of their ways.

While Paul would definitely challenge those who claimed sinless perfection this side of glory, the better translation is "mature," for several reasons. First, Paul declares himself to be a member of this group, for the verb in verse 15 is first person plural. Second, there are various nuances that attend to the word group *teleios*, used in 3:12 (translated "arrived at my goal"). Elsewhere Paul can use a term having the same root with different nuances in the same passage (cf. Rom 12:3; 2 Cor 4:8). Third, the general tone in this section does not seem ironic, unlike Paul's frustrated comments in 2 Corinthians 10:1: "I

---

1. Troels Engberg-Pedersen, *Paul and the Stoics* (Louisville: Westminster John Knox, 2000), 93.
2. Reumann, *Philippians*, 559.

appeal to you—I, Paul, who am 'timid' when face to face with you, but 'bold' toward you when away!"

What would a "mature" believer look like? Paul probably has in mind the general picture of a devoted follower of God, as found in the Greek translation of Deuteronomy 18:13, "You must be *teleios* before the Lord your God," in contrast to the nations who practice sorcery, witchcraft, and the occult (cf. also the "willing mind" in the LXX of 1 Chr 28:9). The mature believer serves God alone, and with perseverance. James picks up this theme in his statement: "Let perseverance finish its work so that you may be mature [*teleioi*] and complete, not lacking anything" (Jas 1:4, see also 1:25; 3:2).

As Paul encourages the Philippians to "take such a view of things," he uses the same verb as in 2:2–5, the passage wherein he encouraged unity among the Philippians.[3] He asked that they think with the same attitude as Christ. Thus a mature believer embraces the humility expressed by the Lord as evidence by his death on the cross. A mature believer follows Jesus' example of obedience (2:8), not on her own strength, but through the power of resurrection (3:10). The mature believer holds all earthly things lightly and views everything (money, prestige, happiness) through the lens of resurrection hope.

How to Disagree Charitably (3:15b – 16)

Paul acknowledges in the second half of 3:15 that perhaps some may think otherwise. How likely was it for the Philippians to dissent from Paul? It is difficult to tell, but his overall stress on unity suggests that at the least, they were given to different opinions with frustrating regularity. What might they question? Paul uses the demonstrative pronoun "this" (NIV translates "such a view of things"), which likely points back to the previous several verses. While they might disagree "on some point" (i.e., on minor issues that can be solved through friends talking together), Paul would insist that his gospel is not up for debate, though earnest seekers after Christ may vary in their methods for attaining a deeper relationship.

Paul is not worried about the content of the Philippians' differences of thought, because these questions deal with minor issues. But he is concerned that they manage these differences by turning to God for guidance. Paul declares that God will inform them of his will through revelation. Herein lies the foundation for unity—corporate prayer seeking God's guidance. How often are we content with a church vote, or do we instead participate in behind-the-scenes machinations to shape our local church to fit our agendas? Do we hold a passive aggressive posture that nods agreement to a decision, but deeply resents it and harbors ill will?

---

3. The Greek verb is *phroneō*; see comments on pp. 7, 89.

Paul stresses that when everyone in the community lays their ideas, hopes, and convictions before God openly, God's will can be discerned. Perhaps Paul imagines this will happen in their gatherings as he notes to the Corinthians: "When you come together, each of you has a hymn, or a word of instruction, a revelation, a tongue or an interpretation. Everything must be done so that the church may be built up" (1 Cor 14:26). Paul's prayer for the Ephesians sounds a similar note: "I keep asking that the God of our Lord Jesus Christ, the glorious Father, may give you [plural] the Spirit of wisdom and revelation, so that you may know him better" (Eph 1:17).

Paul's concern in 3:16 is that the Philippians might take a few steps back in their faith journey. He pleads with them to hold onto what they already have and continue in their current trajectory. He asks them not to abandon what they "have already attained" in their lives of faith. Paul uses this verb elsewhere, always with the idea of future hope (e.g., 1 Thess 4:15). He goes on to ask them to stay the general course, to "live up to" what they know is true; he uses the same verb as in Galatians 5:25, where he instructs the Galatians to "keep in step" with the Spirit.

Imitate Paul and Other Believers (3:17)

Paul comes full circle in 3:17–21 from his opening verses in this chapter. He again alludes to the believers who claim circumcision and other ethnic hallmarks are essential for all God's people, Gentiles included. But for those who embrace the cross of Christ with its suffering and ultimate resurrection, the end is great joy, a transformed body, and peace everlasting with Christ. Several questions arise from these verses, including the best way to interpret Paul's call to imitate him and the identity of the "enemies of the cross."

The first word in 3:17 is unknown outside of Paul's work, which is a fancy way of saying that it appears Paul created it! He adds the prefix "with" to the noun "imitator." Why? Likely he wants to stress that the Philippians *as a group* should imitate him. Twice in 1 Corinthians Paul encourages the Corinthians to imitate him. In 1 Corinthians 4:14–17, Paul notes that he is the Corinthians' father and thus desires that they imitate him just as children learn how to live by imitating their parents. In 11:1, Paul culminates his argument about eating meat sacrificed to idols by asking them to imitate his example. He hopes to bring everyone to Christ, and he seeks the good of others, not his own good. It is what the Corinthians should emulate.

In both of these cases, one can hardly accuse Paul of self-aggrandizement. Moreover, Paul asks that communities imitate each other. He reminds the Corinthians of the Macedonian churches (Philippi, Thessalonica, Berea) and their generous spirit in giving to the needy in Judea (2 Cor 8:1–6), and he asks the Corinthians to do the same. He points to the churches in Judea as examples for the Thessalonian churches to follow (1 Thess 2:12). These examples show that imitation in the ancient world was not limited to an individualistic, personal, private sphere, but involved the community living in the public square.

Some might be surprised at this emphasis on imitation, since Paul has stressed throughout the letter that the Philippians should be of one mind and think the same thing. Yet for Paul, and for any ancient Jew or philosophical Gentile, right thinking leads to correct actions. For Stoics, right understanding led to control of passions. For Jews, right thinking led to the worship of the one true God. For Christians, right thinking leads to a life that mirrors the life of obedience and service of Jesus the Messiah.

Sadly, in some Christian circles today, right thinking is viewed as an end in itself. Doctrines are used as a bludgeon against other believers' differing views. In some cases, believers have separated thought and deed, relegating the latter to secondary status lest they give any hint of works righteousness. Paul's communities would never have imagined a system where thoughts and deeds were disconnected. The goal of right thinking was to improve one's actions. That is why all good teachers encouraged their students to follow their actions. Perhaps an analogy would help. Most tennis players would love to apprentice with tennis masters Roger Federer or Rafael Nadal or the Williams sisters. By listening and watching, the avid tennis player's game would improve. In a similar way, watching a dedicated believer obey God and seek his will leads the novice believer to grow in spiritual disciplines and godly reactions.

Paul's call to imitate him has come under fire recently in certain scholarly circles as being more about power and control[4] and about eliminating personal differences so that everyone talks and acts like Paul himself. Imitation has the ring of imperialism to it.[5] Paul's call to imitate him makes him appear a bit uppity. Beneath this concern is the sense that Paul is misusing his authority by coercing others to be like him. Indeed, it is wise to guard against capricious extensions of authority, and plenty of Western Christians have been part of churches whose senior pastors rule as totalitarian chiefs. But Paul is not supporting that picture of leadership here. He has no authority other than

---

4. Elizabeth A. Castelli, *Imitating Paul: A Discussion of Power* (Louisville: Westminster John Knox, 1991): "The thesis of this study is that the notion of mimesis functions in Paul's letters as a strategy of power. That is, it articulates and rationalizes as true and natural a particular set of power relations within the social foundation of early Christian communities" (15).

5. Joseph A. Marchal, *Hierarchy, Unity, and Imitation: A Feminist Rhetorical Analysis of Power Dynamics in Paul's Letter to the Philippians* (SBLAB 24; Atlanta: Society of Biblical Literature, 2006), 115–56.

persuasion over any of his congregations, who are free to leave the group at any time and who could join a synagogue or return to paganism.

We know from an early second-century letter by the governor of Bithynia, Pliny the Younger, to the Emperor Trajan, that some people accused of being Christians admitted that they had joined the group but had left it.[6] None of Paul's congregants are trapped into going along with what Paul says, and he has no other way to enforce their obedience than his declaration of the gospel.

Furthermore, Paul is not asking the Philippians to imitate his style of dress or learn Aramaic. Distinct language and dress are part of every culture. But when in Greco-Roman cities to which Paul preached the gospel, their cultural practices included idolatry, sexual immorality, acceptance of infanticide, and other practices that Jews deemed sinful, Paul did ask that the new Gentile Christians imitate his way of life, for he understood the moral principles of God.

Paul's desire that they imitate him signals a key element in the Christian life, namely, that "the walk must match the talk." Interestingly, Paul is the only New Testament writer to ask that his congregants imitate him. This "is the result of his radical insight into the gospel as the communication of God's saving power in Christ and his total awareness of human impotence vis-à-vis that divine power."[7] Paul also never speaks of having followers — only coworkers, fellow soldiers, and fellow prisoners (1 Cor 10:17; 2 Cor 4:5; Col 4:10). Finally, Paul stresses that he imitates Christ, and it is this imitation that he wants his congregants to follow (2 Cor 4:7 – 11; 1 Thess 1:6). Note too that Paul never asks those churches that do not know him personally (e.g., Rome or Colossae) to imitate him.

In modern terms, we might imagine Paul as a coach who both shows and tells his players what to do. I recall when my son played high school football, he had a coach who would routinely send him out on the field with the following words, "Don't throw an interception." Of course, the body cannot *not* do something; it has to form a picture of what to do. The coach would have been better off to encourage him to "throw a tight spiral" or to "step into the throw." Paul is following this tactic by showing the Philippians what godly behavior looks like. It is easier to mimic a positive action than to avoid a "don't."

---

6. Pliny the Younger, *Letters* 10.96 – 97, writes, "Others named by the informer declared that they were Christians, but then denied it, asserting that they had been but had ceased to be, some three years before, others many years, some as much as twenty-five years." See www.earlychristian writings.com/text/pliny.html

7. David Stanley, S. J., "Imitation in Paul's Letters: Its Significance for His Relationship to Jesus and to His Own Christian Foundations," in *From Jesus to Paul: Studies in Honour of Francis Wright Beare* (ed. Peter Richardson and John C. Hurd; Waterloo, ON: Wilfrid Laurier University Press, 1984), 141.

Paul's example suggests a model of apprentice and master rather than student and teacher. This model of education was commonplace around the Mediterranean world, with its emphasis on manual labor and handmade crafts and a predominantly illiterate population. Boys learned their father's trade; girls learned housekeeping and childcare from their mothers.[8] Men and women worked in shops with their children helping them. Slaves (male and female) were apprenticed to master weavers or potters, to learn a trade that would add income to the family. People apprenticed or learned by watching and then imitating the master.

What would our churches be like if we saw ourselves as apprentices trying to learn new skills and better ways of doing things from those who have had long experience in the ways of prayer, tithing, joyful living, and trust in God? What if we recognized that we also stand as "masters" before apprentices, that our actions should demonstrate a Spirit-filled walk? I wonder if we in the U.S. shy away from thinking about ourselves as "masters" to apprentices because it places greater responsibility on us to behave in a manner worthy of the gospel. Conversely, perhaps we rebel against considering ourselves apprentices, for we'd rather go our own way, find our own path, do it ourselves. But Paul uses the apprentice model because he knows that to claim Christ as Lord is to submit to Christ's daily rule and to commit to an eschatological reality of raised bodies. The resurrection truth informs daily suffering and the importance of the body.

Reject the Enemies of the Cross (3:18–19)

Paul draws a sharp distinction between those believers who follow his gospel of participation in Christ and those whom Paul labels as "enemies of the cross of Christ." His description here is cryptic, prompting contradictory interpretations, and any firm conclusions on the enemies' identity outruns the evidence. I suggested earlier that this group is connected with the "evildoers" noted in 3:2.[9] If so, these enemies are promoting circumcision of Gentiles as necessary for full membership in Christ's church. The scales tip in favor of viewing these "enemies" as self-identified believers who minimize the cross and its attending suffering.

In 3:18 Paul describes their behavior with the verb "live" (Greek, "walk"), a favorite of his in describing the Christian life. He also speaks of "their mind … set on earthly things" (3:19), using the verb "to think, have an attitude,"

---

8. Women could run the family estate if their husbands were fighting in the military or if the family was wealthy, for Roman women could inherit property and money. See Lynn H. Cohick, *Women in the World of the Earliest Christians* (Grand Rapids: Baker Academic, 2009), 225–55.

9. See pp. 164–66 for a discussion of "evildoers."

which he has used extensively in this letter to describe the believer's attitude and accompanying behaviors and practices. This suggests that these people claim to live the Christian life. Notice too that they are enemies of the cross, which suggests they take some position relative to the cross; "they are not merely neutral outsiders."[10]

Paul understands himself connected to them in some way, for he weeps at their position ("with tears," 3:18); he is most saddened to see those who have professed Christ turn away.[11] His sadness comes from how close these people are to embracing what God has done for them and then stepping away. It is unlikely that his tears reflect his frustration in being in chains and being unable to address the situation in person, for Paul has earlier indicated that the chains have actually emboldened other believers and served to advance the cause of Christ. Perhaps Paul is even personally familiar with some in this group, thus compounding his sorrow.

Paul lists several characteristics of this group. First, they behave "as enemies of the cross of Christ." Since the cross represents service, suffering, and sacrifice, we should assume that these enemies downplay the servant nature of the faith and reject the element of suffering that believers take upon themselves. They are destined for "destruction," Paul says, because "they have abandoned Christ by adopting a lifestyle that is totally opposed to the redemptive work of the cross."[12] The cross represents suffering, as in the Christ hymn, Jesus became "obedient to death — even death on a cross" (2:8), and Paul's own hope that he might "know the power of his [Christ's] resurrection and participation in his sufferings, becoming like him in his death" (3:10).

Paul charges next that "their god is their stomach, and their glory is in their shame" (3:19). These accusations are connected with Paul's final statement that "their mind is set on earthly things." The references to "stomach" and the contrast between glory and shame remain an enigma. Perhaps Paul connects stomach with eating practices of the Jews, pointing us to his earlier comments about the "evildoers" who promote circumcision. As Paul declared to the Galatian Gentiles, if these men underwent circumcision, they are then required to do the entire law (Gal 5:3), which would include restricted table fellowship. Paul accuses these agitators, those who tried to compel the Gentile male believers to be circumcised, of wanting "to avoid being persecuted for the cross of Christ" (6:12). Those who see the Messiah as a piece to be fitted into the existing puzzle of Jewish life, who understand Jewish rituals and practices as essential to every believer's life, are still living in the present age. Paul, of

---

10. Bockmuehl, *Philippians*, 230.
11. Fee, *Philippians*, 369.
12. Ibid., 371.

course, never renounces his Jewish heritage, only its relative importance next to life in Christ.

Or perhaps Paul denotes pagan converts who have slid back to their old ways of indulging at pagan festivals and glorying in their old gods. They could represent a libertine fringe of the Christian movement. They sanction gluttony, expression of sensual desires, and the pursuit of fame. Paul would certainly lament any group of believers who turned from godly living to indulge their passions and follow after worldly goods and goals.

We may have two examples of this sort of believer. Revelation 2:20 refers to the prophet Jezebel (perhaps a derogatory label), who encourages believers to continue participating in pagan festivals, thus preserving their membership in trade guilds. Again, the "strong" in Corinth boast in their decision to eat meat sacrificed to idols because, they rationalize, "an idol is nothing" (1 Cor 8:4–8). No doubt a wing in the Christian movement justified their participation in former pagan festivals as a way to keep a foot in both the pagan and Christian camps.

Perhaps in the end, Paul's genius is revealed in his fluid and encompassing descriptors of this group. Regardless of whom he intends, those who despise the cross and live for today face destruction in the end. Those who set their minds on earthly, fleshly goals have only those as their reward. But Paul sees beyond that; he is captured by an eschatological vision of bodily resurrection.

Watch for Our Savior from Heaven (3:20–21)
Paul sees beyond natural sight to the vision of God's triumphal reign in Christ, and he wants the Philippians to live in that hope as well. But to do so, they must reorient their thinking and priorities. I grew up in south central Pennsylvania on a small farm, and we had a saying, "Make hay while the sun shines." That meant that when a couple days in August looked free from afternoon thundershowers, farmers busied themselves mowing, drying, and baling the hay. I recall one frantic afternoon when all hands were called upon to load the bales in wagons and truck beds to get the hay into the barn before the skies opened.

In a much more dramatic way, Paul asks the Philippians to reimagine their daily priorities, their commitments, their values, their treasures, and their goals, all in light of the gospel promises. These final two verses draw a striking contrast to the activities and fate of the enemies of the cross. Instead of ruin, the Philippians will enjoy heaven; instead of a god of the stomach, they will welcome the Savior of the world; instead of dying in one's shame, their lowly bodies will be transformed into the likeness and glory of the Son.

The opening sentence of 3:20 includes a noun not found elsewhere in the New Testament, *politeuma*. The term was used in wider Greek circles to indicate commonwealth or citizenship. It has the idea of an ethnic group living abroad in a foreign city. It carries the sense of being an active body that regulates its constituents. Both Jews and Greeks used it to describe the body politic of a polis or Greek city. Importantly, it also carries the sense of exile or colony — a group whose main social body lives in a distant homeland. What we should not hear in this term is modern democracy — one person, one vote, and civic duties incumbent on all citizens — not least because few people were citizens of Rome or of their city.

Paul seems to use this term to describe the Philippian church for two reasons. First, it stresses their unity as a group set apart from the other groups within the polis. That is, they have a unique identity in their town. Second, it tweaks the term's general meaning in Philippi, which stressed that city's status as a colony of Rome. Philippi held the highest possible status of any city outside of Italy and was justifiably proud of that honor. Paul transposes such honor to the heavenly kingdom. Even as Rome exists currently, so too Paul stresses that the Philippians' commonwealth also exists in heaven — it is more real than the seven hills guarding the "eternal" city, Rome.

Another possibility is that *politeuma* is borrowed from the enemies of the cross, who chose to identify their "Christian group" with a somewhat common Jewish label of Jews living outside their homeland. If so, Paul turns the label on its head by noting both that Jews and Gentiles in Christ are members of this commonwealth, and that its homeland is not part of this present age but is rooted in the age to come.

Perhaps the phrase "our citizenship is in heaven" sounds less real to our ears. But the verb tense used here is in the present — this heavenly home exists now. Moreover, this heavenly home is not just a future example of what we have now, but is of a totally different nature. In this new place, love rules, sin is banished, and joy covers all things. And believers today actually have an address in this place! We are not ultimately defined by the earthly situations and circumstances. The medical diagnosis, the shattered dreams, the broken relationships, the list of regrets — they don't ultimately define where we live or who we are. To the Philippians, Paul says that they are an ethnic group currently living in exile. To the Corinthians he writes that they are being transformed into Christ's image, with ever-increasing glory (2 Cor 3:18), knowing that their earthly tent (body), if and when destroyed, has "an eternal house in heaven" (5:2).

Our Savior Will Come (3:20)

Paul explains that from this exalted place, the Lord Jesus Christ, our Savior, will come. In Paul's time, townspeople would pour out beyond the city walls and line the main street into the city to honor a victorious general. Josephus describes Emperor Vespasian's welcome to Rome, hailed as Benefactor and Savior. Everyone—men, women, children—left the city and lined the street to catch a glimpse of the triumphant new emperor.[13] Likewise, the people of Antioch lined the main road into their city to welcome Titus, Vespasian's son, fresh from his victory over Jerusalem.[14] Everyone wanted to celebrate with the victorious army.

By happy chance I once happened to be in London for the Queen's speech, an annual event where Queen Elizabeth II ceremoniously opens Parliament. Roads were blocked to make way for the stately parade of matching cavalry and the horse-drawn carriage with Her Royal Highness inside, waving and smiling. After a brief ceremony in the Parliament building, she retraced her steps back to the palace. As an American tourist, it was grandeur beyond anything I'd seen. I was happy to wait the hour or two to see this event. This example of awaiting and watching a head of state hardly merits mention compared to the greatness of Christ's return, when he will be welcomed by the entire body of believers worldwide. We all recall standing alongside our hometown street as the high school band marched past, and our hearts swelled with emotion. Paul wants us to draw on that picture and magnify it a million times. It is this great event in which the *politeuma* of the saints takes part.

Our Transformation (3:21)

Paul goes on to say that believers have something life-changing awaiting them. When Jesus the Savior returns, he will transform the believer's body, a body of humiliation, so that it will share the likeness of the body of glory that is Christ's. Two points bear mention. First, Christ is identified as "Savior" here, a rare appellation in the New Testament (see John 4:42; Eph 5:23; 2 Tim 1:10; Titus 1:4; 2:13). Paul perhaps chooses this term because it was also used to venerate Caesar. For example, in an important inscription from Priene that recalculates the yearly calendar based on Augustus's birthday, Caesar is called "Savior."[15] Yet I detect a note of irony here in Paul, for Caesar's feet are of clay, and even his subsequent apotheosis (becoming a god at his death) did

---

13. Josephus, *Jewish War* 7.4.1.

14. Ibid., 7.5.2.

15. The fragment reads in part, "Since Providence, which has ordered all things and is deeply interested in our life, has set in most perfect order by giving us Augustus, whom she filled with virtue that he might benefit humankind, sending him as a savior ... that he might end war and arrange all things...." For a discussion of this inscription and the gospel of Mark, see Craig A. Evans, "Mark's Incipit and the Priene Calendar Inscription: From Jewish Gospel to Greco-Roman Gospel," in *Journal of Greco-Roman Christianity and Judaism* 1 (2000): 69; see http://craigaevans.com/studies.htm.

not promise a returning victory over all forces of evil in the world. Thus Paul may be subtly mocking the minuscule expectations of Augustus Savior, in comparison with the ultimate power and goodness of Christ the Savior.

Second, Paul may have used "Savior" because those "enemies of the cross," who despised Christ's suffering, also had no true sense of Jesus as Savior. Most Philippians wanted safety and security through military might, and when they found a man who could deliver that, they identified him as savior. Perhaps Paul's opponents saw safety in standing under the umbrella of Judaism, an accepted religion. But Christ the Savior has a much more radical view of the world's problems, and a much more invasive solution. The problem is sin, through and through, and the solution is new heavens and a new earth, complete with new, transformed bodies.

Christ "will transform our lowly bodies." The core of this verb is the Greek word *schēma* ("form"), which Paul uses in the phrase "being found in appearance [form] as a human" (2:7). Again, our bodies are currently in a state of humility or humiliation, even as Christ accepted humiliation and was obedient unto death (2:8). Paul may describe our bodies here as "lowly," or he may emphasize that in our earthly bodies we experience weakness and suffering.[16] Paul is not decrying our fleshly existence; rather, he notes that our current life is one of affliction in this present evil age. But when we are transformed, we will share in the likeness of Christ. The adjective "like" (3:21) combines *morphē* with the prefix "with" (*syn*). The Christ hymn in 2:6–7 explained that though the Son was in very nature (*morphē*) God, he took the *morphē* of a slave. And we saw the cognate verb in 3:10, as Paul longed to "become like [Christ] in his death."

Now in 3:20–21, Paul draws together two themes discussed throughout the letter, especially in the Christ hymn. Paul explained there that the nature or character of God was to *not* take advantage of status, privilege, or position. Christ did not consider his equality with God as something to be used for his own advantage. Further in the hymn, we find that Christ died on a cross. Ancient ears would not be surprised to hear this, for it was a common fate for slaves. This thread of the hymn, then, stresses the supreme social shame endured and embraced by Jesus on our behalf. It is this aspect of his death that Paul desires to know, "becoming like him in his death" (3:11).

Hellerman argues that in this hymn and subsequent argument, Paul turns the Roman social virtues upside down. The Roman *cursus honorum*, or "formalized sequence of public offices that marked out the prescribed social pilgrimage for aspiring senatorial aristocrats," was upended and replaced by a

---

16. Fee, *Philippians*, 382, n 28.

cursus pudorum or an ignominious course.[17] Paul desires for himself and all other Philippian Christians of means to forego the path of earthly honor and instead embrace service for others. To become like Christ in his death is to become a servant of all until one draws their last breath.

But there is another part of the hymn that describes Christ's deity taking up human flesh — the incarnation (2:7). Christ is in the form (*schēma*) of humanity. This too Paul connects with believers in 3:21, noting that our present bodies will be transformed (trans-*schēma*-ed). Christ's human form was both humble and obedient, which led to his dying on the cross. So too, Paul says, we participate in his (Christ's) suffering. But the glory is always and only Christ's. His is the victory over sin and death; ours is the sure hope of transformation to his likeness.

But it is wrong to assume that this is all about us! This transformation of the saints to conformity to Christ's glorious body is but one piece of his full victory over all powers, putting all things in subjection to him. Christ came to save sinners; he came to give life abundantly. But he also came to right the destruction plaguing creation. It is not enough to save human souls; he must vanquish death once for all, subjecting all powers, all of creation under his just and loving hand. Paul writes the same sentiment in 1 Corinthians 15:20 – 28, that God has the final word, and that word is victory. Victory over sin, evil, and death.

The following hymn captures this beautifully:

This is my Father's world, O let me ne'er forget
that though the wrong seems oft so strong, God is the ruler yet.
This is my Father's world: why should my heart be sad?
The Lord is King; let the heavens ring!
God reigns; let the earth be glad.

Maltbie Babcock (1858 – 1901) penned those words in 1901. A pastor at First Presbyterian Church in Lockport, New York, he regularly walked in the morning, exclaiming to those he greeted, "I'm going out to see my Father's world." Lockport is about twenty miles from Niagara Falls. On a trip to the Holy Land in 1901, he was struck down suddenly by illness. In the flyleaf of his Bible, one finds these words: "Committed myself again with Christian brothers to unreserved docility and devotion before my Master."[18]

---

17. Joseph H. Hellerman, *Reconstructing Honor in Roman Philippi: Carmen Christi as* Cursus Pudorum (Cambridge: Cambridge University Press, 2005), 1 – 2.

18. *This Day in Presbyterian History: Daily Devotional Readings in Scripture, the Westminster Standards, and Presbyterian History* (August 3, 2012). See www.thisday.pcahistory.org/2012/08/august – 3-maltbie-babcock-composer/.

The Cross

Paul speaks of enemies of the cross. Because he puts the article in front of "cross" and defines it as Christ's, we know he is speaking directly about Jesus' cross, the cross on which Jesus took the weight of the world's sins. But who can possibly be a friend of a cross? Would not everyone want to be an enemy of that mechanism of torture and terrorism? Undoubtedly no one in Philippi would be under any illusions about the pain associated with it. Most would have seen such executions, and even children were not shielded from such torturous sights.

Today we marvel at the cruelty meted out by the Roman officials, and rightly so. But in focusing on the physical pain of crucifixion, we can lose sight of its equally important function in the ancient world as a social shaming tool. Families avoided shame at all costs, even choosing suicide rather than face a trial or accusation of wrongdoing. The book of Hebrews reminds us that Jesus took up the cross, "scorning its shame" (Heb 12:2). These "enemies of the cross" mentioned in Philippians may have focused, not on denying the forgiveness of sins that Jesus' death brought, but rather on the shame that attended death by crucifixion. To claim allegiance to a crucified leader was to open yourself to utter social disgrace and embarrassment. If the social currency was honor, the crucified one had less than zero in his purse.

Today we don't feel the pull of pagan festivals, and we thus might not connect ourselves with a label like "enemy of the cross." This is especially true because we see the cross primarily in relation to forgiveness of sins, less for its shaming quality. Our Western culture is less an honor/shame culture; we admire individuals who chart their own path, who care little for society's assessment of them. So it is hard for us to appreciate the shame aspect of the cross that reinforced the social hierarchy of the Roman world.

Nevertheless, like the ancient world, we operate with a "me first" mentality. We excuse impoliteness if it serves the overall effort to get ahead. And we often live by the maxim that "the end justifies the means," whether we own up to it or not. So at the level of individualism, we, like those enemies of the cross two thousand years ago in Philippi, resist the cross's call on our lives. That call insists that others come first, and not only when it is convenient.

Who Are the Others?

Who are these "others" who come first? Not just family, neighbors, and fellow church members; these are also the ones who ask you to carry their load one mile (but you take it two miles, Matt 5:41). These are the ones who cheated you out of a promotion or swindled you out of your retirement savings. Recall Jesus' answer to the question, "Who is my neighbor"? The answer—a Samaritan—has rung down through the ages and left humans without excuse.

Dr. Feng-Shan Ho (1901–1997), from the Hunan province of China, is one example of someone who understood the shame of the cross and embraced it. He lost his father at age seven, and the Norwegian Lutheran Mission helped his family and educated him. He earned a PhD in political economics from the University of Munich in 1932, and it was his skill in the German language that helped land him the position of Chinese Consul-General of Vienna in 1938–40. When Hitler annexed Austria in March of 1938, there were approximately 185,000 Jews living in that country, 120,000 of them in Vienna. Against direct orders from the Chinese ambassador in Berlin, Ho gave over 2,000 visas to Jewish families, allowing them to flee the Nazis. He also interceded directly for Jews. On one occasion, his neighbor's (Lilith Sylvia Dorn) brother was taken to Dachau. Feng-Shan personally sought Karl's release. Yet he expected no fanfare, no reward, no ticker-tape parade.

His daughter notes that he lived in accordance with the Chinese saying, "A good deed performed for others to see is not truly a good deed."[19] Jesus similarly cautions his disciples not to let the left hand know what the right hand is doing and to eschew the most important seat at the table. Indeed, Feng-Shan died in relative obscurity in San Francisco at age ninety-seven. His motivation seemed in part to resist imperialism in any form. His generation of Chinese had felt the sting of humiliation of one hundred years of Western imperialism in China, and he chose to extend compassion to the Jews who were experiencing horrific persecution. But his pastor, Rev. Charles Kuo, noted, "He knew he had received many gifts from God. He felt that they were not given to him solely for his own benefit, but to do for others, for his fellow man."[20]

Dr. Ho was a founding member of the Chinese Lutheran Church in San Francisco, and he wrote his memoirs, *Forty Years of My Diplomatic Life*.[21] *Yad Vashem*, the Holocaust memorial in Jerusalem, awarded the title "Righteous Among the Nations" posthumously to Dr. Ho. But these awards did not motivate his actions, and he sought no special honor. Indeed as he wrote to his wife on New Year's Day, 1947, "The gifts Heaven bestows are not by chance. The convictions of heroes not lightly formed. Today I summon all spirit and strength, urging my steed forward ten thousand miles."[22]

---

19. Manli Ho, in *China Daily* (Sept. 26, 2007), 11.
20. Pierre Moulin, *Dachau, Holocaust, and US Samurais: Nisei Soldiers First in Dachau?* (Bloomington, IN: AuthorHouse, 2007), 182.
21. Feng-Shan Ho, *Forty Years of My Diplomatic Life* (Pittsburgh: Dorrance, 1990).
22. Moulin, *Dachau*, 182.

Embracing the Cross

Each generation faces evil and the challenges to human life and well-being. A *National Geographic* article in 2012 did an exposé on a crucifixion that occurred in Yemen.[23] A woman reported that a man had been killed and crucified, hung for three days as a message to others not to resist the ruling militia. Here we are in the twenty-first century, and crucifixion is still used as a method of terrorizing the population. For Christians in Paul's time to support someone who was condemned to such torturous death was courageous indeed. As in Yemen today, few would stand with the crucified man, knowing that such punishment could await them. These early Christians certainly had great courage to stand firm in the face of such torture.

Nevertheless, Paul as a Roman citizen would not have faced crucifixion. Thus when Paul speaks of imitating him, both he and his audience realize that from a legal perspective, many of them probably could not imitate Paul's Roman citizenship and its attending advantages. Did this knowledge shape his presentation or his reception by those to whom he preached? Did anyone from the crowd ever yell to him that he's asking them to do more than he'd ever be expected to do? We do not know. This may be because when Paul wrote, Christians were not being crucified or thrown to the lions as they were in the next few centuries. Paul seems to have used his citizenship only as a vehicle to get him to Rome and to secure safe passage from Philippi *after* he spent a night in prison. In other words, his citizenship did not prevent his suffering, nor did it ultimately save him from execution.

Rather, he used its advantage subversively to promote opportunities to preach the gospel in places that noncitizens were unlikely to reach. His mission was not to die on a cross, but to preach to as many cities as he could. His citizenship did not prevent him from getting beaten or shipwrecked.

---

23. Joshua Hammer, "Days of Reckoning," *National Geographic* (September 2012). http://ngm .nationalgeographic.com/2012/09/yemen/hammer-text.

CHAPTER 12

Philippians 4:1 – 3

LISTEN to the Story

¹Therefore, my brothers and sisters, you whom I love and long for, my joy and crown, stand firm in the Lord in this way, dear friends! ²I plead with Euodia and I plead with Syntyche to be of the same mind in the Lord. ³Yes, and I ask you, my true companion, help these women since they have contended at my side in the cause of the gospel, along with Clement and the rest of my co-workers, whose names are in the book of life.

Listening to the text in the Story: Exodus 32:31 – 35; Psalm 69:16 – 36; 133:1 – 3.

These three verses really belong in chapter 3 as the conclusion of Paul's argument that began in 1:27. We can trace both verbal and thematic links through these chapters, and we find that Paul has been leading up to this crescendo of eschatological hope and practical gospel living since he enjoined the faithful in Philippi to stand fast against the world's onslaught, bind themselves to each other in the unity of the Lord, and focus on the sure hope of Christ's victorious return.

EXPLAIN the Story

Connections through Key Terms and Themes with Previous Chapters

At least two key terms on which Paul builds his argument in 4:1 – 3 occur earlier in this letter. (1) In 4:1, Paul encourages the believers to "stand firm," using the same verb as in 1:27 when he admonished them to "stand firm in the one Spirit" and with a single purpose. It is no accident that both in 1:27 and in 3:20 – 4:1 Paul refers to the Philippians' citizenship established in Christ and the injunction to stand firm. In 1:27, the call is to stand as one people, one church united in the gospel. In 4:1, Paul asks the church to stand together and hopes that two leaders, Euodia and Syntyche, will work together toward the same goal, the advancement of the gospel.

(2) Paul calls on Euodia and Syntyche "to be of the same mind," repeating the phrase used in 2:2 (see discussion there). We cannot overemphasize Paul's conviction concerning the unity of the local church body, that in Christ, believers think with a renewed, transformed mind-set that privileges others above themselves. We might narrow this concern a bit more, that the disunity among the leaders, the *episkopoi* (overseers) and *diakonoi* (deacons) (1:1), is worrisome to Paul.

Paul's language in 4:1 overflows with affectionate terms for the Philippians. He loves them, repeating the adjective "beloved" twice.[1] He longs for them and considers them his "joy and crown." Paul uses similar language in 1 Thessalonians 2:19, when he speaks of boasting about the Thessalonians on the Lord's return. Fee suggests a similar eschatological scope here, linking Philippians 4:1 with the previous passage stressing the Lord's coming. Paul indicated in 2:16 that the Philippians' steadfastness promises to allow him to boast in his labor among them.

How often today do church leaders, youth directors, parachurch leaders, and missionaries imagine their relationship to their congregations with such affection and with such eschatological vision? Usually we hear sad stories of pastors who valued the wealthy or prominent congregants, finding their joy and crown among the things of this world. Paul, however, believes that these ragtag former pagans will be his grounds for boasting on the Lord's return. Paul speaks not of self-congratulatory, prideful boasting, but boasting that represents God's faithfulness in and through Paul's ministry.

As to themes, while some argue that the situation described in 4:1–3 about Euodia and Syntyche is minor, unimportant, or incidental,[2] most recent commentators hold that Paul's concern for unity between these believers is central to the letter, if not the primary reason for sending it. Thurston notes that their situation is representative of the general disunity rampant among the Philippians,[3] while Peterlin suggests that the dissension between them marks the key issue facing the congregation.[4] Osiek[5] and Fee[6] argue that Paul has been building up to this culminating plea for unity made from the begin-

---

1. The NIV translates the first occurrence as "you whom I love" and the second one as "dear friends."

2. O'Brien, *Philippians*, 479.

3. Bonnie B. Thurston and Judith M. Ryan, *Philippians and Philemon* (SP; Collegeville, MN: Liturgical, 2009), 142.

4. Peterlin, *Paul's Letter to the Philippians*, 101–2.

5. Osiek, *Philippians, Philemon*, 109.

6. Fee, *Philippians*, 385–86.

ning of his letter. One need only read 1 Corinthians 1:11–3:23 to understand how vital church unity is to Paul. Any possible factions must be resolved and reunited so that Christ's body might be whole. And Paul's unprecedented mention of their names suggests a high degree of concern.

Characters in 4:1-3

The language and themes represented in verses 1–3 clearly fit with the overarching burden of Paul's message to the Philippians—stand fast in the hope of Christ, and stand together in the Spirit. United in the single cause of the gospel, Paul desires that they model his focus and passion, desiring to know Christ deeply and reflecting Christ's obedience in service to God and the church. But what are the specific nature of the conflict and the specific descriptions of the persons involved? It is to those important questions that we now turn.

Paul gives us only tantalizing hints about who "Euodia" and "Syntyche" are, and from those commentators try to fill out the picture. The fact that they are named suggests that they are important in the community. Fee notes how rare it is for Paul to give the name of a person with whom he has a disagreement (see Hymenaeus and Alexander in 1 Tim 1:20; 2 Tim 2:18).[7] Euodia's name means "good journey" or "pleasant," and Syntyche's name is related to the goddess Tyche, the goddess of Fate or good luck (Fortuna in Latin). Both are well-attested Greek names and suggest a background of poverty, low status, and perhaps even slavery.[8]

Presumably Euodia and Syntyche were of equal social status. The verb "plead with" may signal that both women were in a subordinate position relative to Paul. We cannot tell by their names whether they were from Philippi or were a traveling missionary pair, similar to Tryphaena and Tryphosa (Rom 16:12). Paul also notes that their "names are in the book of life."[9] This phrase recalls Paul's joyous note of hope in 3:20–21 that points to the Savior who comes from heaven for his own—those whose names are recorded in the Lamb's book of life (Rev. 21:27).

Perhaps the church in Philippi met in several houses, much as it did in Corinth. If so, these women may have led their respective house churches. We hear of Nympha (Col 4:15), Lydia (Acts 16:15, 40), and Priscilla and Aquila (Rom 16:3–5) having churches meet in their homes. They had influence over others, but we need not assume that such influence was formal or related to

---

7. Ibid., 390, n 27.

8. Richard S. Ascough, *Paul's Macedonian Associations* (Tübingen: Mohr Siebeck, 2003), 125.

9. Other occurrences of this phrase include Exod 32:32–3; Ps 69:28; Dan 12:1; Luke 10:20; Rev 3:5; 13:8; 17:8; 20:12, 15; 21:27; 22:19.

holding a title or office. In the first century, the social system of patronage was strong, and Paul drew on that when he stayed with Lydia on his first visit to Philippi. She opened her house to Paul and his group, giving them shelter, food, and safety. Patrons had responsibilities toward their clients (friends), and the latter were expected to show public honor in return. Patrons often had political power in the town or trade guild. They expected support for their projects and goals. Rival groups formed around different patrons.

Within the city of Philippi, it is often assumed that women in general held high positions. But such assumptions are based on a faulty reading of the evidence, because most are relying on inscriptions and texts that speak of Macedonian queens from the late classical and Hellenistic periods. Others suggest that women were active in the religious life in Philippi, because so many of the cults were dedicated to goddesses, such as Artemis/Hecate/Diana. But this conclusion rests on the faulty assumption that women were drawn more toward goddess worship and men to the worship of gods. In reality, both men and women worshiped gods and goddesses.[10]

While patrons often held great informal power within a community, and it is possible that these women were patrons of Paul or of the Philippian church, most commentators believe they were (also) part of the group of *episkopoi* ("overseers") and *diakonoi* ("deacons") (1:1). Philippians is the only letter in which Paul notes these groups in his greetings. This unusual feature, along with mentioning these women by name, likely indicates that the women belong in one of these categories. The fourth-century church father Chrysostom claimed that these women were the "chief" or "head" of the church in Philippi.[11]

Both terms took formal shape in the second-century church, developing into a single bishopric overseeing numerous elders and deacons in the parish. But in the first century, the office responsibilities were more fluid, and a church could have several bishops. The term *episkopoi* is found in Acts 20:28 in Paul's address to the leaders of Ephesus (see also 1 Tim 3:2; Titus 1:7; cf. 1 Pet 2:25 [as a title for Jesus]). Here and in Acts 20, Paul uses the plural. Deacons include Paul himself, Phoebe, Timothy, Epaphras, and Tychicus;[12] Paul speaks more generally about deacons in 1 Timothy 3:8, 12. Twice Paul refers to Christ as a deacon or servant (Rom 15:8; Gal 2:17, although in Galatians he speaks rhetorically).

We have no single person other than Christ named as overseer in the New

---

10. Cohick, *Women in the World of the Earliest Christians*, 159–93.

11. Chrysostom, *Commentary on Philippians*, Homily 13.

12. Deacons: Paul (1 Cor 3:5–6; 6:4; Eph 3:7; Col 1:23, 25), Phoebe (Rom 16:2–3), Timothy (Phil 1:1), Epaphras (Col 1:7), and Tychicus (Eph 6:21; Col 4:7).

Testament. This leads Peterlin to conclude that since no woman is named an *episkopos* in apostolic or postapostolic periods, Euodia and Syntyche could not have been *episkopoi*.[13] But since no individual man (except Jesus Christ) is so titled, this begs the question. Moreover, the passage in 1 Timothy 3:1–13 uses the generic masculine category to speak of overseers and deacons. True, Paul indicates that an overseer should be married, or married only once, or only to one wife. Since the Romans did not practice bigamy, this text likely asks that an overseer not remarry, a common virtue at this time (known as *univira*). Paul enjoins deacons also to have one wife (3:12), but he also speaks of women as deacons, which suggests that his statement that deacons have one wife was not to be taken as a requirement.

Several pieces of evidence are brought forward to argue that Euodia and Syntyche should be considered *episkopoi*. First, given that patronage was so important and early churches met in homes, it seems likely that these women functioned in some leadership capacity. Second, Paul's designation of the women as coworkers is used to identify itinerant missionaries as well as resident leaders (1 Cor 3:9; Phil 2:25; Phlm 1; 3 John 8).[14]

While we can speculate as to whether Euodia and Syntyche were overseers or deacons, there is no doubt that Paul calls them his "co-workers," who have labored alongside him in efforts for the gospel. Other people identified as Paul's coworkers include Timothy, Titus, Priscilla and Aquila, Apollos, Philemon, Urbanus, Epaphroditus, Mark, Aristarchus, Demas, and Luke.[15] Within this group, some traveled and preached, some remained in towns to disciple and lead house churches, and some served as Paul's liaisons with the churches. Indeed the variety of responsibilities evidenced in this category suggests that if Euodia and Syntyche were deacons, we still might not know exactly what they did! Such fluidity is consistent with the wider Greco-Roman world's assemblies and trade guilds. Ascough notes that terms on inscriptions are inconsistent with no standardization of meaning.[16]

Euodia and Syntyche: Be of the Same Mind (4:2)

Paul enjoins these women "to be of the same mind." Most commentators hold that these two women were in disagreement with each other. But a few have recently argued that these women were together *against* Paul. Joseph Marchal argues that Paul tends to distinguish his views from others and to

---

13. Peterlin, *Philippians*, 107.

14. Osiek, *Philippians, Philemon,* 111–12.

15. Timothy (Rom 16:21; 1 Thess 3:2), Titus (2 Cor 8:23), Priscilla and Aquila (Rom 16:3), Apollos (1 Cor 3:9), Philemon (Phlm 1), Urbanus (Rom 16:9), Epaphroditus (Phil 2:25), and Mark, Aristarchus, Demas, and Luke (Phlm 24).

16. Ascough, *Paul's Macedonian Associations,* 131–33.

stress sameness, with himself as the model. These women, who hold influence in the church, have drifted from Paul's teachings or expectations, and Paul entreats them to return to their former close relationship.[17] Marchal's argument relies on both feminist and postcolonial reading strategies and presumes that Paul insists on sameness within his circles of influence. Even aside from his reading strategies, Marchal underappreciates Paul's openness to discuss any disagreements he might have with those in his churches. And he undervalues Paul's statements that all believers are in Christ, so that the call to imitate Paul is only one example of what imitating Christ looks like. Moreover, Paul holds up other (unnamed) leaders for the Philippians to emulate (3:17).

What differences might these two women have had with each other? The only inference we can draw is from Paul's explicit concern, which suggests the situation is serious. Thus those who think it is a petty difference[18] cannot adequately explain why Paul "calls them out" in front of the whole church. Some suggest a theological dispute, but it seems odd that Paul would not instruct them further on how to resolve it. If it was a minor theological difference, he would likely not have taken the time to bring it up. If it was a serious theological or church procedure error, Paul would have specified the correct doctrine (see Paul's comments in 1 Cor 5).

Most likely, Euodia and Syntyche have disagreed on how to live out their faith in Christ. Several possibilities present themselves. Perhaps they are at odds over how to best relate to the wider imperial environment. Marchal notes that the verb "contended at my side" carries a military overtone, portraying them as co-combatants with Paul in the fight against the imperial cult.[19]

Or perhaps they struggled in how to accommodate their social class or rank with their Christian walk. In the ancient world, friendship as a social category was *agonistic*, that is, highly competitive. The political and social structures of this time encouraged people to outdo each other. Our sense of friendship today can carry a sense of competition, and we all have had friends who needed to be "one-up" on us. But our ideal friend is one who accepts himself or herself and us without competing. In Paul's day, the political instability and the social pressures to always gain honor and avoid shame shaped the category of friendship. Thus these two women, part of the leadership team with Paul, may understand their "friendship" in typical, worldly ways, competing with each other for honor and influence in the church.[20]

17. Marchal, *Hierarchy, Unity, and Imitation*, 148.
18. O'Brien, *Philippians*, 478–79.
19. Marchal, *Hierarchy, Unity, and Imitation*, 33.
20. Ibid., 35.

Third, a related possibility is that these women are in a court battle. Peterlin postulates that we might have here a situation similar to that found in 1 Corinthians 6:1 – 8, wherein believers were taking each other to court.[21] Supporting this view is the fact that Paul calls for a mediator, much as he does in the Corinthian situation.

Finally, perhaps these women disputed over administering social aid to the poor in their midst. If they were patrons and deacons, they would likely have been responsible for aid to the destitute in their midst. Perhaps a situation similar to Acts 6 arose in Philippi, maybe between the two house churches led by Euodia and Syntyche. Indeed, we can think of a number of possible situations where through misunderstanding, miscommunication, and different assessments of need, Euodia and Syntyche came to a fork in the road. Paul asks that they join hands and go forward together in Christ, and he desires "the true companion" to facilitate this reconciliation.

Whatever their differences, Paul "pleads with" them, a verb that carries the sense of encouraging, consoling, even begging. Using the same verb in Romans, Paul puts forward an appeal for the Romans to join him in prayer (Rom 15:30) and to watch out for those who cause dissensions (16:17). Paul uses this verb when sounding the call to holy living as he challenges the Thessalonians to walk worthy of God, the one who called them into his kingdom and glory (1 Thess 2:12; 4:1).

These two women should have "the same mind in the Lord." The phrase is a word-for-word repetition of the request leveled to the entire church in 2:2 ("like-minded"). Paul is appealing to Euodia and Syntyche to put aside their personal ambitions or agendas and serve the other as they serve Christ together. It is not unheard of for believers to clash over ministry goals. Paul and Barnabas did so over whether to include John Mark on their second missionary journey. These two men failed to reach an agreement, and so each pursued his own course (Acts 15:36 – 41). Yet Paul's later letters demonstrate that the situation over Mark was resolved (Col 4:10; Phlm 24); perhaps this is why Paul can speak so encouragingly to these coworkers, for he too faced struggles in ministry, and in the Spirit worked through them toward reconciliation.

True Companion, Clement, and the Rest (4:3)

The strange Greek word *syzygos* has puzzled translators and commentators. Paul indicates that this genuine "companion" ("yokefellow") will help rebuild the relationship between Euodia and Syntyche. We have no evidence that the Greek word is a proper name, *Syzygos*; most likely it refers to a person

---

21. Peterlin, *Philippians*, 127.

well-known by the Philippians. Suggestions include Epaphroditus, who is likely bringing this letter with him, so he would understand Paul's concerns and be able to convey them well to the women. Another option is Timothy, though he is arriving later than Epaphroditus. Fee suggests Luke, who probably stayed in Philippi for several years, based on inferences from the "we" passages in Acts 16 and 20.[22] Whoever this person is, he is trusted by Paul, and he believes will also be well received by the Philippians.

This "true companion" has some standing in the community and thus can support the reconciliation efforts between the two women. Paul leaves unsaid the specific form this help will take, but it must take into consideration the valiant history of service for Christ exhibited by Euodia and Syntyche. The reconciliation effort will not challenge the women's dedication to the gospel, nor will it question their membership in God's family. Rather, it will embolden them to serve each other as they serve Christ. This posture would serve the church well in Philippi — and today. Each local congregation should look within their own ranks for a *syzygos* to heal wounds, restore relationships, and refocus service selflessly to one another as unto Christ.

The name Clement is well attested; the Latin name is Clemens, a common slave name. Paul does not indicate whether this man is from Philippi or is a traveling missionary. He concludes by noting all the rest of his coworkers, whose names are in the book of life. Why does Paul mention Clement and the others? Is it an implied challenge to Euodia and Syntyche that other coworkers are able to be of the same mind, and thus so they too should strive for that goal? Or is Paul noting these other people to highlight the profound appreciation he has for the women, as they number among those who have risked all and who have a share in eternal life?

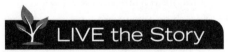 LIVE the Story

Reconciliation and the Mediator

Reconciliation is a noble endeavor; the unnamed figure to whom Paul points is entrusted with a task often relegated to secondary status until the fight breaks into the open and threatens to consume everyone. Paul understands the speed with which the fire of animosity can spread through a congregation, and thus we sense an urgency in his message to his *syzygos* to mediate between Euodia and Syntyche.

What might this mediator say if he were to engage a local American church or place of business today? In my own experience as a mediator in

---

22. Fee, *Philippians*, 394–5.

the workplace, I discovered three important points. First, a mediator must be trustworthy. They should keep a secret and hold confidential all interactions with the persons or groups in disagreement. Second, a mediator must be fair. By this I mean that the mediator must be committed to hearing each person's story with an open mind and open heart. Third, a mediator, especially a believer negotiating a truce between two other believers, must pray for a heartfelt love for those working toward reconciliation.

This approach takes time, energy, and a desire to see God change everyone in the process, including the mediator! I came away from this process with a chastened realization that I judge motives too quickly, I fail to forgive fully, and I doubt the strength of God's amazing love working in believers' intent on honoring God with their commitment to reconcile. What stands out most to me in the reconciliation process is the sense of divine victory when believers (and mediators) lay down their personal rights and agendas for the sake of the other. When that happens, everyone in the room realizes they are in the divine Presence, a holy place indeed.

John Paul Lederach

John Paul Lederach is a mediator of a different sort — the kind who faces bullets and mobs as part of his job bringing two sides together.[23] He worked with leaders in Nicaragua, Somalia, and the Philippines. He writes of a time in 1987 when he was awaiting a flight from Honduras to the United States. It was a well-known secret that Nicaraguan resistance troops camped in Honduras, and as he watched out the airport window, a helicopter fleet took off towards Nicaragua, returning in about an hour. As one landed close to the terminal, the pilot's face was visible except his eyes, hidden behind his dark sunglasses. A few hours later, the same man reappeared, a Honduran military official, who was waiting for an incoming plane. Lederach recalls thinking *What did he just do on the border, this very afternoon? Whose lives did he take?* Then "a righteous disdain floated in my pacifist mind."[24] Nothing prepared him for the visitor received by the colonel — a young girl with metal braces supporting her spindly legs. *The colonel is a father like me!* The thought stunned Lederach, and he concluded, "In the end, an enemy is rooted and constructed in our hearts and minds."[25]

Such experiences led Lederach to move from conflict resolution to reconciliation. Psalm 85:10 became central in working out this concept: "Truth and Mercy have met together. Justice and Peace have kissed" (his translation).

---

23. John Paul Lederach, *The Journey toward Reconciliation* (Scottsdale, PA: Herald, 1999).
24. Ibid., 46.
25. Ibid., 47 (italics original).

Lederach noticed that the psalmist treated these ideas as living embodiments. So in his training workshops on conflict resolution, he personifies each of these ideals and asked the participants to treat each concept as a person. To each of these "persons" the group asks, "What is Truth (or Mercy, Justice, Peace) most concerned about in the midst of a conflict?"[26] An individual from the group is chosen to be the voice of each of these "persons" and is addressed as Sister Mercy or Brother Justice. The group dialogues with these "people" rather than pitting the four ideals against each other. Lederach is convinced that these four voices must be heard together, not seen as contradictory forces. "We are not asked to choose between rain or sunshine. Each is different, but both are needed for sustaining life and growth. Such is the case with Truth and Mercy, Justice and Peace."[27]

Lederach uses these insights within the church as well, noting that the goal of reconciliation is a healed relationship, in both the personal and social sense. The church is a place "of Truth-discerning and Truth-telling. It is a place for vulnerable transparency.... It is a place of accountability. It is, after all, a place where we journey toward each other and toward God."[28]

---

26. Ibid., 53.
27. Ibid., 61.
28. Ibid., 132.

CHAPTER 13

Philippians 4:4–9

 LISTEN to the Story

> [4]Rejoice in the Lord always. I will say it again: Rejoice! [5]Let your gentleness be evident to all. The Lord is near. [6]Do not be anxious about anything, but in every situation, by prayer and petition, with thanksgiving, present your requests to God. [7]And the peace of God, which transcends all understanding, will guard your hearts and your minds in Christ Jesus.
>
> [8]Finally, brothers and sisters, whatever is true, whatever is noble, whatever is right, whatever is pure, whatever is lovely, whatever is admirable — if anything is excellent or praiseworthy — think about such things. [9]Whatever you have learned or received or heard from me, or seen in me — put it into practice. And the God of peace will be with you.

Listening to the text in the Story: Psalm 64:10; 95:1–2; 97:12; Habakkuk 3:17–19.

By now the reader is hardly surprised to hear the call to rejoice, for Paul rings this bell consistently throughout the letter. He rejoices though he is imprisoned, for Christ is preached regardless (perhaps because of) his dismal circumstances (1:18). He rejoices with the Philippians at their mutual exercising of their faith (2:18) and imagines their joy in receiving back Epaphroditus (2:28). He begins chapter 3 with a general call to rejoice (3:1), one that he echoes here. Paul is filled with joy as he prays for them, encouraged by their growth in the gospel (1:4–5, 25). He hopes to have even greater joy as they grow together in unity (2:2) and stand firm in their faith (4:1; see also 2:29).

Verses 4–9 sound staccato notes, exhibiting a "clipped, almost terse, style,"[1] typical of the endings of Paul's letters. But their content carries a surprising punch. On the surface, his words might appear as common sense platitudes to which anyone in the Greco-Roman world could assent. But a

---

1. Fowl, *Philippians*, 180–81. He points to 1 Cor 16:13; 2 Cor 13:11; 1 Thess 5:16–22.

second read makes clear that these exhortations are "much more substantial, demanding, and even subversive for the Philippians."[2]

 EXPLAIN the Story

The Context of This List of Virtues

Admittedly, these verses have puzzled commentators. Reumann believes 4:4–7 are "miscellaneous exhortations" unconnected to the previous verses, but echoing 3:1.[3] His sentiments tally with others that 4:4–9 are among the most contested verses in Philippians, not because their meaning is unclear, but because they seem out of step with Paul's argument. They seem to fit best as concluding remarks to the letter. For example, the phrase "finally" in 4:8 suggests the end of the letter. Yet as O'Brien notes, this expression can also indicate a transition or a new point in an argument (see 1 Thess 4:1).[4] Bockmuehl argues that Paul includes 4:8–9 to develop the implications of his charge to rejoice and pray.[5] Thus we can translate the expression as "in addition" or "beyond that."[6]

How do these verses connect with 4:10–20, Paul's "thank you" section? Fee argues that Paul's conclusion begins already with 4:4–9 — an epistolary ending that is longer than what most commentators expect. He offers three observations. First, Paul's letters do not exhibit a uniform pattern in his conclusions.[7] Second, here and in 1 Corinthians 16:15–18, which seems to be an interruption by Paul (a recommendation letter for Stephanas, Fortunatus, and Achaicus, noting their gift), Paul's appreciation and thanksgiving lie at the heart of the letters' closing. Third, 4:10–20 are lengthy because the letter fits the category of friendship letter[8] and because Paul exhibits rhetorical flourish. Fee concludes: "These will be the final words left ringing in their ears as the letter is concluded, words that have had to do with 'their concerns for the apostle.'"[9] This community has a close relationship with Paul, so it makes sense for him to include a lengthy segment detailing the gift's importance both to Paul himself and to their witness to the gospel.

2. Ibid., 181. "Joy is the appropriate response when one rightly perceives the unfolding of God's drama of salvation even in the midst of suffering and opposition."

3. Reumann, *Philippians*, 634.

4. O'Brien, *Philippians*, 348, 499.

5. Bockmuehl, *Philippians*, 249.

6. Ibid.

7. Fee, *Philippians*, 399.

8. I critique Fee's emphasis on the friendship letter in the introduction, pp. 8–10.

9. Fee, *Philippians*, 402.

Rejoice in the Lord Always (4:4)

Paul begins his concluding remarks in a manner similar to 1 Thessalonians 5:16–17: "rejoice always, pray without ceasing." Interestingly, both passages speak about church unity just before the charge to rejoice (Phil 4:1–3; 1 Thess 5:12–15). While our tendency today is to individualize this message, Paul speaks here to the church, perhaps in a worship context. He may even be reflecting back to the Christ hymn and its promise that every knee will bow and every tongue confess that Jesus Christ is Lord, to God's glory. This same God and Christ hear every supplication, every prayer, and grant the supernatural peace that only the Lord of all creation can provide. Paul joins with the psalmist, "Rejoice in the LORD, you who are righteous, and praise his holy name" (Ps 97:12; see also 64:10; 95:1–2).

The source of the Philippians' joy is participation in God's unfolding story of redemption. Paul noted in the previous chapter that such participation includes suffering (3:10), a reality he pointed to in 1:29—that the Philippians are called not only to believe in Christ, but also to have the privilege of suffering for him. The joy that comes from participation in witnessing to the gospel is not an end in itself, but a by-product.[10] It is the fruit of life in the Spirit (Gal 5:22). This joy comes not from achievement but from abiding with God, no matter what.

The Meaning of Gentleness (4:5)

In verse 5 Paul gives an injunction ("let your gentleness be known to all") and a statement ("the Lord is near"). Two key interpretive issues concern us: What nuances should be attached to the rare New Testament term "gentleness," and does "near" carry a spatial or temporal sense? To help with the first question, we should look at the adjective's use in 1 Timothy 3:3; Titus 3:2; James 3:17; and 1 Peter 2:18, as well as the cognate noun's use in Acts 24:4 and 2 Corinthians 10:1. The psalmist in Psalm 85:5 Septuagint (= 86:5 Hebrew) uses this word group to speak of God's compassionate character. Note also the *Wisdom of Solomon* 2:17–20, a second-century BC work, which records here the words of the ungodly about the righteous man:

> Let us see if his words are true,
> and let us test what will happen at the end of his life;
> for if the righteous man is God's child, he will help him,
> and will deliver him from the hand of his adversaries.

---

10. Fowl, *Philippians*, p. 182.

> Let us test him with insult and torture,
> so that we may find out how *gentle* he is,
> and make trial of his forbearance.
> Let us condemn him to a shameful death,
> for, according to what he says, he will be protected.

Osiek postulates that Paul might be using this word group to define the appropriate posture of endurance to be demonstrated by the Philippians in the midst of public harassment.[11] Furnish likewise suggests that the Christians' livelihood was continually threatened by the wider community's hostility toward the new faith, and that Paul is counseling them to forgive those who are hostile (see also 1 Thess 5:15).[12] Reumann notes that the term, while hard to translate, has a comfortable home in Greek, going back to Aristotle, where the word suggests reasonableness or fitting.[13]

Most likely Paul intends that the Philippians engage their neighbors with mercy and compassion. Do they do so in the hope that the latter will convert? That is, does Paul suggest this gentle posture as a missional tactic? Probably this demeanor is to reflect the believer's transformation, irrespective of its possible reception by others. The gentleness, mercy, and joy that should characterize a believer's life might be attractive to an outsider, or it might be the cause of ridicule. Regardless of the reaction, the call to gentleness is rooted in modeling Christ's own "meekness and gentleness" (2 Cor 10:1).

The Lord Is Near (4:5)

The phrase "the Lord is near" puzzles commentators because the range of "near" extends from temporal (coming soon) to spatial (next to me). Paul does not speak with apocalyptic fervor in Philippians, though in 1:10 he does mention the "day of Christ," and in 3:20–21 he encourages believers that the Savior Christ will return from heaven to conform them to his glorious body. In these two cases, the emphasis is on a future date at which time Christ's full power will be revealed. Reumann argues that this phrase is eschatological, underpinning Paul's ethics. "Because the Lord is near, exhibit patient steadfastness, stop being anxious about everything."[14]

However, since Paul mentions prayers in verse 6, the spatial sense of God's presence attending a believer's prayers should be considered. In this sense, Paul's words are similar to Psalm 145:18, "The LORD is near to all who call on

---

11. Osiek, *Philippians, Philemon*, 115–16.
12. Victor Paul Furnish, *The Moral Teachings of Paul: Selected Issues* (3rd ed.; Nashville: Abingdon, 2009), 145.
13. Reumann, *Philippians*, 611–13. See Aristotle, *Eth. Nic.* 5.10 1137a 31-b 27.
14. Ibid., 635.

him, to all who call on him in truth" (see also 119:151). Paul does not include any conjunctions linking this sentence to the previous sentence or the next, making it difficult to say whether he is reflecting back on what he has just written or ahead to what he will say about prayer. In the end, it might be best to conclude that both meanings are possible, and even intended by Paul.[15]

Prayers and Peace (4:6 – 7)

"Don't worry, be happy" might be a catchy phrase sung to a zippy tune, but it is far from Paul's serious injunction against worry or anxiety. For Paul, the lack of anxiety is rooted in the conviction that the Lord is near. Anxiety is worry without purpose or effecting change, as though one spins in circles, going nowhere. Anxiety must be addressed through prayer, not by being more self-aware or pursuing *apatheia*, the self-mastery promoted by the Stoics, a perfect indifference to situations. The goal is not to be divorced from suffering or to float above it, but to embrace its reality and to see in it the potential to strengthen one's witness, perseverance, and maturing in the faith.

Denise, a close friend of mine, captured Paul's meaning well as she talked about her long battle with cancer. Often one feels alone in the struggle, and it is easy to worry about the "what ifs." If I die, what about my three school-aged children? What about my husband? What about my aging mother? Worry is a signal that our gaze has shifted to the swirling clutter of events at our feet. We must lift our head and raise our eyes to the throne of God, to the figure of Jesus present with us. This act of faith must be repeated and strengthened. My friend spoke words like these to me when I expressed my fear of flying on a transatlantic flight. Her words brought me up short; I was allowing my mind to cycle through imagined scenarios rather than live in the present moment, where God is sovereign.

Instead of worrying about possible harassment by neighbors or the health and well-being of those in prison (such as Paul), the Philippians are encouraged to pray to God. Jesus encouraged his listeners to remember that God cares for them, for he knows they need food, clothing, and shelter (Matt 6:25 – 34). Paul experienced the provision of life's necessities, as he states later in this chapter (Phil 4:11 – 14). But in 4:6 he is likely thinking of the persecutions and troubles the Philippians face because of their testimony of faith. Certainly such testing can result in anxiety about having work and food to feed one's family.

The prayers Paul envisions should be characterized by "thanksgiving" (see Col. 3:15). Paul does not suggest that we can thank God for specific answers

---

15. Fee argues that Paul uses here an "intentional double entendre," *Philippians*, 407. See also Fowl, *Philippians*, 183.

even before they happen, as though a believer can define how God will act and that God just gives his stamp of approval. Instead, the thanksgiving Paul has in mind is an act of the will, a conviction of the heart. It is a defiant claim against the powers of this world and its idols, declaring that God is on the side of his people; nothing life throws at them will sever that bond (Rom 8:31–39). Fee notes that when we thank God *in* all things (not *for* all things), we are declaring our dependence on him.[16]

Prayer Brings Peace (4:7)

The result of such prayers is not a bigger house, more money in the bank, success at work, and good health news. The result is priceless—"the peace of God." Such peace knows no earthly parallel and often defies explanation, because it is unrelated to external circumstances. We do not imitate this peace; in this sense it is different from the love of Christ that surpasses knowledge. The latter we are to imitate, however imperfectly (Eph 3:19; 5:1–2).[17] The former is a gift from God, pure and simple. It exists not only within a believer's heart but is shared in the community. In Ephesians 2:14–18 Paul explains that the peace of Christ makes possible the joining of Jew and Gentile into one body. So, too, it brings the Philippians together, for the one mind and the singular love that is to be their focus (Phil 2:2) is that same collective mind that is guarded by God's peace.

Paul's use of the term "guard" gives a nod to Philippi, which garrisoned Roman soldiers, and might also draw on his own situation imprisoned by the Praetorian Guard in Rome. Such language calls to mind the precision in fighting techniques, the discipline and ruthlessness of the Roman military machine. In Paul's choice of words, we see his concern that the Philippians marshal their thoughts, taking them captive to obey Christ (2 Cor 10:5). He knows that the world never stops its relentless efforts to shift a believer's focus from God's kingdom to its own values and ideals, putting self first.

C. S. Lewis, in his classic *The Screwtape Letters*, includes a discussion about prayer. The head demon, Screwtape, writes to his nephew, the new tempter Wormwood, on how to erode the power of his man's prayers. First, Wormwood must have his new believer focus on how he feels, not on what he says. The point is to *feel* forgiven, or brave, or loving, not to actually forgive another, or summon courage, or will to love. Second, the man's focus should not be on God as God really exists, but on a composite picture taken from the various experiences the man has had with God, from Sunday school pictures to church art. Screwtape writes of the disaster (from his perspective) that

---

16. Fee, *Philippians*, 409.
17. Fowl, *Philippians*, 184.

results when the man praying directs his prayers "not to what I think thou art but to what thou knowest thyself to be."[18]

Paul speaks of the Philippians' hearts and minds being guarded by God's peace. We should not imagine that Paul is speaking here about feelings and thoughts, for his meaning is broader and deeper. Osiek notes that the heart was seen as the seat of personality, and the mind as that which deliberated and then acted accordingly.[19] Paul speaks here of the surrendered will, the broken heart, the yearning soul, and the convicted mind. The prayer of such a believer transforms their world—and their own life.

The key terms in verses 6–7 include joy, prayer, thanksgiving, and peace—these represent Paul's vision of spirituality, as they are all subsumed "in Christ." Eastern meditation practices promise peace and calm, and moralistic, therapeutic Deism suggests that a loving God must heed our prayers for pleasure and ease. But the believer's *joy* is rooted in the truth of the gospel; Christ's death and resurrection assures us of new life in new heavens and a new earth. The church's *prayers* testify to the conviction that God hears and answers and works for our good, the good of his church, and the good of his creation. The believer's attitude of *thanksgiving* is a testimony to the belief that God will accomplish his promises, and the believer's *peace* is the matrix of the church here and now, the glue that holds the body of Christ together.

Know the Truth, the God of Peace (4:8–9)

Tertullian famously asked: What has Athens to do with Jerusalem?[20] His point is that Greek philosophical thought, depending as it does on human wisdom, should not dictate Christian teachings and God's revelation. What, then, of Paul's collection in 4:8 of six Hellenistic virtues? Is Paul baptizing Greek philosophical categories? Is he asking the Philippians to carefully examine their culture's values and goals as they live out the gospel before their neighbors? Is he asking the Philippians to take what they can from their Gentile heritage,[21] or is he presenting Christianity as public truth?[22] How would one know whether Paul is critiquing the wider use of these virtues in order to reshape them in Christ, or is trying to build bridges to aspects of the pagan culture that agree with the Christian gospel?

---

18. Lewis, *The Screwtape Letters*, 22.

19. Osiek, *Philippians, Philemon*, 116.

20. Tertullian, *On the Prescription of Heretics* 7. Tertullian is not against the use of reasoned arguments, careful exposition, and persuasive rhetoric per se, but rather the claims that the philosophies such as Stoicism, Aristotelianism, Platonism, and Epicureanism hold the final word on matters of the cosmos and the human condition.

21. Fee, *Philippians*, 415, adds that these values must be "understood in light of the cruciform existence that Paul has urged throughout the letter."

22. Bockmuehl, *Philippians*, 250, argues this has profound implications for Christian apologetics, that a "Christian ethic . . . can at least in part be formulated in openly accessible terms."

Examining Paul's framework helps us sort this out. Notice that Paul speaks first of the Lord's nearness, then of the peace of God and Christ Jesus, and after the list of virtues he speaks again of the God of peace. This language regulates the options for interpretation. Moreover, Paul includes only one of the four classical cardinal virtues (justice), without mentioning self-control, prudence, or courage. This suggests Paul is not interested in baptizing the culture, but is making links that can be nuanced in Christ. Furnish suggests that in this list Paul presupposes a possibility that good moral assessments can be made within the wider community; "this is not to say, however, that Paul regards society as itself the *source* of moral insight or ethical norms."[23]

The Philippians are to think about themselves in a new way, to be citizens of a different sort, because their kingdom is of a different nature. Paul uses the language available to him, but places it within a different paradigm of reality. This new reality witnesses to the cross, resurrection, and return of the Savior, Jesus Christ. Fowl notes: "Paul has throughout the epistle been providing the Philippians with the resources they need to deploy that language within the context of a Christ-focused, cruciform common life."[24]

Furnish notes that this list of Hellenistic virtues is unparalleled in Paul, but it is not uncharacteristic, as Paul provides lists of acceptable moral postures elsewhere (e.g., 2 Cor 6:4–10). Paul focuses here on "the broader, public setting in which moral choices have to be made and acted upon,"[25] which is why he repeats the term "whatever" six times. Fowl insists that the six nouns are not special in themselves, and Paul could have picked six other terms. "It is their application in specific ways in particular circumstances that reveals something significant about them."[26] Paul feels free to laud truth and justice, but qualifies the content of those virtues as that which is consonant with the gospel of Christ, as seen in Paul himself (Phil 4:9).

Whatever is true. My philosophy colleagues often say, "All truth is God's truth." But how do we know what is truth? Pilate asked Jesus that very question (John 18:38). Ironically, Truth in the person of Jesus was standing in front of Pilate, for Jesus had declared himself as "the way and the truth and the life" (14:6). But Pilate scorned the kingdom Jesus preached and rejected God's true message of grace.

The phrase "whatever is true" has personal meaning for me. Right after my sister died, a friend quoted this entire verse to me as a reminder that believers are never separated from God's love (cf. Rom 8:38–39). I was to cling to that hope by continuing to think about and renew my mind on the

---

23. Furnish, *Moral Teachings of Paul*, 147, italics original.
24. Fowl, *Philippians*, 187.
25. Furnish, *Moral Teachings of Paul*, 146.
26. Fowl, *Philippians*, 185.

completeness of the gospel. I confess that all I could remember was this line, "whatever is true." I would repeat this numerous times a day, willing myself to see beyond the moment to the eternal truth of the resurrection that is truer than my present grief. Paul notes to the Corinthians that love rejoices in the truth (1 Cor 13:6).

Whatever is noble. The term "noble" (*semnos*) goes back at least as far as Aristotle, who defines it as between "obsequiousness and stubbornness."[27] Paul is more likely thinking of Proverbs as a backdrop. In Proverbs 8:6, the term is used alongside truth and righteousness, in the context of speaking rightly. In 15:26, it describes those gracious words that are pure in God's eyes. In the Pastoral Epistles this term is included in discussions concerning the proper character traits of those serving in leadership positions in the church (1 Tim 3:8, 11; Titus 2:2).[28]

Whatever is right. This word is the adjective *dikaios,* related to the cognate noun "righteousness" (*dikaiosynē*) and verb "justify" (*dikaioō*). Paul twice quotes from Habakkuk 2:3–4, "the righteous/just will live by faith" (Rom 1:17; Gal 3:11). Clearly this term does heavy theological lifting for Paul. In Philippians 1:7, however, Paul uses this term outside the conversation about salvation, where he speaks of the correctness of his views about the Philippians: "It is right [*dikaios*] for me to feel this way about all of you." Here in 4:8, Paul probably wants to include both the theologically rich texture of righteousness as well as the broader meaning of what is right or just. For Paul, this virtue is rooted in God's character and God's salvation plan in Christ, which shapes a believer's reality and actions.

Whatever is pure. This term carries both a moral and a ritual connotation. Both Jews and Gentiles recognized sacred space, such as temples (or the one temple in Jerusalem), and the necessity to be pure when in the "home" of the deity. Paul's frequent designation of the church as the temple of God (1 Cor 3:16; 2 Cor 6:16; 11:2; Eph 2:21), or believers individually as God's temple (1 Cor 6:19), signals the importance of purity for the church. Paul also contrasts the impurity of sexual immorality and idolatry with the holiness that should characterize believers, as well as Christ's purifying of Gentiles and Jews to make them one holy dwelling place for God.

Whatever is lovely … admirable. The fifth and sixth terms are not found elsewhere in the New Testament, and the latter does not occur in the Septuagint either. However, Paul uses the cognate noun of "admirable" in 2 Corinthians 6:8 in defending his conduct as an apostle, stating that he commends himself whether others speak about him with bad report or "good report," for

---

27. Aristotle, *Ethica Eudemia* II.III.4, see Fowl, *Philippians,* 185, for discussion.
28. The cognate noun *semnotēs* is used in 1 Tim 2:2; 3:4; Titus 2:7.

he speaks the truth. The term translated "lovely" occurs in Esther 5:1, refer-ring to Esther's beauty; in Sirach 4:7 it describes deference to those in higher status, in the context of remembering the poor, and the pleasing words of the wise, which make them loved by the people (20:13).

Live out the virtues. After listing six virtues, Paul shifts his language to add that believers are to reckon or consider anything that is "excellent or praiseworthy." In verse 9 he explains his intentions with this list, namely, that the virtues must be exercised in the context of the gospel and life in the church. The Philippians must judge all things based on the gospel message they received and the behavior they observed in Paul that matched that mes-sage. Even more, they must put into practice virtuous deeds — this charge by Paul matches the philosophers and Jewish sages, who regarded virtue to be embodied and demonstrated, not merely discussed.

Live out God's peace. Paul concludes with the promise that "the God of peace will be with [the Philippians]." Why give such assurance? Paul has just encouraged them to follow what he has taught them and what they saw in his actions (3:17; see also 1:30). Recall too that in his first visit to Philippi (Acts 16:11–40), Paul exorcised a demon from a slave girl and was beaten, jailed, and asked to leave the city. Moreover, he writes while chained to a Roman soldier. It is understandable that the Philippians might pause before following all that Paul did and taught. Such emulation could run them right up against the town council, the Jewish community, their patrons and employers, even their own family members. Thus Paul stresses that their journey is guarded and supported by "the God of peace." It is the Christian hope that both awaits a Savior (3:20–21) and enjoys a God who provides peace in the moment. Paul likewise encourages the Thessalonians (1 Thess 5:23), the Corinthians (1 Cor 14:33; 2 Cor 13:11), and the Romans (15:33; 16:20) to hold to the God of peace for their sanctification and in the midst of persecution.

A question from 4:9 arises in our own context, namely, our culture's accu-sations that Paul seems overly confident, if not downright arrogant, in holding himself up as a model for Christian living.[29] It is crucial to remember that Paul does not hold himself up as a *sinless* or *perfect* example; he made that clear in 3:12. Instead, he asks the Philippians to imitate his own attitude and behaviors only *as those model Christ* — that is, only as they are excellent, praise-worthy, and so on. O'Brien notes that Paul introduces verse 9 with a relative pronoun that looks back to "these things" in 4:8, restricting the scope of his call to model his behavior to only that which is "excellent and praiseworthy."[30] Paul also held up Timothy and Epaphroditus as important models

---

29. See the commentary on 3:17 for more on this issue.
30. O'Brien, *Philippians*, 508.

(2:19–30), and he desires the entire community to be of a single mind and focus (2:2–5), which implies that they look to each other for examples of modeling Christ. Far from encouraging hero worship, Paul's statement in 4:9 should be a standard expectation of all Christian leaders. Pastors or leaders who do not invite others to imitate them on their journey of faith should rethink their sense of calling and understanding of ministry. However, any pastor who puts himself or herself up as an exclusive model of Christian character and behavior should be avoided as power hungry.

 LIVE the Story

Virtues Today

Paul's list of virtues offers us an opportunity to think about the church's relationship with the wider, often secular, culture. Fee concludes that "being 'in Christ' sanctifies whatever else one is and does, so that what is honorable, lovely, and pleasing, as long as it [is] also worthy of praise, is also embraced by life in Christ."[31] Paul's words offer us ballast against two extremes — baptizing the American culture with its representative democracy and free market economy as God-given, and promoting a "counter-cultural" posture that rejects the status quo.

Paul invites the Philippians to engage with the ideas present in the marketplace and homes, to ponder what they have assumed to be correct, and to put all things under the light of Christ. Today perhaps Paul would be asking that we evaluate the claims that all truth is relative, or known only through personal experience. He might encourage us to engage with the cultural claims that tolerance is the highest virtue, and no one can "call out" another concerning their personal behavior, even if that includes overt sins such as adultery or stealing. The sentiment suggests that since none of us is perfect, we have no right to judge others. How far have we sunk from Paul's vision of a unified, pure congregation?

Joy and Peace, Truth and Rightness: The Power of Transformed Lives

The gospel transforms lives. It takes the weak of society and gives them a supernatural strength to overcome adversity and suffering, to hold real joy deep down in the core of their being. This they claim in Christ. Paul asks the Philippians to reflect on what he taught them, what they received from his teachings (4:9). They are to remember his actions and attitudes during his previous visits to their city. In Acts 16:11–40 we see how Paul spoke

---

31. Fee, *Philippians*, 417, n 17.

courageously, underwent beatings and imprisonment, and healed a woman possessed by a demon. The power of the gospel was clearly portrayed, and its life-changing power was felt by Lydia, the jailer and his family, and the slave girl. This power of transformation continues to remake lives and reshape villages. Below are four examples of such conversions, following loosely Paul's four verbs used in 4:9.

1. *The gospel transforms villages:* **learning** *the gospel of* **peace**. A friend of mine worked for several years with an international NGO serving the poor around the world, specifically in delivering food and helping to alleviate food shortages. In 2002, he traveled to Cambodia and tells this story.

> One senses in Cambodia a bustling momentum. The past sits so painfully in the background that while it still aches, people eagerly move into the future. But the old wounds impair that movement. The atrocities of genocide by the Khmer Rouge in the late 1970s can and should never be forgotten. People remember. The loss of a child is not something that one "gets over." A childhood stolen by the execution of parents is never regained. The broken trust of a genocide that altered life in unspeakable ways is not easily rebuilt.
>
> Fast forward thirty years and journey three and a half hours by truck outside of Phnom Penh. Then hop onto a "moto"—smaller than a motorcycle, bigger than a moped (able to leap rice paddies in single bounds)! The moto is necessary because there are no roads to many of the villages where people live. There are paths, not roads. You will come into a cluster of stick huts, elevated by poles. You will hear the clucking of chickens, the snorting of hogs. You will smell a goat's pen, and you will see a pack of naked boys splashing in a murky swimming hole shared with their water buffalo. It is hot. Perspiration beads and rolls like a soaking from a summer rain.
>
> When I talked with the villagers, I heard something far different than what you might expect from the recipients of a humanitarian program. Instead of hearing about simple things like water, shoes, increased rice production, or education, the dominant theme actually was life transformation and reconciliation—the joy of knowing forgiveness and love in Christ.
>
> They talked about their personal histories—citing how they used the family's money for gambling rather than the children. They had beaten their family, not loved them. Some of the people are not only old enough to remember the re-education camps of the Khmer Rouge, but also to have worked in them. In Cambodia, many people who worked on behalf of the Khmer Rouge just assimilated back into

society. Many people did awful things, partly for survival and self-preservation. Many have never known what it is like to trust, to forgive and be forgiven.

Reconciliation is not well understood or practiced—and it is even harder in the "ground zero" of a village that functions in an open and communal lifestyle. People cook outside, wash their clothes outside, bathe outside, work outside, nap outside—all in the open for the watching world. Yet when transformation happens in a life, it is visible. The whole village finds out. No secrets. And it is not just about the abandonment of destructive behaviors, although often it includes that. It is about real peace coming to people who are sincerely ashamed of—and publicly confess—what they may have done to survive atrocity. The repentance is far more public than in a Western context. Healed relationships are observed by a close-in audience.[32]

*2. The gospel transforms lives: **receiving** the gospel of joy.* Heather King was raised in the church, but left it for a life of unrestrained hedonism, drug use, and sex. In her book *Redeemed*, she recounts how she made her way back to the church from alcoholism.[33] As King tells the story, the founder of Alcoholics Anonymous, Bill Wilson, started the group out of self-preservation. On a business trip after becoming sober, he was standing in a hotel lobby faced with a choice: to go to the bar, or not. He chose instead to look at a directory for church phone numbers and called a clergyman. "This far-from-perfect man [Wilson] who desperately needed help himself ... by some divine grace, intuited it would come from helping someone else."[34]

She cites Richard Rohr, a Franciscan priest who observed that the opposite of control is not letting go, but *"participating in something larger than ourselves."*[35] This happened to King during her month-long stay in rehab. Women with whom she had nothing in common invited her into their "stories, their joy and pain, their jokes, and they broke me open."[36] She discovered

---

32. Ben Homan, President, Langham Partnership USA (US affiliate of Langham Partnership International). This story occurred during Ben's work as president of Food for the Hungry. "The reign of the Khmer Rouge in Cambodia ranks as one of the most disastrous in modern history. It could be persuasively argued that it was, in fact, the worst. Scholars currently investigating mass graves in Cambodia now estimate Pol Pot's three-and-a-half year reign led to the deaths of approximately two million people.... Literally overnight, entire cities were emptied. Property was abolished. Money became worthless. Homes and families were destroyed.... Thousands were executed immediately. Overnight, Cambodia became a nation of slaves." (Excerpt from Mekong.net)
33. Heather King, *Redeemed: Stumbling toward God, Sanity, and the Peace That Passes All Understanding* (New York: Penguin, 2008).
34. Ibid., 130.
35. Ibid., 131. Italics original.
36. Ibid.

that this is possible only by allowing one's ego to be crucified, "a consent to be emptied," as Jesus emptied himself (Phil 2:5–7). She notes, "Pleasure is shallow, but joy has pain in the middle of it. Pleasure comes and goes, but joy has eternity in it."[37] King expresses the eschatological vision Paul paints for the Philippians, a view of such supreme majesty that all earth's pleasures fade, because it becomes clear they cannot last.

Yet people still seek the hollow pleasures this world offers. One popular book in that regard is *Eat, Pray, Love,* by Elizabeth Gilbert. The book challenges Christians, as Dani Nichols notes,[38] for Gilbert presents an authentic, genuine self, vulnerable and searching, exposed to the reader. Nichols notes how often Christians attempt to protect themselves from honestly speaking with their spiritual leaders. Moreover, Christians can project onto them a perfection that is not based in reality. We want to hear spiritual platitudes that make us feel good about ourselves, rather than search our hearts or have God search our hearts and test our actions. Gilbert's appeal is her openness about being imperfect and thus is admired as being authentic. Often believers feel they must project an image of perfection, having it together. Such a posture is not only inauthentic and inaccurate; it is also harmful — to the believer herself, the church, and the wider, watching world. Paul's call to imitation is framed with the admission that he has not achieved perfection (3:12). We should likewise not pretend to have done so. The world deserves our honesty, and God requires it.

*3. The gospel transforms lives: **hearing** the gospel of **loveliness**.* My husband puts Scripture passages to music, and one of my favorite songs is Habakkuk 3:17–19. It was also my sister's favorite song, and she asked him to sing it at her wedding. Two days before the wedding, he got a terrible cold and lost his voice. We were beside ourselves and prayed earnestly for healing. The morning came, and still no voice. Noontime, and still just a squeak. But about 3 p.m., his voice grew strong, and for the 5 p.m. wedding, he sang beautifully. About 7 p.m., he lost his voice again. He laughed, saying that he had only asked that he might sing for the wedding, but he should have asked for more!

Habakkuk 3:17–19 demonstrates incredible faith in the face of utter devastation:

> Though the fig tree does not bud,
>   and there are no grapes on the vine,
> though the olive crop fails
>   and the fields produce no food,

---

37. Ibid., 7.
38. Blog by Dani Nichols on 8/21/10: http://everydaychristian.com/blogs/post/8130/.

> though there are no sheep in the pen
>> and no cattle in the stalls,
> yet I will rejoice in the LORD,
>> I will be joyful in God my Savior.
> The sovereign LORD is my strength;
>> he makes my feet like the feet of the deer,
>> he enables me tread on the heights.

Habakkuk stands firm—and even rejoices—not in his circumstances, but in the God who is exalted above any situation. For God makes the prophet's feet like those of a deer, so he can scale the heights. He climbs above the emptiness of his world, the parched and desolate land. On the heights, he sees more clearly the power and love of the God who strengthens him.

About four years after this beautiful wedding, my sister died in an accident. Her tombstone is engraved with the final words of Habakkuk, "The sovereign Lord is my strength. He makes my feet as a deer; he enables me to go up on the heights." In the midst of grief that tears holes in your side, a believer can sing with Habakkuk that death—of crops, farm animals, and even God's own people—does not have the final word. Jesus Christ is God's final word. Like Habakkuk, we can ascend to the heights.

4. The gospel transforms lives: **seeing the gospel of respect and joy**. More is caught than taught as children watch parents and teachers, toddlers imitate older siblings, and coworkers look for guidance to more experienced members of the staff. The life of joy and peace, of choosing the noble and the admirable, is not an easy one. It takes discipline to be thankful, to pray without demanding specific answers, to commit to a life of selfless service based on the reality of Christ in you. Fowl comments that the joy Paul speaks of in this passage is a by-product, not an end in itself.[39] This is not the joy of achievement or accomplishment, but of abiding with God no matter what. Generally speaking, the moral excellence of Christ does not stand over against the moral depravity of everyone else. "Instead moral excellence in Christ works to expose and stand as an alternative to false or merely apparent excellence in the surrounding world."[40] This insight invites us to ask how we can distinguish between what is good in the sense of conventional wisdom, and what is excellent in God's sight.

One way we can develop such discernment is to speak with believers from around the world. They often can see our own blind spots, or even just our own cultural assumptions, more clearly than we can appreciate them

---

39. Fowl, *Philippians*, 182.
40. Ibid., 188.

ourselves. For example, recently I listened to a sermon from a Thai pastor studying for his PhD in the United States. In his study of a gospel passage, he spoke rather off-handedly about the benefits of monarchy in Thailand, over against the growing democratic activists. It was a first for me to hear that democracy was not necessarily better than monarchy, that a benevolent ruler could be better than "one person, one vote." I realized I had a default position, based on my heritage as an American, that our democratic form of government was somehow enshrined in the Bible. But this sermon reminded me that our form of government, however laudable, is not the only way to express scriptural principles of justice and equity.

Distinguishing the Excellent from the Good

Moreover, Fowl notes that Paul indicates here that the way to tell the excellent from the good is by cultivating a godly lifestyle. It means practicing the communal life of selfless giving, focused on others, sincere and steadfast. "If Christians order their common life in a manner worthy of the gospel, if they master the convictions and practices appropriate to life in Christ, they will be able to discern what is truly excellent."[41] Our current public space has taken some Christian terms and adjusted their meaning to its own purposes. Christians absorb the new meanings without reflection, in part because the practices that informed the language have fallen away.

For example, many believers today wear a cross necklace; however, in Paul's day, the cross was used as state torture. Why can we use the cross as jewelry now? Fowl says because "Christian language about the cross has all too often been detached from the practices and convictions which made it such a potent image for someone like Paul."[42] As someone who regularly wears a cross necklace, I had to think a bit about Fowl's claims. I realized that I wore it most in graduate school, when I was in a "secular" environment. Wearing my necklace reminded me of my personal convictions and was also (in my mind) a witness of my identity as a Christian. Ironically, I viewed my jewelry not as capitulation to a worldview that sought to tame the cross's message, but as a stand against the domestication of the gospel. In the end, Fowl's overall argument is important, for it reminds us that the potential is always there to neutralize the radical message of the gospel, to soften its rough edges and dim its trumpet call to live a life extravagantly devoted to God.

Fowl's argument prompted soul searching on my part—always a good thing. If he had pronounced that the wearing of cross necklaces signaled

---

41. Ibid.
42. Ibid.

weak commitment or unreflective absorption of secular ideas (which he does not), the claims would slide into judgmentalism. Instead, Fowl raises the crucial distinction located in these verses between the content of godly truth and worldly wisdom. He points to 1 Corinthians 1:18–2:16, a passage that explains how wisdom and truth look different to people with dissimilar grids of evaluation. This calls to mind the stereotype of Christians wagging their fingers in another person's face—they are judgmental and judging. Sadly, this is a fair portrait of some Christians. To avoid this, other Christians refrain from making any evaluations at all. This is also not what Paul would have in mind.

This truth was brought home to me during a discussion over lunch with a dear friend. She noted that a friend of her sister's has been in a secret adulterous relationship for over fifteen years. Yet this woman goes to church regularly, participates in a women's Bible study, and is considered a member of good standing in the community. My friend noted that at times, however, the woman declined to read the Bible study material, when it seemed to be "judgmental." What became clear in our conversation is that this woman (and sadly, she is not alone in the churches) separated her devotion to God declared in word and song on Sunday morning from her ethics lived out during the week. For Paul, one's gentleness and joyous spirit is intimately connected to the posture of transparent, humble prayer that exposes the soul to God's healing and correcting touch. God's reach extends over the community, drawing them together as they praise and pray together.

CHAPTER 14

Philippians 4:10–20

 LISTEN to the Story

> ¹⁰I rejoiced greatly in the Lord that at last you renewed your concern for me. Indeed, you were concerned, but you had no opportunity to show it. ¹¹I am not saying this because I am in need, for I have learned to be content whatever the circumstances. ¹²I know what it is to be in need, and I know what it is to have plenty. I have learned the secret of being content in any and every situation, whether well fed or hungry, whether living in plenty or in want. ¹³I can do all this through him who gives me strength.
>
> ¹⁴Yet it was good of you to share in my troubles. ¹⁵Moreover, as you Philippians know, in the early days of your acquaintance with the gospel, when I set out from Macedonia, not one church shared with me in the matter of giving and receiving, except you only; ¹⁶for even when I was in Thessalonica, you sent me aid more than once when I was in need. ¹⁷Not that I desire your gifts; what I desire is that more be credited to your account. ¹⁸I have received full payment and have more than enough. I am amply supplied, now that I have received from Epaphroditus the gifts you sent. They are a fragrant offering, an acceptable sacrifice, pleasing to God. ¹⁹And my God will meet all your needs according to the riches of his glory in Christ Jesus.
>
> ²⁰To our God and Father be glory for ever and ever. Amen.

Listening to the text in the Story: Psalm 1:3; Proverbs 13:2; Isaiah 27:6–9; Jeremiah 11:19; Acts 17:1–9; 18:1–18.

The early second-century AD philosopher Epictetus declared, "He is a wise man who does not grieve for the things which he has not, but rejoices for those which he has."[1] Jim Elliot, the twentieth-century missionary killed in South America by a people group he was trying to reach with the gospel,

---

1. Epictetus, *Fragments* 129 (see http://perseus.uchicago.edu/perseus-cgi/citequery3.pl?dbname=GreekFeb2011&getid=1&query=Epict.%20Fr.%20129). A similar quotation is found in *Fragments* 2, *From Arrian, the Pupil of Epictetus* (LCL; trans. Oldfeather), 443.

said, "He is no fool who gives up what he cannot keep to gain that which he cannot lose."[2] The former speaks from within Stoicism, a philosophical system that taught contentment is achieved by distancing oneself from the pain and struggle of the world. The latter quotation reveals the Christian hope that pain and struggle are more than compensated by the riches of God in Christ (Rom 8:17-18).

The first-century AD philosopher and social critic Seneca wrote, "It is better, however, to get no return [from an ungrateful person] than to confer no benefits. . . . In order to discover one grateful person, it is worthwhile to make trial of many ungrateful ones."[3] In this he reflects the competing sentiments of his day, which insisted both that those who gave must do so without thought of praise, and that those who received were expected to respond in kind or with gratitude. Paul and the Philippians lived within these rules of the game and sought to live out the gospel's call to extravagant giving and receiving.

As we explore these eleven verses, we must keep several points in mind. Perhaps more than ever, we must read this passage within its historical context. Much mischief is wrought when we pluck the passage from its first-century surroundings. Second, we must not forget the warm tone that has permeated this letter to this point; Paul clearly thinks highly of the Philippians. Finally, this passage speaks most directly about money and finances; however, for Paul, all things, including money, are in service to the gospel by those whose lives are reshaped in Christ.

EXPLAIN the Story

Three Main Questions (4:10-13)

Three main questions emerge from this passage. First, why does it take Paul so long to thank the Philippians? Why does he wait until the end of the letter? This might be classified as a question about Paul's rhetorical style. Second, why does Paul's thanks sound so hollow or listless? Why does he seem to vacillate, to hesitate in his tone? This question is best answered by exploring the social conventions of Paul's day. Third, why did the Philippians contribute to Paul's ministry when Paul did not accept gifts from other churches for his personal ministry, such as the Thessalonians or the Corinthians?[4] This question focuses more acutely on Paul's theology of ministry.

---

2. Jim Elliot, from his journal, October 28, 1949. *The Journals of Jim Elliot* (ed. Elisabeth Elliot; Grand Rapids: Revell, 1978), 174. To see a photo of the journal page, see www2.wheaton.edu/bgc/archives/faq/20.htm.

3. Seneca, *Letters to Lucilium* 81.1-2.

4. Paul did collect money from his churches for an offering to the Judean churches.

Before diving into these questions, we might pause to ask what Paul hoped to accomplish in this passage. Bockmuehl holds that Paul wants to strengthen his "warm and natural relationship"[5] with the church, to fortify their partnership with him in the common cause of the gospel, and most important, to build up the unity of the community. To this last point, Paul leaves to the end of the letter any direct discussion about gifts and money. This move communicates his set of priorities, namely, that their unity and standing firm in the face of suffering and persecution, were of supreme importance. Their financial gift to Paul is an expression of their steadfastness, a testimony to their hope that God meets the needs of his people.

First Question: Why Wait to Thank the Philippians?

Now for our first question: Why did Paul wait until the end of this letter to thank the Philippians for their financial gift? As hinted above, this question arises often because of an assumption that Paul's primary intention in writing this letter was a thank-you note. Perhaps Paul was concerned that he could easily become dependent on one church, and so he vacillates by giving a less than exuberant response to their gift. The question about whether Paul vacillates will be looked at in more detail below.

Even if we assume for the moment that Paul deliberately waited until the end of the letter to bring up their gift and his grateful reception of it, modern Western readers often impute negative motives and attitudes to Paul because he seems to drag his feet, seemingly wasting time talking about his own imprisonment and their divisions. However, other cultures might judge Paul too abrupt if he got straight down to business at the beginning of this letter.

For example, I learned while living in Kenya that I was much too abrupt in my interactions with Kenyans. They expected me to ask about their well-being, their families, and their work. What would have been a quick question in the States was a short conversation in Kenya. And I was much the better for it—it taught me to focus on the individual and his or her circumstances, and place my question or request within a larger social and relational context. Far from "buttering up" the person before asking the question, this social convention allows both the parties to enjoy each other as people, without a utilitarian edge. This example could be multiplied across cultures and through the centuries. We do well not to impose our own social conventions on the biblical text, but rather allow it to shine its light on our customs.

Returning to our question of why Paul waits to thank them, it is most likely because his appreciation is best understood from the context of their partnership. He saw the Philippians as his fellow participants in the sharing

---

5. Bockmuehl, *Philippians*, 257.

and living out of the gospel. Their collective convictions have been tested by outside forces, enemies, and opponents, who sought to weaken their resolve. Paul speaks into their real and present concerns about his safety and their own. Support for this interpretation can be found in 1:3–7, which emphasizes the partnership (*koinōnia*) Paul shares with the Philippians, repeated in 4:14 (cf. also 4:10, 18). By waiting until the end of the letter, Paul gives two lasting impressions. First, he is concerned about their disunity and their spiritual growth. Second, the final note left echoing in their minds and hearts will be one of appreciation for their gift.

Second Question: Why Give a Weak Thank You?

Our second question looks at Paul's apparently weak or ambiguous thank you. This assessment arises for at least two reasons. First, Paul gives two qualifying clauses (4:11, 17) that suggest to some that Paul is not actually thanking them; he may even be belittling their gift as not necessary. Second, Paul indicates that their gift is in fact a gift to God, and thus he has less reason to be grateful. A full answer to this question requires that we explore the first-century social world. As we do, we must examine friendship and patronage systems, which overlap. Additionally, friendship protocols included the giving and receiving of favors and material gifts. And in any interaction, economic or social, interpersonal engagement was the norm.

In the ancient world, economic exchange was also personal exchange. Friendship, patronage, buying and selling—all these things happened within the honor/shame culture, which supported a complex hierarchy of social status and rank. That means that Paul might paint himself as a client of the Philippians if he were to thank them effusively for their gift. Or he might seem to hint that the Philippians need to give more because he, their father in the faith, was in prison. Thus what seems like Paul tiptoeing around this issue of thanks for a gift is really in a delicate dance trying to avoid stepping on social toes.

After exploring the world of social reciprocity, we will return to Philippi and Paul's ministry around the Aegean, paying special attention to his work with the Thessalonians and Corinthians (where we will explore our third question). But first a closer look at the social world of giving and receiving in Paul's day.

The ancient systems of friendship and patronage. From the time of classical Athens and Aristotle's rumination about friendship, to imperial Rome and its stress on social hierarchy and patronage, the philosophers of the age reflected on the nature of friendship, obligation, and the giving of gifts. Aristotle spoke of reciprocity and "proportional exchange and *charis*"; the Roman patronage system grew from the Greek system.[6] A complexity of the patronage system is that it can be expressed on an individual level or on a group level. Both women and men could be civic patrons during the Roman imperial period, and in this way women had political influence, albeit informal.[7] Again, both men and women served as patrons for men and women clients; in this sense the patronage system was "gender blind." However, friendship was understood as between equals, and in the Greek and Roman social systems, men and women were not seen as social equals (all other things such as wealth and social status being equal).

The social convention of reciprocity permeated the ancient cultural world. "This convention dictates that when a person (or persons) is the recipient of good in the form of a favour or a gift, the receiver is obligated to respond to the giver with goodwill and to return a counter-gift or favour in proportion to the good received."[8] To the ancients, friendship contained what we would consider an economic element, as did patronage. "Thus friendship and patronage relationships are different manifestations of the same underlying phenomenon."[9]

Seneca provides a useful example of the complexity of patronage and friendship. He extols true friendship as one of life's highest goods, and also as a basic need.[10] Friendship should be based on virtue, especially the virtue of loyalty or *fides*, not on utility. But Seneca knew that exchange of goods was a basic part of friendship (as well as patronage), and he was troubled by the dilemma this caused, as exchange was not the purpose of friendship. He solves this problem by declaring that virtue has exchange (giving and receiving) as its natural by-product.[11] Seneca shares with his contemporaries the belief that the ungrateful friend or client is deplorable.

The theme of virtue as foundational for friendship is prominent in Cicero, an eminent orator of the first century BC. He declares, "It is virtue, virtue which both creates and preserves friendship."[12] If one lacks virtue, friendship

---

6. Carolyn Osiek, "The Politics of Patronage and the Politics of Kinship: The Meeting of the Ways," *BTB* 39/3 (2009): 144. Paul uses the latter term, *charis*, which is translated as "gift" or "grace," ten times in 2 Cor 8:1 – 9:15. Osiek continues, "My own reading and consultation with experts in Greco-Roman social history has led me to take the side of those who say that there were definite patterns of personal patronage established in the East long before the arrival of Roman social customs" (146).

7. Ibid., 145.

8. G. W. Peterman, *Paul's Gift from Philippi: Conventions of Gift Exchange and Christian Giving* (SNTSMS 92; Cambridge: Cambridge University Press, 1997), 3.

9. Ibid., 4.

10. Seneca, *Letters to Lucilium* 109.

11. Seneca, *On Benefits* 4.20.

12. Cicero, *On Friendship* 27. He calls friendship the handmaid of virtue (22). For the entire text see www.fordham.edu/halsall/ancient/cicero-friendship.asp.

is unattainable. Cicero urges that a friend's character must be beyond reproach and that friends should have harmony in their views on the purposes and aims of life. A true friend shows fidelity and loyalty. Yet he also cautions that a person must be mindful of his own reputation and thus should not continue in a friendship that could harm one's reputation. Given the political intrigue swirling around Cicero[13] and his own personal experience, he knew that those you counted as friends one day could later be your undoing.

Patronage implied social inequality between a *patronus* (patron) and a *cliens* (client), while a friend (*amicus*) could be of the same social rank, but need not be.[14] One reason for this overlap of conventions is the "fundamentally instrumental nature of Roman friendship, [which] was a corollary of the underdevelopment of rational, impersonal institutions for the provision of services."[15] When one finds terms such as *amicus* (friend) describing a relationship between men of unequal status, it is probable that such relationship is one of patronage. Clients were determined to be inferior to their patrons in terms of status and resources, and thus in literature the terms *patron* and *client* are often avoided so as not to insult the latter. But clients showed no such hesitancy in declaring themselves clients on inscriptions that honored their patron.[16]

For example, in an elaborate inscription by a client honoring two of his patrons, the man describes himself as both a friend (*amicus*) and a client (*CIL* 13.3162). The inscription highlights that a client might have more than a single patron and that friendship and patronage language overlaps.[17] The patronage relationship is reciprocal; thus when someone is given an *officium* (gift), that person is in the gift giver's debt. The patron-client relationship is basically instrumental, and the Latin words used to describe the exchange are *officium, beneficium, meritum, gratia*.[18] The first term, *officium*, carries the sense of favor and was used at this time as "the concrete expression of the *fides* implicit in such relationships."[19]

The gift given might be political or financial help, to which the client responds with loyalty and *fides*. The latter term carries the "implication of submission to a superior power as well as confidence in protection."[20] Thus

---

13. Cicero was assassinated by Mark Antony in 43 BC.

14. Richard Saller, *Personal Patronage under the Early Empire* (Cambridge: Cambridge University Press, 1982), 11.

15. Ibid., 13–14.

16. Richard Saller, "Patronage and Friendship in Early Imperial Rome: Drawing the Distinction," in *Patronage in Ancient Society* (ed. Andrew Wallace-Hadrill; New York: Routledge, 1989), 54.

17. For a discussion of the Thorigny Marble inscription from Gallia Lugdunensis (3rd century AD), see ibid., 56–57.

18. Saller, *Personal Patronage*, 15.

19. Ibid.

20. Osiek, "The Politics of Patronage," 144.

loyalty and favoritism are expected, inasmuch as both patron and client are to look out for each other's interests first. To capture the interpersonal dynamics, a "'kinship glaze' is superimposed on the language surrounding the relationship to dull the crassness of the situation for the client."[21] Language of friendship and kinship, such as terms like father or brother, is used to protect honor. And we should not underestimate how important the exchange of honor is, for clients must honor their patron. This does not always translate as demeaning for the client, for if the patron has power, the client stands close enough to reflect some of that glow.

Friendship and kinship. Osiek remarks that the New Testament offers some of the best literary remains for understanding "the social relations of non-elites in the early Empire."[22] Paul uses *charis,* which carries overtones of benefaction, gift, and returned favor, but primarily we find the language of kinship. Such language is prominent in other religious groups and associations, such as the mystery cults of Mithras, Magna Mater, and Isis, and also in Jewish groups. Osiek cautions, "Contrary to what modern readers might think, it does not connote egalitarian relationships, but rather stresses unity and harmony."[23] Nor should we confuse the use or nonuse of patronage language for the presence of its structure in the community. With Paul's use of *charis* we have the introduction of patronage connotations.

Paul the patron? Would Paul have served as a patron in the congregations he started? They might consider him a patron, for he was their superior guide in spiritual matters, and he was their educator. Some even considered his baptizing activities as patron-like, and in Corinth, he sought to minimize such an interpretation (1 Cor 1:14–17). Another activity that might cast Paul as a patron is his mediation between Onesimus and Philemon. A patron was expected to mediate conflict between his or her clients. Notice that in Philemon, Paul acts as a worthy benefactor by being indirect and delicate in handling Philemon's honor as a house church leader.

Paul the client? Would Paul have served as a client to any church member? A complicated example of this possibility is Phoebe, of the church of Cenchreae. Paul describes her as his *prostatis* ("benefactor") in Romans 16:2. However, Paul is recommending her to the Roman church, an unusual move for an apparent social inferior, Paul, to make for his social superior, Phoebe. In this case we have an example of the "reversals of relationship [that] are possible when there are different dimensions of status."[24]

---

21. Ibid.
22. Ibid., 146.
23. Ibid., 147.
24. Ibid., 149, based on a personal conversation with Richard Saller.

To better understand this case, we can look to a similar situation exhibited by Junia Theodora, a social elite from Corinth lauded for her hospitality and business and political connections that she offered to her compatriots of Lycia traveling through Corinth. Perhaps Phoebe (not likely from the elite social class) had business in Rome and could be trusted to deliver the letter by Paul. If she had higher status than Paul, his introduction of her to the believers in Rome would enhance his status as one who was under her protection.[25] If she was of lesser status than Paul, his statement that she was his patron elevated her status and added weight to her function as Paul's official voice and representative to present and perhaps expound the letter (cf. Eph 6:21; Col. 4:7 about Tychicus). We might also see here an example of humility on both sides: Phoebe is humble in allowing herself to be recommended by Paul, and Paul is humble in stating she is his *prostatis*. If this is the case, we have an example of the gospel infusing and remaking the status-conscious system into one that models the humility of Christ.

Indeed, it has been noted that patronage in the early church does "not depend on wealth, birth, and education, but rather is constructed from a new and different form of status."[26] Exchange is based on service and implies mutuality. In this believers might take their cue from the philosophers, artists, and writers of the day who were clients to patrons. However, these patrons sought the former to enhance their own status. The artist's skill acted as a type of social power. Again, while a philosopher might have a patron, the latter was likely also a disciple in that the patron accepted what the philosopher said. Thus the philosopher has an important good "that the patron wants and cannot acquire him/herself."[27]

In the case of the Philippians, we might think of Euodia and Syntyche as perhaps like Philemon, who owes Paul his very life and thus should accede to his request to welcome Onesimus as a believer. Paul's authority, therefore, is not to demonstrate high social status but rather the status of the father in a family. Or perhaps Paul serves as their patron, reconciling the two of them, as he did Philemon and Onesimus. Paul praises Euodia and Syntyche as coworkers and wants them to unify because he, their patron, will be blessed. Thus like Philemon and Onesimus, so too these two women are under their "father figure," Paul (cf. 1 Tim 5:4). Again, in the matter of financial giving, Paul navigates the rocky waters of the social conventions supporting patronage and friendship, as we will see below when we examine the individual verses of this passage.

---

25. Ibid.
26. Ibid., 150, citing a private conversation and expressing Richard Saller's sentiments.
27. Ibid.

Summary of argument thus far. We argued that Paul placed the thanksgiving of the Philippians' gift at the end of his letter to emphasize his appreciation. We also noted that he does thank them in 1:3–7. In both cases he emphasized their partnership with him in the gospel. The second question examines the alleged lackluster thanks, and we have showed that Paul's enthusiasm for the gift is great; however, he directs his joy toward the Philippians' evident spiritual sacrifices made to God, evidenced in this gift. Paul must negotiate the intricate social codes of patronage and friendship of his day, so that he does not imply either that he is the Philippians' client or that he is obligated to respond in kind to their gift. God will supply their needs, even as he rejoices at their generous giving to him, and by extension, to the gospel.

This careful examination of the social conventions helps modern readers in two ways. First, it encourages them to step into Paul's world, the world of the early church. This adventure back in time allows for a closer, more careful reading of the letter. We begin to imagine the Philippians' daily exchanges and see what Paul accepts about his culture, and what he seeks to modify under the gospel. Second, looking at another culture's social conventions holds up a mirror to our own culture. How is our culture similar in its expectations of friendship? Are loyalty and gift giving primary features, or do we stress other characteristics? What should be retained in our culture's expression of friendship, and what should be challenged by the gospel? As we think about possible answers to these issues, we must turn to our third and final question.

Third Question: Why Did Paul Accept Funds (Ungraciously?) from the Philippians?

The third question points to the charge that Paul was ungracious to the Philippians. For example, he did not use the typical verb for thanks, *eucharisteō*. Did he avoid a robust thank-you because he was embarrassed about money, or was he ashamed that he could not be self-sufficient? Was Paul disinterested in money, as something with little theological value? Paul is hardly embarrassed about asking for money, as evidenced by his lengthy exposition on giving in 2 Corinthians 8:1–9:15. In this passage Paul lauds the Philippians (and other Macedonian churches) since in the midst of great trial, "their overflowing joy and their extreme poverty welled up in rich generosity" for funds to be sent to churches in Judea (8:2). Nor does Paul advocate self-sufficiency, as shown by his "in Christ" refrain that rings throughout his letters — never, "in Paul." In fact, he boasts that in his weakness, God is shown to be strong (12:9–10).

Paul's relationship with the Thessalonians and Corinthians. Yet our third question looks not simply at the letter to the Philippians, but compares Paul's message to them with his words to the Thessalonians and Corinthians. Specifically, in Philippians Paul reveals that he accepted financial support from them for his personal ministry.[28] However, Paul indicates to the Corinthians that he did not accept donations for his personal ministry from his churches (1 Cor 9:12–16) while he was living in their city, and to the Thessalonians he underlines that he was not a burden to them, but rather worked to earn his keep while ministering in Thessalonica (1 Thess 2:9). The danger is not simply inconsistency on Paul's part, but the possibility that he is flattering the Philippians. A flatterer was the opposite of friend, as detailed by Plutarch, and was to be avoided at all costs.[29]

Threefold problem with financial support. Paul understands the problems of financial support as threefold. First, financial support can be a barrier to evangelism (1 Cor 9:12). Second, it can be a burden to the local church (2 Cor 11:9; 1 Thess 2:9). Third, it can replace friendship as the supreme virtue. In Philippians 4:15, we find the phrase "shared with me in the matters of giving and receiving," which is "a social metaphor denoting friendship [that] becomes a Christian appellation for financial fellowship in missionary work."[30] With this insight, we see that the Philippians understood Paul's hesitancy in accepting funds for his direct ministry while working among them. For reasons not preserved for us today, it seems that Philippians did not run the risk of seeing Paul as a huckster or sham artist, as was the danger in Thessalonica (1 Thess 2:4). They did not worry that Paul would be claimed as a client of one or more groups, as emerged in Corinth (1 Cor 1:11–16). Was it his imprisonment and subsequent miraculous release that demonstrated beyond doubt to this church that Paul's ministry was to be supported (Acts 16:25–35)? Did the jailer and/or Lydia fully grasp the concept of suffering partnership in Christ for the gospel, and therefore Paul warmly accepted their money?

Fee wonders if Luke's presence in Philippi might account for this unique financial arrangement. He suggests that the unnamed mediator in 4:3 ("my true companion") is most likely Luke, who stayed in Philippi for several years after Paul planted the church and thus was well known there.[31] Moreover, Luke was likely with Paul for part of his imprisonment in Rome, as witnessed by Paul's note in Colossians 4:14 (see also Phlm 23). In this scenario, Luke's

28. Fee, *Philippians*, 444.

29. Plutarch, *How to Tell a Flatterer from a Friend* 7, notes that a flatterer has "no fixed character of his own, and not seeking to lead the life suitable for him, but shaping and modeling himself after another's pattern, is neither simple nor uniform, but complex and unstable, assuming different appearances, like water poured from vessel to vessel, ever in a state of flux and accommodating himself entirely to the fashion of those who entertain him" (LCL ed.)

30. Peterman, *Paul's Gift from Philippi*, 8.

31. Fee, *Philippians*, 394–95. The "we" narrative occurs in Acts 16 with the journey to Philippi, and then does not pick up again until 20:1–5, about four to six years later.

presence would act as a solid wall of defense against the twin threats of placing Paul as the church's client or as a self-promoting mercenary.

Summary of Arguments Surrounding Philippians' Gift

The questions swirling around Paul's acceptance of the Philippians' gift for his own ministry force us to dig deeply into Paul's understanding of ministry. They also reinforce the need to examine Paul's letters with a historically sensitive perspective. The results of our exploration include that Paul's literary decision to leave until last his full expression of thanksgiving for their gift was predicated on (1) his conviction that friendship, partnership in the gospel, and the spiritual growth and unity of the Philippian church far exceeded any financial arrangements, and (2) his belief that his final words about receiving his gift with joy would ring joyously in the Philippians' ears.

We discovered that the ancient protocols for patronage and friendship are markedly different than our own and thus account for what we might perceive as a lackluster or half-hearted response from Paul. Finally, we noted that Paul's message of relying on God alone is not compromised by his acceptance of financial support from the Philippians, for they understand they are but God's servants used to facilitate the spread of the gospel, and they willingly stand with Paul in his trials.

As we shift our attention to 4:10–20 directly, the passage connects with Paul's message throughout the letter in several significant ways. As noted above, it serves as an *inclusio* with 1:3–11 in stressing the key themes and vocabulary in the letter. For example, the notion of "beginning of the gospel" is found in 1:5 and 4:15. Again, the term *synkoinōnia* ("share with me") is found in both 1:7 and 4:14. Philippians 4:10–20 also includes key vocabulary found throughout, such as the verb "to think," "have this attitude" (1:7; 2:2–5; 3:15, 19; 4:2, 10). The refrain to "rejoice" resounds (1:18; 3:1; 4:4, 10), as does the theme of sacrifice (2:25, 30; 4:18). These verbal and thematic connections suggest that 4:10–20 is not a separate letter stitched onto other letters to the Philippians by a later scribe.

Contentment Is God's Gift (4:10–14)

Years ago my sister-in-law had a salesperson come to her door. In the course of their conversation, the Bible was brought up, and this salesperson said that his favorite verse was, "I can do all things." My sister-in-law paused, waiting for the man to finish the verse "through him who gives me strength," but the second half of the verse was never mentioned. Ironically, I do not think the man made a sale, which indicates that in fact he could not do all things! It is possible that this man simply did not realize that the verse attributed strength to God, not to humans. Both today and in Paul's day, human strength and self-reliance are seen as the highest goods and greatest achievements. But that is not Paul's opinion, nor is it the burden of his message here. Instead, Paul exalts God's work in sustaining him and even prospering him in adversity.

Paul begins 4:10 with a backward glance to when Epaphroditus came to him in Rome and recalls, "I rejoiced."[32] Paul rejoices not simply in their gift, but more basically in the Lord, because the gift confirms their partnership with Paul in the gospel. The saying, "It's the thought that counts," fits in a limited way here. First, Paul's joy comes from their *thought*, that is, from their thinking about him. He uses the verb "to think" (*phroneō*) twice in this verse (translated "concern" in the NIV). We have seen this word eight times so far in this letter, and its meaning is elastic. Fowl sums it up nicely as intending the "particular disposition toward a Christ-focused pattern of thinking, feeling, and acting."[33] This disposition stands together with believers in times of trial and struggle. This is in sharp contrast to the mind-set of some (then and now) who engage in ministry only as long as they are stroked and applauded.

Second, the thought counts not only to Paul, but also as reflective of the Philippians' spiritual health. Paul expresses his joy that they are blooming again, or are growing, using a verb (*anathallō*) found nowhere else in the New Testament (translated in NIV as "renewed"). It is used in the Septuagint Psalm 27:7, "my flesh flourishes" or "blooms anew."[34] We also find it in Sirach 1:18: "The fear of the Lord is the crown of wisdom, making peace and perfect health *to flourish*" (NRSV). In Sirach 11:23 – 24, the author extols God's blessings: "The blessing of the Lord is the reward of the pious, and quickly God causes his blessing *to flourish*. Do not say, 'What do I need, and what further benefit can be mine?' Do not say, 'I have enough, and what harm can come to me now?'" Paul suggests a similar sentiment, noting that he has enjoyed plenty and has submitted to humiliation, all through God's strength. Paul did not mistake the "good times" as being of his own doing.

Paul notes that "at last" the Philippians have accomplished their goal of giving a gift to him (4:10). The idiom translated "at last" should not be understood as Paul saying "finally!" with a churlish edge to his voice. Rather, Paul communicates that he understands their struggles in completing their desire to give to him. He knows that the Philippians repeatedly thought about him with concern but were thwarted in their response. We do not know what prevented them; perhaps it was their poverty (2 Cor 8:1 – 2) or the inability to

---

32. O'Brien, *Philippians*, 516.
33. Fowl, *Philippians*, 193.
34. Pers. trans. (Ps 28:7 in the NIV, translated from the Hebrew, reads "my heart leaps for joy"; NETS translates "my flesh revived").

deliver their funds to Paul because of the distance from Philippi to Caesarea, where Paul was first imprisoned. This verse testifies to "the mutuality of their partnership and ... [to] the attitude of concord and Christ-like service which the letter extols."[35] Fowl suggests, far from rebuking the Philippians for the delay of their gift, that Paul makes clear that he knew their delay was beyond their control. Their desire was always to help, but their ability to do so was temporarily lost.[36]

Paul Faces All Things in and through God's Strength (4:11–13)

The language in these three verses sounds very Stoic, but also contains virtues that are as far from Stoicism as one can get. Paul uses the term "contentment," common in Stoic material, but indicates that he knows what it is to be humiliated or humbled (4:12), hardly an ideal for Stoics. Nor is Paul declaring his indifference to circumstances, a Stoic virtue, for he declares that he rejoices (4:10) and enjoys plenty (4:12). In 4:11, Paul states his position in general terms, namely, that he is content, and in 4:13 he explains why such an assertion is possible.

In 4:11, Paul describes his situation, one in which he has learned contentment even as he celebrates partnering with the Philippians in gospel work. Paul had thanked them previously for sending Epaphroditus to meet his needs (2:25), and we should not downplay the importance of such care. Prisoners at this time were on their own for basic needs, relying on outsiders to send food. Given that Paul acknowledges their gift with joy in 2:25 (and 4:10), probably here he wants to develop the concept of need.

What does it mean to be "in need"? Paul suggests such a situation is in contrast with contentment. Thus we must ask: What constitutes contentment? The Stoics held that contentment or self-sufficiency was achieved as the individual became indifferent to his/her surroundings. The Stoic looked to virtue to find contentment. "Virtue was found within oneself independent of others,"[37] wrote Seneca of being reconciled to circumstances that he could not change. *Apatheia* or detachment was the goal. Paul seeks not self-sufficiency, but Christ-sufficiency. Contentment is living in Christ, the sure hope (1:19–20), the unfailing promise (2:9–11), the Savior who will come again (3:20–21). Such contentment leads not to indifference but to service; not to detachment but to active engagement with the world, "becoming all things to all people so that by all possible means I might save some" (1 Cor 9:22).[38]

35. Bockmuehl, *Philippians*, 260.
36. Fowl, *Philippians*, 193.
37. Ibid., 194.
38. The adjective for "content" used in 4:11 (*autarkēs*) occurs in the cognate noun form in

This contentment was not something Paul attained overnight, but he "learned" it through his experiences. Thus he invites each reader and congregation to embrace for themselves this high goal of contentment. Presumably this learning of contentment is another example that Paul would want believers to follow. Note that such contentment is not synonymous with happiness, excitement, or success. Philippians 4:12 outlines the humiliation, the deprivation, the emptiness that characterized his walk. Yet at other times he had plenty, with his stomach filled. The contentment comes from the supernatural strength, the "power of his [Christ's] resurrection" (3:10) that reshapes perceptions and values to conform to the reality that Christ is victorious over sin and death (cf. Rom 8:1; 12:1 – 2; Eph 2:4 – 7).

Moreover, Paul says that he "learned the secret of being content," but here the expression carries the sense of knowing something hidden. The verb "learned" was used in the mystery cults for learning secrets. Paul picks up on the revelatory nuance to stress that his "knowledge" reflects the wisdom and love of God. In the Beatitudes, we find the same verbs "to be filled" and "to hunger" as are used here: "Blessed are those who *hunger* and thirst for righteousness, for they *will be filled*" (Matt 5:6).

Philippians 4:13, a verse often misquoted and misinterpreted, stands as Paul's summary statement on contentment. The verb and the participle both carry the meaning of "strong." Together the verse pulsates with power — but whose power? The NIV uses "him," while other English translations insert "Christ" to make explicit Paul's meaning. The Greek text, however, can refer either to God or to Christ. Given that Paul begins this section by rejoicing in the Lord (4:10) and speaks throughout this letter of being "in Christ," the balance tilts to understanding Christ as the one who strengthens Paul.

Paul reflects a similar sentiment to the Corinthians in describing God's grace to him. In 2 Corinthians 12:9, he writes that God's "grace *is sufficient,*" a verb similar to the word "contentment" in Philippians 4:11. Paul continues that his condition of weakness (i.e., insults, hardships, and persecutions) serves to magnify God's power and concludes, "Therefore I will boast all the more gladly about my weaknesses, so that Christ's power may rest on me" (2 Cor 12:9). The "power" is similar to the participle used here in Philippians, "who give [me] strength."

This is not a special strength only for Paul, for in 4:14 he will speak of the Philippians' partnership with Paul in his trials. In the same way, Paul enjoins

---

2 Cor 9:8 and 1 Tim 6:6. To the Corinthians, Paul assures them that God will bless them so that they have what they *need*; in 1 Timothy, we read, "godliness with *contentment* is great gain." Both quotations reflect a context of financial gain, but push beyond that limited scope to see contentment rooted in the all-sufficiency of Christ.

the Ephesians, "Be strong in the Lord and in his mighty power" (Eph 6:10). The strength that Paul learned is available to all believers — to face the humiliations, setbacks, deprivations, as well as the times of fullness.

Partnership Is the Church's Gift to Each Other (4:14)

Verse 14 begins with a conjunction rarely used by Paul.[39] It connects this sentence with the previous four verses. Here Paul comes closest to offering a direct thank-you with his phrase "it was good of you."[40] But notice that Paul does not say that it was good of them to give him money for his ministry. Instead, he indicates that they shared with him in his troubles, probably referring to his imprisonment (see also 1:17; the same verb, without the prepositional prefix "with," occurs in 4:15). The idea is that the Philippians were partners in Paul's ministry. He indicated as much earlier in the letter when he encouraged them to stand firm as they faced suffering and struggles, just as they saw in Paul (1:29–30).

How does Paul's description of his relationship to the Philippians challenge our current models of church giving and involvement? From the pastor's perspective, does he or she relate to the congregation as co-partners in the ministry? From the congregation's standpoint, do they embrace the struggles and hardships of their pastor(s)? Can pastors say that they have no needs because Christ strengthens them? Can the congregation say that their pastors have no needs, because they stand with them in participating in the struggles of ministry? Is church giving subsumed under the larger heading of partnership in the gospel? The possibilities for dynamic fellowship and a deepening walk with God through the strength of Christ invites each of us to accept the implicit challenge found in these verses and to rethink how we understand giving.

History and Future of the Philippians' Giving (4:15–20)

"I remember when...." "Do you remember when...?" How often these phrases echo at holidays or reunions, at birthdays and graduations. As generations gather, grandparents recall the silly antics of a toddler who now stands before them graduated from college. Former roommates laugh at the foibles of their college years, and parents wonder "where did the time go?" as their lastborn has her own baby. My cousin reminds me of a crazy stunt she pulled with my sister, and a part of my own history is restored. My brother shares his recollections of our beloved Pappap, and my own childhood is enriched. Memories keep us connected to who we are and to each other.

---

39. See Phil 1:18; 3:16; 4:14; also 1 Cor 11:11; Eph 5:33.
40. Bockmuehl, *Philippians*, 262.

My husband and I have friends in ministry with whom we shared years of service and trials. In one case, we were newly married couples serving an inner city community of Cambodian refugees. The friendship in ministry continued as we both entered full-time mission work in international health-care missions. We share the joys of children's marriages and the deep sorrows of parents' passing. In another case, our friendship began in the crucible of mission service in Africa and continues as God directs us to different areas of the globe for continued service in his church. And when we meet, our visits always include moments of memory sharing, reestablishing our friendship, and reaffirming our identity together in Christ.

Thus when Paul sketches the history of the Philippian church's faithfulness to the gospel and to his particular ministry, he invites them to reclaim and embrace their own identity in Christ. Their gift to Paul invited the apostle to reflect back with great joy and appreciation on their lengthy ministry together. We must remember this aspect of the passage, so as not to get tangled in the weeds of words. This is especially important because Paul's language here draws on the commercial world, and to our ears that strikes a utilitarian note. But to a first-century ear, the chords ring of friendship, and hopefully for today's readers we will learn a new song or at least a new verse to a familiar song celebrating memories of faithful friends serving in Christ.

In 4:15–19, Paul continues the commercial language found in the previous verses. The verb "to share" can carry financial overtones. The phrase "in the matter of" is a technical one that means "into the account of." The phrase "giving and receiving" likewise is found in many ancient records of transactions. The term "credited" in 4:17 can also mean "profit" or "return." And Paul's declaration in 4:18 that he has received full payment again reflects transactional language. This vocabulary is interwoven with liturgical language of sacrifice, shaping what could sound utilitarian into a celebration of faithful giving that enriches the community.

Giving and Receiving for the Gospel (4:15–16)

Nothing is duller than a braggart, and nothing so sweet as praise from a friend. In 4:15–16, Paul commends the Philippians' steadfast friendship in the nitty-gritty of gospel work. They stood by Paul in word and deed, and Paul responds with gratitude, a posture that fit the conventions of the day. Cicero, a Roman senator and friend of Julius Caesar, noted that services rendered should be remembered by those who received them, but not by the one who provided the services.[41] Said another way, those who receive should brag about their patron, but those giving should keep their lips sealed about their

---

41. Cicero, *On Friendship* 71. Cited by Fee, *Philippians*, 439 n 11.

own good deeds. A century later, Seneca echoed Cicero's sentiments. "In the case of a benefit ... the one should straightway forget that it was given, the other should never forget that it was received."[42]

Two phrases in Philippians 4:15 require a closer look, namely, the statement that the Philippians were with Paul from "the early days of your acquaintance with the gospel," and that they shared with him in "giving and receiving." The first phrase likely points to the time recounted in Acts 16, when Paul first arrived in Philippi during his second missionary journey (see also the reference in Phil 1:5, "from the first day until now"). Their forgiveness of sins and newfound acceptance by the one, true God involved a new beginning with a new "family," a new community, and a new mission or purpose in life.

The second phrase looks at the language of giving and receiving, drawing on the complex interrelated conventions governing economic exchange, patronage, and friendship. Paul may be using this language a bit tongue in cheek, with a touch of irony that one could speak of gifts exchanged between believers as contained within the sphere of economic discourse. He uses the social conventions, but he reshapes them in light of the gospel. As Bockmuehl notes: "Full mutuality in friendships and other equal relationships were essential if an outstanding debt of obligation was not to degenerate into discord or dependency."[43] Fee warns of another pitfall, that of competition between friends, leading to "one-up-manship."[44] Paul steers between being dependent and competitive by focusing on the singular goal they shared, namely, the advancement of the gospel and their common identity in Christ.

Paul reviews here the Philippians' giving to him. Their giving extended beyond Paul's residence in Macedonia, but it did include immediate assistance when he stayed in Thessalonica directly after leaving Philippi. Paul begins with the larger picture in 4:15, noting that when he left Macedonia, their giving continued. Paul traveled to Corinth by way of Athens (Acts 17:13–18:1). After being in Corinth for an unspecified amount of time (but at least a few Sabbaths), Silas and Timothy arrived from Macedonia with financial gifts that enabled Paul to leave his tentmaking with Priscilla and Aquila and devote all of his time to preaching (18:5). Paul refers to this in 2 Corinthians 11:8–9, when he defends his decision to accept gifts from the Macedonian brothers and sisters, speaking there specifically of the Philippian believers.[45] Thus their

---

42. Seneca, *On Benefits* 2.10. Cited by Fee, ibid.
43. Bockmuehl, *Philippians*, 263.
44. Fee, *Philippians*, 453.
45. Fee (ibid., 441, n 14) notes that at several places in 2 Corinthians Paul hints at this (2 Cor 1:16; 2:13; 7:5), but 11:9 makes clear that Paul can use "Macedonia" and "Philippi" interchangeably.

gifts sent to support him in Corinth remained a significant measure of their commitment to Paul and his ministry in Christ.

In 4:16, Paul narrows his focus, highlighting that even when he was next door, so to speak, in the city of Thessalonica (about ninety miles away on the *Via Egnatia*, a "superhighway" of the day), the Philippians sent financial help to him "more than once." This was much appreciated, although it did not cover all his expenses, as indicated in 1 Thessalonians 2:9: "Surely you remember, brothers and sisters, our toil and hardship; we worked night and day in order not to be a burden to anyone while we preached the gospel of God to you" (see also 2 Thess 3:8).

Paul reflects with joy on the steadfast support of the Philippians. The gap in time between their gifts was only a lack of opportunity, not an indication of their lessening commitment. In a sense, their perseverance matches Paul's own — although Paul traveled extensively and the Philippians remained in their city, both demonstrated remarkable loyalty to each other.

Giving for the Gospel (4:17–18)

Having praised the Philippians for their steadfast giving, Paul does not want them to draw the conclusion that he is flattering them so as to gain more gifts. He provides another qualifier ("not that") in 4:17, as he did in 4:11. He further clarifies his intent by using *doma* for "gift," because it does not carry the sense of payment; rather it described the exchange between friends. The term is found in Ephesians 4:8 in an Old Testament quotation that describes the gifts given by Christ: "When he ascended on high, he took many captives and gave gifts to his people."

Further distancing himself from any hint of maneuvering for a gift, Paul speaks of their "credit," using the term "fruit." The images of growing and harvesting are ubiquitous in the Old Testament (Ps 1:3; Prov 13:2; Isa 27:6–9; Jer 11:19) and are found throughout Jesus' descriptions of discipleship. For example, Jesus likens a believer to a branch that bears much fruit if it remains connected to the vine (John 15:1–8). He warns that false prophets will come, but that "every good tree bears good fruit, but a bad tree bears bad fruit. . . . Thus, by their fruit you will recognize them" (Matt 7:17–20). Paul continues this imagery, having first hinted at it in 4:11 with his claim that they had at last "renewed" (or re-bloomed) their concern for him. In 1:11, Paul includes in his prayer for them the hope that the Philippians will be filled "with the fruit of righteousness that comes through Jesus Christ."

Epaphroditus has delivered their gift, and Paul declares that it not only more than met his needs, but it also testified to the Philippians' commitment to the gospel. In 4:18, Paul declares, "I have received full payment," as though he was writing out a receipt. He states this not because someone in Philippi may think that perhaps Epaphroditus skimmed something off the top, but merely to note that the gift abundantly provided for Paul. Paul makes clear in his next sentence that he is thinking not only of an accountant's book, but also of service to God.

Paul likens their gift to a "sacrifice, pleasing to God." In both cases, money is involved, for a sacrifice costs money. A person buys an animal or carries the firstfruits of harvest and places it on the altar in reverence and obedience to God. The greatest example of such obedient sacrifice is Christ's own death, as Paul noted in the Christ hymn (2:8). To the Romans Paul states explicitly, "God presented Christ as a sacrifice of atonement, through the shedding of his blood—to be received by faith" (Rom 3:25; see also Eph 5:2). He later adds that believers should respond to this gift by offering themselves as "living sacrifices" (12:1–2; see also Heb 13:15–16), a paradox that penetrated deep into the Philippians' understanding of the gospel.

In sum, Paul's context included two competing social norms, namely, showing gratitude for a gift and engaging in the hierarchy of patronage relationships. It was inexcusable for anyone to be ungrateful, and it was unthinkable that anyone could step out of the informal social network of patronage. Paul must thank them without suggesting he is beholden to them or insulting them by reinforcing their client status as those who owe him their lives since they heard the gospel from him. This passage shows Paul's skillful maneuvering through this minefield. (1) He has previously noted their close relationship in being committed to the gospel. (2) He flattens the hierarchical relationship by identifying himself as a slave (1:1), not an apostle. This means the Philippians are less likely to think of themselves as Paul's clients who must continually pay back a great debt. (3) Paul prevents them from imagining themselves to be his patron, which might lead to a compromising of the gospel's message or Paul's freedom in Christ. He prevents this move by noting that their gift was to the ministry, not to himself. Their gift allowed for spreading the gospel in Rome among the most unlikely group—the Praetorian Guard!

In 4:18 Paul states what the Philippians believe also to be true, that their gift to Paul was really a gift to God, to the gospel, in obedience to Christ. Thus, Paul cannot reciprocate, because the gift was not meant for him to begin with. It was not "his" money—it was God's money. There is an important twofold message here. First, to the giver: you must reckon your gift as unto God, not to any person or entity. There is great freedom in that acknowledgment, but no glory from humans. Second, to the recipient: you must reckon the gift as God's, to accomplish purposes that might not line up with your own dreams. Paul never imagined that his hope to visit Rome would be accomplished with free transport chained to a Roman soldier! But the recipient should note that the gift is not designed to build up his or her ego or reputation; in fact, it might lead to humiliation. But God will be exalted, in his time and for his purposes.

Verse 18 not only concludes Paul's explanation that the Philippians' gift is a sacrifice, but it also looks ahead to verses 19–20, which highlight God's response to such sacrifices. Just as Paul was filled to overflowing from their gift, so too he promises that God will meet all the Philippians' needs with great abundance. The common verb connecting verses 18 and 19 is *plēroō*, which means "to fill, fulfill" (trans. "supplied" in v. 18, "meet" in v. 19).

Giving from God to Meet Believers' Needs (4:19–20)

Throughout the centuries, believers cling to the promise proclaimed here in Philippians that God will meet their needs. The hymn "Be Thou My Vision" expresses this conviction well:

Riches I heed not, nor man's empty praise,
Thou mine Inheritance, now and always:
Thou and Thou only, first in my heart,
High King of heaven, my Treasure Thou art.[46]

Paul identifies God as "my" God, and the needs as "your" (the Philippians') needs. The choice of "my" is curious, as throughout the letter it has been clear that the Philippians worship the same God Paul does. Even more, 4:20 will identify "our" God and Father. Probably Paul is continuing his thought about the gift given to him and thus to God. From one perspective, Paul might say, "This is *your* gift to *me*." In this case, Paul could then say, "*My* God will respond." Or perhaps Paul is staking his own reputation on this declaration of God's character. In the opening lines of this letter, Paul notes that he thanks "my" God (1:3; see also Rom 1:8: 1 Cor 1:4). In such cases, it is Paul's personal testimony, his experience with "my" God, that lends further weight to his pronouncement that God will act, and will do so with all-surpassing generosity and fullness.

Yet we know through Paul's own words that the Philippians are poor, and it may be tempting to understand Paul as promising wealth to them. The immediate context shows that money is certainly part of the discussion.

---

46. This anonymous text is attributed to Celtic Christianity of the medieval period. Mary Byrne translated the poem into English in 1905, and in 1912, Eleanor Hull put it into the verses we now sing. The hymn was published in *Church Hymnary* (1927). See Erik Routley, *An English-Speaking Hymnal Guide* (ed. Peter W. Cutts; Chicago: GIA Publications, 2005), 21. www.ctlibrary .com/ch/1998/issue60/60h037.html.

But Paul is at pains to expand from coins to spiritual blessings of strong faith and godly righteousness. Yet I want to be careful here and not "spiritualize" Paul's meaning. He believed that God could heal miraculously—Paul performed such miracles, even raising a man from the dead (Acts 13:9–12; 14:3; 16:16–19; 20:7–12; 28:3–9). When he states that God will meet their needs, he knows a God who offers physical aid.

How should the phrase "the riches of his glory" (4:19) be understood? Some see the phrase functioning adjectively, reading the text as God extending his glorious riches to us. Others stress that it refers to the location from which the riches flow, namely, "from [God's] heavenly presence and power."[47] These riches come from "the ineffable and eternal glory in which God dwells."[48] Paul elsewhere describes such glory as a believer's destiny: "We all, who with unveiled faces contemplate the Lord's glory, are being transformed into his image with every-increasing glory, which comes from the Lord, who is the Spirit" (2 Cor 3:18). The beauty, power, and majesty of the cosmos and the subatomic particle—and all in between—belong to our God.

Our want and our abundance are both opportunities to know better the hand that cannot fail to fill us with "immeasurably more than all we ask or imagine" (Eph 3:20), the one about whom Paul can sing, "Oh, the depth of the riches of the wisdom and knowledge of God! How unsearchable his judgments, and his paths beyond tracing out!" (Rom 11:33). Fee rightly observes, "True theology is doxology."[49]

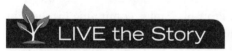

LIVE the Story

God's Healing Power

Throughout the centuries and around the world today, believers are witnesses to God meeting their needs through healing (and other miracles).[50] My father, a medical doctor, visited Pakistan a few years ago. He testifies to the healing of a woman bedridden for four to five months, a mother of three. He and a medical team were traveling to Afghanistan, and as they were passing through Pakistan, this woman's husband asked my father to come and see her. A local Baptist missionary had seen her several times, and he also wanted the team to visit her.

---

47. Bockmuehl, *Philippians*, 267.
48. Fee, *Philippians*, 453.
49. Ibid., 455.
50. See Craig Keener, *Miracles* (2 vols.; Grand Rapids: Baker Academic, 2012). See also Timothy Stafford, *Miracles: A Journalist Looks at Modern Day Experiences of God's Power* (Bloomington, MN: Bethany, 2012).

Her diagnosis was lupus erythematosis, probably not obvious to the doctors in Pakistan. Systemic lupus erythematosis (SLE) is an autoimmune disease, which means the body's immune system mistakenly attacks healthy tissue. This leads to long-term (chronic) inflammation. The underlying cause of autoimmune diseases is not fully known, and there are no cures.

My father realized the family had neither the funds nor the availability of current medical treatments to help her. Even more, there was no medical possibility for a cure. The case was a hopeless one, and then the husband asked for prayer. As my father tells it, "With her husband's permission, I laid hands on her and prayed for healing, unaware that twenty to thirty relatives had now gathered in the next room." The team then left and continued their journey to Afghanistan. About three days later, the team learned that the woman they had prayed for had gotten out of bed, unassisted, and prepared the evening meal, and each meal since. Three months later, after a mullah had come to appraise the situation, it was to be recorded that "a busy American doctor had visited etc., and as a result of his prayers, this was to be recorded in their history as a miracle."

Meeting Needs Not Endorsing the Prosperity Gospel

Paul does *not* imply that God promises health and wealth, as though God is a great vending machine that dumps out blessings if we put in a few coins. This (admittedly crass) description of God's character has been called the "health and wealth gospel" or "the prosperity gospel," which I believe is one of the greatest dangers to the Christian faith today. This "gospel" holds that God will bless his followers with wealth and health as they give payments of tithes and offerings. Because it promotes that every believer should be healthy and wealthy, if a believer is not, then one of two options is left: either God has failed them, or they have failed God. Yet God never fails to love us, and we can never fall so far that God cannot reach us (Rom 8:31–39), for his love operates now and extends into eternity.

A statement from the 2010 Lausanne Congress lays out the concerns with clarity.[51] God's miraculous grace and the Holy Spirit's power operate around the world today; however, the working of that power is not automatic or under a human's directive. Material wealth and human health can be signs of God's blessing, but they can also be achieved by corrupt means and thus are not in themselves signs of God's favor. In the same way, poverty and/or illness are not always signs of God's disfavor or the human's sin. In the end, the

---

51. See www.lausanne.org/en/documents/all/twg/1099-a-statement-on-the-prosperity-gospel .html ("A Statement on the Prosperity Gospel," first draft by Rev. Dr. Chris Wright, edited by Rev. Dr. John Azumah, in collaboration with Rev. Prof. Kwabena Asamoah-Gyadu).

human efforts and power of "positive thinking" that underpin the prosperity gospel movement around the world shares with the ancient Stoics the desire to make it by their own ingenuity and effort. While the Stoics strove for indifference and the modern health and wealth gospel wants more of what the world has to offer, in the end Paul would say to both that our sufficiency is in Christ.

Thankful Hearts

Luke tells of Jesus' healing of ten men with leprosy and asking them to go to the priests to show they were now clean. Only one returned to Jesus, fell at his feet, and thanked him. This man was a Samaritan, Luke notes. Jesus asked where the other nine men were; why did they not also return to give praise (Luke 17:11 – 19)? This story highlights a typical human propensity to fail to offer thanks. Only one in ten properly thanked Jesus and praised God loudly. I do not think those statistics have changed much since Jesus' time. That is why we must read Paul's thanks to the Philippians with such care. Then and now, the charge of ungratefulness is damning, and the accusation against Paul of giving a "thankless thanks" hovers over our letter. Such an indictment invites us to ask deep questions about how we interpret a document.

It also highlights that we are reading a document from two thousand years ago. The New Testament was written to real people with real problems, in a real language that everyone in the Roman empire used. The gospel was communicated through current images and drawing on Old Testament images, so the first-century Philippians heard the message in ways that fit their world. We can think of this as the *particularity* of Scripture. The claim that Jesus was a historical figure means that history is important.

But we also know that our own situation and history affect how we understand the world. We have our culturally sensitive and appropriate ways of expressing the Christian life and message. And what 4:10 – 20 reveals to us in the West in the twenty-first century is that we thank people differently than did those in the first century. Our customs are different in part because our social arrangements are not based on patronage or complex hierarchies that include slaves and freedmen and freedwomen. We must be sensitive to our social distance from the first century.

Reading the Bible invites us to explore not only another world, but our own world as well. It invites us to examine how we thank people, for example, or how we engage in sharing meals or helping the sick. What we discover is that even today, around the world believers show their thanks, eat meals, and care for the ill in different ways. This realization allows us to think deeply about *why* Paul acted as he did, digging below the surface expression of his beliefs to where the gospel was informing his actions. It is at that level that we can engage in imitation.

Treasure, with Strings Attached?

Handling money and gifts is as difficult today as it was in Paul's day, if for different reasons. Jesus' words, "Where your treasure is, there your heart will be also" (Matt 6:21), ring as true then as now. We confront similar situations concerning the giving and receiving of gifts, both at the individual and the corporate levels. On a personal level, some people struggle to accept any gift, because they feel it will tie them to the giver. We all have received gifts "with strings attached," often unspoken strings. Paul's teaching on gift giving takes issue with that form of giving, for it places the recipient in the difficult position of pleasing the giver rather than God, and it puts the giver in a position of power over the recipient.

Others struggle to give gifts because they worry that there will not be enough left for themselves. The Philippians offer a wonderful model of giving freely, come what may. Indeed, much did come their way, and yet they never lost the desire to give to the outreach of the gospel. Their poverty did not hold them back; in fact, it seemed to encourage them all the more. Today, a similar statistic holds true—those who make an average living tend to give a higher percentage of their income to their churches than the wealthy. Yet sadly we also hear today in churches the phrase, "I want to make lots of money so I can give more to the church." This passage cuts that sentiment off at the knees. Giving is a habit, a mind-set, not something that should be delayed until one has "enough" to give.

At the church level, we might say that some churches follow the "golden rule," that those who have the gold make the rules! In this passage Paul declares that they alone, the Philippian church, have supported his ministry from the beginning. Yet the church gives no evidence of directing or manipulating Paul's ministry, teachings, or actions. They do not think of him as responsible to meet certain criteria or goals as contingencies for their gifts. Their relationship is such that Paul can level direct warnings and critiques at their disunity without seeming to fear financial reprisal. Probably part of this godly reciprocity rested in their shared conviction that their gift to Paul was really their gift to God, to the gospel, in obedience to Christ. As such, Paul cannot reciprocate, because the gift was not meant for him to begin with. It was not "his" money—it was God's money.

Unappreciated Service

One area of ministry that this passage might address indirectly is that feeling of being unappreciated in one's service to the church. Probably we have all felt taken advantage of or undervalued at some point in our ministry. It might be true, humanly speaking, that others were ungrateful. How can churches work against this human tendency? Paul and the Philippians offer a good model, because their reciprocity involved not only their engagement with each other, but also a firm and unwavering appreciation that God was active in each other's place of ministry. Paul knew that the Philippians faced real struggles, and they followed Paul's tumultuous career with prayer and concern. It was a triangle relationship with Christ at the pinnacle, and the Spirit at the center of the triangle.

This passage in Philippians invites all believers to think about two issues. First, if you are feeling unappreciated in your ministry, visualize doing your ministry as offering a sacrifice to God. Imagine yourself before Christ placing your ministry on an altar and believing that its sweet aroma will please him. Also, ask yourself how you are supporting those who serve with you. Do you see them standing with you in partnership? Do you imagine their acts of service as gifts on the altar? Above all, is there a pervasive attitude of rejoicing in the ministry? No better refrain can be offered than has been given to the Philippians, "Rejoice in the Lord always. I will say it again: Rejoice!" (4:4).

A second issue that this touches is the very nature of service to God. Jesus once showed two types of service to God: a wealthy man contributing much money to the temple, and the widow giving two pennies, all she had (Luke 21:1–4). The sort of service that is generally lauded is the sort that applauds the wealthy, the stylish, the influential, the celebrity. This is precisely the sort of figure whom Jesus cautioned his disciples against emulating. Paul too paints a far from glamorous picture of ministry, but at the same time, he holds out one that transcends the pettiness of our own human existence. Would we even know about the Philippian church had Paul not written about them? Did they send out a great apostle? Did they have great wealth to influence communities? Yet they possessed far greater riches and influence in their perseverance in supporting Paul, standing against the allure of the world's charms, and even holding fast in the face of persecution. They could do this because they viewed things from heaven's vantage point; that is, they had an eschatological perspective. They kept glancing up from their work to see if indeed it was now that Christ was returning (3:20). They continued in their faithful ministries, sensing that such brought them into the presence of God with sacrifices pleasing to him (4:18). We do well to follow such an example.

CHAPTER 15

Philippians 4:21–23

LISTEN to the Story

²¹Greet all God's people in Christ Jesus. The brothers and sisters who are with me send greetings. ²²All God's people here send you greetings, especially those who belong to Caesar's household.

²³The grace of the Lord Jesus Christ be with your spirit. Amen.

Listening to the text in the Story: Psalm 67:1–7; Revelation 1:4–5.

EXPLAIN the Story

In all of Paul's letters he offers closing remarks. Those in Philippians are brief in comparison to others, such as the long list of friends greeted in Romans 16:1–27 (see also 1 Cor 16:19–24; 2 Cor 13:12–14; 1 Thess 5:25–28). Paul uses the plural imperative as he asks that each saint be greeted. To whom is Paul referring? Some wonder if Paul is calling on the overseers and deacons mentioned in Philippians 1:1 as those responsible to make sure the letter is read to all.[1] Regardless of whom he intends, Paul is asking his own greetings are delivered to each saint "in Christ Jesus." This clause probably modifies both the greetings and the saints. Thus Paul greets them in the Lord, and each saint is also in the Lord.

Paul extends the greetings from those with him, although only "those who belong to Caesar's household" are singled out. These people were likely imperial clients, slaves, or freedmen and freedwomen who were part of the extensive entourage that managed Caesar's vast estates and civil affairs. Bockmuehl puts forward an interesting theory that some of the names noted in Rom 16 might be members of Caesar's household. For example, the household of Aristobulus (16:10) might refer to those connected with a grandson of Herod the Great. Again, Narcissus's household (16:11) could refer to members of

---

1. Bockmuehl, *Philippians*, 268.

the household of Tiberius Claudius Narcissus, an influential freedman whose power peaked under Claudius (AD 41–54). Finally, Herodion, a fellow Jew, is mentioned in 16:11 between the households of Aristobulus and Narcissus, perhaps indicating that "through his own family background among imperial freedmen ... Paul himself may have had personal connections with the civil service, and that at least one of his relatives or acquaintances in that official hierarchy had become a believer in Christ."[2] Such connections might link Paul closer to the Philippian church, located as it was in the Roman colony of Philippi. The Philippians too might have connections (patrons, family members) who knew people in the imperial household.

Paul's closing sentence (v. 23) reflects the promise and hope of the church, namely, that Christ's "grace" would cover, protect, guide, and sanctify until the day of his coming. Paul asks that this grace "be with your spirit," that one spirit in which they stand firm (1:27). This prayer expresses the hope given by the risen Christ to the disciples, showing through the Old Testament Scriptures that "the Messiah will suffer and rise from the dead on the third day, and repentance for the forgiveness of sins will be preached in his name to all nations.... I am going to send you what my Father has promised" (Luke 24:46–49). That promise was fulfilled on Pentecost with the coming of the Spirit, and it is on that story of salvation that Paul reflects as he pens his final sentence to the Philippians.

 LIVE the Story

Expressions of Grace

Paul closes with a prayer that the grace of Christ be with them. Philip Yancey explores the nature of grace lived out between individuals as people stretch out in faith that others will embrace them. Sometimes the call to act with grace seems impossible. Yancey tells the story of Daisy,[3] one of ten children who was born in 1898 to an alcoholic father. He kicked her mother out of the house when she was little, and Daisy's hate for him grew with each passing year. When the children grew to adulthood, the father vanished, only to reappear many years later, a sober believer who asked forgiveness for his past sins. Eventually all his children did accept his pleas for forgiveness, except Daisy. Though his last five years were spent living with her sister eight houses down the block, she never visited him. When Daisy's daughter, Margaret, stopped for a visit, near the end of his life, the father thought he was seeing Daisy.

---

2. Ibid., 270.
3. Philip Yancey, *What's So Amazing About Grace* (Grand Rapids: Zondervan, 1997), 77–81.

"Oh Daisy, Daisy, you've come to me at last." Yancey writes that the others in the room did not reveal Margaret's identity, for "he was hallucinating grace."[4]

Grace exposes our self to ourselves. Victor Hugo's novel about forgiveness and grace, made famous by the musical of the same name, *Les Misérables*, highlights the infectious capacity of grace.[5] At the beginning of the story, prisoner 24601, Jean Valjean, wanders the streets after his release from prison. A bishop, M. Myriel, gives him shelter, but that night Valjean steals some silver and flees. In the morning the police capture him and return him to the bishop's house. Expecting the bishop to applaud the thief's capture, the police are stunned when the clergyman hands him two silver candlesticks. The bishop declares that he has given all these silver objects to Valjean; thus the latter is not a thief. With this act of grace, the bishop breaks the chain of "un-grace" that had imprisoned Valjean.

In hopes of establishing a new life, Valjean breaks his parole and becomes a factory owner and official in his town. But a police officer, Javert, doggedly tracks the "criminal" and eventually locates him. Valjean must be on the run again. Yet at the moment when Javert is in his power, Valjean refuses to kill him; indeed, he sets him free. This gift of grace from a man whom Javert defined as "bad" because he was a criminal undoes his "black and white" world, and he commits suicide. Similar to Daisy in Yancey's story, Javert ultimately turned away from receiving grace and forgiveness.

Grace and Forgiveness to Move Forward

Miroslav Volf draws from the ethnic and religious conflict that swept over the former Yugoslavia to understand more deeply grace-filled actions. He makes the crucial, but often counter-intuitive, point that in extending grace or granting forgiveness, you are implying that the recipient has the need to receive grace or forgiveness. "To forgive is to name and condemn the misdeed. The same is true of God. God doesn't just condemn and *then* forgive. God also condemns in the very act of forgiving."[6] That is what makes accepting God's forgiveness and grace so difficult at times.

To illustrate this truth, he writes of his friend "Esther," abandoned by her alcoholic mother at age nine. Years later, Esther searched for the woman she vowed never to love. When she found her mother, Esther begged forgiveness for those years when she did not call or write. Esther waited for her mother

---

4. Ibid., 77.

5. Victor Hugo, *Les Misérables* (1862; trans. Charles E. Wilbour; New York: Barnes & Noble, 1996).

6. Miroslav Volf, *Free of Charge: Giving and Forgiving in a Culture Stripped of Grace* (Grand Rapids: Zondervan, 2005), 166.

to ask forgiveness for abandoning her. When none was forthcoming, Esther said, "I love you, I'm okay, Mommy. My life has turned out okay, and I forgive you for everything."[7] At this, her mother wept and repeated over and over, "I'm so sorry." Esther realized at that point that her mother's guilt had such a hold on her that she was unable to face it, but her daughter's love overcame the power of her shame.

The grace of Christ *is* with us. Amen.

---

7. Ibid., 186.

Scripture and Apocrypha Index

Proverbs

Isaiah

Jeremiah

Ezekiel

Daniel

Habakkuk

1 Corinthians

2 Corinthians

Galatians

Ephesians

Philippians

Subject Index

Author Indexes

Ancient Authors

Modern Authors

We want to hear from you. Please send your comments about this book to us in care of zreview@zondervan.com. Thank you.